Postjournalism
and the death of newspapers

**The media after Trump: manufacturing anger
and polarization**

By Andrey Mir

2020: To my Mom and Dad

Table of contents

Introduction: The Great Pivot from advertising to reader revenue 5

1. Scheduling the extinction of newspapers 10

   When newspapers die *10*

   Accelerators and decelerators of newspaper extinction *12*

   It is already on its way *15*

   Old media and COVID-19: news demand surged, business crumbled....17

2. The Trump bump: commodifighting Trump...21

   Trump-addicted..*21*

   Few succeed, many fall *26*

   Media impact and impact on media *27*

   Who got trumped more, Fox News or the New York Times? *29*

3. Why did journalism even appear?..34

   The printing press released a tidal wave of literacy man-hours *34*

   Venetian avvisi *36*

   From avvisi to gazettes *38*

   The press: inception *40*

   The influencers of the early Modern era *42*

   Siblings: journalism and the public sphere *46*

4. How society used to pay for journalism 53

   The two types of journalism: paid from below and paid from above *53*

   The eternal failure of selling news *54*

   Lenin's Iskra: the first attempt at the membership model....................*59*

   Advertising distortions of the media: the audience as commodity........*64*

5. Business of old media: the monopoly is gone 69

   Watchdogs prefer the paywalled garden *69*

   2014: advertising hit rock bottom and punctured it *74*

Journalism in search of a cute little monkey 80

In the meantime: marketing turns into journalism 89

6. Materiality of old media: the medium was the message 96

From journalism of fact to opinion journalism 96

Everything is a policy statements when headlines are clickbait 100

Factoid. Validation by dissemination 110

From factoid to fake news 117

The quantum theory of media 120

The quantum leap to the hamsterization of journalism and cannibalism of news teasers 128

7. Who will pay for journalism? 133

No future for paid content. Except for paid from above 133

Money talks 137

When concerned billionaires and Big Tech care about journalism 141

Philanthropy funding: paying for the pushing of pressing issues 150

The Guardian and the genesis of the membership model 157

Membership as a new business model 163

Membership and the donating audience: paying for others to read ...168

8. Why subscription mutates into membership 173

The media as a notary service: news validation instead of news production 173

Soliciting subscription as donation 176

Does donscription work without Trump? 178

9. From making happy customers to making angry citizens: journalism follows money 185

Ad-driven media: merchants of happiness 185

Reader-driven media: negativity bias 195

Inducing demand, the news media reshape the audience 198

Subscription solicited as donation: a new and unexplored cause of media bias 201

10. Manufacturing anger. The post-'propaganda model' 209

The moral of Lippmann's elitism *209*

The Propaganda model: the basics *211*

Functions of media: an ongoing process of change *213*

The Propaganda model revised *217*

A new and weird reader revenue *218*

Flak *220*

Ideology of threat *236*

Sourcing: opinions' supply *239*

Ownership of the media: it is not what you think it must be *257*

**11. Postjournalism: from the world-as-it-is
to the world-as-it-should-be** **262**

How did we get here? *262*

Donscription: subscription solicited as donation *265*

Impact for sale *266*

Negativity bias *268*

Activism *269*

Repudiation of standards *272*

Discourse concentration *287*

Post-truth: too good to be true *293*

Postmodernism unbound *301*

12. Polarization: dividing, electrifying and uniting **322**

Polarization is a media effect *322*

Affective polarization *325*

Agenda-setting polarization *329*

Rebound agenda-setting polarization *335*

Ideological polarization *337*

13. Understanding media effects: instrumental vs. environmental **340**

McLuhan's Figure/Ground Analysis *340*

From instrumental to environmental *342*

3

Media literacy: against instrumental relativism 345

14. The residual needs for journalism and the desperate needs of journalism 353

Newspapers as a discourse Holy Grail 353

The really immortal qualities of good-old journalism 361

– 30 – 367

Conclusion: an ascent from the maelstrom..370

Bibliography 381

Introduction: The Great Pivot from advertising to reader revenue

Fake news is an overhyped issue. The greatest harm caused by media is polarization, and the biggest issue is that polarization has become systemically embedded into both social media and the mass media. Polarization is not merely a side effect but a condition of their business success.

The recent surge in polarization originated from the advent of social media, which unleashed the authorship of the masses. In this newly emerged horizontal communications, alternative agendas were gradually shaped. It soon became apparent that this direct representation of opinions forms very different agendas than those shaped by the more traditional representative form of opinion-making, the news media.

The clash between the alternative agendas of social media and the mainstream agendas of the news media entailed political polarization, which produced two waves of anti-establishment movements.

The first wave was caused by the initial proliferation of social media in the early 2010s, when digitized educated progressive urban youth ignited the Arab Spring, the 'Occupy' movement in the US, the protests of 'indignados' in Europe and worldwide protests against the old institutional establishment.

The second wave of polarization started in the mid-2010s, when social media had permeated society deeply enough to reach and influence those who are older, less educated, less urban, and less progressive. As a result, the rise of conservative, right-wing and fundamentalist movements affected elections and social life around the world. In a sense, Trumpism continued the 'Occupy Wall Street' movement but on a completely different demographic basis.

The grassroots activity of the digitized masses, having been enabled by social media, not only fueled alternative agendas but also returned the favor to social media by providing higher user engagement. User engagement is the fundamental factor of social media's business. Thus, through the strive for user engagement, the business of social media happened to be tied to political polarization. There is nobody's evil intent or conspiracy behind such settings; the hardware of this media environment just requires this software – polarization.

***

In parallel, a seismic shift occurred in old media. The 'hardware' of the news media business has drastically changed, too. Over the last 10–15 years, both advertisers and audiences have fled to better platforms, where content is free and far more attractive and ad delivery is cheaper and far more efficient. The classical business models of the news media, news retail and ad sales, have been shaken up so violently that it is hard now for the media to survive.

Ad revenue in the media has declined much faster than reader revenue. The media were therefore forced to switch to the reader revenue business model aimed to sell content. However, as content is free on the internet, it is hard to sell. People almost always already know the news before they come to news websites because they invariably start their daily media routine with newsfeeds on social media. Increasingly, therefore, if and when people turn to the news media, it is not to find news, but rather to validate already known news.

Thus, the reader revenue the news media now seeks is not a payment for news; it is actually more a validation fee. The audience still agrees to pay for the validation of news within the accepted and sanctioned value system. After switching from ad revenue to reader revenue, the business of the media has mutated from news supply to news validation.

***

The mass media business is desperately searching for appropriate pitches and formats for this last-resort business model amid the shrinking revenues. New forms of funding are tested, among which the most promising appears to be philanthropy funding and the membership model. Philanthropy funding, most often accumulated via foundations, assumes that the media outlet picks up a pressing social issue and pledges to cover it for a grant or continued funding from a foundation. This form of funding inevitably leads journalists to excessively focus on chosen triggering topics instead of covering a wider spectrum. Under this form of funding, the media surrender a part of their newsroom autonomy to foundations, which have their own understanding of what is important for society.

The membership model has married the motives of philanthropy funding with traditional subscription. Within the membership model, a media outlet defines a noble cause and offers the audience the opportunity to join the cause and support journalists through donations. However, such 'noble causes' always happen to be, in fact, the most potentially donatable causes. Eventually, the membership model has come to calling readers to pay not for news but for the public service of the media outlet, which has pledged to cover certain social issues or just cover news from a certain angle or within a certain value system.

The radical difference between traditional news retail and the membership model is that the payer is not a reader. The membership payers do not pay to get news for themselves (they already know the news), they pay for news to be delivered to others. The membership model leads the media to set a certain agenda and promote certain values, pitching for money from the most active part of the former audience – now the donating audience.

The validation fee and the membership model are similar in their impact on journalism. They require newsrooms to operate with values, not news. This slowly forces journalism to mutate into crowdfunded propaganda – postjournalism.

***

The desperate attempts of the media to replace the faded business models with a hybrid form of reader revenue coincides with political polarization spurred by social media.

During the time when the membership model was tested and its relative viability proved (the Guardian, De Correspondent and others between 2013–2016), social media empowered alternative agendas and boosted polarization insomuch as it caused the political shocks of Trump and Brexit. The philosophy behind reader revenue in the form of membership appeared to be in tune with the rise of politicization. The leading mainstream media, previously sticking to paywalls, started to promote the noble cause of democracy as a cause of journalism, to which the audience was invited to join.

The media has started pitching subscription as membership. The transactional offer of selling news has turned into philanthropy soliciting. The news media have started soliciting subscription as donation.

With this shift, subscribers gradually turn into two new categories of payers:

1) those who pay a validation fee for the news validation service of the media, and

2) the donating audience contracting the media to influence others.

Both types pay the news media not for news but rather for impact. They incentivize the news media to sell impact.

***

Thus, a completely new business model has been formed in the media, herein called the 'donscription' model, when the subscription actually represents some hybrid of a validation fee and donation. This sort of reader revenue is not based on retailing news; it is based on validating the value of news and promoting agendas.

Because the largest mainstream media outlets in the US, both liberal and conservative, performed incredibly well in commodifying Trump in the form of subscriptions solicited as donations to the cause, the rest of the media market has started moving in the same direction. The media are increasingly pitching their services as a noble cause in the hopes of attracting audience support in the form of donations or time spent.

This model of media business predefines the mode of agenda-setting. The media are incentivized to amplify and dramatize issues whose coverage is most likely to be paid for. Only news and opinions which help to solicit support and donations can pass editorial scrutiny. This leads to the narrowing of the scope of agenda-setting to a number of the most worrisome and well-paying topics and also to making those topics even more worrisome. The setting incentivizes not just the search for triggering issues but also triggering coverage. At some point, the media start seeing nothing but the issues that are able to trigger donations and support from the audience.

Not only do the media have to address 'pressing social issues', they must also support and amplify readers' irritation and frustration with those issues. The more concerned people become, the more likely they will donate. Ideally, the media should not just exaggerate but should also induce the public's concerns.

As the Trump bump (the subscription surge in some leading US news media) showed, the most triggering issues are political topics that polarize the audience. Covering polarizing issues for better soliciting of support, the media are incentivized to seek and reproduce polarization for the next rounds of soliciting. They change the picture of the world and they change their audiences, agitating them into more polarization, for profit.

***

Reliance on either ad revenue or reader revenue incites the media to paint two different and even opposite pictures of the world. The media relying on ad revenue makes the world look pleasant. The media relying on reader revenue makes the world look grim. The decline in the media business caused by the internet has not distorted the picture of the world in the media; it has distorted the habitual distortion.

There is no evil plot, nor 'liberal bias', nor 'right-wing conspiracy' behind it. Such are the environmental settings of a media industry that is losing its ad revenue and news business to the internet. The media based on the subscription-membership business model must push pressing political issues and therefore be polarizing. This is their survival mode. They will not extinguish social and political conflicts but rather fire them up.

The media system based on ad revenue manufactured consent. The media system based on soliciting the audience's support manufactures anger. The ad-driven media produced happy customers. The reader-driven media produces angry citizens. The former served consumerism. The latter serves polarization.

Thus, the entire media environment, comprised of both new and old media, rewards now the rage and polarization of their actors and users. Polarization has become the software of digital capitalism.

All that we knew about journalism was related to a news business funded by advertising. Nowadays, the necessity to pursue reader revenue, with the news no longer being a commodity, is pushing journalism to mutate into postjournalism. This book is about the origins and propelling forces of this mutation. The book explains why polarization is a media effect and, therefore, why polarization studies are media studies.

1. Scheduling the extinction of newspapers

Surrounding every technology are institutions whose organization – not to mention their reason for being – reflects the worldview promoted by the technology. Therefore, when an old technology is assaulted by a new one, institutions are threatened. When institutions are threatened, a culture finds itself in crisis.

Neil Postman.

"Me? Personally? I'm neither pessimist nor optimist... I'm an apocalyptic!"

Marshall McLuhan.

When newspapers die

I believe it was Ernest Hemingway who once said that any story is a tragedy, you just need to tell it honestly till the very end.

The last newspaper generation is comprised of people born in the early 1980s. Up to their coming of age in the 1990s, when the internet entered their homes, they saw their parents reading and subscribing to newspapers and magazines. Members of this generation are *digital migrants* because they have already transferred their news and entertainment consumption onto the internet. But they at least have had not only the sensorial but also the economic experience of interacting with papers. They have some readers' consumer skills and remember the myth of newspapers' significance.

For those born in the 1990s and socialized in the 2000s, PCs, laptops, smartphones and all sorts of gadgets were already all around. These kids, the millennials, were the first digital generation, the *digital natives*. They might have had a sensorial experience of interacting with paper, but, statistically speaking, they do not know how to buy it at the stand or how to subscribe to it.

Moreover, they do not have any need to purchase papers or magazines. In their rare encounters with the press, the press is most likely given to them for free. The digital natives see newspapers either as an artifact of the past or as a promotional channel. They do not have the economic or social experience of interacting with newspapers as a commodity or an agenda supplier. The worst thing is that their same attitude is extrapolated to journalism in general.

The next digital generation, generation Z, has not even had a sensorial experience with the press. Hundreds of thousands of today's students have never even touched a newspaper.

The *digital natives* (who have no newspaper experience) will displace the *digital migrants* (who have some newspaper experience) at the commanding heights in the economy, politics and households by the mid-2030s. At that point, nobody will know how to consume newspapers. Newspapers are in decline because of economic and technological factors, but their life span is measured by demographic factors. They will exist as an industrial product for no longer than the mid-2030s at the latest. After that, newspapers will become historical artifacts, sometimes items of vintage consumption or antiquary interest, and sometimes artforms – just as McLuhan saw the destiny of some media after they cease doing their entitled job and become obsolescent.

It will take a while for the industry to go through economic shrinkage, but the process is already well underway. The press industry will collapse sometime between now and the mid-2030s.

So, the inevitable death of newspapers poses no dissenting question. It is a historical fact that just needs some time to complete its occurrence. The question is the methodology of the time-to-event calculation.

***

The death of newspapers will most likely happen instantly and simultaneously in different countries with little to no variations related to local specificities. The collapse of the press will occur everywhere around the world at approximately the same time, despite the fact that some countries demonstrated positive trends in press development recently. For example, during the early 2010s the press faired comparatively well, even slightly increasing its circulation, in China, India and some other countries, most likely due to ongoing urbanization in these regions.

Historically, the proliferation of the press lasted almost four centuries, starting with first German newspapers in the 1600s. As the emergence of newspapers was most likely linked to the liberation of the national bourgeoisie – liberation from local princes or colonial powers – print media appeared in different countries in different periods. However, each subsequent technological wave of mass media expanded across the planet ever more rapidly. Whilst radio and TV spread over decades, the internet spread its tentacles throughout the world in a mere 20 years. Social media captured the world instantly; for them, the areas of proliferation were demographic rather than geographical.

Social media thus equalized the pace of media evolution across the world's countries. Therefore, the factors impacting the decline of newspapers appeared everywhere at once and simultaneously, if looked at from a historical perspective.

The most important of these factors were:

1) The media lost its monopoly over agenda setting because the internet offered an alternative, crowdsourced mode of agenda-setting;

2) Audiences and advertisers migrated to better platforms that provided more efficient advertising; and

3) The competition for time spent with media has become extremely intense; new and newly arriving digital media are much more efficient at capturing users' attention, leaving newspapers, and old media in general, with an ever-shrinking share of our daily time.

Accelerators and decelerators of newspaper extinction

The process of newspaper extinction has accelerators and decelerators.

The social media proliferation serves as the main economic and technological accelerator for newspaper extinction. However, demographic factors are the defining ones in terms of calculating the time remaining for the press as an industry. The time left for the last newspaper generation to live and hold commanding heights in society and households sets the time limits for newspapers. But this also maintains these time frames, serving as a decelerator of the newspaper decline. People who remember the myth of newspapers and have newspaper-consumption skills might be willing to support newspapers for far longer than it will ordinarily be provided by market factors – but not longer, of course, than the lifespan of these people.

The market is already ready to drop newspapers, but society is not. The commercial demand for newspapers has already almost vanished, but the social demand has remained rather strong.

***

The social demand for newspapers will also create some country-specific decelerators for the process of newspaper decline.

In the countries with stronger state regulations or more authoritarian regimes, the authorities will see newspapers as a traditional and still valuable channel for communicating with their popular base. Even though this audience is also moving to the digital reality, there will be a shared belief that newspapers still matter to the older generation. Therefore, the authority will financially support newspapers long after it makes sense from an economic perspective.

Another similar decelerator in such countries relates to the ability of local newspapers to provide a well-controlled communication channel for the local authorities. Amid the alternative agendas on the internet, which cannot be controlled at the local level whatsoever, local newspapers can preserve valuable agenda-setting opportunities for local princelings. Besides, the digital backwardness of some places can give newspapers a place to live a little while longer there. Thus, an *authoritarian demand*, related to local specificities, will decelerate the pace of newspaper extinction in some regions.

***

In the countries with free markets and developed democracy, a social demand will also decelerate the pace of newspaper decline. The myth of newspapers, or the belief that newspapers are important for democracy, held by the older generation and desperately promoted by newspapers themselves, allows newspapers to survive and sometimes even to thrive far beyond the 'purely' market logic. Society and local communities can also support newspapers as an element of their habitual social landscape.

This is already happening: many subscribers, if not the majority, pay not for news (which they consume in other ways) but simply for newspapers to exist. Foundation funding, the membership model, and other forms, essentially, of donations are becoming more present in the media business. Having almost lost the traditional business model comprised of reader and ad revenue, newspapers themselves have started to either ask for donations directly or solicit subscription as donation.

This change in funding has profoundly impacted agenda-setting, a fact that has gone unnoticed by the public. In general, asking for subscription as donation causes the media to politicalize, radicalize and polarize agendas, contributing to general political discord in society, a phenomenon that will be explored in detail later. For now, it is important to acknowledge that there are factors besides market demand that are allowing newspapers to survive longer than the market itself would provide. These decelerators of newspaper extinction are powerfully transforming the nature of the latest (and the last) newspapers, a phenomenon that has not yet been explored properly.

***

Nevertheless, whichever decelerators afford newspapers a few more years of survival, the time limit of the industry's demise is defined by demographic factors. New communication technologies triggered the process of newspaper extinction, the market speeds it up, and social habits slow it down; but it will be demographics that will eventually frame it in time.

Whether it be authorities' beliefs in the significance of newspapers for addressing the popular base, or the audience's beliefs in the significance of newspapers for preserving democracy or community, these beliefs are tied to generational factors. When the generation associated with these beliefs are gone, newspapers will be gone, too. There will be no reason for them to exist. Market excuses have already vanished, and social reasons are tied to the remaining lifespan of the last newspaper generation.

However, the major events of extinction will happen well in advance of the last newspaper's final days. The industry's collapse will be instantaneous due to the technical aspects of production and distribution. A cheap good with low added value can provide sufficient revenue only when a sales turnover is significant, which, in turn, requires expensive infrastructure. This infrastructure will collapse not after the turnover drops to near zero, but merely down to 50–60–70%, depending on the efficiency of the operational model.

Continuing support of an operation with no prospect of covering debts makes no sense. Of course, some philanthropic billionaires or foundations can breathe some life into the body of newspapers beyond their commercial demise, perhaps even up to the end of the allotted time of the last newspaper generation. However, it is obvious that there will be very few of them, and the vast majority of newspapers will collapse much earlier, when the social decelerators cease to compensate for the impact of the economic accelerators.

In other words, the critical point-of-no-return for the collapse of the system of newspaper production and distribution will be reached well before the social demand falls to zero. This tectonic event will happen in about mid- to late 2020s. Thereafter, a long trail of residual newspaper shutdowns will continue until the mid-2030s. No longer, no sooner.

The newspaper industry is therefore heading towards five years of agony followed by 10 years of convulsions, before its death. Some nostalgic production of newspapers for vintage use may of course remain afterwards, but it will be a matter of arts, not industry.

It is already on its way

The critical events will look like a tsunami of dramatic shutdowns of giants. However, newspaper extinction is already underway. The signs of it are just less noticeable or wrongly interpreted as a cyclical crisis. Newspapers are cutting jobs and downsizing the scale of operations as they try to move from print to digital. All these activities look like the search for a solution and create the illusion of possible adaptation. Observers may expect a rebound, but the crisis is not cyclical, it is existential.

The shutdown of smaller newspapers started long ago. In the American media market, which is not just setting the tone but is still the strongest in the world, the first noticeable shutdown was that of the *Ann Arbor News* in 2009, which made Ann Arbor the first city in the US to lose its only daily newspaper.[1]

What was foreseen by media-futurologists in the early 2010s started being noticed by investors and publishers by the late 2010s. In 2017, Warren Buffett said that, "most newspapers, including his own, are doomed."[2] He only made some reservations regarding the *New York Times*, *Wall Street Journal* and *Washington Post*, as they had succeeded in selling digital content; he assumed they would be able to survive.

***

Of course, the prophecy of the world's most famous investor should be taken very seriously, however I beg to differ with him with regard to the lucky chosen three exceptions he promulgated.

Unlike the past, the future does not exist in a fixed state. When speaking about the future, one should specify the time frame. In the future, there is no future-at-large. A close-horizon future is completely different from a far-horizon future. Those three newspapers might survive longer than others, but no longer than the last newspaper generation.

The CEO of one of the three, the most successful in digital subscriptions (the *New York Times*), Mark Thompson in 2018 was more precise in defining the remaining lifespan of print. As quoted by *CNBC*, he said that,

---

[1] Edmonds, Rick. (2009, June 16). "Why Ann Arbor will be the first city to lose its only daily newspaper." Poynter. https://www.poynter.org/reporting-editing/2009/why-ann-arbor-will-be-the-first-city-to-lose-its-only-daily-newspaper/

[2] Ingram, Mathew. (2017, February 28). "Warren Buffett says most newspapers, including his own, are doomed." *Fortune.* https://fortune.com/2017/02/28/buffett-newspapers-doomed/

"I believe at least 10 years is what we can see in the U.S. for our print products," Thompson said on "Power Lunch." He said he'd like to have the print edition "survive and thrive as long as it can," but admitted it might face an expiration date.

"We'll decide that simply on the economics," he said. "There may come a point when the economics of [the print paper] no longer make sense for us."[1]

Thompson assured that the *New York Times* was "pivoting": "Digital subscriptions, in fact, may be what's keeping the *New York Times* afloat for a new generation of readers." But he also admitted that, at the time, "Without question we make more money on a print subscriber."[2] (this changed during the pandemic lockdown in 2Q 2020[3])

This is an issue. While there are some rare examples of successful and sometimes even skyrocketing growth of digital subscriptions for some leading newspapers, mostly following the effect of the so-called *Trump bump* (reviewed in the next chapter), the digital growth might be more arithmetic than monetary. Newspapers simply undercharge digital readers in order to attract as many digital subscriptions as possible in the hope of increasing subscription prices someday in the future. But the digital subscription price cannot be as large as the print one – neither logically, nor psychologically.

Not only do bravura reports on digital subscription growth relate to very few papers, they also do not reflect, for many, the real business gains. The push for digital subscriptions might help to grow the audience numbers, but less so the business results.

As John Paton, the promoter of the "digital first" media strategy, once sadly admitted, "Print dollars are becoming digital dimes."[4] (Since then, worse has happened: they have turned into mobile pennies.) But expenses remain in dollars. I also once happened to come across a media org's data, according to which a seven-dollar decrease in print revenue was compensated for by only a one-dollar increase in digital revenue. The

---

[1] Ell, Kellie. (2018, February 12). "New York Times CEO: Print journalism has maybe another 10 years." *CNBC*. https://www.cnbc.com/2018/02/12/print-journalism-may-last-another-10-years-new-york-times-ceo.html

[2] Ibid.

[3] The New York Times Company reports 2020 second-quarter results. (2020, August 5). https://investors.nytco.com/news-and-events/press-releases/#data-item=The-New-York-Times-Company-Reports-2020-Second-Quarter-Results.

[4] Ingram, Mathew. (2013, November 18). "John Paton says what most media CEOs won't about paywalls — they are a short-term tactic at best." *GigaOm*. https://gigaom.com/2013/11/18/john-paton-says-what-most-media-ceos-wont-about-paywalls-they-are-a-short-term-tactic-at-best/

traditional business of the media has been collapsing much faster than the digital one has been growing.

Old media and COVID-19: news demand surged, business crumbled

The COVD-19 pandemic disrupted the previous prognoses regarding newspaper extinction. More precisely, the prognoses withstood, but the time remaining for the collapse needs to be revisited.

Generally, the COVID-19 outbreak was beneficial to the media, but the quarantine was not. At the beginning of the pandemic, the media was in a high level of demand that they had not experienced in a long time. News media traffic skyrocketed. COVID-19 made journalism great again.

But the quarantine did to the media what it was supposed to do to the virus. The quarantine demolished the business of old media, perhaps even more effectively than it stopped the pandemic. As the economy in general went into decline, advertisers began withdrawing or freezing their contracts.

***

The pandemic and quarantine impacted old media differently. Because the populations of entire countries became locked up in their homes, television had a chance to improve its standing. The quarantine boosted the ratings of major TV networks by 30–60%.[1] But television faced strong competition from other 'stay-at-home' media, such as streaming movie services and video games.

Furthermore, advertisers have tasted life without spending on TV commercials. Some of them froze budgets, while many others looked for other more efficient channels. Considering the general shift in consumer lives and the economy towards more digitalization during and after the quarantine, there is no guarantee that advertisers' budgets will return to TV at the previous levels.

As for radio, it was an old medium that suffered least from the rise of the internet, mostly because people generally listen to radio in their cars, as driving prohibits the use of other gadgets. Car listening provided the forced media consumption that secured, to some extent, radio business in the era of the internet.

---

[1] Bond, Paul. (2020, March 23). "Ratings skyrocket for cable news amid wall-to-wall coronavirus coverage." *Newsweek.* https://www.newsweek.com/ratings-skyrocket-cable-news-amid-wall-wall-coronavirus-coverage-1493836

The quarantine took the cars off the streets. The decrease in traffic was 60% overall and as high as 90% in some areas.

At home, radio does not seem to be a medium of choice when the entire sensorium is not restrained by driving and is free to explore all the amazing digital seductions. The quarantine hit radio severely. However, not for long. The traffic has gradually been restored, and radio has had an opportunity to fully recover. It will be neither the pandemic not the internet that will kill radio. Its mortal threat will be the self-driving car.

***

Newspapers were the most dramatically impacted by the pandemic, which greatly accelerated the process of its extinction. "We are all going to jump ahead three years," said Mike Orren of the *Dallas Morning News*[1].

He was an optimist. Newspapers have most likely jumped right to the end. Ken Doctor in *NiemanLab* observed how COVID-19 spurred newspaper strategies "that publishers had hoped could wait a while longer". Among them were "cutting print days, corporate consolidation, or even closing down offices". Doctor concluded that, thanks to the coronavirus, "tomorrow's life-or-death decisions for newspapers" suddenly became "today's."[2]

Indeed, print across the globe started to cease being printed; not in the mid-2020s but now. Murdock's News Corp suspended print editions of 60 local newspapers in Australia.[3] In Russia, three mainstream papers: *RBC*, *Vedomosti* and *Izvestia* put printing on hold until better days.[4] Canadian papers started laying off journalists and limiting printing to Saturday editions only, with observers stating that, "Our media is on the brink of mass failure." [5] The British Independent Community News Network, which

[1] Doctor, Ken. (2020, March 31). "Newsonomics: Tomorrow's life-or-death decisions for newspapers are suddenly today's, thanks to coronavirus." *NiemanLab*. https://www.niemanlab.org/2020/03/newsonomics-tomorrows-life-or-death-decisions-for-newspapers-are-suddenly-todays-thanks-to-coronavirus/

[2] Ibid.

[3] Meade, Amanda. (2020, April 1). "News Corp to suspend print editions of 60 local newspapers as advertising revenue slumps." *The Guardian*. https://www.theguardian.com/media/2020/apr/01/news-corp-to-suspend-print-editions-of-60-local-newspapers-as-advertising-revenue-slumps

[4] Мишина, Ирина. (2020, 30 марта). «Бумага стерпит? Коронавирус серьезно ударил по печатным СМИ». *Новые Известия*. https://newizv.ru/news/society/30-03-2020/koronavirus-ubivaet-poslednie-pechatnye-smi-no-oni-ne-sdayutsya

[5] Bernhard, Daniel. (2020, March 27). "Our media is on the brink of mass failure." *The Toronto Star*. https://www.thestar.com/opinion/contributors/2020/03/27/our-media-is-on-the-brink-of-mass-failure.html

represents 108 UK hyperlocal publishers, warned that communities across the UK would lose their independent press in the coming weeks.[1]

Newspapers cohabit the same ecological niche as the virus – they both need physical contact with people. Physical isolation prevented the distribution of newspapers even more effectively than that of the virus.

Strikingly, all of this happened amid the skyrocketing traffic on news media sites. The pandemic was crunch time, when journalists worked hard and did their best. The demand for news was huge, but it did not pay off.

***

Halted distribution and business troubles were not the only issues that physical isolation from readers brought to newspapers. Unlike radio and TV, print is a physical news medium. The very materiality of newspapers had been deemed their most attractive feature, which allegedly played an important role in slowing down their decline. People were said to like the smell of ink and holding paper sheets. During the pandemic, this previously saving grace of tactile interaction with newspapers became a major threat to the press.

The pandemic changed the tactile habits of the masses. Millions joined the ranks of germophobes. This shift in tactility might have an environmental and long-lasting impact on print media that will complete the fatal blow dealt by the disruption in distribution and advertising.

The state of affairs in the print industry led the *New York Times*' Ben Smith to publish a column with the speaking title "Bail out journalists. Let newspaper chains die."[2] The forecasts that seemed to be distant quickly became reality.

Without sponsors and governmental intervention, newspapers will start dying earlier than previously scheduled. However, even sponsors and governments will ask: Why paper? Indeed, why? The coronavirus became a new and powerful accelerator of newspaper extinction.

***

When predictions about the death of newspapers first appeared circa 2010, they caused a range of denial reactions – from chuckling in the general public to defensive sarcasm in the industry. As one of those who developed

---

[1] Abbott, Matt. (2020, March 25). "An open letter calling for support of ICNN members in this time of global crisis." ICNN. https://www.communityjournalism.co.uk/an-open-letter-calling-for-support-of-icnn-members-in-this-time-of-global-crisis/

[2] Smith, Ben. (2020, March 29). "Bail out journalists. Let newspaper chains die." *The New York Times*. https://www.nytimes.com/2020/03/29/business/coronavirus-journalists-newspapers.html

and delivered these ideas to industry investors and professionals[1], I personally witnessed their passing through the stages of denial, anger, bargaining, depression and acceptance, as life has steadily been converting the predictions into reality.

At some point, the professionals accepted that this was happening but started 'bargaining'. 'Yes, the printed press will be gone, it is obvious,' they argued, 'but journalism and its accompanying media business will transition into digital forms.' Many of the shutdowns that happened were indeed presented as the transition to the digital.

No, this will not happen. Journalism as we know it will not survive the transition into the digital space. The relocation of old print newsrooms into the digital environment will not solve the problem. They will be, and are, facing there the same issues that online-media newsrooms already struggle with: namely the absence of a reliable business model for news production.

The least obvious and yet most shocking aspect of the discussion about the death of newspapers is the fact that we are discussing the fate of journalism, not just papers. This is neither a cyclical crisis nor a matter of transition; this is the end of an era. To understand this, it is necessary to analyze the ways in which print journalism was organized, for what social demand and what business supported its social functions.

In the bigger picture, the emergence of the internet is an extinction event for humankind in its biological form anyways. The death of newspapers is just a tiny ripple on the turbulent surface of the stormy sea.

---

[1] I developed the concept in a number of articles in Russians outlets such as *Slon, Forbes, The Moscow News, Nezavisimaya Gazeta* and others starting 2009 and in the book: Miroshnichenko, Andrey. (2011). *When newspapers die.* – Мирошниченко, Андрей. (2011). *Когда умрут газеты.* М: Книжный Мир.

2. The Trump bump: commodifighting Trump

A good newspaper is a nation talking to itself.

Arthur Miller

Trump-addicted

Everybody discusses how the media suffer. Let us discuss how they profit; at least some of them. A lay witness might observe very confusing signals from the media market in recent years. On the one hand, the decline of newspapers and the general crisis of journalism are widely acknowledged. On the other hand, the role and the all-permeating presence of the media in social life seems to have grown exponentially, and the leading media likes to report strong readership and viewership numbers.

The confusion is well-founded and reflects the real state of affairs. The industry is dying, but some media organizations are thriving. They are first and foremost the American mainstream media that found a way to capitalize on politics in 2016. They include not only leading TV news networks, such as *Fox News, CNN* and *MSNBC*, but even some newspapers, such as the *New York Times* and the *Washington Post*, which have been showing outstanding results, too.

The success of the mainstream American media, that sent such mixed signals to the media industry, was linked to the *Trump bump*, the surge in readership numbers and viewership ratings based on the feverish interest of the public in Donald Trump that was spurred and exploited by the media.

***

Why have the media become so "obsessed with Trump"?[1] The quick answer was given by Les Moonves, the chairman of *CBS*, at the beginning of the presidential campaign in February 2016, when he said that, "It may not be good for America, but it's damn good for *CBS*. The money's rolling in.... This is fun".[2]

---

[1] LaFrance, Adrienne. (2016, September 1). "The media's obsession with Donald Trump." *The Atlantic.* https://www.theatlantic.com/technology/archive/2016/09/trumps-media-saturation-quantified/498389/.

[2] Cornwell, Rupert. (2016, March 19). "Donald Trump might not be good news for America, but he's great news for the TV networks." *Independent.* https://www.independent.co.uk/voices/donald-trump-might-not-be-good-news-for-america-

Being preoccupied with the idea of exposing Trump, the media consciously afforded enormous exposure assets to him for free from the beginning of the 2016 presidential campaign. In exchange, they received growth in audience attention and an increase in circulation and revenue. This is how and where the so-called Trump bump started in the media[1] (initially, 'Trump bump' was slang for the economic growth seen in some industries attributed to Donald Trump's electoral victory).

By March 2016, Trump had gained media coverage that was the equivalent of about $2 billion in advertising (Figure 1). By comparison, Hillary Clinton had earned about $746 million in free media at the time, and Bernie Sanders' free media totaled about $321 million.[2]

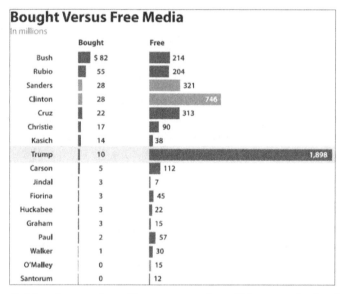

Figure 1. Paid and earned media coverage of candidates at the beginning of the election campaign (by March 2016). Sources: mediaQuant, SMG Delta. By *The New York Times*.[3]

---

but-hes-great-news-for-the-tv-networks-a6941441.html.

[1] *The Economist*. (2017, February 16). "Traditional media firms are enjoying a Trump bump. Making America's August news groups great again." https://www.economist.com/news/business/21717107-making-americas-August-news-groups-great-again-traditional-media-firms-are-enjoying-trump-bump.

[2] Confessore, Nicholas, and Yourish, Karen. (2016, March 15). "$2 billion worth of free media for Donald Trump." *The New York Times*. https://www.nytimes.com/2016/03/16/upshot/measuring-donald-trumps-mammoth-advantage-in-free-media.html.

[3] Ibid.

Trump's deeds and tweets were not only highly attractive but also sold very well. The period since the 2016 election has been extremely successful for the leading American media. Because of the Trump bump, the *New Yorker,* the *Atlantic[1]* and the *Washington Post[2]* doubled or tripled their subscriptions in the first year of Trump's presidency.

In July 2018, the *Washington Post's* vice-president of marketing, Miki Toliver King, presented a report showing a correlation between marketing efforts and subscription success (Figure 2). However, if we overlay the key events of Trump's campaign and presidency onto the subscription growth curve, we will see another pattern of correlation, a more obvious one. It was not a 'marketing bump'; it was the Trump bump.

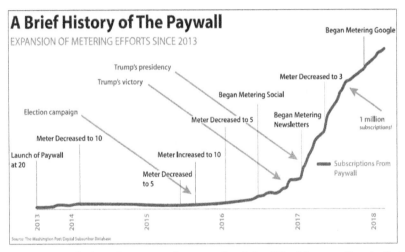

Figure 2. Correlations between the growth of the *Washington Post's* digital subscriptions and marketing strategy or Trump-related events. Source: World News Publishing Focus, WAN-IFRA[3]; Trump-related events are added.

The real symbol of the Trump bump is the *New York Times.* The Gray Lady made unprecedented progress during the first year of Trump's

---

[1] Doctor, Ken. (2017, March 3). "Trump bump grows into subscription surge – and not just for the New York Times." *The Street.* https://www.thestreet.com/story/14024114/1/trump-bump-grows-into-subscription-surge.html.

[2] Stelter, Brian. (2017, September 26). "Washington Post digital subscriptions soar past 1 million mark." *CNN.* http://money.cnn.com/2017/09/26/media/washington-post-digital-subscriptions.

[3] Veseling, Brian (2018), 'Washington Post puts emphasis on creating paths to subscription', *World News Publishing Focus, WAN-IFRA*, 30 July, https://blog.wan-ifra.org/2018/07/30/washington-post-puts-emphasis-on-creating-paths-to-subscription.

presidency. At the beginning of the campaign, the *New York Times* had slightly over 1 million digital subscribers to its news products. The paper almost doubled this number by the time of Trump's inauguration. As of December 2017, the *New York Times* had 2.2 million digital subscribers for its news product; by August 2020, this number had reached 4.4 million.[1] All these numbers set the world records for digital subscriptions to the news media product (Figure 3).

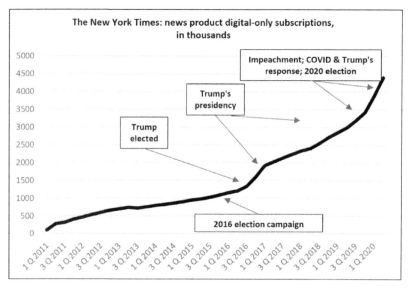

Figure 3. The *New York Times*: news product digital-only subscriptions (in thousands). Source: The New York Times Company's press releases[2]. It is also necessary to take into account that marketing efforts, such as discounted offers, might have affected the dynamic of subscription, too.

Television benefited from the Trump bump as well. For *CNN*, 2016 was the most profitable year in the organization's history.[3] Those shows and TV hosts that focused heavily on Trump received a ratings boost, among them Stephen Colbert, Rachel Maddow and Trevor Noah.[4] "Saturday Night Live"

---

[1] The New York Times company reports 2020 second-quarter results. (2020, August 5). https://investors.nytco.com/news-and-events/press-releases/#data-item=The-New-York-Times-Company-Reports-2020-Second-Quarter-Results.

[2] The New York Times Company's press releases. http://investors.nytco.com/press/press-releases/default.aspx.

[3] Mahler, Jonathan. (2017, April 4). "CNN had a problem. Donald Trump solved it." *The New York Times Magazine*, https://www.nytimes.com/2017/04/04/magazine/cnn-had-a-problem-donald-trump-solved-it.html.

with Alec Baldwin as Trump increased its viewership 44% in the 2016–2017 season.[1] For political reporters, the daily White House press briefing has turned "into a career launching pad like it's never been before." As *BuzzFeed News'* Steven Perlberg put it, "It's a good time to be a reporter covering Trump if you like money and going on TV".[2]

Donald Trump made the mainstream American media great again. An old saying among reporters goes 'If it bleeds, it leads.' An appropriate contemporary version might be "If it's Trump, it leads." *Columbia Journalism Review* reported that even placing international stories in American outlets is getting harder – unless they directly involve Trump.[3]

The same goes for book publishing. In 2018, as noticed by Brian Stelter,[4] each book at the top of the *New York Times* best-seller list has had one thing in common: President Trump. Even children's books fell to the Trump bump. Stephen Colbert's children's book *Whose Boat Is This Boat?*, which he made out of Trump's post-Hurricane Florence comments, held №1 on the Amazon respective category for a while.[5]

The Trump bump also resulted in an admission surge in journalism schools.[6] This fact additionally strengthened the illusion that the industry was on the ascent.

---

[4] Adalian, Josef. (2017, March 3). "8 TV Stars who have seen their ratings soar due to Donald Trump." *Vulture*. http://www.vulture.com/2017/03/trump-bump-stephen-colbert-rachel-maddow-tucker-carlson.html.

[1] Littleton, Cynthia. (2017, October 1). "'Saturday Night Live' season 43 opens strong but shy of last year's turnout." *Variety*. https://variety.com/2017/tv/news/snl-season-43-ratings-7-million-ryan-gosling-1202577326/.

[2] Perlberg, Steven. (2018, May 14). "It's a good time to be a reporter covering trump if you like money and going on TV." *BuzzFeed News*. https://www.buzzfeed.com/stevenperlberg .

[3] Schwartz, Yardena. (2018, January 30). "Freelancing abroad in a world obsessed with Trump." *Columbia Journalism Review*. https://www.cjr.org/covering_trump/trump-impact-foreign-reporting.php.

[4] Stelter, Brian. (2018, April 16). "Every top New York Times best-seller this year has been about Trump." *CNN*. http://money.cnn.com/2018/04/16/media/trump-new-york-times-best-selling-books/index.html

[5] Fischer, Sara. (2018, October 9). "The Trump political media frenzy is just getting started." *Axios Media Trends*. https://www.axios.com/newsletters/axios-media-trends-86a9bc0e-6086-4964-be84-eb659fbfc36f.html

[6] Tullis, Matt. (2018, September 10). "How Trump Is Making Journalism School Great Again." *The Daily Beast*. https://www.thedailybeast.com/how-trump-is-making-journalism-school-great-again

Few succeed, many fall

For many in the industry, the business reports from the *New York Times* and the *Washington Post* created an illusion that there is a magic recipe for digital transformation – you just need to find it. Many newspapers and online news outlets have been trying to introduce paywalls (frankly, they have not many other options left) in attempts to replicate the success of the *New York Times*, but all have been in vain.

The stark divide between the few successes and the majority failings quickly became evident. In December 2017, Mathew Ingram wrote in *Columbia Journalism Review* that, "A rising Trump tide will not lift all boats – some will be swamped."[1] He explained this by stating that, "Just from a purely financial perspective, there are not going to be enough people who are willing to pay for subscriptions to multiple outlets." The other reason proffered was that many local newspapers had lost "touch with their local markets after decades of chain ownership" and were not able to solicit support in the form of subscriptions from local communities.

It appeared that what the *New York Times* and other mainstream media were doing was a specific sort of business that could not be replicated in other conditions or at the local level.

***

In July 2019, Joshua Benton from *NiemanLab* attempted to analyze why digital subscription numbers for *Los Angeles Times* happened to be far below expectations despite the fact that the newspaper had "limitless" support from billionaire Dr. Patrick Soon-Shiong, LA's richest resident who had bought *Los Angeles Times* in 2017.

Twenty years ago, in print, *Los Angeles Times* was a worthy rival to the east coast capitals' papers. Benton drew up an interesting table which demonstrated that whilst the large metropolitan dailies were once comparably similar in terms of print circulation, their digital formats were drastically different: all bar the *New York Times* and the *Washington Post*, suffered dramatic falls. (Figure 4).

Benton tried to analyze *Los Angeles Times*' marketing strategy to find an explanation for the disappointing numbers. But a glance at the table he posted suggests another answer for the metropolitan papers' decline amid the *New York Times* and the *Washington Post* blossoming: too much local news, too little Trump. The chart best explains the correlation between

---

[1] Ingram, Mathew. (2017, December 27). "A rising Trump tide will not lift all boats – some will be swamped." *Columbia Journalism Review.* https://www.cjr.org/analysis/trump-facebook-2017-publishers-social-media.php.

business outcomes and engagement with the Trump bump. "A rising Trump tide will not lift all boats – some will be swamped"[1], indeed. As a matter of fact, only a few flagships have sailed mightily.

Newspaper	2002 print circ	2019 digital subs
The New York Times	1,113,000	2.7 million
Los Angeles Times	965,633	170,000
The Washington Post	746,724	1.7 million
New York Daily News	715,070	27,000
Chicago Tribune	613,429	100,000
Newsday	578,809	25,000
Houston Chronicle	552,052	37,000
The Dallas Morning News	521,956	72,000
San Francisco Chronicle	512,129	57,000

Figure 4. Source: Joshua Benton, *NiemanLab*[2]; Benton made a reservation saying he was as generous as possible in interpreting some numbers, as they may include double-counted subscribers.

Media impact and impact on media

To those lucky few, the commodification of Trump appeared to be a game-changer. Historically, there have been no such political events quite so beneficial to the media, except for revolutions and wars. The value of this occurrence is particularly poignant because it is taking place amid the closing scenes of the media industry tragedy.

As Martin Gurri stated in *The Revolt of the Public and the Crisis of Authority in the New Millennium*, "Media people pumped the helium that elevated Donald Trump's balloon, and they did so from naked self-interest" (Gurri, 2018, p. 361). Comedian Michelle Wolf made this point even more

---

[1] Ingram, Mathew. (2017, December 27). "A rising Trump tide will not lift all boats – some will be swamped." *Columbia Journalism Review*. https://www.cjr.org/analysis/trump-facebook-2017-publishers-social-media.php.

[2] Benton, Joshua. (2019, July 31). "The L.A. Times' disappointing digital numbers show the game's not just about drawing in subscribers – it's about keeping them." *NiemanLab*. https://www.niemanlab.org/2019/07/the-l-a-times-disappointing-digital-numbers-show-the-games-not-just-about-drawing-in-subscribers-its-about-keeping-them/

graphically at the White House Correspondents' Dinner on April 28, 2018, when she blamed the congregation:

> He's helped you sell your papers and your books and your TV. You helped create this monster, and now you're profiting off of him.[1]

This did not all happen at once. In 2016, they covered Trump as a celebrity and political wonder, which made the election campaign saleable. After the shock of his victory, the mainstream media learned how to commodify the Trump scare.

This invention has had a global impact, as it showed the media that taking a political side can not only be moral but also profitable. Thus, the politicization of media business began. It was not controversial for the conservative media. The conservative media earned money from what they promoted. But the liberal media profited from what they fought against. For them, it might cause a conflict of interest. The liberal media profited from a phenomenon against which they stood. By the standards of good old capitalist corporate ethics, they would have been obliged to declare this conflict of interest to regulators, consumers and shareholders.

The commercial motives behind the media coverage of Trump remain unrevealed to the public. Meanwhile, such analysis allows the assumption that the mainstream media not only commodified public fears while profiting from them, but also created a new materiality for these fears to be reiterated, thereby increasing those fears and their profitability for the media, but in so doing set up a disastrous feedback loop for society.

Business stimuli for the media to cover Trump's every move contributed to a media environment favorable to Trumpism. Meantime, the media themselves became more and more politicized and contributed to the surge of polarization in society. What used to be accepted as natural for *Fox News* became common for all the media, including those who had previously tried to display impartiality, a stance they abandoned to move to a political side. This happened literally over two–three years and in no small part because of business reasons.

Another byproduct of the commodification of Trump by the media relates to the screening effect of the Trump bump. Being 'obsessed with Trump,' the media paid much less attention to other circumstances that brought Trumpism into the world. It appears that the same effect of the

---

[1] Perlberg, Steven. (2018, May 14). "It's a good time to be a reporter covering Trump if you like money and going on TV." *BuzzFeed News*.
https://www.buzzfeed.com/stevenperlberg/white-house-reporters-tv.

media's obsession that served Trump's ascension is now preventing the public from understanding the real causes and forces behind Trumpism.

Who got trumped more, *Fox News* or the *New York Times*?

The media coverage of Trumpism – much like the coverage of any liberal vs. conservative stand-off in recent times in other countries – exposed multilayered asymmetric media polarization. The mass media have become polarized in their attitude towards Trump or similar triggers in other countries – Brexit/Johnson in the UK, Jair Bolsonaro in Brazil, AfD in Germany, Scott Morrison in Australia, Narendra Modi in India, Viktor Orbán in Hungary, Andrzej Duda in Poland, and so on.

***

The first polarizing divide in media cuts through media platforms. It is commonly recognized that the right-wingers and conservatives are more active on the internet, leading the internet to be accused of being an instrument or amplifier of the right. It is also true that the right is less represented in traditional media, particularly with regard to the mainstream media, as those media are mainly controlled by people with social, educational and cultural backgrounds that do not favor right-wing views.

In a sense, the activity of the right on the internet is forced upon them – they are offset thereto. The internet provides opportunities they do not have in the traditional media. The idea that the internet as a medium is beneficial to the right specifically is a misconception: the internet and social media are beneficial to those who are underrepresented in the mainstream media.

In the early 2010s, the internet and social media became a place of forced representation for those who digitized the first – the young, urban, educated, and progressive. They expressed and realised their agendas through social media, which eventually led to political polarization and the wave of protests exemplified by the Arab Spring and the Occupy Wall Street movement. Those who digitized next were older, less urban, less educated and more conservative. Their previously unrepresented agendas became expressed on the internet by the second half of the 2010s because they were non-represented and therefore forced out of the mainstream media into the digital world.

So, the polarization of political views between old and new media is not political but rather media ecological: the opinions suppressed in the legacy media find a release in new media. In the early 2010s, this was the polarization between the young progressives and institutional establishment. In the late 2010s, the shifted demography of social media use enabled a new vector of polarization – between the conservative masses and the liberal institutional establishment. As this shows, the conflict between social media and the mainstream media is always the conflict between the underrepresented and the establishment.

The left and the right constantly accuse internet platforms of serving their rivals. But, of course, the internet and social media are not homogeneous in their political content. The most accurate assessment perhaps is that because the established media are burdened with regulations, affiliations and the risks of public backlashes, radicals, dissidents and other suppressed movements tend to seek out less pressurized spaces to vent their agendas. The internet, and social media in particular, provide just such an environment for the underrepresented to create their own networks and 'stand-alones'. It is this that creates the deluded impression that such groups have conspired to capture the digital space entirely.

***

The second polarizing divide in media splits media formats. The press, radio, TV and the internet with its news websites, blogs, social media platforms, influencers, dark web networks, etc. have become asymmetrically polarized into political camps based on their formats.

The press is occupied predominantly by progressives and liberals, while radio, TV and the internet allow more diverse representation. This asymmetry can but only lead one to the conclusion that this is the mode of media consumption that predefines the political bias/non-bias of formats.

Literacy media either stick to professional and therefore non-political standards or tend to host centrist, liberal and progressive views. Meanings need to be placed in a written text linearly, one-at-a-time, but connectedly; this requires elaboration, prioritization, structuring, selection and the packaging of thoughts, which makes the production and consumption of the press an inherently rational and taxing process. Whilst conservative views are not entirely excluded from this activity in the print format, the leading newspapers everywhere tend to be rather liberal in nature. Literacy as a sensory feature of a medium correlates with a certain mindset.

This sensory-ideological predilection of the media formats was unequivocally revealed as a statistical fact. In 2016, among the top 100 largest newspapers in the US, only two — the *Las Vegas Review-Journal* and the *Florida Times-Union* in Jacksonville — endorsed Trump. Democratic nominee Hillary Clinton received endorsements from 57 newspaper editorial boards across the country. Four more did not endorse Clinton, but explicitly advised readers to vote against Trump.[1]

As for electronic formats – radio and TV – they do not have such specific sensory-related cultural 'requirements' imposed upon those who may use them. They are not literacy-centric; to such an extent that they do not even require literacy at all. McLuhan (1964) called radio a "tribal drum" and stated that electronic media with their audile-tactile mode of perception created the "Global Village" (he later suggested the term "Global Theater").

A noteworthy fact is that the most-watched cable news in the US is *Fox News*, a TV network that leans to the conservative side. Bearing in mind that TV is likely to be more powerful in shaping moods than print, the domination of Fox News over MSNBC and CNN to a certain extent compensates the conservatives for the domination of the liberals in the print media. However, *MSNBC* and *CNN*'s combined viewership (1.9 M + 1.7 M primetime viewers in May 2020) slightly exceeds that of *Fox News* (3.4 M).[2]

The digital format also does not have any sensory requirements or pre-dispositions for the consumption of its media to be governed by the users' political beliefs. Other factors are at work here: all opinions are equal, but those views which are suppressed in the mainstream media are particularly motivated to make themselves be more prominent in digital media simply because of the 'difference of pressure' between old and new media.

All in all, despite all the conspiracy theories about the liberal bias of the mainstream media and the internet having been captured by the alt-right, the distribution of formats between political camps is not political but 'media ecological'. The specific sensory characteristics of particular media consumption sometimes predefine (visibly so in literacy media) the cultural and, to some extent, political profile of users.

In general, though this correlation might be very tenuous, the mass media with a greater dependence on literacy (the press), because of the cognitive requirements of linear reading, might be slightly predisposed to incline towards more elaborated and educated views, while the mass media with less involvement of literacy, such as radio and TV, are free of this 'bias'.

---

[1] Wilson, Reid. (2016, December 6). "Final newspaper endorsement count: Clinton 57, Trump 2." *The Hill*. https://thehill.com/blogs/ballot-box/presidential-races/304606-final-newspaper-endorsement-count-clinton-57-trump-2.

[2] Joyella, Mark. (2020, June 2). "Fox News dominates May ratings, but CNN prime time jumps 117%." *Forbes*. https://www.forbes.com/sites/markjoyella/2020/06/02/fox-news-dominates-may-ratings-but-cnn-prime-time-jumps-117/#569c814c1e6d.

Additionally, it can be assumed that the institutional mass media (old news media and online news media), due to their journalistic heritage, might be slightly predisposed to incline towards the views of the educated and political elites, while media platforms which do not have such roots in journalism are rather free of this 'bias' and can provide a conduit to a broader range of views, with a natural predisposition to reinforce more radical views.

***

The third polarizing divide in media severs media organizations themselves. Due to media conditions shaped in the mid-2010s, news organizations were forced to choose a side. Even those news outlets that had once been mainstream and impartial now needed to participate in polarization because of the declining business of the news media. Old business models were failing, and the only successful strategy seemed to be to attract an audience by taking a political stance in the hope of monetizing this through subscriptions or advertising.

However, the media is spread across the political spectrum unevenly. Their ideological distribution was predefined partly by the format (print, digital) and partly by journalistic tradition.

Researchers from the Berkman Klein Center for Internet & Society at Harvard University conducted a study on media polarization and published their results in 2018 in a seminal book, *Network Propaganda: Manipulation, disinformation, and radicalization in American politics* (Benkler, Faris and Roberts, 2018). They concluded that the media landscape in the USA exhibits asymmetry in polarization. The left side of the spectrum is more dispersed and attenuated; it also has broader areas adjacent to the center. The right side, in contrast, is denser, 'heavier' and more detached from the center.

At the time when they conducted their research, this asymmetry was "between the right and the rest of the media landscape" (Benkler, Faris and Roberts, 2018, p. 51.). While the right side was always more detached from the center, denser and, therefore, more radicalized and mobilized, the most significant changes, presumably, happened and continue to happen in "the rest of the media landscape". Thus, the authors pointed out that,

> The leading media on the right and left are rooted in different traditions and journalistic practices. On the conservative side, more attention was paid to pro-Trump, highly partisan media outlets. On the liberal side, by contrast, the center of gravity was made up largely of long-standing media organizations steeped in the traditions and practices of objective journalism.[1]

In other words, right-leaning media were always partisan. They did not suffer a noticeable metamorphosis while adapting to the Trump-era media environment. The mainstream media, on the other hand, used to stand for the non-partisan position of objective journalism prior to 2016. Even the fact that they were often accused of 'liberal bias' demonstrated that the bias, if it existed, was not that obvious and conventionally admitted.

After three years of Trump's presidency, the definitions "mainstream media" and "liberal media" have become synonyms. Whilst the conservative media have always stuck to their side of the spectrum, the mainstream media ("the rest of the media landscape") have only recently taken a side. The suspected bias became the overt stance. As the progressive magazine *The Nation* described this transformation,

> In the past, *Fox News* stood out for the nakedness of its partisanship and the purity of its ideology; now, both *MSNBC* and *CNN* are mirror versions of it, tailoring their programming to the demands of their Trump-loathing audiences.[1]

Therefore, the discussion about the changes in journalism during the Trump era is predominantly about the journalism of the mainstream, liberal media. These are the ones, not *Fox News* or *Breitbart*, who used to be "steeped in the traditions and practices of objective journalism". (And that is why this book rests mostly on samples from the mainstream media when it describes the transition of the media system from journalism to postjournalism.)

---

[1] Faris et al. (2017, August 16). "Partisanship, Propaganda, and Disinformation: Online Media and the 2016 U.S. Presidential Election." The Berkman Klein Center for Internet & Society at Harvard University. https://cyber.harvard.edu/publications/2017/08/mediacloud

[1] Massing, Michael. (2018, July 19). "Journalism in the Age of Trump: What's missing and what matters." *The Nation*. https://www.thenation.com/article/archive/journalism-age-trump-whats-missing-matters/

3. Why did journalism even appear?

> Prior to movable type, much of the literature available in Europe had been in Latin and was at least a millennium old.
>
> *Clay Shirky. "Cognitive surplus", 2010.*

> It is quite likely that most of the first fifteen presidents of the United States would not have been recognized had they passed the average citizen in the street.
>
> *Neil Postman. "Amusing Ourselves to Death", 1985.*

The printing press released a tidal wave of literacy man-hours

Journalism as a profession and social institution emerged circa the 16–17th centuries. Three main factors can be identified that contributed to the rise of early journalism:

1) the printing press liberated a huge amount of free time of the *literati* from the need to copy manuscripts

2) the increased literacy of merchants and the middle class (driven, again, by the printing press and rapid proliferation of books) spurred their appetite for recorded news, and

3) the commercial proliferation of Venetian *avvisi*, initially private newsletters, which later evolved into public newssheets, or *gazettes*.

***

Elizabeth Eisenstein wrote in *The Printing Press as an Agent of Change* (1979) that, in the past, the copying of manuscripts kept scholars in early Medieval Europe extremely busy. She noted that,

> This point is especially important when considering technical literature. The difficulty of making even one 'identical' copy of a significant technical work was such that the task could not be trusted to any hired hands. Men of learning had to engage in 'slavish copying' of tables, diagrams and unfamiliar terms. (Eisenstein, 1979, KL 1315).

There was nothing noteworthy about the fact that manuscript copying kept educated people busy. Something outstanding happened, however, when the Gutenberg invention, the printing press (circa 1450), liberated them from this meaningless job, "producing a new situation which released time for observation and research" (Ibid., KL 1315).

The printing press turned thousands of scholars and scribes into thousands of writers who, all of a sudden, had nothing to write. The printing press took predefined content away from them, leaving them with a desperate need to find out on their own what to write about.

This was clearly a revolutionary situation. A new medium not only took over the job of an old one but also liberated people's time and skills, allowing them to do something new. A new medium always creates new opportunities, which, in fact, become duties: the feasible becomes the inevitable. This is how a medium-as-an-instrument turns into an environmental force that reshapes the environment.

It was indeed just such an indirect environmental media effect of the printing press that enabled the emergence of the so-called *Respublica literaria*, the Republic of Letters, the international network of scholars. The appearance of an army of literate individuals eagerly searching for something worthy to be scribed onto paper – something 'noteworthy' – resulted in them recording everything and anything that came across their avid gaze and minds. Within their scholastic network, they started exchanging newsletters brimming with philosophical thoughts, local political and general news, and social or historical observations. Essentially, all these same topics were seen in the early blogosphere, before social media started applying algorithms for shaping interpersonal communication.

The emancipation of educated man-hours, multiplied by network effects, directed intellectual power toward the exploration of nature and society. Next came the Scientific Revolution and then the Enlightenment.

***

The surge in original writings, spurred by the availability of millions of educated man-hours, made the recording of current affairs a sort of duty for the literati. The search for something noteworthy engendered a recording criterion that we now call 'newsworthy'.

Respublica literaria became a network of correspondents that supplied not only scholarly treatises but also religious, political, local and global news to each other and to the noble houses and the clergy. As many literati commonly served at courts, they became correspondents for princes and bishops. A new genre of court correspondence emerged that focused on political, royal, military and religious events, with reports on commerce, prices, battles, marriages, alliances, taxes, shipments and the populace's wellbeing. Herein we already see the structure and format of the news media, that has remained in place up to today.

This scholarly/court correspondence created the flow of political and business newsletters, reflecting the newly appeared supply and demand for news. Interestingly, it was the plethora of literate people having the time and ambition to record current news which most likely was the driving force behind this activity. So, it was the supply that spurred the demand, not the other way around. The political, religious and business elites became accustomed to reading news from other lands, liked it, and wanted more.

Thus, the impact of the printing press on the formation of journalism at first had nothing to do with the printing of newspapers. Rather, it was the creation of a network of writers whose literary man-hours were released from the humdrum chores of manuscript copying. With great gusto they launched themselves into the task of exploring and recording reality in all its forms.

Venetian *avvisi*

Between 1500 and the 1550s, Venice had already become famous for its regular handwritten recurrent newsletters, *avvisi*. Being such a central maritime and commercial hub in Medieval Europe, Venice was the source of a huge amount of commercial and political data that arrived with ship captains and letters delivered by ships. *Avvisi* combined merchants' and captains' accounts of what they witnessed overseas with the *literati*'s correspondence from foreign courts, thereby creating valuable reports about affairs that could impact trade and politics.

As English bibliophile and publisher John Camden Hotten wrote in his introduction to *An Early News-Sheet: The Russian Invasion of Poland in 1563* (translated from an earlier Latin historical account),

> To Venice is generally accredited the earliest newspaper. Its commercial position, in the early part of the sixteen century <...> rendered the dissemination of news necessary for the trade of the city. The ships of Venice then covered all the seas <...> The arrival of the ship in the Adriatic, the content of its cargo, the price of commodities, together with some account of the new island, its wonderful people and marvelous products, would form the staple of the news-sheet of the hour. This document was in manuscript, written in a legible hand, and copies were affixed here and there at different points of the city - the news-rooms - for the immediate perusal of those merchants who chose to pay a gazzetta[1] for the reading. (Hotten, 1874, p. 7-8.)

Interestingly, Hotten's use of the word "staple" as applied to information is reminiscent of the same use of this word by Harold Innis. Starting his political-economic explorations with the impact of staple products, such as cod, fur, wheat, lumber and the like, on the political and economic development of North Atlantic and Canada, Innis moved on to study transportation and then communication systems. Eventually, he came up with the idea that information is a staple in its own right, and, as with any staple, it empowers those who control it. The ways in which information circulates and is stored reflect, or even predefine, the profiles of entire civilizations. In *Empire and Communications* (1950), Innis showed that stones with hieroglyphs or clay tablets were durable and heavy, meaning they were 'time-biased' media that underlay the rigid and hierarchical Egyptian and Sumer civilizations. Conversely, light and easily transported papyrus, a 'space-biased' medium, enabled Rome to be administratively flexible and govern a large, centralized empire.

Precisely in accordance with this logic, *avvisi*, the newssheets with information about prices and current affairs, became a Venetian staple in their own right and were highly valued across Europe. The technology of *avvisi* came to Rome and then was replicated in many cities and noble houses.

***

The first *avvisi* were accounts of a diplomatic and intelligence nature. It can be said that journalism emerged, in part, from espionage based on in-court intelligence and the collection of data from rumors and open sources. Wars, politics and commerce were tightly intertwined, which is why *avvisi* were of such high value, not only to courts but merchants and captains as well.

Another source for *avvisi* emerged from the professional job of scribes. There, in Venice, the *scrittorie*, initially the scribes' workshops, became the first news agencies sometime in the early 16th century. Historian Andreas Würgler even used the notion of 'news dealers' when describing this early journalism. Scribes-turned-to-journalists gathered, reproduced and sold information, often oral accounts or gossip from merchants and captains. It was also assumed that some scribes could use information they picked up from copying someone's records or private correspondence.

This is how Würgler described the sources of news and the proliferation of news business:

---

[1] A Venetian low-valued coin of that time.

Thanks to cheaper paper the news slips could not only be enclosed in diplomatic, but also in business and scholarly correspondence. Around 1530, Italian news dealers began to assemble the news sources from the diverse circulation streams and send them to others on a regular basis for a fee. These *Avvisi* have been characterized as a kind of outsourcing of diplomatic news traffic, yet they were also interesting for wider audiences because they collected news from other sources, including business, intellectual, religious or private circles. Whoever had connections to the *Avvisi* writers or news dealers could have relevant weekly news sent to them for a set price.

The *Avvisi* marked the transition to the commercialization of news distribution. In the 1550s, they also began to circulate among princes and the city elites of the old German Empire, and from the 1570s onwards they reached large parts of Europe. (Würgler, 2012.)

An important detail: Venice did not have a guild of copyists, as was the case in many other cities.[1] A guild permit was not required, nor were guild restrictions applied to anyone who wanted to enter the market. Any literate person with good connections in the seaport and in the cafeterias around the Doge's palace could engage in the profession. As a result, strong competition created a vibrant market and a quality product that could be exported to other markets.

Therefore, professional journalism appeared more than half of a century before the first newspaper was printed (1609). This was purely commercial journalism: it sold news, nothing else.

From avvisi to gazettes

Print historian Mario Infelise provided an interesting etymological analysis of how *avvisi* turned into *gazettes*. He pointed out that these two were initially different entities:

> It should be remembered that the system of *avvisi* existed from at least the fifteenth century, but was mostly the concern of courts and princes, and political and religious circles more generally. On the other hand, the *gazettes*, as we will see, bring about the emergence of a new public. (Infelise, 2016, p. 243.)

---

[1] Zamburlini, Ilaria. (2013). "The early beginning of journalism: the case of Venice and its "gazzette" between 15th and 16th Century."
https://www.academia.edu/9872964/The_early_beginning_of_journalism_the_case_of_Venice_and_its_gazzette_between_15th_and_16th_Century.

As is widely known in narrow circles, the word *gazzetta* stems from the name of a low-denomination Venetian coin. However, the word *gazzetta* is also a diminutive of Italian *gazza*, magpie, a bird that is regarded in many cultures as a chatterer. Due to its noisy nature, the bird also metaphorically represents a person who makes a lot of noise and whose talk is cheap, a chatterbox.

As often happens in derivational morphology, it is likely that word *gazette* assimilated both meanings. The coin gave its name to a product that could be bought for the low value of this coin, but also the 'chatterbox' bird connotation perfectly matched the new phenomenon of *gazette* as it was perceived at the time (and continues to be).

***

The consonance between the coin's name and the name for a magpie allows for the interesting semantic reconstruction made by Infelise. He provided a set of accounts according to which, in many European languages at the time, the word and the phenomenon of *gazette* was used disparagingly. He assumed that *gazette* was a vernacular term for *avviso* and was often used to mock the low credibility of this new medium. The term also related to a type of junk-news media consumption as we would call it now. Infelise gave an example from the 1694 French language dictionary:

> GAZETTE, sub. f. Booklet, flying sheet published weekly, and which contains news of various countries. *Gazette of France, of Holland. Printed Gazette. Handwritten Gazette.*
>
> One refers figuratively to someone who is eager to learn news, and who spreads it around everywhere, as a *Gazette. That woman is dangerous, she is the gazette of the neighbourhood, she is a true gazette.* (Infelise, 2016, p. 256; translated from French by the quoted author.)

Basically, compared to *avvisi* and particularly to books, *gazettes* were received by the public similarly to how social media content is regarded nowadays; i.e. compared to the legacy media – simply as fake news. This is the fate of any new medium that emancipates news consumption from the previously established order.

***

However, Infelise also emphasized that *gazzetta* in Italy also meant something very cheap or pennyworthy. He pointed out that this word was used as an epithet for other things whose third-rate, cheap nature was meant to be highlighted. Infelise mentioned that educated people often complained that theater, a noble art, was brought to the streets and *piazzas* by third-rate artists, whose performances were usually rewarded by the public with the cheapest coin, *gazzetta*. Contemporaries called them *commedianti della gazzetta* (Ibid., p.260).

Infelise then made a very interesting assumption:

> Very frequently these street performers sold booklets and broadsheets concerning their performances. <...> It is plausible that the two products with similar features were assimilated and that the *gazzetta*, then a current coin of low value, tended to identify them—at least that was the intention of many who were inclined to discredit the sheets which reported notorious and unsubstantiated news (Infelise, 2016, p. 260.)

Indeed, travelling comedians and vagrants could, or even had to, be both peddlers and distributors of news. Their job was very similar to that of news suppliers (and, for example, the captains and merchants mentioned before). They all distributed news from far away. Perhaps itinerant comedians even sold 'aftermarket' and third-rate *avvisi* or, this time exactly, *gazettes*.

Referring to both the theater being degraded to *piazza* performances and *avvisi* being turned into *gazettes*, Infelise concluded that, "Something similar happened each time a cultural product conceived for use by the higher levels of society began to broaden its audience" (Ibid., p. 259).

This lowering of status naturally imparted a negative connotation to newspapers, which is still sensed today. Social media are not even paid for with the lowest value coin; they are free. And such is the value and trustworthiness of their content. This had already been witnessed throughout the history of media.

However, even being frowned upon at the time, the *gazette* proved "the capacity... to involve a wider audience and become an object of market value compared to the *avviso* – although both continued to be handwritten" (Ibid., p. 259).

The press: inception

Avvisi for the nobles and *gazettes* for the emerging general public became so popular that they created the news network that connected Venice, Rome, and other Italian and European trade and political centers (Infelise, 2002; Palazzo, 2016). These newsletters brought together business/political correspondence, proto-newswire agencies and news business.

German historian of newspapers Ludwig Salomon in his *Allgemeine Geschichte des Zeitungswesens* (*General History of the Press*, 1907) pointed out that the noble houses, trade companies and municipalities readily paid significant honoraria to authors of newsletters. As honoraria were most often paid on a regular basis, annually, this may be considered the first case of news subscription. The earnings of some authors were so significant that writing these newsletters became their profession and even business. The newsletters made by professionals were the most reputable, of course, so that they were copied and publicly sold.

Having learned from Venice and Rome, these professionals created the bureaus, the first news agencies, in Nuremberg, Strasbourg and other political and trade hubs. The richest European merchant family at the time, the Fuggers, established their own news agency that covered international trade activity and all the events that could impact the family business. By the 17th century, the Fuggers' newsletters were so reputable that many politicians and businessmen subscribed to them. Contemporary business news agencies, such as Bloomberg and some others, have developed the model of news trade first introduced by the Fuggers. In addition, as Würgler pointed out, the professional approach of the Fuggers facilitated "the cultural transfer from Italian Avvisi to German newspapers" (Würgler, 2012).

Despite the fact that this medieval news network, and the papers sold in it, were occasionally used by the noble houses for influence and propaganda, the underlying primary motivation was purely market driven. The first newssheets supplied nothing but news on a commercial basis. This was news paid *from below* – by the end user.

Thus, by emancipating the thousands of literati and scribes from the time-consuming labor of manuscript copying, the printing press shaped journalism and thereby created the market for news. On this well-tilled soil, print newspapers started growing in the 17th century.

***

Being natural hubs for trade, politics and information, seaports logically provided both supply and demand for news business to emerge. Arguably the first 'proper' newspaper, *Courante uyt Italien, Duytslandt, &c.,* which began circulating in Amsterdam in 1618, stemmed from this: it supplied news related to the sea trade.

'Proper' is written in quotes here because there was a debate regarding what counts as the first newspaper. Some media historians along with the World Association of Newspapers[1] consider the German newspapers of

---

[1] World Association of Newspapers. "Newspapers: 400 Years Young!" https://web.archive.org/web/20100310235015/http://www.wan-press.org/article6476.html

1605–1609 as the first ones. Others, such as Stanley Morison, pointed out that those first German papers were rather newsbook or pamphlets, while Amsterdam's *Courante* set the specific newspaper standards of format and news delivery used in the press ever since. *Courante* was printed in broadsheet format (a single *folio* sheet), while most other early newspapers were pamphlets printed in *quarto* format (Morison, 1954).

These differences in formats mattered. Ideas and manifestos, being a part of the *literati*'s discussion, better fit the book format, which pamphlets inherited. The listing of news, prices and goods for the general public, is better suited to publication on a broadsheet. The novel medium was in search of the most appropriate format that would appeal to both the elites and the masses, while at the same time suit the type of information being conveyed.

The Venice and Amsterdam seaport approach to trading news about trade was replicated three centuries later by the *Wall Street Journal*. The information about the supply and demand within the stock market is similar to that of the medieval seaports. News about goods, prices, shipments, war and peace matter. Starting with selling the daily bulletins containing the news about stock and bond prices on the New York Stock Exchange in the early 1880s, Charles Dow and Edward Jones[1] thereafter added analysis, columns, sports, general news and political coverage. The trade bulletin eventually evolved into the influential newspaper, hence compressing the 500-year transformation of commercial journalism into several decades.

The influencers of the early Modern era

Journalism did not last long as a purely commercial news retail enterprise. Soon after the potential political influence of newspapers became clear, the noble houses took political control over publishing and either funded newspapers directly or gave them a permission to do business on selling news, which they nevertheless strictly controlled.

This was the time when the monarchs, dukes and barons redefined their domains in the religious, political and ideological struggle with the papacy and each other. As Hotten wrote,

> Religious disputations were the principle topics in the early part of the sixteen century, and therefore we find the pamphlets of time - for these were the first news-sheets - mostly occupied with the arguments and anathemas of

---

[1] Dow Jones & Co. Inc., "Dow Jones History – The Late 1800s."
http://www.dowjones.com/TheCompany/History/History.htm

the reformers of Northern Europe, and the Catholics of the South. (Hotten, 1874, p. 6-7.)

The print press armed the leaders and preachers (of which Martin Luther, of course, is the best example) with a new and advanced tool for disseminating propaganda. The public space of the printed word, easily copiable and hence much more transportable, durable and powerful, than the oral word, was created by printed pamphlets and newspapers.

***

The papacy and the ruling houses needed to keep up. Along with restriction and censorship, they got into a game of publishing pamphlets and newspapers. These publications were licensed by the authorities and were expected to represent their views. They might have been directly sponsored by the courts or earned money from selling copies and later advertising, but their very existence was only possible because the rulers granted permission for their existence and closely supervised their content. In Germany (the 1600s), France (1631), and Russia (1702), the first newspapers did not emerge from the demands of readers but were created by the decrees or under the patronage of the ruling houses.

This type of mass media created a different sort of journalism – political journalism. Political journalism produced news coverage that was in the interests of the patron and rested on the respective business model. It did not sell news *downwards*; it sold agendas *upwards*. Political journalism was directly licensed by the authority, implicitly sanctioned by a political patron or in some other way affiliated with a political player. In return, political journalism either received direct funding or obtained permission to do news business and sell the news. News retail, however, in this case, was not self-sustainable business; it was framed by a political license.

If political coverage in commercial journalism stemmed from the necessity to cover the conditions for commerce, political coverage in politically patronaged newssheets was of the primary interest.

***

La Gazette in France (since 1631) laid out the standard of a political publication for years to come. It was issued under a royal license and was supervised by Cardinal Richelieu, who was also a contributor and personally supplied most international news.

Although its publisher and editor Théophraste Renaudot was a progressive public figure and a man of the Enlightenment, the role *La Gazette* played in mind control and agenda-setting was obvious. The paper served as a guardian for the monarchy in the ideological fight against the rebellious aristocracy in a turbulent time of religious disputes. As Elizabeth Eisenstein put it,

> In France the regency of Louis XIII saw the last meeting of the Estates General before 1789; it also saw the founding of the first royally sponsored newspaper in Europe. The replacement of the volatile assembly by the controlled weekly Gazette is a concurrence symptomatic of the importance Cardinal Richelieu attached to print in his state-building objectives. (Eisenstein, 1979, KL2728.)

As a doctor, Renaudot was also the physician of Louis XIII, King of France. From the very beginnings of journalism, this is a clear illustration of how close editors could be to those in power. Louis XIII himself was a frequent anonymous contributor to *La Gazette*. Interestingly, according to Salomon, in 1894, when historians found the lost king's military correspondence of 1633–1642 and compared it to the reports published in *La Gazette*, they detected some significant differences and redacted information (Salomon, 1907). Théophraste Renaudot clearly copyedited and cut his king's writings. Renaudot defined what words coming out of the sacred source were newsworthy. This is similar to a priest's function. Renaudot was most likely the first among the most famous editors who absorbed and radiated, with some rational interference and arbitrary adjustment, the will of the highest and mightiest authority.

In a sense, the power of the news editor rose above the power of the king – and, paradoxically, for the sake of the king's power. Renaudot knew what was best for the king better than the king. This is something akin to the doctor's power: the doctor is allowed to subordinate the patient for the sake of the patient's wellbeing. This power of subjugation through the creation of their reality often gave the media an illusion of power and, not uncommonly, they fell into the trap of abusing that power, still evident today.

This reflects the further development of political journalism: journalists and editors collectively knew what was best for the elites, and they knew it better than the elites themselves, as they did it professionally. They became a new caste of priests.

Under the communist Soviet regime, this function of journalism was much more direct: Soviet journalism was the ideological vanguard of the Communist party. More generally, translated into common language, political journalism was the ideological vanguard of the ruling class.

***

Nevertheless, *La Gazette* was also an early capitalist enterprise that used the privilege of sanctioned agenda-setting for profit. Presenting a yearly 1631 compilation of *La Gazette*, Renaudot emphasized the practical utility of the information the newspapers supplied: "the merchant will no longer seek business in a besieged or ruined city, nor the soldier employment in countries where there is no war" (as quoted in Blair & Fitzgerald, 2015, Chapter 9).

Its business was built, first, upon access to the highest (literally) sources, including the best political and diplomatic exclusives. Second, and most importantly, its business was built upon a monopoly protected by power, at that time – through direct and restrictive licensing.

The elites always cared about their agenda's monopoly, applying different measures of direct and indirect regulations to protect their monopoly over minds from alternative agendas. This political monopoly always had a small but pleasant business side effect for the media, the ideological vanguard of the elites: they could also sell news to the general public.

***

Thus, historically, newssheets appeared as a business instrument first and foremost. They provided valuable overseas information for merchants and noble houses. Providing commercial information was the first function of the newly emerging journalism.

However, the power of the news supply was instantly recognized by the powerful. The technology of newssheets was quickly taken under their control, and the news was allocated under the auspices of political influence.

Originally being the second function of journalism, political influence quickly became the primary goal of the press. Newspapers joined pamphlets, leaflets and other printed products in the ongoing religious and political struggle of the national noble houses with the papacy, reflected also in many local conflicts within nation-states emerging in the lands of Roman Catholicism.

As a political instrument, newspapers were directly paid, patronized, licensed or otherwise controlled by the princes and bishops. Most generally, news retail was the secondary business of local newspapers and was allowed on the condition of loyalty to, and promotion of, the interests of the local barons. However, this use as an instrument for political influence and commercial informing unleashed an unpredicted environmental effect of the new medium.

Siblings: journalism and the public sphere

When used by a person, a fence is an instrument to protect and defend. When used by a culture, a fence is an environmental force that transforms a nomadic tribe into a settled civilization.

The phonograph was intended by Edison to be used to record telephone conversations. What worked out in reality was the capability of this sound-recording instrument to detach the listening of music from the time and space of performance. After coming into common use, the phonograph and its sound-recording/replaying successors created show business, pop culture, the cult of celebrity and, eventually, the phenomenon of Trump, among other astonishing things.

The internet was meant for communication but created a new space for civilization to resettle.

These examples demonstrate how any instrument, when (and if) its use grows from personal to social, creates an environment and unleashes its own environmental force that does not necessarily comply with its originally intended instrumental task.

In the case of newspapers, the switch from an instrumental function into an environmental force can be best illustrated by the *dictator's dilemma*. The dictator needs better communication for better governance. But enhanced communication improves the exchange of information and ideas. The accelerated exchange of ideas very soon introduces alternative options, then incites alternative decisions and eventually undermines the monopoly of the dictator over the only 'right decision'.

The unprecedented exchange of commercial and political information in pamphlets and newspapers empowered merchants and bourgeois as a new social class and eventually provided capital to seek political power. The new class had neither the birthright nor the right sanctified by divine authority. But the merchants and the bourgeoisie acquired some money and some new communication opportunities. The printing press and new means of communication – leaflets and newssheets – enhanced commerce and governance. But they also enabled what Jürgen Habermas described as the "public sphere".

***

By the "public sphere", Habermas meant "a sphere which mediates between society and state, in which the public organizes itself as the bearer of public opinion." He put the appearance of the public sphere into historical context when the princes were forced to give up a part of their formerly absolute power. The public sphere was organized on the "principle of public information which once had to be fought for against the arcane policies of monarchies and which since that time has made possible the democratic control of state activities" (Habermas, 1974 [1964], p. 50).

According to Habermas, the main condition for the public sphere to appear is an ability of private individuals to assemble and form a public body in an unrestricted fashion and with "the freedom to express and publish their opinions about matters of general interest" (Ibid., p. 49).

An important starting point for the public sphere to appear was a divorce between the private interests of individuals and power interests of rulers. Habermas linked the rise of the bourgeois public sphere to "disintegration of the feudal authorities (church, princes and nobility)." The church, for example, lost the monopoly over personal choice when individuals' relation with religion began to be thought of as a 'private matter'. Indeed, this was something unheard of at the time. Similarly, princely authority became detached from the economic and political self-awareness of individuals when the public budget of lands and cities was separated "from the private household expenses of a ruler" (Ibid., p. 51).

As a result of the disintegration of the feudal authorities, the economic and social behavior of individuals became unshackled from the regulations of the princely households. Individuals earned the freedom of economic and religious choice. Power and private individuals became separate social entities.

With their divorce, mediation between them became necessary, both top-to-bottom and bottom-up. As Habermas pointed out, before that, when people and lands still belonged to the princes or church, the authorities represented "their power 'before' the people, instead of for the people" (Ibid., p. 51). After the authorities became separated from the 'private matters' of individuals, they needed representation of their alienated will to each other. The bourgeois public sphere, essentially, was a public body representing the collective 'private matters' of individuals, of the newly emerged class of the bourgeoisie, to the power and religious authorities.

***

Habermas directly linked the emergence of the bourgeois public sphere to journalism. This link clearly illustrates a typical 'resolution' of the dictator's dilemma:

> The bourgeois public sphere could be understood as the sphere of private individuals assembled into a public body, which almost immediately laid claim to the officially regulated "intellectual newspapers" for use against the public

authority itself. In those newspapers, and in moralistic and critical journals, they debated that public authority on the general rules of social intercourse in their fundamentally privatized yet publically relevant sphere of labor and commodity exchange. (Habermas, 1974 [1964], p. 52.)

Newspapers, thus, became a deliverer of the new class's will. This view suits the classical political-economic approach that has its roots in Marxism, according to which communication and ideology are functions of the *superstructure* reflecting or serving to solve the contradictions in the *base*, which is comprised of the economic forces and relations of production.

However, a different view regarding the cause and effect in the rise of the public sphere can be proffered by media ecology. This was not that the "intellectual newspapers" got involved in politics, but the other way around: the advance of printing technology and the emergence of pamphlets and newspapers enabled the unprecedented social autonomy and political self-awareness of the new class of the bourgeoisie. The dictator's dilemma always arises not from the dictator's will but from the development of communications.

The chicken-or-egg debate regarding the media or the public sphere's precedence might be alluring, but regardless of its competitive part, it is obvious that the simultaneous emerging and parallel development of the media and the public sphere was mutually predefined. The evolution of the media as an instrument of commercial and political communication created the conditions that led to the formation of modern society, both in its economic and political dimensions.

Habermas pointed out that early newssheets that were "mere compilations of notices" turned into daily political newspapers that fulfilled the important role of literary journalism in the second half of the 18th century. In other words, the early commercial newssheets shaped agendas only through the set of news presented, while the later political dailies came *with* their own agendas.

It might still be a debatable 'chicken-or-egg' situation as to whether the media evolved within their own logic and led society or if they themselves followed the social-economic changes, but Habermas highlighted that it was this political involvement aligned to party affiliations that led the media to recognize their public role. In his Encyclopedia Article, Habermas quoted Karl Bücher, a German economist and the founder of journalism as an academic discipline:

Newspapers changed from mere institutions for the publication of news into bearers and leaders of public opinion – weapons of party politics. This transformed the newspaper business. A new element emerged between the gathering and the publication of news: the editorial staff. But for the newspaper publisher it meant that he changed from a vendor of recent news to a dealer in public opinion. (As quoted in: Habermas, 1974 [1964], p. 53.)

The sequence of the bourgeois and then socialist revolutions was catered to by a vast number of political newspapers in the late 18th century through the 19th century. Every small political group mandated the establishment of a press arm to mobilize their followers and ensure their 'true ideals' were faithfully carried out. Habermas noted that in the revolutionary year of 1848, over 200 journals were established in Paris between February and May alone (Ibid., 53). Thus, political journalism appeared – alongside the party system, electoral democracy and class struggle.

***

At approximately the same time, in the mid-19th century, in England, France, Germany, and the United States, the transformation began from "a journalism of conviction to one of commerce." Habermas did not specify the reasons for this transformation, but they obviously related to the series of fundamental technological advancements that made newspaper production incredibly cheap:

- 1814: the invention of the cylinder press, which was powered by a steam engine that printed on both sides of the paper sheet and ran four times faster than the latest flatbed press,
- 1843: the invention of the rotary press, which was able to print millions of copies in a single day;
- 1844: the invention of pulp-based paper (instead of the more expensive cotton-based paper); and
- 1884: the invention of the linotype machine, which allowed the casting of entire lines instead of letter-by-letter typesetting.

In the capitalist spirit, all these inventions were introduced almost immediately, rapidly speeding up the production of the press, simultaneously cheapening its cost. The growth in the cost efficiency and speed of printing increased the affordability of newspapers. The press proved to be the first truly industrial mass product.

The affordability of newspaper production and consumption affected the political application of the press. The bourgeois press, which had already become the elite press by that time, was complemented by the labor press, which flourished in the late 19th century and the first half of the 20th century until the advertising business model buried it.

Simultaneously, the affordability of the press spurred on an entrepreneurial view of the media. The penny press appeared, aimed at the wider urban population. The penny press introduced a new business model that was independent from political funding and political supervision and focused on the interests of the masses. The yellow press as well as investigative journalism appeared. Newspapers became the *mass* media.

Without digging deep into the technological and economic circumstances of the development of newspapers, Habermas underlined how the evolution of the media contributed to the development of the public sphere. He wrote:

> In the transition from the literary journalism of private individuals to the public services of the mass media the public sphere was transformed by the influx of private interests, which received special prominence in the mass media. (Habermas, 1974 [1964], p. 53).

***

Journalism first appeared in the form of handwritten Venetian *avvisi* as a product of the printing press, even before the first newspapers were printed. The printing press freed a sufficient number of literate man-hours to be redistributed from book copying to event recording, and therefore prepared the societal conditions needed for regular news to appear. The early development of newspapers walked journalism through the stages of their technological, social and economic development, pairing journalism with respective processes in society enabled by the same media evolution.

The early development of journalism can be grouped into three stages.

1. Early commercial journalism grew out of Venetian *avvisi* in the 16th to early 17th centuries. The funding model for this type of journalism was news retail, selling news to end customers, initially the nobles and clergy, then to merchants and the general public across the network of the largest European cities. This stage was very significant for the emergence of the profession, yet it was very short-lived, as the ruling elites immediately recognized the influential power of newspapers.

2. The political journalism of the religious and bourgeois and then labor struggle in the 17–19th centuries. First used by the princes and bishops for better governance, newspapers became a means of political struggle and facilitated revolutions. From this point on, newspapers also began to be a media platform for the public sphere in the Habermassian sense.

3. The mass media of the second half of the 19th century until the present. Technological innovations of the 19th century made newspapers cheap, and they became a truly industrial mass product. Since then, their commercial and political impact has rested not on the access of the literates, but on their affordability to the masses. Different funding models became possible: political sponsorship, news retail, advertising sales and different combinations of them. In addition to the elites' political newspapers, different types of mass media emerged, such as the labor press, the penny press, the business press, and all possible types of press specified by the social-demographic and consumerist characteristics of its audience. The new technology of mass communication led to the emergence of new types of non-literary and therefore even 'more mass' mass media, such radio and TV. In this period, the public service provided by journalism was based on its capacity to appeal to the elites and the masses through attractive news content or direct political messaging.

***

Different countries went through these stages at different paces. Some countries skipped some early stages or the entire period of newspaper journalism because the development of journalism started there later, sometimes in the era of radio, TV, or the internet, when those became the main platforms of mass communication.

A curious fact: the first American newspaper, *Publick Occurrences Both Forreign and Domestick*, was shut down after the first issue was published in 1690. The British governor banned the printing of the paper for "reflections of a very high nature" and for failing to obtain a correct printing license.[1] There was no local press until 14 years later. The locals read British newspapers or their locally reprinted leaflets. Then, local newspapers appeared in the east coast's port cities, logically having repeated the path of Venetian *avvisi*: from sea-trade news to political influence. Very rapidly, American journalism moved from news retail to the stage of the national-liberation bourgeois movement, when the national bourgeoisie fought with the colonial power for independence.

It is worth noting that bourgeois revolutions of the second stage of newspaper development created a profound esteem for newspaper journalism in societies, despite all the criticism it received. The press is still significant in people's perception in countries that went through bourgeois revolutions at the time when the printing press was the only technology of

---

[1] Shedden, David. (2014, September 25). "Today in media history: First colonial newspaper published in 1690." *Poynter*. https://www.poynter.org/reporting-editing/2014/today-in-media-history-first-colonial-newspaper-published-in-1690/

mass communication. The myth of newspapers is very strong in Germany, the UK, France, the USA, and Russia – compared to Canada, for example, where newspaper journalism is not perceived as particularly sacred and rather shares its mythological significance with later media, such as radio and TV. No bourgeois revolution – no strong tradition of newspaper journalism.

***

The emergence and development of journalism has been linked to a large and turbulent historical period. This period is framed as the Modern age in history, as capitalism in political economy and as the Gutenberg era in culture. This period is approaching its demise on all three fronts.

With regard to the chicken-or-egg dilemma, out of those three intertwined eras – the Modern age, capitalism and the Guttenberg era, – the latest, the culture based on printing, has obviously already come to the end. The main medium of that era, print, has ceased to be significant. First, electronic media, then digital media wiped out the leading cultural role of print. Coincidentally, modernity with its Age of Reason and capitalism with its industrial political-economic settings, are also being discussed as soon to be coming to an end.

Such has been the historical background for reviewing the fate and the future of journalism amid the forthcoming death of newspapers.

4. How society used to pay for journalism

If you are going to blame "capitalism" for the faults of the press, you are compelled to prove that those faults do not exist except where capitalism controls.

Walter Lippmann. "Public Opinion", 1922.

A newspaper is not only a collective propagandist and a collective agitator, it is also a collective organiser.

Vladimir Lenin. "Where to Begin?", 1901.

The two types of journalism: paid from below and paid from above

From their very inception, newspapers essentially represented one of two types of journalism based on their respective business models. Commercial journalism sold news to readers; political journalism sold agendas to patrons.

Of course, such pure archetypes are rarely witnessed in reality. Instead they are more like the two poles that frame the range of social functions of journalism practiced within the bounds of these business models.

Journalism is inherently designed to sell news *downward*, to the end user – a reader. However, as it is an intrinsic part of a whole social context, journalism inevitably switches to selling agendas *upwards*, with some news traded *downwards* as a side business.

This gives us two ultimate 'ideal' models of the media business. Journalism is either paid *from below* by those who want to read news or paid *from above* by those who want others to read news. These two opposing models, in different mixes, have been employed by journalism throughout it 500-year-long history.

Business models and political pressure predefined the ways the two modes of journalism perceived the world. Serving its readers, commercial journalism sought to portray the *world-as-it-is*. Serving its patrons, political journalism sought to picture the *world-as-it-should-be*.

Thus, from the very beginning, journalism became the battleground for what we now differentiate as truth and post-truth.

News-selling journalism sells news *downwards* to the readers, while agenda-selling journalism sells agendas *upwards* to the patrons. They both create agendas, but for news-selling journalism, the news is a commodity and the agenda is a byproduct, while for agenda-selling journalism, agenda is the product and is used either to sell it *upwards* to the patron or to attract the audience in order to sell this audience to the payer(s).

On the one hand, as news-selling journalism produces a commodity for direct trade, it is regulated by market forces – the invisible hand of the market and reputation. On the other hand, agenda-selling journalism is paid *from above* and is therefore regulated by the political needs of its patrons or contextual needs of advertisers. This regulation may manifest itself in various forms such as financial patronage, juridical licensing, indirect sanctioning, allocative financial control and the like.

Agenda-selling journalism is inevitably more complex. It can only succeed in selling agenda *upwards* if and when the readers read its product. This apparent restriction actually creates an additional business opportunity. It enables agenda-selling journalism to produce a commodity of 'double-conversion': the product of agenda-selling journalism must be sold *upwards* to the sponsors (agenda) and can also be sold *downwards* to the readers (news).

Later developments brought more sophisticated forms of control over agenda-setting within the agenda-selling type of journalism. The direct political control by authorities over newspaper agenda-setting was complemented and replaced by the indirect control of advertisers. Nevertheless, advertisers still made journalism portray the *world-as-it-should-be*.

The eternal failure of selling news

Informing people is seen by default as the foundation, justification and social mission of media business. According to this view, journalism is supposed to sell news; however, it has never happened in the pure form. Even in cases when journalism was intended to be paid *from below*, historically it always ended up being paid *from above*.

Even the 'purely' news-selling business of the early Venetian handwritten newsletters in the 16th century was immediately acculturated by power. As Hotten accounted,

In 1536 the Venetian possessions and factories in the East were attacked by the Turks <...>. As may be imagined, the people of Venice were extremely anxious to hear the news from fleet; so the first regular monthly journal was established by the government to supply this information, and men were paid to read the particulars at the principle points of the city. But the heads of the Republic were fearful of the spread of the false news and opinions dangerous to their position, so they ordained that no sheets should be issued but such as were sanctioned by the Doge and his Council. (Hotten, 1874, p. 8-9.)

It is indeed fascinating how an account from 1874 regarding events of 1536 mirrors the issues of 2017, when 'fake news' was named the 'word of the year' by Collins Dictionary. The network of alternative news was considered to supply false news that endangered the established institutions. The ruling class discussed (and applied) measures to regulate this alternative news environment by introducing mechanisms of content filtering and restriction. The same issues and solutions are now discussed regarding the alternative news environment of Facebook and other social media.

***

Those early seaport newsletters of the 16th–17th centuries – the Venetian *avvisi* and Amsterdam's first newspaper *Courante* – were all immediately appropriated by the elites to deliver something else. The alleged *news* business was always just a carrier for something else to be delivered – some other good (advertising) or built-in agendas of political patrons.

The identification of a purely *news* business (or the purely informational function of journalism) would be simple. This journalism should be paid predominantly or even exclusively *from below*, by readers who consume news to stay updated on affairs or just out of curiosity. The role of the payer is crucial for defining the function of journalism.

News itself is a very paradoxical commodity. It always 'needs' to be read; it is always in some kind of demand *from below*. But there is always someone *from above* who wants to pay for certain news to be delivered to the public. And those *from above* – those in power or advertisers – want to pay to deliver the right news much more than those *from below*, who are willing and able to pay to receive news.

The value of news as a carrier for agendas and advertisements is much higher than the value of news as a commodity in its own right. As a result, the audience always surrenders the right to pay for news to those *from above*. The elites and advertisers reorganize journalism into a subsidized

55

news service in which news becomes a sort of chum for attracting fish to gather around.

**

The pay *from above* takes over the pay *from below* also because of its higher economic efficiency for the media. Transaction costs in retail are always higher than in wholesaling. Collecting a small fee from the widespread audience requires an additional costly infrastructure; the wholesaling of the audience to a smaller number of big payers is much more cost-efficient.

All things being equal, newspapers that only sell news to readers will lose out to newspapers that sell news to readers and sell readers to advertisers (or political sponsors). The business model encompassing both news retail and audience wholesaling is always a better commercial strategy than just news retail. Hence, from a commercial perspective, any newspaper will readily switch from news retail to audience wholesaling if it is offered such a business opportunity.

As such, historically, this became the typical outcome. There was always someone *from above* who came and forced or seduced the media to sell the audience *upwards*, not news *downwards*. First, these were political patrons, then political parties, then advertisers. The physically dispersed nature of the audience, the high cost of retail money collection, the political and financial persuasiveness of the elites and the organizational specificity of news business have made journalism predominantly paid *from above* throughout its history.

The occasions when journalism tried to earn money from serving the audience, not the elites, meaning predominantly selling news *downwards* and not agendas *upwards*, did not last long. The first news bureaus in the 16th century, the Venetian and Roman *Scrittoria*, aimed to produce news purely for the sale of that news. The noble houses and members of the elites were the first end users, and they quickly realized the importance of spreading the 'right' news. Politics swallowed news business because politics is always the best business of all.

**

The next attempts to make journalism being paid *from below* happened in the late 19th century.

Everyone knows that Gutenberg's printing press enabled the Scientific Revolution and the Protestant Reformation, but few are aware that newspapers became the true mass media because of a sequence of relatively small technological improvements in the 19th century.

A series of inventions in the course of the 19th century introduced the cylinder press powered by the steam engine, the rotary printing press, wood-pulp paper, and, finally, the linotype. These inventions significantly reduced the production cost of books and newspapers, and dramatically increased their speed of production. The advent of quickly printed cheap newspapers made large scale circulation not only possible but inevitable.

This spurred major structural changes in the offerings of the printed press, facilitating the appearance of the likes of 'penny press' and 'labor press'. With the advent of cheaper and more affordable newspapers journalism, once again, attempted to sell news to the end user, rather than agendas to the elites. This did not stem from someone's noble intent to free journalism from elites' control; this was a business opportunity created by the low production cost.

**

The penny press appeared in the USA in the 1830s. These papers sold for only one cent – compared to six cents for regular old newspapers (Kaplan, 2013, p. 6). They represented a completely different business model. The cheaper production expenses lowered the cost to enter the newspaper market. "Newspapers' prices were dropping, yet publishers did not require extensive capital to reach and hold a readership," as Kaplan wrote (Ibid., p. 7). Reader revenue drove the development of the mass newspapers, and the growing circulation attracted advertisers.

The switch in the media's business model from dependence on political parties to dependence on the audience changed the nature of media coverage. Pre-existing newspapers had been partisan propaganda outlets maintained by political parties or politicians. As journalism historian Barbara Friedman stated[1], "Political parties considered newspapers as extensions of what they did. They were tools. The point was to discredit and even savage the opponent with falsehoods". The penny press papers "revolutionized content by declaring their independence from political parties and concentrating on news rather than opinion" (Nerone, 1987, p. 378).

Reliance on mass opinion and financial sustainability made newspapers independent from direct political subsidies and party control. Kaplan pointed out that the economic transformation of the daily paper from partisanship to appealing to the broader masses changed papers' political identity and rhetoric. The new business model changed journalism. "No

---

[1] Seidenberg, Steven. (2017, July 1). "Fake news has long held a role in American history." *ABA Journal.* http://www.abajournal.com/magazine/article/history_fake_news

longer dependent upon party subsidies but instead driven by the profits to be gained from large circulation and advertising," wrote Kaplan, "<Papers> … embraced political independence, even objectivity. Papers ceased to address their audience in political terms – neither as citizens, nor as fellow partisans – but instead as consumers" (Kaplan, 2013, p.13).

***

The tabloids and yellow press originated from this type of journalism. Furthermore, investigative journalism is also rooted in the penny press. Journalism, in general, learnt to pay more attention to the interests of the audience it served.

Catering to the tastes of the crowd for better copy sales, the penny press directed much of their attention toward criminal stories. The inclination for the mass-circulation newspapers to attract their readers through coverage of sensational crime stories is notoriously illustrated by the media hysteria whipped up around the murders of London prostitutes in the 1880s by the mysterious "Jack the Ripper", perhaps the first world-renown *media criminal*.

The heightened interest in crimes prompted journalists to acquire the methods and very investigative mindset of the police and private detectives. The first investigative journalists were pushed not so much by social consciousness but by market competition, which forced them to dig deeper to find sensational cases and atrocities hidden from the public. This was what made their names and consequently increased their earnings.

With the further growth of newsrooms' financial independence and urban-class demand for social justice, the principle of investigative journalism turned toward social issues and conflicts, paving the way for muckraking journalism in the early 20th century and then contemporary watchdog journalism.

The penny press also signified the final shift of the media from an artisan type of professional activity to an industrial business. The mass media became a 'culture industry', perhaps the first of a kind, precisely in the sense that Horkheimer and Adorno (1947) assigned to that notion: not just a serving an ideological mechanism but a sustainable capitalist industry in its own right.

***

This continuing reduction in production costs resulted in greater circulation figures, which made advertising more efficient, thus attracting ever more advertisers. In addition, by the end of the 19th century, the economy in general moved towards a mass-market consumer society, with its growing reliance on advertising. Consequently, this maximization of the audience morphed the business into selling this audience to the advertisers rather than selling news to the audience.

Gross advertising income between 1870 – 1880 for the mass American newspapers increased from 40% to more than 50%, subsequently rising to 60–70% by the 1900s, a level at which it remained throughout the twentieth century (Kaplan, 2013, p. 12). The new, purely commercial form of the media's dependence on the elites was formed, which was later described by Herman and Chomsky as the Propaganda model (1988).

Whilst the penny press's attempt to escape from being paid *from above* may have failed, it nevertheless changed the media environment by making journalism independent from direct political control. The relations in the love triangle of 'the media – the masses – the elites' thus became more complicated.

Lenin's *Iskra*: the first attempt at the membership model

Revolutions always relied on the dissemination of new, alternative and disruptive agendas undermining the previously established order. Almost all revolutionary thinkers and leaders were publicists, many were journalists, and some even worked as professional editors. The names of John Milton, Benjamin Franklin, Jean-Paul Marat, François-Noël Babeuf, Karl Marx, Vladimir Lenin, Leon Trotsky and many others belong to the history of journalism as much as to the history of revolutions.

The printing press, of course, gave the revolutionaries new opportunities. It can be said that the very notion of revolution appeared after the invention of printing, as previous upheavals had been riots and coups. A riot is based on a collective emotional impulse and a coup can be conspired as an oral plot, but a revolution requires an ideological justification that is formulated, expressed and transferred into action by means of disseminated text.

Respublica literaria, the international community of scholars, could supply a sufficient quantity of authors. But the size of the audience was limited by the affordability of reading to those who were literate and able to pay for books and papers. In the 16th–18th centuries, revolutions were the privilege of the educated elites – first the aristocratic, then the bourgeois ones.

In the 19th century, revolutions became the business of the masses. For this to happen, the abundance of not only revolutionary publicists, but also revolutionary readers was required. The cheapening of mass printing and the growing affordability of newspaper production led to this outcome.

***

The cheapening of newspaper production stimulated the rise of the labor movement. Similar to the aristocracy and bourgeoisie centuries before, a newly formed proletariat class recognized its own identity and claimed its rightful place in the societal structure. As was the case with its predecessors, it did it by means of revolutionary pressure and, therefore, via an ideological – meaning textual – justification.

The growing affordability of newspaper production facilitated this process. Along with cheaper mass newspapers, such as the penny press and the evening press, the labor and communist/socialist press appeared.

Before the proletariat even became self-conscious, progressive intellectuals came forward to be its voice. Armed with newspapers, they spearheaded the new class's struggle.

The central place in this cohort, of course, belongs to Karl Marx with his *Neue Rheinische Zeitung* (1848–1849). This newspaper was affiliated with the leaders of the Communist League, which commissioned the famous Manifesto of the Communist Party (1848) written by Marx and Engels.

Neue Rheinische Zeitung offered fellow revolutionaries the opportunity to buy shares in the project and donate to the cause. Even though the sale of shares alluded to the prospect of profit, in reality everyone understood that this was more a form of contribution. In today terms, this business model can be called 'philanthropy journalism'. Some insignificant amount of advertising was also sold to, what one can easily assume, sympathizers.

An interesting fact: The Communist League counted no more than 300 members, yet what was essentially its party's newspaper printed up to 6,000 copies per issue. (Vasilyeva, 1977, p. xviii). Those funding *Neue Rheinische Zeitung* paid not because they wanted to read the breaking news about the 1848 revolution in Germany (they already knew the news), but because they wanted others to read it. This is a model of funding to which journalism is going to return to during the throws of its dying days.

***

Other publications in this cohort were *Vorwärts!* (Social Democratic Party of Germany, 1876), *Justice* (Social Democratic Federation, Great Britain, 1884), *Le Peuple* (Belgian Labour Party, 1885), *Le Socialiste* (France, 1885), *Avanti!* (Italian Socialist Party, 1896) and others.

As for the US, the Labor Press Project by University of Washington, noted that,

> By the end of the 19th century, working-class newspapers proliferated in cities across the country. Between 1880-1940, thousands of labor and radical publications circulated, constituting a golden age for working-class newspapers. Although both radical and labor newspapers struggled to finance their publications, utopian, socialistic, and independent journalism produced thousands of papers during this period that contributed significant alternative voices to mainstream journalism and society. (Kelling Sclater, 2009.)

One of the most interesting samples of the worker press 'business model' was Vladimir Lenin's *Iskra*.

***

While the Western tradition is inclined to see journalism, in general, as a molder and mirror of public opinion, the Soviet tradition regarded journalism along the lines of Lenin's assertion that it is "not only a collective propagandist and a collective agitator" but "also a collective organizer."

Some observers may conclude that newspapers organize readers through ideas. But for Lenin himself, the organizing principle of the party newspaper had to be employed literally: *Iskra* was the backbone upon which the entire body of the Bolshevik party developed.

This is how Lenin defined the role of the newspaper in his *Iskra*'s article "Where to Begin?" (1901):

> The role of a newspaper, however, is not limited solely to the dissemination of ideas, to political education, and to the enlistment of political allies. A newspaper is not only a collective propagandist and a collective agitator, it is also a collective organiser. In this last respect it may be likened to the scaffolding round a building under construction, which marks the contours of the structure and facilitates communication between the builders, enabling them to distribute the work and to view the common results achieved by their organised labour. With the aid of the newspaper, and through it, a permanent organisation will naturally take shape that will engage, not only in local activities, but in regular general work, and will train its members to follow political events carefully, appraise their significance and their effect on the various strata of the population, and develop effective means for the revolutionary party to influence these events. (Lenin, [1901] 1961, p. 18.)

***

By the beginning of the 20th century, Marxist ideas in Tsarist Russia were very popular among the young intellectuals but also very scattered. The Marxist and labor groups were disconnected due to regime pressure and a lack of information. Lenin wanted to reorganize the scattered and ideologically variable local groups into coherent cells and unite them into a combat-capable revolutionary party.

Iskra was launched in 1900. It was printed in Leipzig, Germany, then smuggled into Russia. Some issues were reprinted by underground printers in Russia. The circulation sometimes reached 10,000. It was funded via crowdfunding among leaders and activists. Some wealthy sponsors financially contributed, too. Among them was even the capitalist-philanthropist Savva Morozov, the fifth wealthiest industrial magnate in the Russian Empire at the time.

Iskra supplied a stream of ideological texts downwards, towards local cells and activists. Thoroughly vetted and adjusted by Lenin and his comrades, the integrated agenda cohered local groups around consistently presented ideological and organizational principles. This was particularly important because many contesting Marxist-revolutionary factions were fighting for local supporters. There were 'economists', 'opportunists', 'liberals', 'revisionists', anarchists, then Mensheviks, etc.

Lenin first tried to co-opt all of them in order to use their financial and reputational recourses (for example, Lenin collaborated for a while with Georgi Plekhanov, the first Russian Marxist and an acquaintance of Engels, as co-editor). But after gaining control over the content and having established his own network, Lenin pushed his own agenda and his own faction, eventually making it the leading revolutionary force that changed the course of world history.

***

The ideological education and promotion of the Marxist-revolutionary agenda, of course, was an important task of *Iskra*. But what impacted the most was not so much the paper's content but its networked effect. *Iskra* became a classic example of McLuhan's idea that it is not the message that impacts the environment but the medium itself. *Iskra* means 'spark' in Russian, and the motto of the newspaper was "Out of the spark shall come the flame". The effect of *Iskra* can be seen as a powerful demonstration of McLuhan's environmental take on media. This effect resided not only in spreading the ideas downwards, but in cohering the upwards efforts of the local groups and activists.

The readers of *Iskra* became its distributors and contributors. The local contributors not only supplied much-valued local news but also helped to maintain an impression of a nation-wide grassroots revolutionary movement led by Lenin. The network of local authors became the network of *Iskra*'s agents, the most valuable and most devoted activists who passed through the filters of the Leninist 'HR' selection. *Iskra* became a 'talent pipeline' for the forthcoming revolution.

As for the 'business model', the local groups were encouraged to buy out small parts of *Iskra*'s circulation for distribution among the local comrades. Even though they often were not able to pay and would receive *Iskra* anyway, their roles of distributors and contributors made them a part of the network, disciplined them, and taught them how to properly react to the commands of the central committee and conduct regular activities.

Within two years, *Iskra* had setup 50 local committees under Lenin's control. *Iskra*'s agents later constituted the core of the Bolshevik party. The leadership of *Iskra* became the organizational committee of the Second Congress of the Russian Social Democratic Labour Party in 1903, the first congress that Lenin attended and impacted (he was in exile during the First Congress). The party split into the more radical Bolsheviks (the majority faction) and the 'opportunist' Mensheviks (the minority faction). And even though the Mensheviks, who were led by the more authoritative-at-the-time Plekhanov, secured the rights over the *Iskra* brand, the revolutionary network – the capable party infrastructure – remained in the hands of Lenin, who immediately launched a new paper, *Vpered* ("Forward"). From that point on, Lenin paid particular attention to the party press.

***

The structure of *Iskra*'s distribution, funding and correspondence became the party structure. The newspaper subscription fees simultaneously became party membership dues. Being an outstanding revolutionary theorist, but also a revolutionary manager, Lenin understood that propaganda alone is not enough to turn a spark into a flame – capable infrastructure is needed.

Under the oppressive conditions of the Tsarist regime (though much softer than those Lenin, and Stalin after him, introduced in the form of the Red Terror and the Great Purge in the 1920–1930s), the institutional formation of a truly revolutionary party was nigh on impossible. Nevertheless, what Lenin invented, in fact, was a networked way to form a structure capable of conducting consistent goal-oriented activities. Long before Clay Shirky (*Cognitive Surplus*, 2010), Vladimir Lenin revealed that

63

networked collaboration can be as efficient as the work of established institutions.

However, Lenin's network collaboration was not entirely horizontal. He created a network in which the will of the creator is vertically inserted by certain resonating content and the invitation to contribute; if successful, these efforts evoke and absorb the horizontal grassroots activity.

**

This hybrid network, with its vertical structure and horizontal contributions, was ideally suited for party building, which was Lenin's primary goal. Lenin's method is still highly applicable today for converting activist, revolutionary and terrorist 'horizontal' potential (including those in the blogosphere and social media) into vertically managed activity.

However, in the form of *slactivism* ('lazy activism' by means of tiny contributions such as small donations or sign/ribbon wearing), Lenin's model also works well for the media, if purely commercial business models (ad revenue, news trade) do not provide enough means and if political or state subsidies are unavailable. Nowadays, the idea of mobilizing readers to join a *cause* is known as the 'membership model'. It is now a business idea which is not founded on party building. But the medium defines the message again – the model of membership evokes the political motives, even if they had not been initially intended.

Thus, this membership model, in which readers pay for a cause, not for news, and which is seen by many as the last resort for a news industry deprived of other business models, was indeed first tested by Karl Marx as long ago as 1848 in *Neue Rheinische Zeitung* and then crystalized in a radical form by Vladimir Lenin in *Iskra*.

Advertising distortions of the media: the audience as commodity

Starting in the late 17–18th centuries, advertising became the leading environmental force in the media market.

This was a mutation of agenda trading: journalism was still paid *from above* by those who wanted others to read news (ads), but the payer(s) did not have direct financial, political or juridical control over publishers (though licensing, censorship or other forms of juridical control by authorities most often remained in place).

Unlike the political patrons with their unified will, advertisers did not have a manifested political will and, in addition, were dispersed. With the development of the advertising-based business model, journalism became more independent.

* * *

The switch from political funding and/or reader revenue to advertising cardinally changed the nature of media business. As Jean Kilbourne put it, "The primary purpose of the mass media is to deliver us to advertisers" (Kilbourne, 1999, p. 75).

Under the model of political funding (and political control), newspapers sold agendas upwards. Under the advertising model, they started selling the audience upwards. The audience was turned into a commodity.

Dallas Smythe, one of the founders of the political economy of communications, in his "On the audience commodity and its work", asked the question: "What is the principal product of the mass media?" (Smythe, 2012 [1981], p. 185).

Seeking to revise the Marxist theory, Smythe questioned a dogmatic Marxist view, according to which the media, as a part of the superstructure, produced influence. He claimed that the dichotomy between base and superstructure became obsolete, as the superstructure is "decisively engaged in production" (Ibid., p. 200). This idea has become widespread in media analysis since Horkheimer-Adorno's 'culture industry', Baudrillard's 'symbolic production' and other similar concepts.

Smythe also repudiated the popular view that the media produce "entertainment, education, orientation, and manipulation" because all these phenomena were rather the effects of mass media content, not aspects of the media themselves (Ibid., p. 185).

According to Smythe, the principal product of the commercial mass media under monopoly capitalism was audience power – by association with labor power. Audience power was produced and sold by the media and bought by advertisers (and, indirectly, by the elites) for "two mutually reinforcing objectives": to promote and sell goods and to promote and sell political agendas. Smythe wrote:

> Because audience power is produced, sold, purchased and consumed, it commands a price and is a commodity. <...>
> What do advertisers buy with their advertising expenditures? <...> What they buy are the services of audiences with predictable specifications which will pay attention in predictable numbers and at particular times to particular means of communication <...>. As collectivities these audiences are commodities. As commodities they are dealt with in markets by producers and buyers (the latter being advertisers). (Smythe, 2012 [1981], p. 187).

65

***

Using the concept of audience power as media commodity, Smythe built his theory of 'audience work' – the efforts the audience unconsciously contributes into goods turnover and market (the elites') sustainability.

For the audience, according to Smythe, this work was not only unpaid – the audience itself paid for it when buying means of communications, such as TV receivers. Smythe even tried to measure audience labor in a monetary equivalent, calculating TV-ad prices, costs of TV receivers and man-hours spent on watching TV or listening to radio.

For Smythe, the phenomenon of the audience's commodification by the media was another example of capitalist exploitation. Capitalism makes people work even in their so-called leisure time. The entirety of human life is included in the capitalist machinery. He wrote: "At the job, you are not paid for all the labor time you sell (otherwise interest, profits, and management salaries could not be paid). And away from the job, your labor time *is* sold (through the audience commodity), although you do not sell it" (Ibid., p. 200.)

Despite the fact that people devote their entire life, both their job time and leisure time, to keep markets rolling, Marxists (and political economists in general) did not notice how the mass media turned the audience into a commodity. Smythe's essay "Communications: Blindspot of Western Marxism" (Smythe, 1977) started a discussion on this matter, from which, essentially, the political economy of the mass media began.

The power of advertising just was not on the radar when Marxism shaped political economy, simply because advertising was not a significant source of revenue for the media from the times of Marx to World War I. "Before the 1880s," Smythe wrote, "the press was mostly supported by money and influence from political parties – not advertisers". Therefore, the press was seen as a means of influence. "The only market involving the sale of newspapers and magazines was that in which people bought them <...> no organized market for the production and sale of audiences then existed" (Ibid., 187).

Having become a significant and then leading source of revenue for the media, advertising has grown into an important political and cultural enforcer. This is another example of how an instrumental use turns into an environmental force. Because of advertising revenue, the media turned from a channel of influence or news trade into an environmental factor that made the audience work for corporations' and elites' sustainability.

***

66

Along very similar lines to Smythe, Edward Herman and Noam Chomsky elaborated their Propaganda model (*Manufacturing Consent: The Political Economy of the Mass Media*, 1988). The Propaganda model describes systemic market-driven mechanisms that lead the media to support the corporate and governing elites.

Among the factors, or filters, that turned the media into effective and powerful ideological institutions that carry out a system-supportive propaganda function, Herman and Chomsky listed, first of all, ownership, profit-seeking and advertising. They even mentioned "the advertising license to do business", implying that only those media who offer the right content to provide "supportive selling environment" for advertised goods deserve advertising money and are therefore allowed to profit and stay on the market.

Thus, purely because of "reliance on market forces, internalized assumptions, and self-censorship, and without overt coercion" (Herman & Chomsky, 1988, p. 306), the media became a propaganda machine. This was not political control or party funding, but advertising (and some other structural factors) that made the media spread propaganda and manufacture consent within the masses.

***

Smythe's notion of audience as commodity along with Herman-Chomsky's Propaganda model are important for seeing how the environmental role of the media depends on their prevailing business model. By the time the mass media reached their historical (cultural, political, business, influential) height, in the late 20th century, their main effect on society had little to do with informing people, the function for which the media usually praise themselves.

The media flourished on ad revenue. News retail was a secondary, often insignificant source of money (sometimes completely absent). Advertisers subsidized news production as a necessary burden, as a condition of the channel's efficiency. In a sense, advertisers paid an institutional fee, on behalf of society, to maintain journalism. The institution maintenance fee gleaned from advertising was so plentiful that it allowed the newsrooms to do whatever they wanted including having a "bureau in Baghdad", as Clay Shirky called it,[1] even though advertisers themselves had never needed any news from Baghdad.

---

[1] Shirky, Clay. (2008). "Newspapers and Thinking the Unthinkable." *Edge.* https://www.edge.org/node/21292

Being perfect for the newsrooms, such relations were not optimal for advertisers. Thus, these relations were doomed to end as soon as advertisers found an alternative way to reach out to their audience.

5. Business of old media: the monopoly is gone

> When a resource is scarce, the people who manage it often regard it as valuable in itself, without stopping to consider how much of the value is tied to its scarcity.
>
> *Clay Shirky. "Cognitive Surplus", 2010.*

> The marriage of capitalism and journalism is over
>
> *Robert McChesney. "Rich Media, Poor Democracy", 2015.*

Watchdogs prefer the paywalled garden

On November 15, 2011, soon after midnight, the New York riot police started a raid to evict the Occupy Wall Street protesters from their camp in Zuccotti Park, Lower Manhattan. Two hundred protesters were arrested, six journalists among them, including two journalists of the Associated Press (AP). They tweeted the news about their arrest. The event had widespread resonance, both in politics (some compared the police raid in Zuccotti Park to the events at Tiananmen Square[1]) and in the media industry[2]. Many outlets and media associations, such as the PEN center, for example, "condemned restrictions on press coverage of police crackdowns" and called the arrests of journalists "an obvious abridgement of the First Amendment."[3]

The next day, AP employees received an email that contained the following, as quoted in *New York Magazine*:

> In relation to AP staff being taken into custody at the Occupy Wall Street story, we've had a breakdown in staff sticking to policies around social media and everyone needs to get with their folks now to tell them to knock it off. We have had staff tweet — BEFORE THE MATERIAL WAS ON THE WIRE — that staff were arrested. (Highlighted in *NYMag.*)[4]

---

[1] Reporters without borders. (2011, November 16). "Journalists arrested and obstructed again during Occupy Wall Street camp eviction." https://rsf.org/en/news/journalists-arrested-and-obstructed-again-during-occupy-wall-street-camp-eviction

[2] Clark Estes, Adam. (2011, November 16). "Press is not forgetting the journalists arrested at Zuccotti Park." *The Atlantic.* https://www.theatlantic.com/national/archive/2011/11/press-not-forgetting-journalists-arrested-zuccotti-park/335423/

[3] PEN America. (2011). "Officials: journalists among those arrested during Zuccotti Park." https://pen.org/press-clip/officials-journalists-among-those-arrested-during-zuccotti-park/

69

New York Magazine wrote that in AP, "The official rules note, 'Don't break news that we haven't published, no matter the format.' (Reuters spells out the same idea plainly in their handbook: 'Don't scoop the wire.')."[1]

As *Hollywood Reporter* put it, "The Associated Press was not happy about being scooped on Twitter by its own employees."[2]

***

The case was widely discussed by media critics. It revealed that journalists must supply news not to the public, but to their outlets. On the background: Twitter happened to be a faster and better tool for covering hot events than even a newswire. The news org had to remind its staffers that they owed news to it, not to Twitter.

The AP representative and the sender of that email, Lou Ferrara, after watching all the nasty commentaries on Twitter, later explained that the first reason why AP staffers should not tweet out news before it got on an AP platform was that 'we put news on our products first. That's what our customers expect.'[3] The second reason was personnel-safety concerns.

This was not an isolated case. All the major media have guidelines, in essence, restricting the rights of their staffers in using social media. "If you have a piece of information, a photo or a video that is compelling, exclusive and/or urgent enough to be considered breaking news, you should file it to the wire, and photo and video points before you consider putting it out on social media," the AP policy reads[4]. The main reason for such restrictions is, of course, to not give away value that constitutes media business.

The case unveiled a fundamental contradiction in principles. Journalism is meant to inform people to make them citizens. It is a core institution that has enabled the development of the Habermassian public sphere. But the institution needs to be maintained. Its public service was paid for either

[4] Coscarelli, Joe. (2011, November 16). "Associated Press staff scolded for Tweeting too quickly about OWS Arrests." *New York Magazine.* https://nymag.com/intelligencer/2011/11/ap-staff-scolded-for-tweeting-about-ows-arrests.html

[1] Ibid.

[2] Nededog, Jethro. (2011, November 16). "Associated Press boss berates staff for tweeting Occupy arrests." *The Hollywood reporter.* https://www.hollywoodreporter.com/news/associated-press-twitter-occupy-wall-street-arrests-262454

[3] Wemple, Erik. (2011, November 16). "Why the Associated Press ordered to 'Knock it off' on Twitter." *The Washington Post.* http://www.washingtonpost.com/blogs/erik-wemple/post/why-the-associated-press-ordered-staff-to-knock-it-off-on-twitter/2011/11/16/gIQAF1O9RN_blog.html

[4] BBC News. (2011, November 17). "Associated Press reporters told off for tweeting." https://www.bbc.com/news/technology-15772243

through news retail or through delivery of advertising. It had not been a problem in the past, if noticed at all. Society agreed to use the public service supplied by business. The public outsourced this service to the media business. But then it was suddenly revealed that the news business actually wants to keep the news for itself, even when the news can bypass it.

***

When the internet allowed news and ads to bypass traditional media, the institution maintenance fee traditionally collected by the media became intolerable for readers and advertisers. Intermediaries have become redundant in many cases, as the consumer increasingly gets along without outsourcing this function. The formerly supplier's market has turned to the market of the consumer. The most terrible thing was that the consumers became the prosumers.

Under these conditions, media orgs came up with ideas to support and preserve their once-walled garden with some artificial restrictive measures. There was the idea, for example, to license journalists in order to distinguish them from bloggers. A legislative initiative in Canada even proposed to "identify those journalists who were dedicated to 'serving the public interest,' and anyone with the professional rank would enjoy certain privileges such as 'better access to government sources.'"[1]

The prohibition on journalists posting the news before supplying it to the wire stems from the same logic. The media try to restore their walled garden by building walls for all who acquired the ability to handle information on their own. If everyone around is hedged in, then yes, you get your fence, too.

***

Watchdogs of democracy prefer to keep their watch in the paywalled garden. But maintaining these conditions artificially is impossible.

The way an instrument is used is under the control of the instrument's owner. But the issue is not even that AP is unable to control Twitter as a better instrument of news delivery. The issue is that this is not an instrumental case at all. This is a new environment in which a media instrument is given to everybody and therefore turned into an environmental force controlled by no one.

It was no coincidence that the ability of the new media environment to challenge, replace and obsolesce old media became apparent at the

---

[1] Ingram, Mathew. (2011, September 7). "No, licensing journalists isn't the answer." *GigaOm*. https://gigaom.com/2011/09/07/no-licensing-journalists-isnt-the-answer/

beginning of the 2010s, when the Arab Spring and the Occupy Wall Street movement rode the first wave of social media proliferation.

"If Twitter is beating your news wire, you have bigger problems", wrote Mathew Ingram, one of the leading media analysts, in 2011, in "Memo to AP: Twitter is the newswire now."[1]

The title of his next column posed the chief question of that time: "What happens when journalism is everywhere?"[2] He wrote:

> When the Arab Spring demonstrations were under way in Egypt's Tahrir Square and reports were streaming out through Twitter and Facebook and text messages and cellphone videos, it was easy to feel superior to the Egyptian government. How could they not realize that information can no longer be contained by blockades or even internet blackouts when everyone has the power to publish? Now the authorities in New York City and elsewhere have been getting a dose of that medicine, with the "Occupy Wall Street" protests being tweeted and live-streamed in real time. As the Associated Press learned this week to its chagrin, we all have newswires at our disposal now.[3]

In 2011, the tone of such revelations sounded alarming but also rather cheerful. What was noticed at the time seemed to threaten the established authorities, but they always deserve to be threatened. As for the media, it was assumed that they should have somehow adjusted to the new challenge.

Nine years and one Trump term later, the tone is different. It is obvious that the new environment threatens the entire established order, including the media, because they are established institutions, too. A challenge has turned into an existential threat.

***

The new media environment does not conflict with the firstborn media. It has simply appropriated their content and deprived them of their business. It has exposed that the old media supplied news not to the public but to the wire. At a deeper level, it has been revealed that journalism thrived not on information but on the lack of information.

Over its entire history, journalism managed to induce unsatisfied demand for information that the audience otherwise would never have even experienced. As Gilbert Keith Chesterton's old joke goes, "Journalism largely

---

[1] Ingram, Mathew. (2011, November 16). "Memo to AP: Twitter is the newswire now." *GigaOm*. https://gigaom.com/2011/11/16/memo-to-ap-twitter-is-the-newswire-now/

[2] Ingram, Mathew. (2011, November 18). "What happens when journalism is everywhere?" *GigaOm*. https://gigaom.com/2011/11/18/what-happens-when-journalism-is-everywhere/

[3] Ibid.

consists of saying 'Lord Jones is dead' to people who never knew that Lord Jones was alive."

The limitation of access to the means of publishing was the crucial factor that environmentally and fundamentally secured the privilege and exclusiveness of journalist status – before any reasoning about journalism quality or social service could even have been taken into account. The lack of access to producing and consuming information, not the information supplied itself, was the core ingredient of the successful media business.

The emancipation of authorship by the internet (Miroshnichenko, 2014) and particularly by social media removed this limitation. Journalism has simply lost the publishing monopoly. It has become clear that it is not the quality of content, nor the social function, but the technological monopoly over content communication that was at the core of the media's existence.

Any attempts to restore this monopoly will obviously fail, as no one can put the toothpaste back in the tube.

Moreover, there is nothing in this environmental change that the media would have been able to fix or prevent. The mass media can decorate and enhance their product however they like but it will be to no avail because their chief issue is on the side of consumption, not production. This now has to do with how news is received, not how it is produced. The media have no control over this whatsoever.

No restrictions on others to express themselves will succeed, as free authorship is the fundamental principle of the post-industrial form of capitalism – the more technologically advanced 'platform capitalism', which is aimed at extracting attention from those given access to instant self-actualization. This is the value of the highest Maslow's rank of needs, and, therefore, it has brought into being the supply-demand relations of the next level, which are inaccessible to old media with their model of industrial broadcasting.

The attempts to secure a paywalled garden for subscription, which have been seemingly successful for some of the largest media outlets in the US under the 'Trump scare', will inevitably also fail after Trump is gone; either then or after the last newspaper generation is gone.

The fundamental technological framework for journalism is vanishing with its monopoly. For journalism, the advent of the internet is not a challenge, it is an extinction-level event.

2014: advertising hit rock bottom and punctured it

Contemporary journalism was maintained in the mass media by two main sources of revenue: readers and advertisers. In the industry in general, ad revenue dominated throughout the 20th century, reaching 80% of total revenue in newspapers.[1]

A critical event happened in 2014, when reader revenue surpassed ad revenue for the first time in a hundred years. According to WAN-IFRA (2015), circulation brought $92.4 billion to newspapers around the world in 2014, while ad revenue only brought in $86.5 billion (Figure 5).

World Press Trends		
	2014	Compared to 2013
Print circulation	$89.9 bln	up 0.4%
Print advertising	$77 bln	down 5.2%
Digital circulation	$2.5 bln	up 45.3%
Digital advertising	$9.5 bln	up 8.3%

Figure 5. WAN IFRA: World Press Trends 2015.[2]

The switch in the dominant revenue sources was presented by some in the industry as a sign of sustainability in readership. The readers allegedly continued to value newspapers for their content.

Indeed, between 2010 – 2014 the reader revenue of newspapers remained at a steady $89–90 billion. However the total newspaper revenue across the globe was in just as steady decline over those years, from more than $190 billion to $179 billion.

However, the most significant outcome of this epochal event in 2014 was not the surpassing of ad revenue by reader revenue, but the dramatic and still continuing decline in ad revenue. It was not reader revenue outgrowing ad revenue; it was ad revenue hitting rock bottom.

Th year 2014 signified a tectonic shift in the business model of the media from funding by advertisers to funding by readers. Journalism had changed its funding model. Instead of being paid *from above*, journalism started being paid *from below*. This shift changed journalism itself. The

[1] WAN-IFRA (2015). World Press Trends 2015. https://www.slideshare.net/WAN-IFRA/250515-wpt-2015-final

[2] Ibid.

environmental consequences of this change have not been reflected upon yet, though they have already started to be sensed in politics, culture and people's mindsets.

***

According to the Newspaper Association of America, print ad revenue in 2013 hit the lowest level since the industry started measuring it in 1950 (in inflation-adjusted dollars). "The decline of newspapers hits a stunning milestone," reported *Slate*.[1] (Figure 6.)

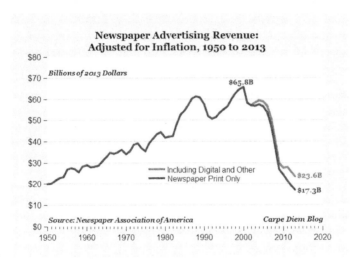

Figure 6. The decline of ad revenue in print. Source: The Newspaper Association of America. [2]

The very fact of industrial measurement indicated that the market started identifying itself. By 1950, the print advertising had matured sufficiently enough for its size to be thus measured. In 2013, it collapsed below the level at which the industry started being measured as an industry. As media analyst Mark Perry noted,

> The decline in print newspaper advertising to a 63-year low is pretty amazing by itself, but the sharp decline in recent years is stunning. Newspaper print advertising revenues decreased more than 50% in just the last five years,

---

[1] Weissmann, Jordan. (2014, April 28). "The decline of newspapers hits a stunning milestone." *Slate*. https://slate.com/business/2014/04/decline-of-newspapers-hits-a-milestone-print-revenue-is-lowest-since-1950.html

[2] Ibid.

from $37.6 billion in 2008 to only $17.3 billion last year; and by almost 70% over the last decade, from $56.9 billion in 2003.[1]

Indeed, the print ad revenue market had grown steadily over the decades in the 20th century but collapsed almost instantly. It took the industry 50 years to triple its revenue and only 13 years to crumble to rock bottom. This dynamic supports the forecast that the industry's agony will be rather quick (though the residual convulsions might continue a bit longer).

Also worthy of note is that the US population in 1950 was about 180 million, while in 2013 it was more than 330 million. Also, the economy in 1950 was just one-seventh of its size in 2013. Considering this, the size of the ad market should have been much bigger in 2013. However, print advertising shrank; so, compared to the growth of the population and economy, its drastic decline looks even more dramatic.

Where have all the ads gone? To Facebook and Google.[2]

***

The mass media are not the best audience gatherers or ad sellers anymore. When the media were the only advertising channel, advertisers reimbursed journalism but overpaid for the service of ad delivery (not to mention the preciseness of this delivery). In the digital realm, new ad services have emerged that are capable of personally customized ad message delivery. This is the simplest and most obvious explanation for why the mass media business will not transition to the digital space. The media as an advertising channel are no longer the most efficient, either in print or on the internet.

Instead of the offline ad monopoly of the mass media, the so-called duopoly of Google-Facebook has formed in online advertising. The duopoly surpassed 60% of the share of global digital advertising in 2019.[3]

In 2014, Google alone had $60 billion in ad revenue compared to the $86 billion of the entire world's newspaper industry ad revenue and $23 billion of American newspapers' ad revenue. In 2019, Google's ad revenue reached $134 billion.[4]

---

[1] Lifson, Thomas. (2014, April 28). "Inflation-adjusted newspaper print advertising revenues now below 1950 levels." *American Thinker*. https://www.americanthinker.com/blog/2014/04/inflationadjusted_newspaper_print_advertising_revenues_now_below_1950_levels.html

[2] The data link to the American newspaper industry, which is the leading one in the world, the trendsetter in media technology and business; similar processes were ongoing in other national markets approximately at the same time and at the same pace.

[3] Dang, Sheila. (2019, June 5). "9 months ago Google, Facebook have tight grip on growing U.S. online ad market: report." *Reuters*. https://www.reuters.com/article/us-alphabet- IV

Experts are now discussing if the duopoly will turn into a triopoly with the addition of Amazon. If Google and Facebook's algorithms are trying to guess what users want to buy, Amazon knows this precisely. The highly technical nature and details of this discussion completely exclude the old media from entering the fray with their method of ad 'carpet bombing'. There is nothing the mass media can do about it. No amount of staff cutting or professional education and no improvements in their content or ad service are relevant amid the advanced ad technologies of the internet.

**

On January 29, 2016, one of Canada's oldest newspapers, the *Guelph Mercury*,[1] printed its last issue.[2] The newspaper had been publishing in Guelph since 1867, the year the first three provinces united into the Dominion of Canada. Thus, the newspaper was a coeval of the nation. Perhaps that was the reason why its shutdown (the paper's, not the nation's) was so broadly and sorrowfully covered in media circles. And not just in the media; the Prime Minister of Canada, Justin Trudeau, tweeted, "Canada loses an institution with the shutdown of the @guelphmercury print edition. Sad to see it go".[3]

The paper remains present on the web and has amalgamated with another local publication, the *Guelph Tribune*, becoming the *Guelph Mercury Tribune*, and somehow continues as a local news site.[4] A year after its shutdown, *J-Source* published an interview with Phil Andrews, the last editor of the *Guelph Mercury*. Here is how the editor answered the question about the newspaper's service to the local community (among other things):

> – How did you see the paper's role in the community?
> – ... We sent someone to Africa because Guelph was connected to a really miraculous fundraising effort that had no corporate backing and it raised a million dollars for a clinic to combat HIV/AIDS in Lesotho. After they hit a million bucks, I sent a guy to Lesotho to chronicle what sort of impact $1

[4] Clement, J. (2020, February 5). "Advertising revenue of Google from 2001 to 2019." *Statista*. https://www.statista.com/statistics/266249/advertising-revenue-of-google/

[1] O'Flanagan, Rob. (2016, January 28). "The Guelph Mercury lived for 149 years." *The Guelph Mercury*. https://www.guelphmercury.com/the-guelph-mercury-lived-for-149-years/

[2] Perkel, Colin. (2016, January 25). "Guelph Mercury, one of Canada's oldest newspapers, quits print editions." *Global News*. https://globalnews.ca/news/2476001/guelph-mercury-one-of-canadas-oldest-newspapers-quits-print-editions/.

[3] Justin Trudeau on Twitter. (2016, January 26). https://twitter.com/JustinTrudeau/status/692034439627419648

[4] *Guelph Mercury Tribune*: About Us. https://www.guelphmercury.com/community-static/2881972-guelphmercury-about-us

million made. When Cardinal Thomas Collins was appointed Cardinal we sent someone to the Vatican to observe it...[1]

Such was a part of the newspaper's role in the small town (population of 130 thousand) as seen by the editor. When advertising was plentiful, a local newspaper could afford to send reporters to Africa and Rome. This is exactly what Clay Shirky called the "Baghdad bureau":

> For a long time, longer than anyone in the newspaper business has been alive in fact, print journalism has been intertwined with these economics. The expense of printing created an environment where Wal-Mart was willing to subsidize the Baghdad bureau. This wasn't because of any deep link between advertising and reporting, nor was it about any real desire on the part of Wal-Mart to have their marketing budget go to international correspondents. It was just an accident. Advertisers had little choice other than to have their money used that way, since they didn't really have any other vehicle for display ads...
>
> The competition-deflecting effects of printing cost got destroyed by the internet, where everyone pays for the infrastructure, and then everyone gets to use it. And when Wal-Mart, and the local Maytag dealer, and the law firm hiring a secretary, and that kid down the block selling his bike, were all able to use that infrastructure to get out of their old relationship with the publisher, they did. They'd never really signed up to fund the Baghdad bureau anyway.[2]

***

Eli Pariser coined the term 'Filter Bubble' when he studied the side effects of the targeting algorithms of the internet platform. Those algorithms aim to deliver content that matches our interests the best. The algorithms analyze our previous preferences (clicks, likes, reposts, connections, time of reading, etc.) and decide what content is the most relevant to us. This is done, of course, for better ad targeting.

In his book *The Filter Bubble*, Pariser made an interesting commentary regarding "a number of mortal blows" that the internet delivered to the newspaper business model. He wrote,

> An advertising pioneer once famously said, "Half the money I spend on advertising is wasted – I just don't know which half." But the Internet turned that logic on its head – with click-through rates and other metrics, businesses

---

[1] Watson, H.G. (2017, February 24). "The last days of the Guelph Mercury." *J-source*. https://j-source.ca/article/the-last-days-of-the-guelph-mercury/

[2] Shirky, Clay. (2008). "Newspapers and Thinking the Unthinkable." *Edge*. https://www.edge.org/node/21292

suddenly knew exactly which half of their money went to waste. (Pariser, 2011, p. 42.)

This is the view of businesses and a digital researcher but not journalists. For the media, that 'half' of advertisers' money was not a waste. This was an institution maintenance fee paid by society for journalism to exist. This was a toll the media collected and spent for a 'bureau in Baghdad', which a concrete advertiser did not have any need for, yet still had to pay for; that is, until the internet freed them from this duty.

If one asks an imaginary arbitrator whether the advertisers' having to pay for a 'bureau in Baghdad' is a fair deal, the answer will most likely be 'no'. For the media, this was an institution maintenance fee, but advertisers obviously overpaid for a service they personally did not order. Such was the consequence of the monopolistic position of the media.

Now, businesses can choose not to overpay. They get an even better ad delivery service to boot. For the media, on the other hand, it's a double whammy; it is not just that the overpaid 'half' of the ad price – the monopoly share of the institutional fee – is gone, but the other half is also in sharp decline.

***

In the early 2000s, local ads, classifieds, and then big ads started moving to the internet. Newspapers began losing funding for their Baghdad bureaus and then for their very existence.

The early impact of ads' migration from print to the web is best illustrated by Craigslist. Newspaper classified advertisements used to bring in $19.6 billion, approximately one-third of ad revenue, at their peak in 2000.[1] Craigslist, eBay, Kijiji and similar sites killed this market by offering people a better service for free (or on the condition of 'freemium' – partly free).

Newspapers' classified ad revenue plummeted to $2.2 billion in 2018. Thus, $17 billion in revenue was quickly wiped out because consumers had migrated to a better online service with the same (or better) functions.

In total, America's newspaper advertising revenue fell from $63.5 billion in 2000[2] to $12.3 billion in 2018.[3]

---

[1] Reinan, John. (2014, March 3). "How Craigslist killed the newspapers' golden goose." *Minnesota Post*. https://www.minnpost.com/business/2014/02/how-craigslist-killed-newspapers-golden-goose/

[2] Kaiser, Robert G. (2014, October 16). "Bad news about the news." *The Brooking Essay*. http://csweb.brookings.edu/content/research/essays/2014/bad-news.html

[3] Watson, Amy. (2019, December 2). "Advertising revenue of U.S. newspapers 2013-2018."

Technologically outdated print advertising is shrinking dramatically and "online advertising is looking more and more like a contest that publishers can't win – not on a large scale, at least," as *Slate* indicated in an article with the title speaking for itself – "The Pivot From Advertising".[1] There are now other online crowd gatherers and ad deliverers that are ten times more efficient.

This is not to mention the new capability of brands and businesses to address their audience directly through their own media channels, made possible thanks to the internet, social media and smartphones. Businesses increasingly prefer to subsidize their own media assets, not someone else's. They themselves become media, using all the technologies of audience attraction developed by journalism over the past 500 years.

Ad revenue was crucially important to the media. Journalism was 80% paid for by advertising in print and even more so on radio and TV. Advertisers' choice to pay for journalism used to be predefined not by better service but by the monopoly; they had no choice. Now, as the monopoly is gone, media ad business is shrinking offline and will not transition to online.

Journalism in search of a cute little monkey

Years ago, resort photographers had a good business, making beach pictures with the vignette "Greetings from Acapulco 1982". Now, everyone has their own camera on their smartphone. The quality might be lower than a professional photographer would offer, but it is satisfactory. Or you can check the picture and try again. Besides, it's always at your disposal and free.

What should resort photographers do? They have found an answer: a cute little monkey (a cute little crocodile or parrot work just as fine). You can pose for a picture with an adorable pet or take a picture on your own device for a fee. No tourist would bring a cute monkey with them to the resort, so this is a unique and monopolistic offer that can potentially induce an impulse to purchase. It might not work as well as photography 30 years ago, but still it is at least something.

The fun part is that the photographer sells not photography but rather a monkey. So, forced by the technological emancipation of photo-authorship,

Statista. https://www.statista.com/statistics/196470/classified-advertising-revenue-of-us-newspapers-since-2000/

[1] Oremus, Will (2017, November 21). "The pivot from advertising." *Slate.* https://slate.com/technology/2017/11/its-time-for-online-media-to-pivot-from-advertising.html

the resort photographer has departed from the art of (resort) photography to the craft of village-fair entertainment and zookeeping.

This is what has happened to journalism, without being noticed and due to the same reasons. Having lost to former customers the monopoly over 'photography supply', journalism is desperately searching for a cute monkey to sell instead.

***

The business model with two main sources of revenue (ads and readers) is not able to support journalism as it once did, so the media are forced to sell something else.

A side business related to content production – a media-allied business – would be the best solution.

Having highly professional writers, many newsrooms launched content studios that produce content for external clients to be published somewhere else.[1] For example, the New York Times Company established T Brand Studio, a sort of content bureau. As its statement claims, "Through T Brand Studio, our branded content studio, we offer our brand partners access to *The New York Times*'s proven recipe for storytelling and work with them to develop industry-leading strategy, creative and distribution."[2]

The small local news site *Richland Source* in Ohio turned photo reporting about homecomings into profitable celebrity-style photo galleries. They do the same with proms and Christmas concerts. This provides a kind of professionally facilitated collective selfies to the local community. As students and families want to see themselves as socialites, these photo galleries are the most visited pages on the *Richland Source* website (10 times more visitors than their average[3]). Sponsor spots in those public photo albums are sold out in advance.

In 2017, *Charlotte Agenda* in North Carolina created a print newcomer's guide that brought in more than $100,000 and provided an unusual case of a purely digital media outlet moving against the grain – into print.[4]

---

[1] Max Willens. (2018, October 4). Publishers are expanding their content studios to do more agency work. *Digiday.* https://digiday.com/media/publishers-content-studios-agency-work/

[2] The New York Company – T-Brand Studio. https://www.nytco.com/products/t-brand-studio/

[3] Hare, Kristen. (2017, November 1). "You can make money off homecoming pics and 9 other simple ideas to borrow from local news." *Poynter.* https://www.poynter.org/tech-tools/2017/you-can-make-money-off-homecoming-pics-and-9-other-simple-ideas-to-borrow-from-local-news/

[4] Hare, Kristen. (2017, June 2). "Charlotte Agenda created a newcomer's guide, in print, that brought in more than $100,000." *Poynter.* https://www.poynter.org/tech-

However, in spite of some experts seeing this case as proof of print's survivability, it was not about print or mass media at all; it was rather an attempt to find a new venture under the brand of the media.

The other moves by *Charlotte Agenda* prove that. It tried to expand its news business with a sister news site, *Raleigh Agenda*, but it failed to find a sustainable business model and closed it in 2016[1]. Instead, *Charlotte Agenda* experimented (successfully) with a print guide in 2017 and planned a move toward business event organizing in 2019.[2]

***

Event organizing is one of the most logical allied businesses for the media, as forums and conferences produce content, too, though in a different form. Thereafter, this content can be used or reprocessed in media outlets in classical media form. Moreover, event advertising, as with the promotion of any information, is a specialty of the media (by which faculty they endanger original event-organizing companies that do not have their own media channels).

The records testify that some media orgs expand to the event-organizing market. In 2018, Vice Media bought an events production company in Brooklyn with a staff of twelve and 300 events per year in its portfolio.[3] The purpose was to promote editorial ventures and provide new services for advertising clients (such as hosting events sponsored by brands).

The *Texas Tribune* is the most recognized event producer among the American and, most likely, world media. The publication earned as much as one-fifth to one-fourth of its revenue on events. A significant part of its event revenue came from The Texas Tribune Festival, "a three-day extravaganza of education, health care, transportation, energy, and other topics that click with the Tribune's audience."[4] This annual event gathered thousands of

---

tools/2017/charlotte-agenda-created-a-newcomers-guide-in-print-that-brought-in-more-than-six-figures/

[1] Mullin, Benjamin. (2016, December 6). "After less than a year, Raleigh Agenda is closing down." *Poynter*. https://www.poynter.org/business-work/2016/after-less-than-a-year-raleigh-agenda-is-closing-down/

[2] Mullin, Benjamin. (2017, March 23). "Despite closing expansion site, Charlotte Agenda plans to book $1 million this year." *Poynter*. https://www.poynter.org/business-work/2017/despite-closing-expansion-site-charlotte-agenda-plans-to-make-1-million-this-year/

[3] Patel, Sahil. (2018, May 4). "Vice buys events company to pitch marketers on experiential events." *Digiday*. https://digiday.com/media/286636/

[4] Ellis, Justin. (2013, September 27). "What makes the Texas Tribune's event business so successful?" *NiemanLab*. https://www.niemanlab.org/2013/09/what-makes-the-texas-tribunes-event-business-so-successful/

attendees, hundreds of speakers and profits from sponsorships and ticket sales.[1] The idea mirrored The New Yorker Festival that started in 2000 as a seventy-fifth anniversary event and became an example for festivals organized by the media.[2] In 2018, the *Texas Tribune*'s events attendance reached 14,382.[3] In addition to the festival, the *Texas Tribune* produces about 60 sponsored and free-for-the-public events per year.

***

Event production is particularly fruitful for industrial and professional b2b publications. Russian publishing house *Glavbukh* ("Chief Accountant") started with a print magazine but eventually turned it into an online consulting system and a nationwide network of conferences and workshops. New industrial and professional standards and practices are always in high demand, and the media format is not the only way to sell such content. Conferences and workshops are a popular vehicle for this content, too.

Along with conferences, *Glavbukh* established The Glavbukh Higher School[4], an educational institution combining offline and online courses for accountants. Graduates gain officially recognized diplomas and increase their professional value on the job market. Thus, media business became diversified by an educational business, which, for *Glavbukh,* long ago surpassed the print magazine in terms of revenue. Of course, the question may arise of what this has to do with media and its original social function, but, frankly, no one cares, particularly in the b2b media market, where the information service of the media prevails over their public function. And particularly when there are no other ways to survive.

Education as a form of content production and communication is an allied business for the media, too. The media can both produce educational content and promote their educational programs, in this way gaining some advantage over original educational companies.

***

Educational business attracts not only b2b media but also the biggest media brands. In 2016, The School of the New York Times offered their

---

[1] Nahser, Freia, (2018, September 27). The Texas Tribune: audience strategy and business model. Medium. https://medium.com/global-editors-network/the-texas-tribune-audience-strategy-and-business-model-376c0a980194

[2] The New Yorker Festival. https://festival.newyorker.com/

[3] Allen, Barbara. (2019). "The Trib effect." *Poynter.* https://www.poynter.org/story-of-the-texas-tribune/

[4] The Glavbukh Higher School. (Высшая Школа Главбух.) https://www.glavbukh.ru/rubrika/129

educational programs to pre-college and professional audiences. "We translate the knowledge and practices of the New York Times into educational experiences for diverse learners," the School proclaimed.[1]

The *New York Times*' educational institution stayed in the shadow of the mothership's main news business and, hence, the general public may well not realize just how large and diverse this new business branch is. First, at the pre-college level, the Summer Academy and the August Writers' Workshop present "a new kind of classroom experience where students can develop skills to guide their educational and professional paths."[2] Second, the "Gap Year is a program for recent high school graduates seeking a transformative intellectual adventure before they go to college or as they consider future plans."[3] Third, the Professional Programs "are designed to provide real-time expertise across a wide range of specializations, including content marketing, virtual reality and writing and criticism."[4]

The School of the New York Times charges tuition fees and offers scholarships – exactly in the way traditional universities do. This is a full-scale educational institution with a brand and self-advertising capacity that many prominent universities would envy.

***

The list of allied businesses maintained by the *New York Times* is not limited to the content bureau and educational programs. The New York Times Store[5] sells memorabilia and souvenirs branded by the *New York Times*. Clients can also buy branded and customized calendars, cookbooks or *New York Times* reprints related to certain data, such as someone's day of birth. The store also offers a lot of *New York Times*-branded clothes, toys and goods of all kinds. In 2014, "the *Times*' 'other revenue,' which includes the store and other brand extensions, brought in 5-10 percent of total revenue of the *Times*, up 3 percent primarily through store sales."[6]

As TV shopping shows say, "Wait! You also can get..." – yes, you also can get vacation and "educational" tours with The New York Times Journeys[7],

---

[1] The School of The New York Times – About. https://nytedu.com/about/

[2] The School of The New York Times – Pre-Gollege. https://nytedu.com/pre-college/

[3] The School of The New York Times – Gap Year. https://nytedu.com/gap-year/#overview

[4] The School of The New York Times – Professional Programs. https://nytedu.com/professional/

[5] The New York Times Store. https://store.nytimes.com/

[6] Moses, Lucia. (2015, July 24). "Publishers set up retail operations to diversify revenue." *Digiday*. https://digiday.com/media/publisher-stores-drive-commerce-preserving-reader-trust/

[7] The New York Times Journeys. https://www.nytimes.com/times-journeys/

which sells journeys that range from New York City tours to cruises around the world.

Others are dipping into tourism, too. In 2017, the *Wall Street Journal* launched the WSJ Business Travel Service, which became a part of its benefits program WSJ+ for subscribers, along with the WSJ Wine Club.[1]

Cross-promotion in the media market has some peculiarities. Goods and services were previously used to attract subscribers. Now, subscription, or more often membership, and some goods or services complement each other and create a new business stream. *New York Magazine*'s membership program "with a bigger focus on food and drink events" not only promotes paid memberships but also the paid events hosted by *New York Magazine*'s experts. It states that,

> There will still be special discount codes and early access to sales at retailers, but more emphasis on exclusive food and drink events, ideally hosted by editors of its Grub Street vertical. Earlier this week, for example, New York by New York members got together to eat an entire pig with food critic Adam Platt and Grub Street editor Alan Sytsma at Gramercy Italian restaurant Maialino.[2]

Special events, sold to the general public and/or with discounts to subscribers, became a mandatory part of all membership programs after the *Guardian* invented this approach in order to have a substitute for subscription in 2011. It aims at subscribers, or now members-donators, but also creates a new stream of revenue by combining subscription and event production (or the production of some other services).

Undoubtedly, this cross-promotional innovation may slightly revitalize the business of media orgs. But it has little to nothing to do with journalism and its social functions.

***

The idea of selling branded 'merch' like Disney or the Transformers' franchise is also quite acceptable to the media. Afterall *Playboy* has long played almost in the same league with Disney: in 2016, the retail value of Bunny-licensed goods sold reached $1.5 billion.

---

[1] Moses, Lucia. (2018, October 10). "How The New York Times uses T-shirt discounts and tours to drive subscriptions." *Digiday*. https://digiday.com/media/new-york-times-shirts-tours-subscription-goals/

[2] Willens, Max. (2018, February 1). "One year in, New York magazine pivots membership program to exclusive events focus." *Digiday*. https://digiday.com/media/one-year-new-york-magazine-refines-membership-program/

But the biggest player among the media in this market is Meredith, parent of *Better Homes and Gardens*, "which accounted for over $22 billion, ... second only to the $57 billion generated by Disney, according to License Global."[1]

Many other publishers are active in brand-licensing, too, including Hearst, with $350 million; Rodale, with $155 million; and Condé Nast, with $150 million in brand-licensed goods sold.

Not only can the media produce branded souvenir merchandise or license their brand to someone else's goods, they also can intervene in completely different markets with their "lines" of products. For example, *Cosmopolitan* launched its own jewelry line and 'Cosmobranded' cosmetic bags and accessories line. *ELLE* launched its own line of fragrances.[2]

***

Other 'cute little monkeys' the media are seeking in order to replace their former business are even funnier.

Hearst Magazines sold a self-rolling yoga mat that was accompanied by a voice assistant yoga instructor. "The mat includes an Amazon Alexa command that turns your device into a yoga teacher and talks you through a flow of the day from *Women's Health*", announced *Cosmopolitan*.[3]

Men's Health not only branded a bag of beef jerky but also made sure it "had the right protein levels without compromising on the taste."[4] Not only is this an allied business, but also the noble function of watchdog journalism is performed here.

"We buy balloons and a helium tank," said the head of the local newspaper *Oktyabrsky Vestnik* (*October Herald*... well, okay, *October Newsletter*) from Russia at a media conference. "We inflate balloons and sell them at local events. It doesn't bring in huge revenues, but it's fairly profitable." As a local newspaper is obliged to cover all local festivities and

---

[1] Willens, Max. (2017, June 13). "Why Time, Conde Nast and other magazine publishers are charging into brand licensing." *Digiday*. https://digiday.com/media/publishers-brand-licensing/

[2] Innovation Media Consulting. (2019). "Licensing and brand extensions: profit or minefield?" *Innovation in Media 2019-2020 World report*. https://innovation.media/newswheel/profit-or-minefield

[3] Narins, Elizabeth. (2018, November 23). "This genius exercise mat rolls itself up like a slap bracelet." *Cosmopolitan*. https://www.cosmopolitan.com/health-fitness/a23941839/self-rolling-yoga-mat/

[4] Southern, Lucinda. (2017, December 11). "Beef jerky and sofas: Why Hearst is expanding product licensing." *Digiday*. https://digiday.com/media/beef-jerky-sofas-hearst-expanding-product-licensing/

be present there, why not sell something celebratory? Yet another allied side business.

In 2017, *BuzzFeed* started selling an internet-connected "precision smart cooktop". It seems that the experiment was so successful that *BuzzFeed* allied with Epoca International, a houseware manufacturer, and Walmart in a joint venture under the brand *BuzzFeed*'s Tasty, a video recipes division complemented by e-shopping. The venture is aimed at producing, promoting and selling spoons, spatulas and other kitchenware.[1]

***

As the media are supposed to be capable of attracting an online audience, e-commerce looks like a logical and prospective solution for establishing an allied business. Many publications have tried e-commerce, though with different outcomes. Even new hybrid half-media/half-e-commerce forms have appeared, such as *PopSugar*, initially a lifestyle online media org that acquired a fashion shopping search engine and turned into a lifestyle media/shopping entity.

The only problem with e-commerce is that, in order to sell something, you need to have this something, and there are a lot of other actors in the market who already have it. With this move, the media enter an area with not even a tiny chance of establishing a monopoly, to which they were once accustomed. They might have an advantage in gathering audience members but not in goods production, logistics and selling. This hybrid zone may be flourishing, and this may continue, but not for media business; rather, it will be for businesses becoming media, a form that all of them must now take.

However, the bigger risk relates not to the uncertainty regarding business success but to the capacity of the media to hold true to their ideals when chasing digital dimes in strange lands of online commerce or online marketing. As *Digiday* once put it,

> Given the challenges of digital media, commerce is a tempting way for publishers to create new revenue streams by extending their brands. But slapping commerce links on articles can lead to the impression that the editorial side is for sale, damaging the publisher's credibility.[2]

---

[1] Kafka, Peter. (2018, March 1). "BuzzFeed has a new business model, so it's selling its own line of kitchen tools at Walmart." *Vox.* https://www.vox.com/2018/3/1/17066402/buzzfeed-walmart-tasty-kitchen-gadget-tools-retail-deal

[2] Moses, Lucia. (2015, July 24). "Publishers set up retail operations to diversify revenue." *Digiday.* https://digiday.com/media/publisher-stores-drive-commerce-preserving-reader-trust/

***

Having lost two major revenue streams coming from the sale of ads and news, the media are trying to apply a multiple revenue approach, similar to a casino's strategy of 'many small bets': bet a little on many numbers in order to increase the probability of a win. It seems to be a reasonable strategy based on a philosophy of trial and error.

This is not, of course, an investment strategy from the industrial era, when you needed to invest significant capital into fixed assets, such as oil platforms, car plants, printing shops, distribution networks and other machinery in industries with a very expensive entry pass and guaranteed profits. This is a strategy from the post-industrial era, in essence a venture investment. The investor will lose something but also can win if they are smart, fast and lucky. A good strategy, but there is nothing specific in it that favors the media; everyone can try. Besides, while the strategy of 'many small bets' reflects a spirit of post-industrial business, it certainly distracts from journalism.

Without the excessive funding guaranteed in the past, mostly by advertising, journalism is reduced to marketing for others or to e-commerce for itself. From the small local newspaper *Oktyabrsky Vestnik* in the frozen north of Russia selling balloons with helium, to world-class media behemoths such as the *New York Times* selling tote bags, everyone in the media market who is struggling for survival is taking this slippery road which results in either being a marketing agency or a media-commerce hybrid akin to *PopSugar*. The need to sell 'something else' is turning the media into sellers of 'something else'.

The question is how the quality of content and independent journalism can be preserved under such conditions. Journalism is turning into marketing. Native advertising has emerged, a prospective format that marries external selling intentions with the editorial journalistic narrative, directly using journalistic tools and styles and mindsets for the marketing of someone else's goods under the guise of media storytelling. The dissolving of journalism's integrity through marketing has intensified.

The wall between advertising and news, the achievement of 20th century journalism, is crumbling. The fall of this wall used to be a dream of advertisers; now newsrooms offer it, and they are even often proud of their achievements in native advertising and other kinds of *advertorials* and *infomercials* – ads built in editorial content. Journalism invites marketing to come in and make itself comfortable. This is a Trojan horse built not by Odysseus but by Hector.

In the meantime: marketing turns into journalism

As the internet emancipated authorship, four types of publishers, or, better, *publicators*, appeared. There are four groups of publicators now:

1. the mass media
2. ordinary people
3. celebrities
4. brands

The firstborn media are still on the market. The internet has not expelled them. The internet uses them as they professionally produce the most attractive and shareable content. Moreover, the internet has offered the mass media even better opportunities for content production and distribution. The internet has just deprived them of a business model that happened to be based on a monopoly over news production and distribution.

At the same time, a huge army of amateur publicators has appeared. The size of this army has already reached half of humankind and will continue to grow until it reaches 85–90% of the Earth's adult population. As these amateur media 'outlets' completely coincide with their audience and witness all the events happening to them, they collectively cover everything and reach out to everyone in an uncountable chaotic array of 'random acts of journalism'.

However, between these two poles of publicators, professional and amateur, there are two more categories of newly emerged media entities whose authorship was emancipated by the internet and whose activity has already begun to threaten journalism from a new angle – that of media professionalism.

***

Celebrities of all kinds are a new type of media that has emerged from amateurs. Celebrities used to depend on the media to maintain their celebrity. But now they are capable of being the media themselves and are sometimes even more prominent than the firstborn media.

Politicians, sports and movie stars, beauty bloggers and vloggers, gamers, streamers, and all kinds of social media influencers have something in common both with ordinary amateurs and the mass media. Similar to amateurs, their authorship was emancipated – they gained access to the public and publication. Similar to the media, they regard their media activity as professional - they are media professionals. Not only do influencers borrow professional journalists' approaches, they also invent new ones.

Another type of publicator has emerged out of the emancipation of authorship related to brands. Brands are becoming the media. Unlike celebrities who learn how to be media on the hoof, brands are inherently professional in any of their activity, including their media activity. Unlike the firstborn media, brands have money to be the media; they also do not need to make money out of being the media. Corporations directly and generously subsidize their media branches, as they are their own assets, redistributing expenses from their former advertising in the mass media.

***

While traditional journalism, seeking to compensate for declining profits, has turned to marketing in order to accommodate advertisers, marketing is gradually morphing into journalism.

Traditional marketing boils down to managing brand information distribution, while a new form of marketing has emerged – content marketing. Content marketing strives to create conditions in which information about the brand spreads on its own.

Brands are now operating as media. Creating relevant and valuable content is no longer an option; it is a necessity. Companies that have nothing to say to their audience will become increasingly marginalized.

The traditional journalism of the media has now been joined by the guerilla journalism of the masses, the celebrity journalism of the Kardashians and PewDiePie, and the brand journalism of the corporations. Whilst each initially started with their own narrow interests, they have become engaged in a media 'arms race' and must evolve to the level of socially significant content.

***

On October 14, 2012, Austrian skydiver Felix Baumgartner leapt from his capsule at an altitude of 39 kilometers. During his freefall, he set a number of world records, including becoming the first man to break the sound barrier without a vehicle.

The project, sponsored by Red Bull, was called Red Bull Stratos[1]. The event was heavily promoted through all media channels, as if Red Bull had launched its own corporate Gagarin (or Armstrong – whomever you prefer).

Just before stepping out of the capsule, Baumgartner said: "I know the whole world is watching now." He was almost right. Over 9 million people watched the live stream of the jump. The next day, YouTube garnered a total

---

[1] Red Bull Stratos.
https://www.redbullcontentpool.com/premium/photography/projects/red-bull-stratos

of 366 million views of the jump. To compare: Neil Armstrong's landing on the Moon in 1969 was watched by 600 million worldwide. On the one hand, there was no YouTube allowing one to watch the recorded video the next day but, on the other hand, the Moon landing was covered by ABC, CBS and NBC, the largest broadcasters at the time.[1] All in all, the Red Bull corporate space jump was covered in the media almost as widely as Armstrong's moon walk. (As for Yuri Gagarin, he was a Russian, so his media coverage remains beyond any comparison.)

Through this event, Red Bull not only dared to organize a state-scale venture, it also managed to cover it on a scale that did not merely surpass that of big media but involved the entire media ecosystem. Basically, it was mainly the coverage that made this event so big. The effect was provided by media coverage that Red Bull maintained itself and initiated in the media and on social media.

***

Many have heard about Felix Baumgartner's jump from the stratosphere. Some have watched funny videos from the Red Bull Flugtag, an annual 'airshow' in which participants build extravagant flying machines and ride them from a pier into a river. Fewer probably know that Red Bull has become one of the first corporations to establish a full-fledged multi-platform publishing house.

By 2014, Red Bull Media House had produced a wide range of media products: four magazines (including a glossy magazine, a popular science title, and the *Red Bulletin* with a circulation of 3.1 million!); Red Bull TV, as well as separate video channels for special projects; online media, including social networking; a music label with a recording studio and online radio; gaming platforms; and films. To cover Baumgartner's space jump, The Red Bull Content Pool website, which covers sports, culture and lifestyle, ran a special section: the Red Bull Stratos Newsroom.

As Brian Morrissey from *Digiday* put it, "Red Bull truly is a media company that happens to sell soft drinks."[2]

***

"So is the *Red Bulletin* marketing or journalism? The answer: both," – stated the *Washington Post*.

---

[1] CNN Library. (2019, August 8). "First Moon Landing Fast Facts."
https://edition.cnn.com/2013/09/15/us/moon-landing-fast-facts/index.html

[2] Morrissey, Brian. (2012, October 15). "What Red Bull Can Teach Content Marketers."
Digiday. https://digiday.com/marketing/what-red-bull-can-teach-content-marketers/

More than this, new media have formed an environment in which brands want to lose control over content they produce – something unheard of in classical marketing, as brands traditionally wanted total control over their brand content. "If you tell great stories, people will do the work for you by distributing it," the *Washington Post*[1] quoted an expert.

In 2010, Coca-Cola presented a new "liquid and linked" content marketing strategy: "Coca-Cola Content 2020"[2]. The idea behind liquid content was to create ideas that would be so contagious that they could not be controlled. Such liquid content should be so interesting that it would provoke consumer conversations without any further interference or control from the company.

Among other things, this new objective has changed the economy of marketing. Companies now have to invest more in content creation and maintaining their own platform, but they can pay less for a distribution channel (assuming the content is popular, of course). Interesting information spreads itself. Content for the Red Bull Stratos project came at a hefty price, but, afterwards, the media story of the stratosphere leap took on a life of its own, generating hundreds of millions of contacts for the brand. Had Red Bull chosen traditional advertising in old media, it would never have had enough money to reach such a vast audience.

***

Brands become media. This is in their genes, as brands produce nothing but content. They also need to attract the audience's attention. So, media production should be their modus operandi, particularly now, when the entire arsenal of media production is available to everyone. Some businesses grow their own media branches; some buy them on the market.

Goldman Sachs produces its own talk show *Talks at GS*, a series of interviews with celebrities and experts that are published on Facebook, Twitter, YouTube, Amazon Prime and Spotify.[3] Dollar Shave Club publishes *MEL*, a men's lifestyle and culture magazine, "the publication extension of the Unilever-owned Dollar Shave Club".[4] The designer fashion online retailer Net-A-Porter publishes *Porter Magazine*, "a fashion magazine for the dynamic, modern woman of the world."[5]

---

[1] Ibid.

[2] Coca-Cola Content 2020. https://www.youtube.com/watch?v=LerdMmWjU_E

[3] Merced, Michael de la. (2018, March 23). "Goldman Sachs takes it homegrown talk show to a wider audience." *The New York Times.* https://www.nytimes.com/2018/03/23/business/dealbook/goldman-sachs-talk-show.html

[4] *MEL Magazine.* https://melmagazine.com/about

Russian search engine Yandex bought *TheQuestion*, the local analogue to *Quora*, the crowdsourced question-and-answer media service.[1] The fintech trading platform Robinhood acquired a media company called MarketSnacks that produces financial podcasts and newsletters for millennials.[2] The purpose was to invite young investors on the platform. Blue Apron, a meal kit delivery service, launched a food podcast in collaboration with the narrative podcasting company Gimlet Creative – in addition to its food recipe blog, a culinary media outlet in its own right.[3] Thematic podcasts are produced by Slack, General Electric, Shopify, Umpqua Bank and many others.[4] SoulCycle, a fitness company that offers indoor cycling workout classes in 88 studios across the US, Canada and the UK, has a 20-person content division that develops its own media business.[5]

It is not only the largest brands that have entered the media realm – mid-size and small businesses are following suit. Those businesses that are not heading there yet should hurry up.

✳✳✳

Those unfamiliar with these new 'corporate media' might say that brands will always talk about how good they are, and this will make their content sound promotional and boring. True, many of them use this new tool in such a limited way. But when speaking about the environment, not the tool, it is clear that the environment forces the new brand media to compete and to compete on the conditions set by the environment.

They compete with all other publicators seeking the audience's attention: the firstborn media, the celebrities and millions of ordinary social media users with hundreds of thousands of talented ones among them. The brands must produce quality content and touch a nerve in order to succeed

---

[5] *Porter Magazine*. https://www.net-a-porter.com/gb/en/Shop/Magazine

[1] Yandex bough TheQuestion by journalist Tonya Samsonova. («Яндекс» купил сервис TheQuestion журналистки Тони Самсоновой. 2019, 12 марта. Секрет Фирмы. https://secretmag.ru/news/yandeks-kupil-servis-the-question-zhurnalistki-toni-samsonovoi-12-03-2019.htm

[2] Marinova, Polina. (2019, March 25). "Exclusive: Robinhood made its first acquisition ever - and it's a financial newsletter." *Fortune*. https://fortune.com/2019/03/25/robinhood-acquires-marketsnacks/

[3] "Blue Apron and Gimlet Creative cook up new food podcast." *Blue Apron Blog*. https://blog.blueapron.com/why-we-eat-what-we-eat/

[4] Steck, Emily. (2016, August 16). "How 7 companies are killing it with branded podcasts." *BlueWing*. https://blog.bluewing.co/best-branded-podcasts

[5] Flynn, Kerry. (2018, November 30). "'Purpose-built for Instagram': SoulCycle has a 20-person team building a media business." *DigiDay*. https://digiday.com/marketing/soulcycle-team-building-media-business/

– absolutely in a journalistic way (or even more advanced, considering their resources). Brand journalism must evolve towards producing socially significant content, entirely in the same way as old journalism had done.

The most advanced brands are able to distance their media from their quarterly sales targets. When Ashley Brown, a manager behind *Coca-Cola Journey* (the online media entity that Coca-Cola's website became in 2012), was asked by the *New York Times* if *Coca-Cola Journey* would accept an opinion column by then-mayor Michael Bloomberg, who spearheaded the campaign against large sugary drinks, he answered that, "Anything's possible. If you want to mention that to Mayor Bloomberg, I would give you my e-mail. We have a belief here that not shying away from tough decisions is a good thing and gives us credibility."[1]

***

Now, when the internet has given everyone their own opportunity to be the media and the firstborn media are losing their grip, brands are developing their own media faculties in the most progressive and professional way, hunting talents from old media, adopting technologies from old media, and developing new media technologies, a venture that many old media cannot afford to engage in as they are preoccupied with their survival.

"Consumers don't care who made the content as long as it's awesome," quoted the *Washington Post*[2] one of the actors in this new media market. The phrase echoes, in a new way, a famous statement of Howard Gossage, an advertising innovator and friend of McLuhan, who said in the 1960s that, "The real fact of the matter is that nobody reads ads. People read what interests them, and sometimes it's an ad." Indeed, people read what interests them, and sometimes it's the news media.

The media activity of brands does not seek to destroy old media. Brands just relocate their resources and efforts toward their own media assets, depriving old media of ad revenue and entering (with those or even bigger money) the media competition themselves. There is no evil plot behind it; this is an environmental setting that has put old media into a new and unexpected niche competition.

[1] Elliott, Stuart. (2012, November 11). "Coke revamps web site to tell its story." *The New York Time*. https://www.nytimes.com/2012/11/12/business/media/coke-revamps-web-site-to-tell-its-story.html

[2] Farhi, Paul. (2013, March 26). "To build brand, companies produce slick content and their own media." *The Washington Post*. https://www.washingtonpost.com/lifestyle/style/to-build-brand-companies-produce-slick-content-and-their-own-media/2013/03/26/741d582a-9568-11e2-ae32-9ef60436f5c1_story.html

The mass media are giving up news and ads to the internet. The decline in ad revenue has surpassed the decline in reader revenue, causing a tectonic shift: the business model that maintained journalism reversed from advertising funding to reader funding. This radical economic change has started transforming the social function of journalism. This economic change was also accompanied by a technological change in the very material base of journalism, and in the ways its very content is produced, packed, delivered and consumed.

6. Materiality of old media: the medium was the message

As an agent of change, printing altered methods of data collection, storage and retrieval systems and communications networks used by learned communities throughout Europe.
Elizabeth Eisenstein. "The Printing Press as an Agent of Change", 1980.

Media is the connective tissue of society... Media is how you know about anything more than ten yards away.
Clay Shirky. "Cognitive Surplus", 2010.

From journalism of fact to opinion journalism

The sixteenth-century Venetian *avvisi*, the first form of the regular news media, could carry, due to their regularity, much more much-needed foreign news than was gathered, simply because of the dearth of news supply. News was extremely valuable, and the shortage of news incentivized the journalism of fact. In reality, there was no other type of journalism at the time. It would have made no sense to publish opinions in *avvisi*; only facts are needed when there is a lack of news.

During bourgeois and religious political revolutions of the Early Modern era, social turbulence and economic development provided an influx of events, and newspapers had a plentiful news supply. But they remained materially constrained – by the size of the paper page and the volume of the folio. The physical limitations of newssheets caused a need for selection. This news selection led the creation of editorial policy. Having an opinion about the news and its political significance became embedded in the process of newspaper production.

Political pamphlets (authorial opinions) and then editorial policy (editors' opinions) created the opinion journalism that dominated the media in the nascent era of the public sphere. Political turbulence and the abundance of news, amid the limitations of the physical nature of the newssheet, increased the use-value of opinion journalism. This value resided in the capability of opinion journalism, through news selection and navigation, to compress an excessive array of facts into comprehensible

96

agendas. The selection of news reduced the flow of news to allow it to fit within the physical limitations of newspapers. This navigation through the news helped people make sense of events. In other words, the abundance and complexity of information needed to be reduced to match the limited carrying capacity of the channel and the limited perceptive capacity of the receiver.

Thus, the increase in the value of opinions was simply predetermined by the imbalance between the excessive news-gathering capacity of the medium and the insufficient news-absorbing capacity of the ecosystem.

***

The advent of telegraph technology made a fascinating breakthrough in news gathering. A rare new type of news, instant distant news, was long undersupplied compared to the news-absorbing capacity of the ecosystem. Growing industrial capitalism and rising capitalist imperialism, both of which aimed at spatial expansion, needed more overseas news to support their growth. The gathering of news from distant places became highly valuable again, as had been the case in the time of the Venetian *avvisi*.

Unlike in the time of the Venetian *avvisi* and for the first time in history, communication was separated from transportation (Carey, 2009 [1989], p. 157). The idea of getting the news from the far-flung corners of the Earth, be it flat or round, not in a year or five months but in a second, was mesmerizing. The telegraph made the news supply from around the world instant, though very expensive at first.

The cost of the telegraph limited not only the number of messages that could be sent but also the size of messages, as the charge for messages was based on the number of characters. This forced correspondents' writing to become concise and substantive. The so-called telegraphic style of journalism emerged. When a conveyed message is literally charged by the letter, nobody will subsidize someone's opinions. Only naked and solid facts were therefore telegraphed. The cost of messages made facts more valuable than opinions, simply by the design of the medium.

The medium also redefined the message structure. The principle of the inverted pyramid appeared, which prescribed the priorities in the structure of a journalist report: the most important information should go first, followed by the details in the order of their diminishing significance. This was (and is), again, a structure catering to the delivery of facts, not the expression of opinions.

In "Technology and Ideology: The case of the Telegraph", James Carey wrote:

> \<The telegraph> snapped the tradition of partisan journalism by forcing the wire services to generate "objective" news, news that could be used by papers of any political stripe.
>
> Telegraph... demanded something closer to a "scientific" language, a language of strict denotation in which the connotative features of utterance were under rigid control. (Carey, 2009 [1989], p. 162.)

***

The telegraph made the local newspapers' coverage of foreign events a matter of high social significance. Never before had local readers been so involved in global politics and in politics in general. Satisfaction of the appetite for national and international news became a part of the daily routine. Armed with the telegraphed news, local newspapers pushed local communities and nation-states towards the global world. Modern journalism emerged.

The higher value of news gathering compared to the value of news absorbing suppressed opinions. Opinions were marginalized to the areas of revolutionary criticism. The value pendulum between facts and opinions swayed back to facts.

The Crimean War (1853–56) proved the incredible commercial value of telegraph news reporting in national and local newspapers. The modern ecosystem of newswire agencies had commenced.

By the end of the 19th century, the cost of the telegraph had decreased, which made it widely affordable. Newspapers became saturated with international news. The demand for guidance in this news kaleidoscope appeared. Opinions and expertise started being valued above mere facts in the media diet. In this new cycle of the evolution, opinion journalism re-established command.

***

Similar cycles happen each time a new mass medium appears and then ages.

It happened again to radio, TV, and the internet. At first, the audience is always fascinated with the technical parameters of a new delivery device. Newspapers, telegraph, radio, TV, the internet – they all initially regurgitated the common effect of the new technologies of news gathering: what is sensed as the *new* in the perception of the medium made its message received as the *news*. Any message put in a new technological shell is considered news, regardless of the content. The new medium makes any message the news. This news is not always necessarily a solid provable fact, but it is factual. In economic terms, the new and unprecedented time-and-space features of news' availability, just recently provided by a new medium, always make facts more valuable than opinions.

When a medium comes of age, it supplies such a large amount of news that it saturates the carrier. Eventually, the carrying capacity of the carrier and the perceptive capacity of the receiver get overwhelmed. Navigation and selection rise in demand, leading to an increase in the use-value of opinions.

Thus, the introduction and then ageing of a new medium correlates runs in tandem with the switch of value between journalism of fact and opinion journalism.

1) When a medium is new, its news-gathering capacity is more valued than the news-absorbing capacity of the ecosystem. This ecosystem is dominated by journalism of fact.

2) When a medium reaches its full news-gathering capacity and oversupplies content above the news-absorbing capacity of the ecosystem, the navigation of facts increases in value. This ecosystem is dominated by opinion journalism.

In other words, up to the point of news saturation provided by a new medium, journalism is more likely to be fact-leaning. When saturation completes and news is in abundance, journalism is more likely to be opinion-leaning.

***

The media have swayed like a pendulum between journalism of fact and opinion journalism for five centuries. Each new medium restarted the cycle.

Now, the question is whether the news-gathering capacity of new digital media and the news-absorbing capacity of the new digital media ecosystem are going to maintain this pendular movement; and, if they are, in what way? Both capacities – news gathering and news absorbing – look either limitless, or limitlessly renewing, in the digital realm. How to measure their waltzing balance (or, more precisely, imbalance)?

In digital media technologies, the speed of news gathering has arguably become the fastest possible. It has become casual for us to routinely not just to get news instantly, but to observe the very development of events in real-time.

The amusement and entertainment value provided by news gathering has also approached its limits. News content is able to trigger all the senses, including tactility – smartphones vibrate when news is delivered. The further evolution of news delivery will make us not just learn or watch news but also sense it.

Thus, on the one hand, all the news-gathering capacities of this new medium, the internet, seem to be exploited. The amount of news is incredible. On the other hand, the news-absorbing capacity of the ecosystem seems to be limitless, too. It can absorb all the news it gathers. So, what shortage should define the value of facts or opinions – the shortage in news-gathering or in news-absorbing capacity?

The issue is that in reality people cannot digest all the news the internet can carry.

While the news-absorbing capacity of media channels and platforms has become limitless, the news-absorbing capacity of the receiver, of us, has approached its biological limits, at least for this type of content. Americans consume media 12 hours per day.[1] Counting weekends, this is twice as much as a full-time job. The media ecosystem gathers and delivers more content than people can process. There is still some unused time remaining, the other twelve hours, that can be filled by further media consumption. But it will not be journalist content whatsoever. Journalist content can barely attract one to two hours (for many – far less) out of those twelve hours already spent by an individual on daily media consumption.

The unlimited news supply amid the limited time capacity of news consumption, according to the rule of the fact-opinion pendulum, has to increase the value of opinions above facts in the news media. In the 2010s, with the widespread internet and social media, journalism tends to be opinion-leaning. Reporting has surrendered to commenting.

Everything is a policy statements when headlines are clickbait

News coming from primary sources was highly significant under the conditions of access scarcity and information deficit. Journalists used to be professional news hunters and gatherers that provided the tribe with info food from original, 'organic' sources.

Now, it is not people who need to get information; it is information that needs to reach out to people. People do not need news hunters anymore; they themselves are hunted by the news.

Within the backdrop of information abundance, it is not primary information that is valued, but the navigation in the ocean of news. The contemporary media have to become opinionated and subjectively biased

---

[1] He, Amy. (2019, May 31). "Average time spent with media in 2019 has plateaued. Digital is making up losses by old media." *eMarketer*. https://www.emarketer.com/content/us-time-spent-with-media-in-2019-has-plateaued-with-digital-making-up-losses-by-old-media

because of the technological settings of the contemporary media environment, where the digital capacity of news gathering has exhausted the news-absorbing capacity of users.

While journalism of fact referred to what is believed to be objective truth, opinion journalism operates with categories of usefulness, efficiency and impact. It is pragmatic, not ontological. As such, it is deictic and subjective by default. In opinion journalism, the primary requirement for news is to fit the picture of the world, not the world itself, as is required from the journalism of facts. Under this ethos, news must be necessarily applicable and not necessarily ontologically true.

***

A massive study of the shift in the presentation of news over the past 30 years, based on linguistic analysis, was conducted by the RAND Corporation in 2019. This was the period when new digital media ceased to be technologically new and had become routinely used. According to the rule of the fact-opinion pendulum between new and old media, this should have brought in an oversupply of facts and an increase in the value of opinions.

The study stated that,

> Over time, and as society moved from "old" to "new" media, news content has generally shifted from more-objective event- and context-based reporting to reporting that is more subjective, relies more heavily on argumentation and advocacy, and includes more emotional appeals.[1]

The researchers highlighted that the shift was observed across platforms. Changes appeared to be the least significant in print journalism but highly noticeable in prime-time cable programming and also in journalism that migrated online.

Print journalism in the pre-2000 period maintained "context- and event-based reporting, reliance on directives, and use of titles and official positions." The post-2000 samples showed a significant shift away from such features. Journalists started using character-centered stories to cover social issues. For example, when discussing homelessness, a story about homeless children would be used.

"Television news has made stronger shifts to subjectivity, conversation, and argument," the study stated. It pointed out that

---

[1] Kavanagh, Jennifer, et al. (2019). "News in a digital age. Comparing the presentation of news information over time and across media platforms." *RAND Corporation.* https://www.rand.org/pubs/research_reports/RR2960.html

Similar to print journalism, television news has shifted from straight reporting that dealt with complex issues and grounded news in the abstract concepts and values of shared public matters to a more subjective, conversational, argumentative style of news presentation.[1]

Broadcast news of the pre-2000 period was more likely to use academic and more precise language as well as complex and argumentative reasoning about causality and contingencies, including the analysis of opposing arguments. After 2000, broadcast news lost much of its academic and precise characterization and became conversational in tone, the study showed.

It is also interesting that prime-time news programs on cable news channels mutated into opinion-based shows with a lot of pundits and experts invited to comment on the issues of the day.

"Online journalism features a subjective kind of advocacy," stated the research. "Online journalism is more personal and direct than print journalism, narrating key social and policy issues through very personal frames and subjective references." Compared to newspaper journalism, online journalism sounds "more personal and subjective, more interactive, and more focused on arguing for specific positions."[2]

The shift in the language and style of news presenting from objective and factual reporting to a more subjective and statement-based delivery contributed to what the researchers called "Truth Decay."[3]

***

According to the Pew Research Center's 2013 report "State of the News Media", 85% of the content of *MSNBC*, the second-largest cable news network, was classified as opinion and commentary, and only 15% as news.[4] For the cable №1, *Fox News*, the proportion was 50/50, and the same ratio was seen for *CNN*, the last of the trio, judging by their ratings.

CNN was founded in 1980 as a 24-hour news channel. It was a pioneer in the genre of instant, around-the-clock and around-the-globe, all-news TV. In a sense, *CNN* was a new medium that revealed the new news-gathering

---

[1] Ibid.

[2] Ibid.

[3] Kavanagh, Jennifer, et al. (2018). "How the style and language of news presentation is changing in the digital age." *RAND Corporation*. https://www.rand.org/pubs/research_briefs/RB10059.html

[4] Bercovici, Jeff. (2013, March 18). "Pew study finds MSNBC the most opinionated cable news channel by far." *Forbes*. https://www.forbes.com/sites/jeffbercovici/2013/03/18/pew-study-finds-msnbc-the-most-opinionated-cable-news-channel-by-far/

capacity of TV. The news was the value, as it always is when a new news-gathering media capacity is introduced.

Both *Fox News* and *MSNBC* were established in 1996, when the TV-capacity of round-the-clock news reporting had already been relatively battered and the ecosystem was approaching the limits of news absorption. These two became more opinionated TV cable networks, which logically resulted in their political inclinations towards the right and the left respectively (with *MSNBC* trying to stick to objective journalism for a while).

But even the initially news-obsessed and for-news-created *CNN* reached the 50% share of opinion by 2013 – long before the media became mesmerised by Trump. The abundance of news made the news less valued and increased the value in the navigation of news, which is commonly provided by expertise, commentaries, and opinions. This was not a partisan impact on TV; this was rather a media environmental effect with the subsequent search, by the media, for a partisan opinionated agenda to lean toward.

In the TV business (and to some extent in print, too), the drift from facts to opinions was reinforced by an economic factor. News production is much more expensive than the production of opinions and expertise. The conversation of pundits in the studio is much more cost-efficient than news reporting from the field. Additionally, amid a sinking business model, the media were pushed towards more opinions by the necessity to cut the production costs. This economy on news production of course resulted in more politicization.

Similar economic- and techno-determinism struck TV networks once again during the COVID-19 pandemic, where news reporting and even studio broadcasting were restricted by the quarantine. TV returned to its archaic 'talking heads' format, now in the form of endless Zoom-like meetings, as this was the simplest and cheapest way to fill air-time with controllably relevant content.

Thus, economic and technical factors also pushed the media to switch from journalism of fact towards opinion journalism over the last couple of decades. The process accelerated in the late 2010s, coinciding with political polarization and likely contributed to it.

***

In the evergreen debates about whether Facebook is a media organization (and whether it should be responsible for content) or just a platform that allows people to express themselves at their own discretion, there was an interesting exchange between the *New York Times* managing editor Joseph Kahn and Facebook CEO Mark Zuckerberg in 2018.

Zuckerberg stated that, "I do think that in general, within a news organization, there is an opinion. I do think that a lot of what you all do, is have an opinion and have a view." Facebook simply "has more opinions," as he noted.

Joseph Kahn replied that such a view isn't just reductionist but outright Trumpian. "The institutional values of most really good media companies should transcend any individual opinion," he said. And to say that journalism can be categorized the way Zuckerberg suggests is "part and parcel of the polarization of society."

As Adrienne LaFrance from the *Atlantic*, who covered the meeting, reported, a pause followed, and then Zuckerberg said, "I think that's fair." He continued, however, that, in a newspaper, publishing opinions in close proximity to the news is "pretty dangerous."[1]

The discussion helps to see the professional self-assertion that blinds the media from seeing the changes in real media performance. The institutional value of the media undoubtedly transcends any individual opinion. Such was an ideal, a creed, that required journalists to follow high standards. But this ideal is maintained by practice less and less when the media 1) get more dependent on reader revenue and 2) get sucked into a highly opinionated environment. The labelling of Zuckerberg's position as a Trumpian view is a blatant example of the readiness or even the habit of a journalist (editor) to take a side. Not just a side: while formally condemning the polarization of society, the editor immediately polarized their debate to the extreme, as the labelling of an opponent's view as Trumpian is something almost akin to the 'Hitler-argument' in the discussion, to extend Godwin's law. It appeared as if the editor turned on the regime of polarization and Trump-labeling, simply out of professional habit.

***

Mark Zuckerberg is hardly impartial in judging the media, of course. But the confusion between facts and opinions in the media, particularly when placed next to each other, has become a notable reason for experts' concern.

The redundancy of news and the competition for readers' attention incentivizes *opinionating* by the media even more when the media promote

---

[1] LaFrance, Adrienne. (2018, May 1). "Mark Zuckerberg doesn't understand journalism. Either that, or he doesn't care." *The Atlantic*. https://www.theatlantic.com/technology/archive/2018/05/mark-zuckerberg-doesnt-understand-journalism/559424/

their products on social media. News teasers and announcements must compete there with clickbait. They become clickbait themselves. All the editors know that they need to exaggerate something in the headline and to make it as catchy as possible in order to grab the attention of an online passerby on social media. The necessity to compete with clickbait makes even fairly factual content sound like a shout, an emotionally charged statement.

Eli Pariser, the author of *The Filter Bubble*, examined the issue in the context of algorithms. Amid the boom of "Potemkin local news sites which republished a mix of valid, truthful wire stories and hyperpartisan propaganda", how should the platforms tell sensational and propagandist clickbait apart from fair journalist headlines and news blurbs? News orgs want to succeed in attracting users' attention and boost their search ranking, too. Pariser wrote:

> This is a harder question than it appears. <...> The *Times* also publishes a mix of hard-nosed journalism and partisan messaging, framed as opinion. Here are some articles that have run on the NYT recently: "Liberals, This is War," "Three Lessons for Winning in November and Beyond," and "Conservatives Are Wrong To Gloat About Kavanaugh." I happen to agree with many of the sentiments in all three – but it's hard to argue they're not pointed political statements.
>
> This contributes to a crisis in trust. Why does the public have such a hard time figuring out what "news" means? Because it's actually confusing![1]

He continued that, "So perhaps it's time to reconsider the whole premise of bundling together hard news and opinion content under the same brand names and domains." In conclusion, Pariser called on publishers to "draw a brighter line around it – a line that both people and algorithms can understand."

This is an important point. Not only is it people who confuse facts and opinions, but algorithms also do it, and perhaps even more so. Algorithms spread media teasers as a brand-certified journalism product, not just without distinguishing between news and opinions, but also in a tone of opinioned statements rather than factual reporting. As it is becoming increasingly rare for people to go any further than reading the news teasers in their newsfeed, the fact-opinion confusion, which stems from the media's

---

[1] Pariser, Eli. (2018, October 12). "Trump's USA Today op-ed demonstrates why it's time to unbundle news and opinion content." *NiemanLab.*
https://www.niemanlab.org/2018/10/trumps-usa-today-op-ed-demonstrates-why-its-time-to-unbundle-news-and-opinion-content/

inclination towards opinions, gets completed by the technological indistinguishability that is passed on and amplified by algorithms.

***

The historic sway of the media back and forth between journalism of fact and opinion journalism formed one of the most important standards of commercial journalism in the 20th century: the sharp distinction between fact and opinion.

This editorial standard was a product of commercial journalism, which learned to serve the audience as customers. The audience wanted to know when it bought facts and when it bought opinions. This rule was particularly important in the quality media. The formal distinction between facts and opinions was technically supported by the format of delivery. In newspapers, opinions were published on a separate page or in visually marked columns.

The internet has injected confusion to the matter, particularly regarding newspapers' websites. Since columns are an important asset (in media with prevalent opinion journalism), they are announced on the home page along with a feature piece and breaking news. As a result, the very striking and subjective headlines of columns, which often express emotionally and politically loaded statements, sit next to the newspaper's brand. The resulting look is so profoundly propagandist that the front pages of the old Soviet newspapers, let say *Pravda*, would have looked modest and even coy amid the ideological intensity of the column headlines that form the impression of the front page of the website, for example, of the *New York Times*, one of the most reputable western publications.

For the editors and people in the media, it is clear that those headlines represent the personal opinions of columnists. They are commonly marked as such, for example, by the standing head 'Opinions' or something similar. But this is not so evident for readers, who are not obliged to easily discern the nuts from the bolts in the media. For many of them, the newspaper looks highly partisan and biased.

***

The competition with clickbait and the necessity to pack the teaser with all the best information end up in the inclination for the media to wind up a modest piece of news into a heavily loaded statement.

In October 2019, a *Reuters* headline read:

Former CIA Director Brennan: Votes were swayed by Russian influence operation.

The news story was unveiled as follows.

1) In the lead: "Former CIA Director John Brennan said on Wednesday that at least some American voters were swayed as a result of Russia's 2016 election interference operation..."

2) In the first paragraph: "Brennan said he was 'sure, personally, that those Russian efforts changed the mind of at least one voter.'"

3) In the second paragraph: "'Whether it was one voter or a million voters, I don't know,' he added."

4) In the last paragraph (out of six): "'How many, in which states, I don't know. Whether it changed the outcome, I don't know,' Brennan said."

Now the headline, again: "Former CIA Director Brennan: Votes were swayed by Russian influence operation."[1] The inverted pyramid, indeed: details are placed in order of diminishing importance. This was *Reuters*, not *Fox News* or *MSNBC*. However, they, too, needed a saleable headline to compete with clickbait for readers' and algorithms' attention.

Once again, such media criticism may relevantly be applied to traditional and mainstream news organizations specifically, as it is they, not partisan outlets, who, presumably, carried the banner of professional journalism based on the standards of impartial reporting and objective analysis.

***

Herman and Chomsky wrote that competition for advertising money incentivized the "sensationalism" of the media, "as in their obsessive focus on the O. J. Simpson trial, the Lewinsky scandal, and the deaths of two of the West's supercelebrities, Princess Diana and John F. Kennedy, Jr." (Herman & Chomsky, 2002 [1988], p. XIV). The purpose of this sensationalism was to attract more readers for a larger advertising outreach, but the outcome of such topic selection was also the depoliticization of media content. This 'by-product' served advertisers and elites: it eliminated the potentially controversial and unfavorable context for ads and contributed to manufacturing consent.

It is only logical that the propulsion behind sensationalism is even more forceful when the media compete for reader revenue. This time, their struggle for the audience's attention is aimed directly at the payer, the audience. But the difference is that the media, within the reader-driven business model, do not avoid politics and pressing social issues. On the

---

[1] Satter, Raphael. (2019, October 30). "Former CIA Director Brennan: Votes were swayed by Russian influence operation." *Reuters*. https://www.reuters.com/article/us-usa-trump-russia/former-cia-director-brennan-votes-were-swayed-by-russian-influence-operation-idUSKBN1XA075

contrary, the media must heavily exploit them. The switch from journalism of fact to opinion journalism supports politicization because politics is the area of the most charged opinions.

The technological need to compete for the weakening and dispersed audience's attention further amplifies political sensationalism. Setting a sensational trap for people's perception, news teasers on social media tend to make everything look like highly expressive and subjective statements. They exaggerate their expressiveness far beyond what would be required for fair fact-based reporting.

The business need for *opinionating* is further aggravated by the historical switch from facts to opinions and by the technological need to compete for attention in a noisy environment.

***

The economically, historically and technologically induced confusion between facts and opinions impacts people's perception and trust.

"Newspaper readers traditionally got cues from the location of articles... Now, for many readers, online publishing amounts to a journalistic stew with ingredients they can't be sure of," wrote Bill Adair in *Columbia Journalism Review*.[1]

When a Facebook link transports you to a story from an unfamiliar publication whose biases are unknown or not clearly labeled and the story is heavily loaded with strong partisanship points, the reader extrapolates their first impression to the entire publication. It does not matter if the editor thinks the story is produced as opinion, placed into a virtual opinion section and marked as opinion. All these strict demarcations exist only in the editor's head.

The study conducted by Pew Research in 2018 showed that most Americans are able to correctly identify only three out of five opinions or factual statements, which is only slightly better than random guesses. Only 26% of adults could recognize all five factual statements, and only 35% could recognize all five opinion statements. Roughly a quarter got most or all wrong.[2]

---

[1] Adair, Bill. (2019, August 29). "Op-ed: Bias is good. It just needs a label." *Columbia Journalism Review*. https://www.cjr.org/opinion/bias-journalism.php

[2] Mitchell, Amy, et al. (2018, June 18). "Distinguishing between factual and opinion statements in the news." *Pew Research Center*. https://www.journalism.org/2018/06/18/distinguishing-between-factual-and-opinion-statements-in-the-news/

Studies show that people's ability to distinguish facts from opinions goes from bad to worse. Among 15-year-olds, only 9% can tell the difference.[1] This issue is most likely irrelevant for them, as they consume content almost exclusively from the internet.

"It's hard to tell if it's their opinion or news...Even facts are opinions," said a participant of a research focus group held by Temple University.[2]

***

It is not that people have a hard time recognizing the facts. They just do not care, until they are asked. People read what interests them, and sometimes it's journalism. They just know that a paper wrote this or TV said that. It is not their concern. It should, however, concern the professionals in the media. And it does, but their concern is limited to their self-awareness that facts are not opinions.

"Media executives want to believe that readers and viewers understand the nuances of journalism and can navigate the space between 'objective' news and obvious opinion. But they don't," concluded Bill Adair in *Columbia Journalism Review*.[3]

"News organizations aren't doing enough to help readers understand the difference between news, analysis and opinion," stated Rebecca Iannucci from the Duke Reporters' Lab. The Lab's study of 25 local newspapers and 24 national news and opinion websites found that only 40 percent of large news organizations provide labels about article types – and nearly all of those only label opinion columns.[4]

The environment now incentivizes opinion in the media for so many reasons (economic, historic, technological) that the distinction between fact and opinions must be enforced tenfold for readers to distinguish it intuitively. And even then, readers will be neither obliged nor concerned with it. They will accept the environment as is, complaining about its wrongs.

---

[1] Anderson, Jenny. (2019, December 3). "Only 9% of 15-year-olds can tell the difference between fact and opinion." Quartz. https://qz.com/1759474/only-9-percent-of-15-year-olds-can-distinguish-between-fact-and-opinion/

[2] Owen, Laura Hazard. (2019, May 3). "'This world is just falling apart': How actual news consumers grapple with fake news and (sometimes) tune out." *NiemanLab*. https://www.niemanlab.org/2019/05/this-world-is-just-falling-apart-how-actual-news-consumers-grapple-with-fake-news-and-sometimes-tune-out/

[3] Adair, Bill. (2019, August 29). "Op-ed: Bias is good. It just needs a label." *Columbia Journalism Review*. https://www.cjr.org/opinion/bias-journalism.php

[4] Iannucci, Rebecca. (2017, August 16). "News or opinion? Online, it's hard to tell." *Poynter*. https://www.poynter.org/ethics-trust/2017/news-or-opinion-online-its-hard-to-tell/

***

Calls for addressing the facts became the most popular guise for opinions in the absence of facts. The very idea of fact has become opinionized, which is certainly an indication of post-truth.

The boom of fact-checking is considered to belong with the era of Trumpism. This is true. But fact-checking itself appeared as early as 1913, when the Bureau of Accuracy and Fair Play was opened in New York by Ralph Pulitzer and Isaac White. The bureau focused on identifying mistakes in print reporting while looking to expose "deliberate fakes."[1]

Fact-checking has risen in significance recently because of the vast amount of freely spreading information on the internet. But the internet and social media are getting used to fake news; it is their natural byproduct. Fact-checking is mostly propelled by the media as their competitive advantage. However, the intensive calls for fact-checking, particularly in the polarized media environment, only reaffirms the issue. Fact-checking often looks like guilty flowers offered to the audience by the media, as the audience subliminally senses that the media are failing in factual reporting.

As strange as it may sound, in the media ecosystem with the prevailing journalism of fact, fact-checking is not needed so much because fakes are too conspicuous. Within journalism of fact, fact-checking is an inner professional filter and rather hunts for errors.

Overwhelmingly propagated fact-checking is a solid sign of the prevalence of opinion journalism. For the media with prevalent opinion journalism, fact-checking has turned from a professional tool to an additional commodity. Fact-checking is for sale next to the fake news it is supposed to fact-check; the former needs the latter.

When opinions take over facts but are dressed up as facts for better impact, literally everything must be, ideally, fact-checked, but it cannot be fact-checked effectively, of course. Not surprisingly, trust in journalism is rapidly dwindling.

Factoid. Validation by dissemination

In their newsfeed, everyone can occasionally get videos of a bear swimming in a backyard pool, a husky dog teaching a human baby to crawl, or a bunch of school bullies harassing a classmate. The video format certifies that those videos are likely to be real. However, after they became a widely

---

[1] Thompson, Kristen. (2019, January 21). "It's a fact." *J-source*. https://j-source.ca/article/its-a-fact/

shared item of content, what is significant about them is not the value of the reality of their content, but the value of the dissemination of that content.

Contemporary news media and news critics have become obsessed with fact-checking or reality checking. However, it is not reality-matching that creates use-value of any disseminated news. It is not even selection (nobody preselected that bear, husky, or bullying video on social media). Social significance in media is not a function of reality reference or selection; it is a function of dissemination, of a scale of outreach.

The newsworthy social significance of a husky teaching a baby, or even of the harassment in school, is not defined by the recording and reporting of the fact. Countless similar videos are recorded and reported but do not become significant news. The social significance of fact is vague until the fact somehow, in some mystic way, hits a certain threshold of dissemination.

At some point of dissemination, the news gains a certain momentum that defines its significance because of its dissemination. Its further spread is predetermined by the previous dissemination. Basically, this means that the dissemination of news is based on the significance it gains through dissemination. The dissemination actualizes the news' potential significance.

According to assumed standards of journalism, news is disseminated because of its significance. But, in fact, news becomes significant because of its dissemination. The quality of newsworthiness rests on the quantity of newsworthiness. This postmodernist self-sublimation of news content accounts for the ability of the media to create a parallel reality, which somehow refers to the objective reality, but is mediated by a peculiar sort of significance gained through dissemination.

***

The validation of news by its dissemination instead of significance resembles a phenomenon referred to as a "factoid". The term was introduced by Norman Mailer in Marilyn Monroe's biography in 1973. According to Mailer, factoids are

> ...facts which have no existence before appearing in a magazine or newspaper, creations which are not so much lies as a product to manipulate emotion in the Silent Majority. (It is possible, for example, that Richard Nixon has spoken in nothing but factoids during his public life.) (Mailer, 1973, p. 18.)

Important is the context in which Mailer introduced the term. By the time he wrote this book, there were two biographies of Monroe that had attempted to build a factual life story of the pop-idol. However, her life was so full of legends, speculations, and rumors – because of her vast media coverage, of course, – that it was hard to tell facts from speculations. Even the people surrounding Marilyn, who seemingly should have been able to testify with facts, instead told legends that would fit the image of her, already created in the public and media perception. She was a media being, a legend, and this, not the real life of the real woman, was what attracted the public to her. In that sense, her real life did not exist; the only life she lived was the life in the media reality, including secrets and omissions, which became facts (factoids) of the media reality, too.

Hence came a genre and approach picked up by Mailer himself. He did not end up producing a historiographic documentary. After digging into biographies, movies, and memoires about Monroe, he used his authorial self to speculate about her and her feelings and the circumstances surrounding her life and death. As his book contained a number of factual controversies, he explained a genre as a "species of novel ready to play by the rules of biography" (Dearborn, 1999, p. 316).

On another occasion, when answering the question of whether it was he who coined the word "factoid" to label "this sort of thing", he said:

> A factoid is a fact which has no existence on earth other than that what's appeared in the newspaper and then gets repeated for ever after. So people walk around as if it is the blooming lively fact. There is all that about her too. She lived in a swamp of legends, lies and factoids. (Mailer, 1988, p. 194.)

***

Since then, the word 'factoid' has entered the lingo of the media and politics. Some new connotations have sometimes been used. Observers have marked out such meanings of factoid as a "quasi-fact", "something that looks like a fact, could be a fact, but in fact is not a fact" and "a brief or trivial item of news or information"[1]; "a little-known bit of information; trivial but interesting data"; and "a brief interesting fact."[2]

Merriam-Webster Dictionary, however, underlines that the suffix '-oid-' traces back to the ancient Greek word *eidos*, meaning 'appearance' or 'form'.[3] Morphologically, a factoid is something in the guise of a fact, instead of a fact.

---

[1] Marsh, David. (2014, January 17). "A factoid is not a small fact. Fact." *The Guardian.* https://www.theguardian.com/media/mind-your-language/2014/jan/17/mind-your-language-factoids

[2] "'Factoid' doesn't mean what you think it does." NPR Ethics Handbook. http://ethics.npr.org/memos-from-memmott/factoid-doesnt-mean-what-you-think-it-does/

[3] Factoid. The Merriam-Webster Dictionary. https://www.merriam-webster.com/dictionary/factoid

Such was the intent of Mailer. In his definition, three aspects are important:

1) Factoids appear in the media and thanks to the media

2) A factoid is a fact of a media reality

3) A factoid is born out of its attraction; it is "a product to manipulate emotion".

Nothing in the definition of factoid refers to the 'real' reality, except for the root of the word itself. It is a fact created by the media, for the media, and validated as true by its dissemination, when 'everyone knows it'. All the reality parameters of a factoid end up in media dissemination. Media distribution is the only reality of a factoid.

***

The factoid was an inevitable environmental outcome of the commodification of news.

Mailer highlighted the factoid's appeal to emotions. Before a factoid is born out of dissemination, it is 'wanted'. Describing how readily Marilyn collaborated "with any near reporter" and supplied them with stories of doubtful veracity, Mailer implied that she unconsciously responded to "the American obsession with factoids" (Mailer, 1973, p. 32). She gave what they wanted. Not just reporters – the public as well. Factoids appeared to satisfy a demand.

In a sense, the actress's life in lies continued the life of her personage created in movies and by the media. As Mailer put it, "For an actor lives with the lie as it were truth. A false truth can offer more reality than the truth that was altered" (Mailer, 1973, p.194).

This maxim works well not only for acting but for the media, too. A factoid is *better* than a lie and *better* than reality.

The problem of the media constructing a false reality is not that a factoid is bad. The problem is that a factoid is good; too good for the audience to want truth instead. The truth is not as good as a factoid is.

Therefore, factoids are good for profit. Being an industrial capitalist enterprise, the media produce a reality that is supposed to be relevant but also has to be marketable. Even non-profit media do this, as they must compete for the public's attention. Thus, the supply of reality in the media is impacted by the necessity to meet the demand.

The commodification of news made the emergence of factoids inevitable. A potentially interesting piece of news becomes tested when disseminated. In many iterations of this process, the media achieve an understanding of what news will become significant when distributed. The media know what

113

snippets of reality are good enough to beget saleable factoids; this is basically the business and the profession of journalism. The media were supposed to make the important interesting, but, instead, they made the interesting important. Having learned to sell factoids, the media reversed public interest into public curiosity.

Being pieces of news commodified in the media, factoids got detached from reality and obtained their own use-value that cannot be disproved by fact-checking or reality checking, because the reality of a factoid is its dissemination. The use-value of a factoid is defined by the relations of demand/supply, not by compliance to reality. In their swirling chicken-or-egg tango, readers want to read what they want, and the media define and supply it. Factoids are the news that is wanted. Journalism is the mastery of factoids.

***

In November 2017, a woman contacted a *Washington Post* reporter and said that she had had a sexual relationship with Roy Moore, a Republican U.S. Senate candidate, when she was 15. The candidate was supported by Trump and had already had a story of similar accusations, so the tip looked promising for the paper. However, when looking for proof, the reporter sensed discrepancies in her account.

A team of *Post* reporters investigated the case over two weeks and found out that the woman was affiliated with Project Veritas, an organization that, "sets up undercover 'stings' that involve using false cover stories and covert video recordings meant to expose what the group says is media bias,"[1] as the *Post* wrote. The paper debunked the plot, published its own investigation, and gained well-deserved praise in the industry for its "journalistic rigor."[2]

It took two weeks and the work of tough professionals not for the story to be published, but for it not to get published. These two weeks and the team effort demonstrate how badly the story was wanted. It has all the ingredients needed for watchdog journalism to do the job. At some point, the woman threatened that if *Post* reporters would not release her story to the public, then she would go to other news outlets. This was a serious

[1] Boburg, Shawn, Davis, Aaron C., and Crites, Alice. (2017, November 27). "A woman approached The Post with dramatic — and false — tale about Roy Moore. She appears to be part of undercover sting operation." *The Washington Post*. https://www.washingtonpost.com/investigations/a-woman-approached-the-post-with-dramatic--and-false--.html

[2] White, Jeremy B. (2017, November 28). "Washington Post claims woman came to them with false Roy Moore abuse story in bizarre plot to discredit newspaper." *Independent*. https://www.independent.co.uk/news/world/americas/us-politics/roy-moore-washington-post-fake-story-woman-veritas-sting-plot-james-okeefe-alabama-a8079216.html

threat: she knew exactly how to lure the press. It was only their professional standards and high reputational and business risks which prevented the *Post* from falling into the trap.

But the story illustrates the power of news being wanted. Not all the media can resist the commercial temptation of factoids and recognize when a factoid begging for publication is a potential fake that can be checked against a verifiable reality, with subsequent reputational or legal risks. Quite often, tips and stories are 'too good to be true' – they are better than true, particularly when they fit some preconceptions and particularly when they are about the likes of Trump, who himself is a media commodity of the highest value.

For some unknown astrological reasons, in that same time period in 2017, whilst the *Washington Post* resisted the temptation, others did not. It was "Journalism's terrible, horrible, no good, very bad week", as *Columbia Journalism Report* labeled it.[1] Several major outlets, including *ABC News, Reuters, Bloomberg, CNN, CBS,* and *MSNBC*, made significant errors and were forced to redact and correct their news afterwards. This came during a particularly packed news cycle – with the Flynn investigation, the Mueller investigation, and other Trump-related hot news, when you would not want to miss out on a good tip if you were going to stay ahead of the pack. The news media always compete for reporting much-wanted news first, and the competition makes factoids wanted even more.

✳✳✳

One of the most notorious cases of the media failure because of a factoid that turned out to be fake was a *Rolling Stone* story in 2014 about "A Rape on Campus" at University of Virginia, based on the account of the alleged victim of sexual assault during a fraternity initiation ritual. The article had dramatic consequences for students and university officials, but subsequent investigations, including one conducted by the police, did not find evidence confirming the described events. The magazine retracted the story, asked the Columbia School of Journalism to review its practices and standards, and even published a review[2] in an attempt to fix the damage done to its reputation.

---

[1] Vernon, Pete. (2017, December 11). "The media today: Journalism's terrible, horrible, no good, very bad week." *Columbia Journalist Review.* https://www.cjr.org/the_media_today/the-media-today-journalisms-terrible-horrible-no-good-very-bad-week.php

[2] Coronel, Sheila, Coll, Steve, and Kravitz, Derek. (2015, April 5). "Rolling Stone and UVA: The Columbia University Graduate School of Journalism report. An anatomy of a journalistic failure." *Rolling Stone.* https://www.rollingstone.com/culture/culture-news/rolling-stone-and-

In May 2015, University of Virginia associate dean Nicole Eramo filed a multimillion-dollar defamation lawsuit against *Rolling Stone*. In the lawsuit, it was stated that,

> Rolling Stone and Erdely's <the author – A.M.> highly defamatory and false statements about Dean Eramo were not the result of an innocent mistake. They were the result of a wanton journalist who was more concerned with writing an article that fulfilled her preconceived narrative about the victimization of women on American college campuses, and a malicious publisher who was more concerned about selling magazines to boost the economic bottom line for its faltering magazine, than they were about discovering the truth or actual facts.[1]

The jury found that *Rolling Stone* and Erdely were liable for $3 million in damages to Eramo. The fraternity sued the magazine, too.

***

The cases of media failures are usually seen as proof of their political biases. The political biases might define what kind of induced reality will be induced, but the very inevitability of reality induction is not ideological. It rests on the commercial need to manufacture a saleable picture of the world. Ideological preconceptions simply accompany the marketing strategy in a chosen or allocated market niche comprised of liberal or conservative audiences. The media define their audience and then manufacture what their audience wants and buys. The wise lawyers of Dean Eramo emphasized in their lawsuit not the ideological preconception but the business intention of the magazine, when they wrote that, a "publisher <...> was more concerned about selling magazines to boost the economic bottom line for its faltering magazine, than they were about discovering the truth or actual facts".

When the media go too far in the commodification of reality in the forms of factoids or when there is someone to resist too-ugly factoids, the media's social constructivism gets unveiled, debunked and sometimes even punished.

However, reality itself in general does not have such an agency to resist the media constructivism. When there is no one to resist, reality is

---

uva-the-columbia-university-graduate-school-of-journalism-report-44930/

[1] Shapiro, T. Rees. (2015, May 12). "U-Va. dean sues Rolling Stone for 'false' portrayal in retracted rape story." *The Washington Post*.
https://web.archive.org/web/20150513080410/http://www.washingtonpost.com/local/pe-story/2015/05/12/2128a84a-f862-11e4-a13c-193b1241d51a_story.html

defenseless before the commercial power of factoids. The scandals occurring from time to time just demonstrate the power of factoid seduction.

From factoid to fake news

The significance of news has always relied on a projected or real attitude of the public. News is defined not only by what happened but also by how people react. That is to say that a subjective measurement of seemingly objective facts has always existed in old media. Of course, everyone takes a subjective view of reality by merely observing it. However, not everyone is able to circulate his or her view on a massive scale, thus making it a social fact – factoid. What is crucial to the power of a factoid is not its falseness, but its dissemination.

Establishing news value by dissemination has become part of the collective survival code. In order to comply with the group and to count on its protection, a member of the group has to believe that what the group thinks reflects reality. The referencing of facts not to abstract truth but to common knowledge is fundamental to the group's social coherence.

The validation of significance by dissemination is also known in rhetoric as *argumentum ad populum* – appeal to the people. Different types of this can be distinguished, such as argument from consensus, appeal to popularity, appeal to the masses, appeal to the majority, etc. They all establish the weight of a view or a judgment by attributing it to the collective authority. The reference to common knowledge creates the bandwagon effect – the phenomenon of communal reinforcement that allows the validation of facts through opinions of others, regardless of empirical evidence.

The cohering effect of validation by dissemination was also well known in propaganda. This was what Joseph Goebbels meant when he said, "Repeat a lie often enough and it becomes the truth."[1]

However much rhetoric or propaganda admit the false or manipulative character of *appeal to the people* and *repetitive-lies-becoming-truth*, a factoid in the media, on the other hand, is neither a falsehood nor manipulation. It is an alternative reality that is widespread enough to sustain its own truth-attestation. For the most part, the media reality does not overlap with any physically or empirically reliably verified reality. Unlike Goebbelsian lies or rhetorical appeals to popularity, a factoid cannot be

---

[1] Stafford, Tom. (2016, October 26). "How liars create the 'illusion of truth'." *BBC*. https://www.bbc.com/future/article/20161026-how-liars-create-the-illusion-of-truth

disproved as something not existing. It exists; it just exists in a specially created space of media reality.

***

Interestingly, a factoid dovetails rather well with the concept of simulation and Baudrillard's simulacrum. If simulation mimics reality and simulacrum replaces reality, a factoid, through repetition in dissemination, induces the reality that people want. A factoid validates its reality via dissemination. Dissemination is the proof of a factoid, meaning dissemination is the reality check of a factoid (that is why fake news is principally immune to fact-checking).

The capacity of a factoid to gain significance simply because of dissemination (as opposed to old-fashioned "dissemination because of significance") also exposes an important trait of factoids in terms of structural semantics: a factoid is self-referential. In Saussurean terms, for a factoid, the signified appears after the signifier gets disseminated. Or, using the more complex Ogden & Richards' semiotic triangle complete with connotative meaning, it can be said that a factoid does not need a referent (denotation) or thought of referent (signification), as its signification appears after its connotation (attitude value) creates a sufficient mass of dissemination.

Factoids also became a convergence point in which the epistemologies of opinion journalism and journalism of fact merged. A factoid is a legitimate hybrid of opinion and fact. The news may or may not refer to the reality; it is irrelevant. What is relevant is if this news is validated by dissemination, i.e. by the real or projected attitude of many. A quantity of opinions turns into a quality of a new type of fact – a factoid.

***

In the pre-digital world, very few had the capacity to generate factoids. Before the internet, the number of journalists in the world hardly exceeded one million. The media possessed avowed and sanctioned authority to construct social reality and to verify any content against the reality constructed by them. Factoids were always a prerogative of the mass media and professional journalism. The social convention about the mass media generally tolerated them. The public was aware of a degree of media social constructivism. For the public, the annoyance of poorly manufactured factoids was compensated for by the enjoyment of their condemnation.

Everything changed when the hordes of unsanctioned authors invaded a new factory of factoid manufacturing – the internet. The number of guerrilla factoid producers suddenly reached 3.5 billion and is still growing. The internet emancipated the factoid from the media and transferred it to social media for it to flourish there. The media lost their monopoly over the factoid, which caused a shock both for the media and the public. What used to be permissible for Jupiter has become permissible for a bull.

The free market of factoids emerged. As factoids became increasingly divorced from reality, the competition for factoid-induced realities has accelerated. Post-truth, the validation of reality through attitudes toward it, is the product of this competition. Fake news is a radical form of the factoid, deprived of the fine quality of those factoids that were masterfully crafted by professionals.

It is now clear that the news media had been just a business incubator for factoids. The miraculous capability of media to induce reality is now being deployed at full blast, when the public itself creates and distributes news, simultaneously transferring all social activities into this induced reality. The tethering of occurrences to the 'real' reality matters less and less.

This is why, by the way, fact-checking is working increasingly less. A curious tendency has appeared: the media replaced the term 'fact-checking' with the term 'reality check', as if they admitted that facts in the media have never been true and have always been factoids and only the reality is the true canon. They are trying to restore the fading link between news and reality. Fact-checking and reality checks are now producing a lot of secondary content aimed for sale, though poorly saleable. Factoids are impervious to either fact-checking or reality checks.

***

Fake news, its father *factoid* and its grandma *canard* are technical, environmental features of the respective stages of media evolution. The validation of significance by dissemination is a fundamental effect of communication media, developed in the form of factoid in old media and explosively evolved in the form of fake news in the new media environment comprised of both old and new media. Factoids have become available to social media. But, being a space of guerilla journalism, they supply fake news to the mass media in return. The rush for attraction often leads old media to use fake news instead of good-old factoids.

To understand fake news, one needs to explore its dissemination, not its falseness. Lies are easy to debunk, but it is much harder to detect why lies are distributed. The definition of fake news through demand (marketable value) rather than through content (lies) or through malevolent producer intentions (propaganda) allows for the exploration of the environmental conditions of post-truth. Fake news is news that is 'wanted' to be shared; falseness is its secondary trait. Not every lie is shareable.

Fake news is marketable misinformation. This, by the way, distinguishes fake news from disinformation. Disinformation is not marketable; it is wanted only by the supplier, not by the receiver. Fake news is wanted by the news consumer as much as by the news supplier in the first place.

Before the internet, the media were the only space of the factoid-induced reality. But the internet fulfills the requirement of the validation of significance by dissemination ten times better than the media. The internet is the environment of free distribution on a scale unimaginable in the media. When the significance of the message is validated by dissemination, the scale of dissemination is the message.

The quantum theory of media

What is the unit of media consumption? What is the tiniest particle in which we receive and consume media content?

The digital media made the switching between streams of content not only easier but also tempting: the lion's share of the content we receive digitally is about clicking the ever-more-interesting links and jumping to somewhere else. It was not that easy to switch between content streams in books; one couldn't do so without switching the books themselves. Newspapers offered a mosaic, but the reader still stayed within the same physical print issue. Old media kept users imprisoned within an allotted chunk of content.

When magazine publishers decided to advertise magazine reading in 2010 (in those romantic times, they still hoped to return the readers to print), they used the image of Olympic swimmer Michael Phelps and the motto: "We surf the Internet, we swim in magazines"[1] (Figure 7).

Indeed, in older and bulkier formats of media, the consumer had no choice but to immerse themselves into a media piece deeper and for longer. There were not many 'withdrawing lures' that would lead one to some other piece without having to materially change the medium – without a costly 'material' effort.

Radio with its tuning knob and television with its remote control started eroding user's loyalty to a linear narrative.

---

[1] Adams, Russell, & Ovide, Shira. (2010, March 1). "Magazines Team Up to Tout 'Power of Print'." *The Wall Street Journal.*
https://www.wsj.com/articles/SB10001424052748703940704575090120113003314

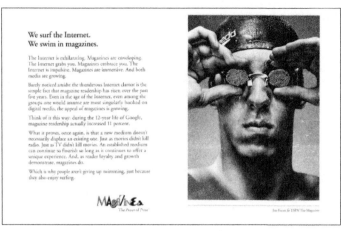

Figure 7. Magazine-reading ad, 2010.

It occurred that the attention span correlates with the length of uninterrupted media consumption, and the length of media consumption correlates with the size of the media parcel. The shrinking of attention spans is a consequence of changes in media formats.

***

So, if the unit of media consumption in old media is equal to what is wrapped – literally – in between magazine and newspaper covers (or TV shows' scheduled times), what is the unit of media consumption on the Internet? It is obviously an endless flow, but what is the quantum of media we receive that our mind is able to register and process?

In 2011, Demyan Kudryavtsev, then-CEO of the major Russian business newspaper *Kommersant*, noted that "a quantum of media expression is no longer an issue of a newspaper; it has shrunk down to an article."[1]

Indeed, prior to the Internet Age, we consumed media content in the form of periodicals (or broadcast shows). A newspaper, a magazine, or a TV program constituted a media consumption unit for the reason of an obvious material nature: it was necessary to 'pack' news into a newspaper or a TV/radio program for its production and delivery.

That is how media brands appeared. The method of production and delivery cut the natural flows of news and thoughts down to deliverable parcels, which became books, newsletters and, later, media brands. When asked what kind of media they read, people of the newspaper generation

---

[1] Miroshnichenko, Andrey. (2014). "What are new media involving us in?" *Slon.* Мирошниченко, Андрей. (2018). «Во что вовлекают человека новые медиа?» *Slon.* https://www.aka-media.ru/foresight/835/

named titles of media outlets: *Reader's Digest*, the *New York Times*, *Fortune*, etc. In practical terms, they read the regular print issues of those outlets, which were the quanta of media consumption.

***

The internet made it possible to deliver content in smaller 'parcels' of separate articles, video clips and alike. This change is often overlooked and underestimated, but it struck one of the biggest nails into the coffin of old media.

By minimizing the size of media consumption from the media issue down to the article, the internet detached content from media brands. The media were thereby deprived of the opportunity to maintain their ownership over content. When content travels in parcels that are smaller than a physically wrapped and salable piece of media (book, magazine, newspaper), it becomes harder or impossible to commodify it under a media brand.

Not only does the business of the news media suffer from this issue, but the news media are even losing the promotional effect from good articles they produce. The reader does not need to associate a good article with a media brand anymore, as he or she receives it as a separate and self-containing quantum of media. The media brand can be shown in some way on the top or below the article, of course, but this type of presence doesn't matter anymore and is rarely even noticed.

Brands mattered when they labeled and, in fact, organized the package/channel of delivery. When the media brand and the package/channel are not the same entity, the user can consume the smaller piece of content directly and 'unmediated' – without seeing or referring to the media brand.

This new quantization of media content deprives the media of the former significance of their branded packaging, thereby killing the commercial value of content. (Many attempts to sell articles separately, by piece, have failed. The earning of that small transaction does not even cover the costs of maintaining the payment infrastructure and associated administrative efforts.)

***

The quantization of media consumption goes further and deeper into the microcosm of media content. As social media, particularly Facebook, have gained momentum, the media quantum – i.e. the elementary particle of media consumption – has become even tinier. These days, an individual article is no longer the smallest unit of mass media consumption. It has been replaced by the smallest bits of media content – headlines, recaps, announcements, teasers, clickbait – destined to attract readers in the social media newsfeed.

The news teaser, not even the article, is now the quantum of media content. As McLuhan once said, "The future of the book is the blurb."[1] The present of journalism is the news teaser. The necessity to attract turns news teasers into news bits and news baits simultaneously.

This change in media content parceling has already been recognized by field researchers. In a study of news consumption conducted by the Associated Press in 2008, a reader told AP that "...news [today] is not the full story, but more like a preview – it's kind of annoying sometimes." Another reader said that he "does not want to be fed bits. I want to know all the details at once."[2]

Even though those accustomed to a larger and more detailed parcellation of media content resist this change (at least they think so when asked), in fact, they can't help but switch to this new mode of fast media surfing. The new generation, the Digital Natives, perceive this mode of media consumption as the natural one. They are simply not familiar with other ways of media packaging that are limited by physical parceling.

* * *

Interestingly, the legacy media had been laying the ground for turning news into news blurbs long before the internet. There was a certain marketing logic behind it. Describing the rise of magazines in America in the 1920s, James Baughman wrote:

> Indeed, perhaps the most successful magazine of the 1920s, Reader's Digest, reprinted abbreviated versions of pieces originating elsewhere. "To be brisk, curt, concise, telegraphic, and bright became the verbal mode of the hour," Charles and Mary Beard wrote. "To print nothing that would take more than 10 or 15 minutes to read became almost a ruling fashion." (Baughman, 2001 [1987], p. 30.)

---

[1] I have made fair efforts to find a proper reference for this quote, searched and asked the experts, collaborators and McLuhan's family members, but did not succeed. This phrase may well happen to be either a part of the oral legacy of McLuhan or one of those McLuhanisms that sound very McLuhanesque but were never actually said by him. The best reference I could find was: The Official Site for the Estate of Marshall McLuhan.
https://www.marshallmcluhan.com/mcluhanisms/

[2] Associated Press. (2008). "A new model for news: Studying the deep structure of young-adult news consumption." As quoted in: Wagner, Earl J., Liu, Jiahui, Birnbaum, Larry, & Forbus, Kenneth D. (2009). "Rich interfaces for reading news on the Web." *IUI'09*, February 8–11, 2009, Sanibel Island, Florida, USA. http://www.qrg.northwestern.edu/papers/Files/QRG_Dist_Files/QRG_2009/wagner_etal_rich_interfaces.pdf

Launched in 1923, "*Time* turned boring newspaper reporting into fun blurbs."[1]

In the 1980s, "*USA Today* embraced a design standard that, in today's terms, seems almost web-like: Its pages were dominated by charts, photos, and shorter blurbs of text."[2] Competitors mocked USA Today, comparing it to fast-food merchandizing, and joked that "it would someday win a prize for 'best investigative paragraph.'"[3] Well, it happened; not the prize, but cutting the size of media narrative down to the paragraph and smaller.

Not only did the shortening of the media narrative happen before the internet, the format of clickbait appeared in old media, too. Magazines put catchy headlines on covers, announcing the articles and luring passersby inside the magazine. Radio and TV used announcements to attract listeners and viewers to certain shows or newscasts. News teasers started shaping a specific genre of media narrative long ago.

However, in old media, the teasers just marketed content. They did not deliver it and did not replace it while delivering.

***

The fact that media content is now consumed in ever-smaller pieces has some evolutionary logic behind it. The function of journalism is to compress the world into a mosaic panorama. This can be done by cutting the flow into parcels. Such were the pre-requisites for better (faster) delivery bounded by the conditions of material production.

In the good-old times, journalism dealt with fairly large sizes of media content not by choice, but by virtue of the available technologies. To print or broadcast content, editors had to pack news into transferable and economically-efficient portions, such as a printed issue or a TV/radio show, scheduled within a certain time frame.

The periodicity was inherent in the old media technologies, and this predefined the size of the issued media parcels. The key thing here was that these technologies taught the audience to consume media in chunks of pre-processed and carefully organized information.

In nature, events, processes or tendencies do not exist in parcels. Their parceled packaging, to which the Newspaper Generations were accustomed,

---

[1] LaFrance, Adrienne, & Meyer, Robinson. (2015, April 15). "The Eternal Return of BuzzFeed. What the online juggernaut can learn from Time, USA Today, and MTV." *The Atlantic.* https://www.theatlantic.com/technology/archive/2015/04/the-eternal-return-of-buzzfeed/390270/

[2] Ibid.

[3] Ibid.

was exclusively the product of certain historical technologies of media production, such as found in print and TV/radio. The publisher was obliged to fill every page (or all of the time allotted to a TV/radio show) with content, not a page more, or a minute less. This operation parceled the natural news flow into chunks, which were the paper issues and TV/radio shows.

***

When material production was based on print/paper, the parcels travelled slowly and had to be quite sizeable in order to fit the optimal proportions of price-quantity-deliverability. But the very idea of news is that it must be delivered faster than anything else; ideally – immediately.

The newspaper, after more than three hundred years of evolution, managed to wrap the news flow into the dailies, the agenda of the day. Radio and TV compressed the world into the agenda of the hour (TV news had already been sensed as a stream). Twitter and other social media platforms deliver the news of the moment.

Morphologically, the flow of news on social media represents the flow of news in the world in the most relevant way. The parceling of news has finally caught up with the natural pace of events by means of quantization into the tiniest news pieces.

The parcels of content in old media were not capable of doing this, as they had to cut artificial chunks out of a natural ongoing flow. And since this operation was performed by individuals, it deviated the flow of information by packaging it into subjectively selected and parceled agendas.

So, media content always 'wanted' faster technologies and, therefore, smaller parceling. With social media, we have approached the quantum limits of media content parceling and the light-speed limits of media content delivery.

The Digital Natives perceive the world in the flow, not in parcels. This is not an issue for them (except for the shortening of their attention span and their screen-scrolling obsession).

***

Physicist Alan Sokal didn't like how postmodernists, Baudrillard specifically, freely manipulated notions and concepts borrowed from real, hardcore science. The famous 'Sokal hoax'[1] aimed to prove that people in cultural studies gladly accept scientific nonsense if that nonsense

---

[1] Sokal, Alan D. (1996, June 5). "A Physicist Experiments with Cultural Studies." *Lingua Franca*. https://physics.nyu.edu/faculty/sokal/lingua_franca_v4/lingua_franca_v4.html

ideologically fits their preconceptions. He wrote an article that stated that quantum gravity is a social construct. The idea was to wrap a piece of complete physics gibberish in progressive leftist clothes. The article was accepted and published in *Social Text*, the leading academic journal of postmodern cultural studies, in 1996. The publication led to a scandal and also made Sokal famous. This case should be a starting point for any study of postmodernism in order to expose the gnoseological limitations of both traditional science and cultural studies.

Now, to give Dr. Sokal yet another reason to be upset: The news bit as the quantum of media content, in essence, represents the wave-particle duality of streaming media consumption.

The internet has shifted the news from a parceled mode of production and consumption to a streamed one. Old media sold media parcels, with the chunks of content packaged at their sole discretion. In contrast, the quantization of content down to the news bit on social media has allowed for the disassembly of the picture of the world into the tiniest particles and their subsequent reassembly into the individually customized newsfeeds streamed on social media.

The newsfeed, which morphologically is a stream, cannot consist of big chunks (such as articles), as Web 1.0 and earlier blog platforms tried to do. Info-parcels are good for periodicals – they created the periodicals; they are the periodicals. However, with regard to the flow, they would clog it. For the stream to flow, the content had to be fluid, squeezable or cut tiny enough.

This not only allows news teasers to be reassembled in any blend for the personally customized newsfeed but also represents something akin to the abovementioned 'wave-particle duality' (sorry, again, Dr. Sokal)

The news bits (teasers, recaps, headlines, announcements, etc.) act as particles when representing pieces of the world picture mosaic. However, when reassembled in a personal newsfeed, they act as the flow, with resonating waves that enable the viral behavior of news on social media.

Thus, more precisely, it is a 'particle-flow duality', which is the most natural way for news to exist. Any other materiality of news, such as parcels of any size, convey not information itself but rather the social-historical conditions of its production/distribution. The method of parceling matters: the parceling is the message. Different media epochs sliced the information flow into content chunks differently, and this made them different social epochs.

***

The number of possible combinations of parcels (the agendas) is much less than the number of possible combinations of particles. Therefore, agendas based on parceling are easier to reduce and manage. This is what journalism is for. Journalism is the fruit of information parceling. News media gatekeeping originated from parcel-binding.

News bits' shepherding on social media, whether by humans (by the Viral Editor) or by algorithms, is making journalism obsolete. Due to the technological difference, not *slicing into chunks* but *blending into flow* is at the core of this new news reassembly operation. There will be no journalism as we knew it in a world without info parceling.

Unlike the case was with parcels, the number of combinations of particles is infinite. Therefore, so is the potential number of personally adjusted newsfeeds on social media. When content is received in the form of flow, not parcels, agendas are the product of personal networks, not the mass media. So, the number of agendas equals the number of users. Everyone becomes their own gatekeeper, depriving the media of this formerly sacrosanct and well-paying job.

However, certain laws of social gravitation start working on social media, eliminating the redundancy of personal news agendas and providing social coherence, even in this highly dispersed news environment. As social significance is the function of quantitative outreach, atomized agendas cannot stay lonely; they immediately start swarming around the centers of social gravitation, or gravitas. Journalism gets replaced by new mechanisms of cohering based on collective selection (the Viral Editor) and algorithms.

***

Media evolution is 'set' to implode the outer environment into the user's operationality. What once was the natural flow of common-to-all alienated events must become the internalized flow of sensations within the induced reality centered on the user.

Content parcellation was the interim stage of media evolution, with media technologies slicing the outer flow of events into increasingly smaller quanta of content. These quanta had to become small enough to be reassembled into the flow of digital events. This is one of the transitional mechanisms that facilitates humans' resettling from the physical reality into the digital reality.

As evolution dictates, only the fittest survive. The obsolescent news media parceling simply does not fit the requirements of flow; the parcels just get jammed in the flow, slowing it down.

This does not mean content parceling will vanish. Larger parcels will simply become the derivatives and the referents for their better, faster cousins, news bits, which are able to flow in the digital stream. News bits and news baits will travel at lightspeed in the mainstreams of newsfeeds, while larger parcels of content will get mouldy in backwaters, being referred to only on occasion.

The quantum leap to the hamsterization of journalism and cannibalism of news teasers

The transition from the parceled to the streamed mode of producing content had a dramatic impact on the quality of journalism. This change in the technology of production caused newsrooms to switch from fixed deadlines to rolling ones, which, in reality, are no deadlines at all, but rather a constant pressure to supply content as much and as fast as possible.

Simultaneously, the 'quantization' of revenue also occurred. As print dollars turned into digital dimes (and then mobile pennies), the media tried to make money from the turnover, not a piece (a parcel). They did not succeed. Instead of money, they ended up chasing traffic, in the hope that traffic would somehow convert into ad revenue. But advertisers migrated to other platforms.

Suffering economically, the media orgs cut jobs. Out of necessity, the remaining staffers have to work more in order to support the content stream simply in an effort to attract impulsive clicks from readers. "We give them three times as many things that are completely unimportant," as Dean Starkman quoted a *Wall Street Journal* reporter in 2011. A decade before, the *WSJ* produced about 22,000 stories per year, "all while doing epic, and shareholder-value-creating, work, like bringing the tobacco industry to heel." The same number of stories was produced by the *Journal* in just six months of 2011, and this count did not include "Web-only material, blogs, NewsHub, etc." [1]

"Do more with less" became the motto of the dwindling newsrooms. *Churnalism* appeared: media staffers used any raw content to publish something in order to keep up with the speed of the flow.

Quantity replaced quality. Instead of thoroughly elaborated masterpieces, journalists started churning out series of oftentimes meaningless news, such as "Sheriff plans no car purchases in 2011," as

---

[1] Starkman, Dean. (2010, September/October). "The Hamster Wheel. Why running as fast as we can is getting us nowhere." *Columbia Journalism Review*.
https://archives.cjr.org/cover_story/the_hamster_wheel.php?page=all

quoted by Dean Starkman, who coined the term 'hamsterization of journalism'. He wrote that,

> The Hamster Wheel isn't speed; it's motion for motion's sake. The Hamster Wheel is volume without thought. It is news panic, a lack of discipline, an inability to say no... But it's more than just mindless volume. it's a recalibration of the news calculus...
>
> The Hamster Wheel, then, is investigations you will never see, good work left undone, public service not performed. [1]

Starkman sagaciously noted other consequences of journalism hamsterization. He wrote that, "the Wheel infantilizes reporters, strengthens P.R.". Indeed, under the condition of production acceleration and rolling deadlines, journalists are forced to use any available hints, pitches and scoops, no matter how empty or un-newsworthy they are. This makes journalists susceptible to any content offers and influences, including those coming from PR-pitches, press-releases and fake news.

***

However, being a champion of good-old quality journalism, Dean Starkman stated that, "the Wheel is not inevitable." He thought the disease is curable.

In 2011, he wrote his famous essay "Confidence Game. The limited vision of the news gurus"[2] (which later became a book), in which he sought to protect journalism as a public service from the digital visionaries such as Clay Shirky, Jeff Jarvis, Dan Gillmor, Jay Rosen, and others.

Referring to high ideals of the past, such as Titan-muckraker Ida M. Tarbell, who dared to stand against Standard Oil's monopoly in 1904 and created, along the way, investigative journalism, Starkman tried to debunk, as he called it, the "future-of-news (FON) consensus" of the digital gurus. He wrote:

> At its heart, the FON consensus is anti-institutional. It believes that old institutions must wither to make way for the networked future...
>
> And let's face it, in the debate over journalism's future, the FON crowd has had the upper hand. The establishment is gloomy and old; the FON consensus

---

[1] Ibid.

[2] Starkman, Dean. (2011, November/December). "Confidence Game. The limited vision of the news gurus." *Columbia Journalism Review.*
https://archives.cjr.org/essay/confidence_game.php?page=all

is hopeful and young (or purports to represent youth). The establishment has no plan. The FON consensus says no plan *is* the plan. The establishment drones on about rules and standards; the FON thinkers talk about freedom and informality. FON says "cheap" and "free"; the establishment asks for your credit card number. FON talks about "networks," "communities," and "love"; the establishment mutters about "institutions," like The New York Times or mental hospitals.

...But if the FON consensus is right, then the public has a problem.

With regard to protecting journalism as a public service, Starkman thought the future of journalism is a matter of the prevailing beliefs in the industry. That is why fancy gurus ("a new kind of public intellectual: journalism academics known for neither their journalism nor their scholarship"[1]) must be dethroned and the lofty principles of journalism must be fought for.

***

However, Starkman's acute revelation of the hamsterization of journalism proved to be good in terms of diagnosis, but not cure. Yes, the public has a problem. No matter who proclaims what, media evolution will pave its way. Regardless of the names and titles of FON gurus or whatever you call those 'prophets' and 'evangelists', they did not lead the processes; they registered the occurrence (if they could prove themselves good enough). This is not someone's evil will that changes the environment. This is an environmental setting that originated from the latest technological improvements, all subjugated to a certain logic of media evolution, that are driving the changes in journalism.

Starkman's 'hamsterization of journalism' was mentioned as one such environmental outcome when the FCC analyzed the threats to journalism. In its 2011 report "The Information Needs of Communities," the FCC noted that,

> ...the broader trend is undeniable: there are fewer full-time newspaper reporters today, and those who remain have less time to conduct interviews and in-depth investigations. In some ways, news production today is more high tech... but in other ways it has regressed, with more and more journalists operating like 1930s wire service reporters – or scurrying on what the *Columbia Journalism Review* calls "the hamster wheel" to produce each day's quota of increasingly superficial stories.[2]

---

[1] Ibid.

[2] Waldman, Steven, and the Working Group. (2011, July). "The information needs of

Starkman's diagnosis of journalism hamsterization was profoundly environmental. "Journalists will tell you that where once newsroom incentives rewarded more deeply reported stories, now incentives skew toward work that can be turned around quickly and generate a bump in Web traffic," he wrote.

The 'FON-gurus' did not arrange the change in newsroom incentives. Clay Shirky, Jeff Jarvis, Dan Gillmor, and Jay Rosen, along with Dean Starkman himself, are among the most prominent thinkers of the early digital era. Nevertheless it was not they who turned the previously parceled content production into the streamed content production, with the rolling deadlines, and the quantum of media content being reduced to the size of news bits that tend to become news baits.

***

The morphological unfitness of the journalistic parcellation of content for better flow in the stream also has an economic dimension.

The quantization of content into news bits creates a paradox that is interesting, yet lethal for good-old journalism. An editor seeks to lure readers by making articles' announcements more attractive and loading them with the most significant information and all the juiciest details from the original articles. Ironically, however, the more attractive the teaser, the more information it carries, thus there is less need for readers to actually follow the link and read the entire article on the media org's website.

The catch is that, while competing for audiences, news teasers do more than just announce the news; they actually *deliver* the news. News bits turn into news baits that do not lure a reader but rather feed him to satiety.

News baits are made to represent media content outside the media brand's own and owned domain. They are set free to work separately and attract readers. They do not belong to the media brand that produced them. News baits are news bits that the media give away for free.

News teasers of the past were not able to do that, as they did not garner enough flows. Three or four catchy teasers on a print magazine's cover did not shape the agenda and did not erode readers' impulse to dive in.

The internet changed this. When recaps, headlines, teasers, announcements, and news baits (accompanied by users' comments) flood one's news feed on social media, they are capable of representing the agenda on their own. There is no need for further reading. Being well-cooked news

---

communities. The changing media landscape in a broadband age." *Federal Communications Commission*, USA. http://transition.fcc.gov/osp/inc-report/The_Information_Needs_of_Communities.pdf

bits, click baits do not evoke clicks when there is a sufficient torrent of them in the flow.

Thus, the side effect of the further quantization of media is cannibalism: the recap devours the original article. Being forced to compete in announcements, the media turn the readers of articles into the readers of recaps.

What this does to media business (or what remains of it) is needless to say. It is impossible to sell announcements; nobody can sell bait to fish.

The quantization of content down to the level of teaser and clickbait on social media dispossesses the media from content they produce even more than was the case on Web 1.0, which delivered separate articles.

***

Legacy media have kept doing their job of news compression better than ever before. If we put the business needs of media orgs aside, it should be noted that news-gathering media technologies have improved dramatically. But there is no good news for the media business in this, as media outlets could end up being hostage to social networks. By adjusting their news to the streams flowing on the networks' platforms in pursuit of a bigger audience, the publishers give up both their news and their audiences to the platforms.

News baits are self-containing bits of media content that, on a statistically significant scale, are capable of feeding everyone's newsfeeds sufficiently enough to shape the panorama of the day. They provide a free service that the new media environment provides to everyone. But it is also a disservice to the media. The gratuitous giveaway of news bits causes the natural weathering of media content that could otherwise have been used by the media for news retail, as was the case in the past.

Under such conditions, media content cannot be a commodity, purely due to technical reasons, no matter how interesting it is. Any attempts to sell content to those who are already overly supplied with this content in the form of news baits, are doomed. There will be no paywalls paid *from below*. All paywalls existing today either are dying relics or represent a different business model: the model of surrogate membership.

7. Who will pay for journalism?

The former audience joins the party.
Dan Gilmor. "We the Media", 2006.

No future for paid content. Except for paid *from above*

As advertising revenue has been lost to internet platforms, many news media have turned to the idea of the paywall, an artificial fence that protects the garden where they grow their beautiful content.

The issue is that nobody will be able to sell news in the future media environment. Not because of the redundancy of content or people's new habit of getting news for free. Those factors will matter, but the primary reason will be a change in the commodity's nature. It is ceasing to be a commodity.

There will be always those who want the audience to spare some time, not money. The best possible content, including news, political reports, financial analysis, sports reviews, you name it – will be supplied to the audience for free in exchange for its attention, not subscription.

Journalism was born when information travelled at horse speed. It was not information but its scarcity that provided business opportunities for the media to thrive. The traditional media business with news retail to the audience and audience wholesaling to the advertisers was viable only under the auspices of a monopoly. Now the monopoly is gone, and content is plentiful thanks to the emancipation of authorship. This environmental shift has turned content from a commodity into a handout.

***

Paywall adherers believe that it is the quality of content that matters. It matters, indeed; but it matters for its successful giveaway as much as for its sale: in order to lure the audience's attention, the giveaway has to be of a high quality. In practice, giveaway outperforms sale: the media increasingly have to give content away more than sell it. The fact of the matter is that value in the media market is now extracted not from content but from the audience's time/attention. So, content is used as bait to attract attention. No business can sell bait to fish. The only party who pays for bait in this relationship is the fisherman – those who supply content.

Another crucial issue for news retail is the technological alienation of content from the producer in the digital environment. In the past, the materiality of content secured the ownership of content to its producer. What was on paper or on air belonged to the brand possessing this paper or this show. The exclusivity of content no longer exists in the environment of 'copy and paste'. Any scoop, no matter how hard it was to obtain, becomes public property in two keystrokes. The better the content, the faster it runs away. In the digital media environment, better-quality content simply has its profitability devoured faster.

Finally, because of the quantisation of content, the media themselves dish out their allegedly saleable content in the form of teasers, news blurbs and announcements even before it is copy-and-pasted, for free, for the same reason – to attract the audience. The packaging of the best news bits into news baits cannibalises the primary articles because, being accumulated and complimented with friends' comments in one's newsfeed, those news bits-baits satisfy the users' need for news without users following the link.

***

There is a myth that some specialized and highly valuable content will be able to preserve its property of a commodity. This myth is false – any high-quality and narrowly specialized content will turn into a high-quality and narrowly specialized lure for a high-quality and narrowly specialized audience. Any specialized content, including business, professional or niche content, can and will be produced and supplied for free by those who want this particular audience's attention, not its subscription.

Let us imagine a powerful investment company that wants to attract financiers to sell them financial products. This company must become a high-quality financial media outlet and build a highly specialized content trap, proving, along the way, its financial expertise and market competence.

In order to succeed, this financial company will copy ideas and approaches that have proved themselves in the media such as *Bloomberg* and the like. It will outbid for talents in the media. It will then create even better ideas, technologies and talents, as it will not be restricted by a lack of funding or the technological burdens of the past. Thus, brand journalism will come to life, employing the best from the past and the most advanced from the present. It will eventually offer high-quality niche media content, but for free, as the most precious value in the new economy is subscribers' attention, not subscribers' pennies. It will make sure the content produced by the company will be shared as freely and widely as possible, across all (relevant) platforms, carrying its brand and expertise.

When this happens, *Bloomberg* will run into problems, as it is their niche. This is just a matter of time. There are already a lot of smaller financial content producers from the financial market, not the media industry, who supply highly specialised financial news and analysis to their desired audiences for free or within their customer ecosystem. Moving into the future, Bloomberg will tend to become rather a trend validator than a news supplier, something akin to a rating agency, whose product serves just as referential background, a part of the landscape.

***

Sports TV rights are the last fortress of paid content in the media (on TV). Sports broadcasting possesses some essential qualities that prevent content from weathering for free. Sports events are strictly scheduled, and broadcasting is tied to the time of the game. People want to see sports together and at the time when the events happen, as the results matter here and now. Viewing that is delayed or divorced from watching together with others, even virtually – the threat to traditional TV – does not fit sports.

Sports events are naturally protected by a wall – a paywall. The rights of the show belong to the leagues, and the leagues make every possible effort to protect content from unauthorized broadcasting. So, when a TV broadcaster buys into the rights, it can create exclusive sports shows, and it can rest assured that its exclusivity will be maintained. These are the ideal conditions for paid content. "Sports obviously is the glue that holds the pay-TV bundle together," – say media experts.[1]

But even this bastion of paid content is about to be destroyed. Too many actors want to use the most attractive content to attract their consumers' attention and secure their consumer loyalty, not subscription. The biggest tech companies, such as Amazon, Facebook, Twitter, YouTube, Verizon and Yahoo, have made their advances in the market of sports TV rights.

In July 2019, Amazon added French Open domestic TV rights to its tennis portfolio. "Amazon's Prime Video subscribers will be able to watch the coverage at no extra cost to their membership," – wrote SportsPro.[2] In 2016–2017, Twitter obtained TV rights for NHL, MLB, PGA and MLS broadcasting. Facebook bought TV rights from UEFA Champions League, NFL, NCAA basketball,[3] and so on.

---

[1] Spangler, Todd. (2018, January 30). "Big Media, Silicon Valley battle for multibillion-dollar sports TV rights." *Variety.com.* https://variety.com/2018/digital/features/olympics-rights-streaming-nbc-winter-games-1202680323/

[2] Carp, Sam. (2019, July 25). "Amazon adds French Open domestic rights to tennis portfolio." *SportsPro.* https://www.sportspromedia.com/news/amazon-french-open-broadcast-rights-tennis-france-televisions

While Amazon used sports TV rights to increase the value of its Prime Video subscription, Facebook used sports broadcasting to increase the appeal of its Facebook Watch, a free video service aimed at attracting viewers and subsequently selling them to advertisers. Facebook bought TV rights and gave away content for free. For the leagues, the content owners, content is paid for. But the traditional media are already excluded from the supply chain.

***

Big Tech is not the only potential suitor for popular content that used to be paid for. The rise of e-sports promises new formats and business models for streaming and broadcasting, for which traditional media simply are not prepared.

Sports betting also creates new opportunities that will be used by those that are more dexterous, whether it be traditional media, OTT streamers or betting companies themselves. As Sara Fischer of *Axios* noted, "Non-media companies, like DraftKings and FanDuel are beginning to integrate more live and on-demand media content into their betting experiences."[1]

Finally, if the content is so good that it can be used by someone to secure fans' attention and loyalty, it must be used for these purposes. As *New York Post* reported, Major League Baseball discussed selling "the internet streaming rights for in-market games to the individual team franchises themselves."[2] The biggest sports goods brands, such as Nike or Reebok, can come up with this idea, too. They can and will buy sports TV rights for attracting consumers onto their websites and other media platforms.

Whoever might enter this business, they will inevitably develop the format in a way that this content requires – with sports commentating, game analysis, sideline and on-field interviews, visual infographics, etc. All the techniques are known, and they are widely elaborated upon by the sports media. However, there is nothing in this type of content that would secure the traditional media's paywall monopoly.

***

[3] Spangler, Todd. (2018, January 30). "Big Media, Silicon Valley battle for multibillion-dollar sports TV rights." *Variety.com*. https://variety.com/2018/digital/features/olympics-rights-streaming-nbc-winter-games-1202680323/

[1] Fischer, Sara. (2018, December 18). "Axios Media Trends." *Axios*. https://www.axios.com/newsletters/axios-media-trends-55b98ed0-2382-4726-bd60-608be1b01057.html

[2] Kosman, Josh. (2018, December 17). "MLB eyes giving teams streaming rights challenging pay-TV model." *The New York Post*. https://nypost.com/2018/12/17/mlb-eyes-giving-teams-streaming-rights-challenging-pay-tv-model/

With a digital device at hand, people cannot help but learn the news that is the most relevant to them. Neither effort nor a fee is required for that. News will find them. When the scarcity of content reverses to its opposite, abundance, people do not hunt for the news, the news hunts for people.

Any kind of content tends to be free under such circumstances. Content morphs from being a commodity into a lure. Fish do not pay for a lure. The only type of price that remains for content will be the price of production. And it will be paid for by those who want the audience's attention, not subscription.

In the digital environment, due to its technological and business specificity, news content will always be paid *from above*, not *from below*, meaning by those who want to deliver it and not by those who want to receive.

Money talks

In 1999, Robert McChesney, one of the leading political economists in the media, published the book *Rich Media, Poor Democracy: Communication Politics in Dubious Times*, in which he introduced the *Media/Democracy Paradox*. He stated that the media formally assumed "a central role in providing institutional basis for having an informed and participating citizenry," but in fact, they thrived themselves while failing real democracy. Despite mass communication penetrating everything, "our era is increasingly depoliticized," he wrote. "Traditional notions of civic and political involvement have shriveled. Political participation (elections 1998) fell to one-third of eligible voters."

The reasons, as McChesney suggested, were corporate control, the concentration of media ownership, profit-seeking and advertising. These structural settings brought the "hypercommercialism and denigration of journalism and public service." He concluded that,

> The media have become a significant anti-democratic force in the United States and, to varying degrees, world-wide. The wealthier and more powerful the corporate media giants have become, the poorer the prospects for participatory democracy. (McChesney, 2015 [1999], p.2.)

This was what he called the *Media/Democracy Paradox*: as the media grew rich, democracy became poor. The book was "about the corporate media explosion and the corresponding implosion of public life, the rich media/poor democracy paradox" (Ibid., p.3). McChesney offered an insightful analysis of the media system and its development in the 20th

137

century. He also gave some recommendations, from the point of view of the political left, regarding media reforms and media activism, partly aimed at fixing the media but also to overcome the influence of the corporate media on democracy.

Strongly critical about the commercial restraints on journalism, McChesney claimed that professional standards could not withstand corporate pressure because of a kind of "Eleventh Commandment" in the commercial news media: "Thou Shalt Not Cover Big Local Companies and Billionaires Critically" (Ibid., p. xvii).

***

The most interesting thing related to this analysis happened 15 years later, when the media system that McChesney described suddenly ceased to exist. All the condemned financial and proprietary dependencies that used to degrade journalism were gone – and journalism with them. In the preface to the 2015 edition, McChesney wrote,

> It is ironic that the journalism hellhole I described in 1998 looks almost like a Golden Age today. Journalism has been in freefall collapse since the early 2000s. <...> With the emergence of the Internet, advertising no longer is tethered to journalism and the commercial basis for sufficient general news production has collapsed. This is a disaster for a political system predicated upon having an informed and engaged citizenry. There is no reason to believe a widespread and effective commercial journalism will ever return. (McChesney, 2015 [1999], p. xxxviii).

And here is one more large quote that deserves to be put here, as it represents McChesney's deep understanding of the underlying changes in the environment and also nicely reflects the changes themselves, historically instantaneous ones. Journalism fell from the heights of glory, corrupted by advertising, to the bottom of a pit where no advertiser is bothered to corrupt it, within a mere 15 years. McChesney wrote that,

> Advertisers provided the vast majority of revenues for journalism in the twentieth century and made news media lucrative. Advertisers needed to help pay for journalism to attract readers and viewers who would then see their adds. That was the deal. Advertisers supported the news because they had no other choice if they wished to achieve their commercial goals; they, of course, had not intrinsic attachment to the idea of a free press.
> In the new era of smart or targeted digital advertising, advertisers <...> purchase access to target audiences directly <...>. *Advertisers no longer need to support journalism of content creation at all.* Advertising gave the illusion

that journalism is a naturally, even supremely, commercial endeavor. But when advertising disappear, journalism's true nature comes into focus: it is a public good, something society requires but that market cannot provide in sufficient quality and quantity.

Like other public goods, if society wants it, it will require public policy and public spending. There is no other way. The marriage of capitalism and journalism is over. If the United States is to have democratic journalism, it will require massive public investment. (McChesney, 2015 [1999], p. lii.)

Further, in his 2015 preface, McChesney discussed measures that could support journalism as a public service, including regulation, public broadcasting, incentives for non-profit media, public subsidies like in some European countries, or something similar to the subsidies that existed, mostly in the form of postal subsidies, in the US in the 19th century, when the American press system "was the freest and most extensive in the world."

He admitted, though, that there could be some legitimate concerns "that public money will lead to a government-controlled propaganda system like one finds in dictatorships and authoritarian regimes or even in the more corrupt capitalist democracies" (Ibid., p. lii). However, he saw public funding and public control as the most viable solution.

This insightful analysis, particularly courageous in admitting the changes in its subject, gives a vivid illustration of how profound changes in the media and journalism have been.

"The marriage of capitalism and journalism is over," as McChesney put it. But the divorce will take some time. Alas, the child of this marriage, the public, will greatly suffer. To understand the details of this divorce, it is necessary to look at the nature of journalism further than back to the 19th century. Besides advertising and public/political subsidies, there was one more business model that participated in maintaining journalism, the pay *from below* model, in which readers buy news. This will not survive the impacts of the internet either. But blended with other residual motives to pay for journalism, it will prolong the agony of the media for another five or so years.

***

Advertising is no longer capable of securing the media's survival; as for news retail, it was never capable of this in the first place. But journalism still seems to be an essential structural element of democracy, at least of the institutional, representative form of it.

So, who will maintain journalism? What funding mechanisms will replace the former institution maintenance fee collected by journalism through news and ad sales?

Everyone in the industry is obsessed with the search for answers, as this is a matter of survival. But few care about the next question: What impact will the change in funding have on journalism?

***

In analyzing corporate control over the communications industries, Graham Murdock distinguished two basic levels of control: the allocative and the operational.

1) Allocative control relates to the power to define goals and determine the priorities of resource commitments.

2) Operational control "works at a lower level and is confined to decisions about the effective use of resources already allocated and the implementation of policies already decided upon at the allocative level" (Murdock, 1983, p. 118).

Allocative control represents the environmental effect of resources spent. It assumes that, through selective funding, the system develops those structures and practices that are paid for and neglects those deprived of resource replenishment. The paid-for structures and practices are incentivized, and the unpaid ones get suppressed. Therefore, the goal of analysis is to identify those incentives and suppressors, why they prevail over others, and what they incentivize and suppress.

To put it simply, operational control rests on the feasibility of intentions; allocative control rests on the viability of incentives.

***

When the modernist idea about the supremacy of human reason over chaotic Nature is pushed to its extreme and people want everything to be rationally reconstructed for a better life and everyone's happiness, the production of meaning ('meaning production') inevitably falls under the operational control of power. Society is seen as a mechanism; one that is complex but manageable by strong and smart enough leadership.

Josef Stalin loved to direct arts, science and the media. He personally decided whether the great Russian poetess Anna Akhmatova, whose life and freedom were mercifully spared by the regime (unlike the life of her husband Nikolay Gumilyov and many other poets), should be published in *Znamya* or *Zvezda* magazines. Adolf Hitler personally commissioned actress and film director Leni Riefenstahl to shoot a movie about the Nazi party congress, the notorious *Triumph des Willens*.

In advanced Western democracies, such operational control of meaning production was unthinkable. Instead, allocative control was responsible for adjustments in the agenda. The ways of culture industries' funding and structuring predefined the global settings and tiny nuances shaping people's picture of the world.

As economy and not politics run the modernisation of society in the West, meaning production is subjugated to economic and not authoritarian forces. During the course of the 20th century, starting in the early industrial times, with Lippmann and Sinclair, then to Adorno and Horkheimer, the Birmingham school, the French postmodernists, and further to Herman and Chomsky, society learned how the media industry was funded and what impacts these types of funding had on agenda-setting. The entire discipline of the political economy of communications appeared in the late 1970s and aimed to explain the wheeling and dealing in the relations between power, capital and the media. Both people in the industry and the general public had become acutely aware of what the driving force was of the media funded by advertising and how those media shaped reality.

All this knowledge has become inapplicable, as the mechanisms they attached to are gone. New funding mechanisms have not been found yet, and there is no guarantee they will ever be found.

However, it is already clear that any attempts to reassemble the business model of journalism based on new principles will inevitably distort the old mechanisms of agenda-setting – at least compared to the distortions that society has been accustomed and adjusted to.

To bring the conclusion to the forefront, those funding mechanisms of the media that are tested now:

1) will not be sufficient for the industry to survive

2) will push what remains of journalism towards propaganda

3) will polarize society even more.

When concerned billionaires and Big Tech care about journalism

In recent years, some new money has been injected into the media industry, shaping a quite obvious trend. Amid the decline of their ancient glory, old media has caught the fancy of billionaires who have just made their fortunes in Hi-Tech.

In 2013, Jeff Bezos, Amazon's owner and one of the richest men in the world, purchased the *Washington Post* for $250 million.[1] The Silicon Valley entrepreneur and philanthropist Laurene Powell Jobs, the widow of Apple founder Steve Jobs, bought the *Atlantic* magazine in 2017.[2] Patrick Soon-Shiong, a billionaire biotech entrepreneur and Los Angeles' richest resident, bought the *Los Angeles Times* for $500 million in 2018.[3] The same year, co-founder of Salesforce.com Marc Benioff and his wife Lynne acquired *Time Magazine* for $190 million.[4]

The pattern resembles the story of 'dollar princesses', the young heiresses of wealthy American families of the late 19th century who went to England to marry a nobleman. The American nouveau riche of the Gilded Age had money but not a noble title. So, they wanted to increase their social standing through aristocratic relatives and acquire noble names for their offspring. For their part, many noble families in England had already passed their heydays and desperately needed a means to maintain the high status they were accustomed to. New money and old titles needed each other.

The same story is sometimes reiterated when new Big Tech money marries old media noble titles.

Aside from such an allegoric generalization, each case of big money marrying into big names has had, of course, its individual motives.

***

In 2007, Patrick Soon-Shiong, a former physician ("the billionaire physician" as *LA Times* called him), read in *LA Times* a story about a woman who could not get medical attention in an emergency room. Dr. Soon-Shiong rushed to the troubled hospital, confronted the doctor in charge and, thereafter, provided a financial guarantee to assist the local authorities with hospital modernization. "The story also helped Soon-Shiong recognize the

---

[1] Bezos, Jeff. (2013, August 5). "Jeff Bezos on Post purchase." *The Washington Post.* https://www.washingtonpost.com/national/jeff-bezos-on-post-purchase/2013/08/05/e5b293de-fe0d-11e2-9711-3708310f6f4d_story.html

[2] Lee, Edmund. (2017, July 28). "Laurene Powell Jobs is buying the Atlantic magazine." *Vox.* https://www.vox.com/2017/7/28/16055162/laurene-powell-jobs-acquired-atlantic-magazine-publisher-steve-widow-philanthropist-nonprofit

[3] James, Meg, & Chang, Andrea. (2018, April 14). Patrick Soon-Shiong — immigrant, doctor, billionaire, and soon, newspaper owner - starts a new era at the L.A. Times. *The Los Angeles Times.* https://www.latimes.com/business/la-fi-patrick-soon-shiong-profile-la-times-20180413-htmlstory.html

[4] Trachtenberg, Jeffrey A. (2018, September 16). "Time Magazine sold to Salesforce founder Marc Benioff for $190 million." *The Wall Street Journal.* https://www.wsj.com/articles/time-magazine-sold-to-salesforce-founder-marc-benioff-for-190-million-1537137165

importance of journalism to his life — and to the life of the community," pointed out *LA Times,* telling the story[1] of its new owner.

The acquisition of *LA Times* by Dr. Soon-Shiong in 2018 was extremely timely. The newspaper was about to cut jobs and close its bureau in DC. This information, as *LA Times* recollected in a touching piece, "spurred him to act 'as desperately fast as possible' to save the paper." As the paper quoted, he said that, "The idea of reducing the newsroom and getting rid of the Washington bureau – I thought if we didn't move, that would be the death knell of the institution as we knew it."[2]

In a different interview, he admitted: "I overpaid. It wasn't the money. It wasn't the business. It was, 'Do we want this paper to exist or not?'"[3]

All the keywords are present here: "save", "institution", "exist". Soon-Shiong's motives were philanthropic (or were depicted as such). Through his own personal financial means, he substituted the vanishing institution maintenance fee for the media and saved the institution; this is portrayed as similar to what he did, for example, when he "rescued six small California hospitals."

A concerned billionaire took on the role of a public interest champion and picked up on a public demand. This is a new way to materialize the invisible hand of society that had previously maintained journalism through purchasing news and ads.

Despite the common view that the rich do not care about the public good, some of them want and, most importantly, are able to compensate for the declining maintenance fee for suffering institutions. Capitalism might be cruel, but capitalists can be caring. Some studies showed, for example, that "chain-owned" newspapers (a rough proxy for stock market traded) "place a higher emphasis on profits over professional or community goals and have smaller news staff" compared to "independent" (often family-owned) newspapers. Respectively, "'independently owned newspapers cover controversial ideas more often' than their corporate chain-owned counterparts" (as quoted in: Benson, Neff & Hessérus, 2018, p. 280). In other words, private owners are generally more humane than the dispersed

---

[1] James, Meg, & Chang, Andrea. (2018, April 14). Patrick Soon-Shiong — immigrant, doctor, billionaire, and soon, newspaper owner - starts a new era at the L.A. Times. *The Los Angeles Times.* https://www.latimes.com/business/la-fi-patrick-soon-shiong-profile-la-times-20180413-htmlstory.html

[2] Ibid.

[3] Pointer Morning MediaWire. (2018, October 3). http://go.pardot.com/webmail/273262/261477187/05a03d1423b5f4e679759d5a65bd9a7e928a25fa68b605d3fec3923ac62eb01a

agency of ownership through stock market. Billionaires can understand the public significance of the media; the market does not.

This is a sort of hybrid allocative-operational control: the rich owners allocate resources for the operational goal to support the public good produced by the media.

***

The story of Amazon's Jeff Bezos having bought the *Washington Post* was initially seen by some as a case of new and fast money marrying into an old and noble name. However, further developments suggest that there was perhaps a cold calculus behind the deal (though 'noblezation' of the fortune through a title affiliation can be a rational business plan, too).

While its leading rival, the *New York Times*, has demonstrated spectacular success in digital subscription (3.4 million at the end of 2019[1]; the world's most), the *Washington Post*, under Bezos's hand, started turning into a hi-tech company that also publishes its own newspaper.

The *Washington Post* developed Arc, a publishing system that covers all publishing needs, starting with news budgeting and content production to managing ad and subscription sales and building the reader community. As *Forbes* reported,

> Arc was initially built by the company to meet its own needs, but after realizing it had built one of the best media tech stacks in the industry, the company began selling it to other publishers. The Washington Post Company now believes Arc Publishing has the ability to become a $100 million business.[2]

The publishing system can become an industrial platform for publishing, as Amazon itself is a platform for online retail. Maintaining a platform for the entire industry, of course, is the next level of media business, for which the *Washington Post* itself might turn out to be just a testing ground and a launching pad.

***

"Arc wants to be more than a technology stack – it wants to be a network," wrote Ken Doctor.[3] Not only has Arc already got on board dozens

---

[1] The New York Times Company reports 2019 fourth-quarter and full-year results and announces dividend increase. Press Release. https://s1.q4cdn.com/156149269/files/doc_financials/2019/q4/Press-Release-12.29.2019-Final-for-posting.pdf

[2] High, Peter. (2019, April 29). "How the Washington Post made its publishing platform a revenue driver." *Forbes*. https://www.forbes.com/sites/peterhigh/2019/04/29/how-the-washington-post-made-its-publishing-platform-a-revenue-driver/#57c905b878cd

of news orgs across the globe, including the *Chicago Tribune* and the *Los Angeles Times*, it also powers "more than 800 sites worldwide"[1] with more than 600 million unique visitors a month (May 2019[2]). This supplies a huge amount of personal data, which itself is a valuable asset in the platform economy, particularly if integrated with the Amazon mothership.

As a content management platform, Arc is attractive to businesses outside the media industry since they are becoming the media, too. In September 2019, the *Washington Post* licensed Arc to British oil giant BP, its first non-media customer. "The energy company will use the tool to publish articles, newsletters and videos to its 70,000 employees across 250 internal websites and a future mobile app," wrote the *Observer*.[3]

Experts have started saying that Arc Publishing is becoming more valuable than the *Washington Post* itself.[4] Thus, thanks to a tech billionaire and his Amazonian take on things, this newspaper has found something else to sell. But this 'something' is not a newspaper at all; it is another 'little cute monkey', though not that little.

It is also obvious that this survival solution is unique. No niche can fit in many 'Amazons', let alone commit the huge technological and financial resources required to create a platform with industry-sized ambitions.

***

The intervention of big money has revived those media orgs who were lucky enough to attract this money. "For the new guard of wealthy West Coast titans, media is the new philanthropy," wrote Sara Fischer in *Axios*.

---

[3] Doctor, Ken. (2018, September 25). "Newsonomics: The Washington Post's ambitions for Arc have grown – to a Bezosian scale. NiemanLab. https://www.niemanlab.org/2018/09/newsonomics-the-washington-posts-ambitions-for-arc-have-grown-to-a-bezosian-scale/

[1] Dol, Quinten. (2020, February 26). "Wrapping your head around the headless CMS." *Built In*. https://builtin.com/media-gaming/arc-publishing-washington-post-headless-cms

[2] WashPostPR. (2019, May 1). "Arc Publishing announces significant investment to support growth, expansion strategy." *The Washington Post*. https://www.washingtonpost.com/pr/2019/05/01/arc-publishing-announces-significant-investment-support-growth-expansion-strategy/

[3] Cao, Sissi. (2019, October 3). "The Washington Post's most valuable asset is now its software, thanks to Jeff Bezos." *Observer*. https://observer.com/2019/10/jeff-bezos-washington-post-publishing-software-arc-licensing-bp-media-revenue/

[4] Williams, Rob. (2019, September 26). "Will Arc Publishing become more valuable than 'The Washington Post'?" *MediaPost*. https://www.mediapost.com/publications/article/341194/will-arc-publishing-become-more-valuable-than-the.html

"And legacy titles, rich with history and cachet, give newcomers access to the talent and infrastructure needed to build influence."[1]

However, concerned billionaires are not the only ones who have sometimes subsidized journalism. As strange as it may seem, the main suppressors of the traditional media business model have become the largest-ever funders of journalism. Google and Facebook, through their different initiatives, have in recent years pledged to donate $300 million each to journalism projects and organizations.[2] "The irony is hard to miss," pointed out Mathew Ingram in this regard, calling these odd philanthropists "the platform patrons" of the media.[3]

Emily Bell highlighted that, "The suddenness of technology companies caring about the financial stability of journalism is not at all coincidental." Funding of the media orgs is part of their lobbyist and marketing efforts. She reminded us that, when Google launched its Digital News Initiative in Europe, "it was a direct response to pressure by EU regulators. The money was allocated from a marketing budget, and amounted to a lobbying exercise." She concluded that, "Facebook, Apple, and Google do things that journalists should be investigating, not profiting from."[4]

***

Besides billionaires and Big Tech buying into the media, there is a vast array of philanthropy initiatives supporting journalism financially. Individual philanthropists, family foundations, institutional funders, corporate partners, and even states such as New Jersey[5] and nation-states such as Great Britain or France are advancing financial initiatives to support journalism, making up for the lost market sources of revenue.

---

[1] Fischer, Sara. (2018, September 18). Axios Media Trends. *Axios*. https://www.axios.com/newsletters/axios-media-trends-53628ed9-1d3a-4fbd-a556-ff99ded1e713.html

[2] Fischer, Sara. (2019, February 19). "Pledges to save local news reach nearly $1 billion." *Axios*. https://www.axios.com/nearly-1-billion-given-to-save-local-news-1550578396-018b9987-a750-4f13-9cb3-f97c8fcec072.html

[3] Ingram, Mathew. (2018, May 16.) "The platform patrons: How Facebook and Google became two of the biggest funders of journalism in the world." *Columbia Journalism Review*. https://www.cjr.org/special_report/google-facebook-journalism.php

[4] Bell, Emily. (2019, March 27). "Do technology companies care about journalism?" *Columbia Journalism Review*. https://www.cjr.org/tow_center/google-facebook-journalism-influence.php

[5] Gabbatt, Adam. (2018, July 6). "New Jersey pledges $5M for local journalism to boost state's 'civic health'." *The Guardian*. https://www.theguardian.com/us-news/2018/jul/06/new-jersey-journalism-local-news-civic-information-consortium

A new business model of journalism appeared, philanthro-journalism, that married non-profit media orgs and foundation funding in the form of grants. In addition to the non-profit media, projects and initiatives aimed at attracting non-profit funding and grants have been created in many commercial media outlets. Even the *New York Times*, the most successful newspaper in the digital market, in 2017 established a division "focused on securing non-profit funding sources for its journalism".[1]

***

These newly emerging forms of funding reflect the global shift from a capitalist economy to an economy of sharing. Donations, fundraising and the like have become just as equally influential financial resources as traditional capital investment.

A number of foundations have proactively become involved in philanthro-journalism. The Knight Foundation, MacArthur Foundation, Omidyar Network, American Journalism Project, Open Society Foundations, Rockefeller Foundation, Bill & Melinda Gates Foundation, C&A Foundation, Ford Foundation, Humanity United, and United Nations Foundation are among them. They fundraise money from private and institutional donors and allocate the proceeds to journalist projects and organizations.

In 2019, Sara Fisher of *Axios* calculated that, "Nearly $1 billion has been committed to saving local news in America over the next several years" in the philanthropy sector. One of the biggest sponsors, the Knight Foundation, pledged to donate $300 million over five years, starting in 2019,[2] which is comparable to the pledged commitment of the Big Tech Behemoths, Google and Facebook. As a financing touchstone, and to put these sums into perspective, US newspapers generated about $25 billion in revenue in 2018.[3]

Clearly, by adding philanthropic programs aiming to maintain other forms and certain themes of journalism (investigative, feminist, minority, environmental, humanitarian, etc.) to this, it is safe to assume that foundations, corporate donations and billionaires' contributions account for a significant amount of media funding. Also, it is safe to predict that non-

---

[1] Wang, Shan. (2017, September 1). "The New York Times is building out a new philanthropic arm in search of nonprofit funding for its journalism." *NiemanLab*. https://www.niemanlab.org/2017/09/the-new-york-times-is-building-out-a-new-philanthropic-arm-in-search-of-nonprofit-funding-for-its-journalism/

[2] Knight Foundation. (2019, February 19). "Knight Foundation focuses on building the future of local news in $300 million, five-year commitment." https://knightfoundation.org/press/releases/knight-foundation-focuses-on-building-the-future-of-local-news-in-300-million-five-year-commitment/

[3] Newspapers Fact Sheet. https://www.journalism.org/fact-sheet/newspapers/

profit funding of journalism will inevitably grow, as the industry will increase the efforts to offset the accelerating decline in the for-profit revenues.

***

When journalism was maintained predominantly by corporations through advertising, the impact of funding mechanisms on agenda-setting was known. To deal with that impact, the industry and the profession established ethical and operational standards: autonomy, objectivity, transparency, fact-checking, a many-sources approach in investigations, a both-sides look at conflicts, a wall between the newsroom and ad sales, etc. These standards were often violated, but the following scandals and condemnations proved that they nonetheless existed and somehow worked.

How will funding by billionaires, through corporate partnerships, and by foundations impact journalism and agenda-setting? New forms of allocative control (incentives through selective funding) have not been properly studied, let alone understood, by theorists and practitioners yet, but they have already impacted agenda-setting. The upheavals related to the rise of conservatism, Brexit, Trump's victory and the resultant election outcomes in many countries, along with the general increase in political radicalization and polarization can be ascribed, at least in part, to the change in funding mechanisms for journalism.

***

Interestingly, the influence of billionaires on the media they purchased poses the least risk, because if and when it occurs, it is highly transparent. When the owner wants or implies that certain standpoints be reflected in the editorial policy or if by some other means they interfere with newsroom autonomy, it is immediately jumped upon by those involved, the experts and the general public. As the risks of losing the all-important social capital are far greater when the financial capital is so large, the owners tend to steer well clear of even the tiniest hint of interfering with any newsroom autonomy. This is not because of their virtuous nature (though they all are no doubt good people), it is because they are watched and are expected to behave in a proper way.

A good example of such public control was shown in 2019, when Jeff Bezos was getting divorced and some intimate evidence of his new relationship was leaked. The entire industry, the experts and the public immediately started watching how the *Washington Post* would cover the scandal. This was important news not because gossip about a billionaire's personal life is newsworthy (though it is, too), but because his personal issues could impact his assets, the industry, investment plans and the stock market in general. (Similar attention was drawn to *Bloomberg* when Michael Bloomberg announced his plans to run for presidency.)

The *Washington Post* somehow managed to cover the delicate issue, though maybe not in the best possible way, uncertain about how to dish out "tawdry gossip and the real news".[1] But the very fact that the newspaper's maneuvering was immediately thrust into the spotlight proved that the control of the media by billionaires can be the least risky path for society because it is the most visible and therefore the most transparent type of influence on the media. Even if a less credible proprietor had interfered and a less credible newspaper had buried the offense, it would have been known to the public "as is" and corrected the attitude toward the newspaper and the agenda produced under such circumstances.

***

Society expects, or maybe it is better to say suspects, that the proprietor may interfere, thus there is some immunity for potential agenda-distortion related to this type of interference.

The same goes for corporation sponsorship of the media. It is always under the microscope, too. When Emily Bell, one the world's leading media experts, compared Google's partnership with the media to the supporting of journalism by billionaires (the aforementioned Bezos and others), she wrote that,

> Individuals who have made money from technology have sometimes used it to support journalism... In all these operations, transparency and a commitment to editorial independence from funding makes for somewhat comfortable relationships. But when it comes to corporate interests, journalists have to be alert to agendas in conflict with their own.[2]

In her opinion, if corporations want to support journalism, it should be done in other ways:

> It can be done through taxation and an expansion of civic media. It can be done through payments into arms-length endowments administered by

[1] Pompeo, Joe. (2019, January 14). "'The first test case': amid the Bezos divorce, the Washington Post tries to sift between the tawdry gossip and the real news." *Vanity Fair.* https://www.vanityfair.com/news/2019/01/the-bezos-divorce-the-post-tries-to-sift-between-the-gossip-and-the-real-news

[2] Bell, Emily. (2019, March 27). "Do technology companies care about journalism?" *Columbia Journalism Review.* https://www.cjr.org/tow_center/google-facebook-journalism-influence.php

separate bodies. It can even be done by changing the incentive structures on their own platforms to elevate and return more money to newsrooms.[1]

Even though the struggling media industry accepts funding from Google and Facebook, people in the media understand whose money they are taking and what is at risk. The same is true for the public. It has even been noticed that "Google has received markedly better press than some of its competitors, notably Facebook." As Bell explains,

> This is in part because it is more mature, and handles relations with the press far better (it has not tried to hide its own influence campaigns, for instance). It also spends more money. The extra money Google provides to journalism is not directly buying favor or dampening dissent, but it is certainly making news CEOs and editors I speak to put Google in a subtly different category from other platforms. Their attitude is that "Google gets it."[2]

However arguable such relations are, they are nevertheless still also in the spotlight. Ethical and regulatory questions are posed. Operational control is almost excluded, and allocative control is understood and watched over.

The same cannot be said about foundation funding of journalism.

Philanthropy funding: paying for the pushing of pressing issues

Funding journalism via foundations is perceived as a positive tendency because no one's individual corrupting will (personal or corporate) can be imposed through such a mechanism. As transactional revenue is steadily falling, foundation funding is welcomed.

However, this growing financial aid comes with a price that few in the industry and nobody in the public is aware of yet. Foundation funding surreptitiously pushes journalism towards activism, incentivizing the mutation of the formerly commercial agenda-setting into sponsored propaganda.

To understand this, the specificity of allocative control employed by foundations needs to be explored. Allocative control means that foundations' resources are directed toward certain specific topics or forms of journalism, while others are ignored. This incentivizes newsrooms to pursue projects

[1] Ibid.

[2] Ibid.

and approaches that will most likely be approved for funding. In their zealous funding search, the media try to meet the expectations of foundations, not those of the audience, the market, or their own.

Therefore, when foundation funding is significant, topic selection becomes quietly conducted by foundations, not by the media. Journalism starts serving foundations, not the audience or society. Agenda-setting is thereby, in part, moving into foundations. A part of the media's autonomy is surrendered because of this.

As foundations are deemed to be useful social institutions that maintain socially beneficial initiatives, no one scrutinizes their impact on the media's autonomy. Foundations are not billionaires or corporations that need to be watched over. The creeping relocation of agenda-setting from the newsrooms to foundations remains unnoticed.

***

The ideological and cultural consequences of the foundation's influence on journalism are not neutral. Before funding the media, foundations themselves need to fundraise. Basically, they offer agendas and ideas in the 'philanthropy market' that not only fit their understanding of public good but also are the most 'fundraiseable'. They are looking for complimentary resonance from individual and institutional sponsors. Fundraising is driven by good people, by responsible and concerned citizens. The ideas and activities selected for funding through fundraising will most likely correlate with the area of civic activism.

No one would condemn civic activism for attempting to forward their ideas and agendas. And this is the issue for journalism. For traditional journalism, public service has been a by-product of news business. For civic activism, public service is the primary goal. These are two different social-economic mechanisms with different approaches to agenda-setting. To put it simply, journalism agenda-setting is panoramic and inclusive, while civic activism agenda-setting is hyper-focused and exclusive.

Foundation funding incentivizes journalism to turn into activism. This is how Murdock's allocative control works: seeking funding within programs announced by foundations, newsrooms select those topics and formats they hope will fit the foundations' preferences, meaning sponsors' preferences, which in turn are selected under the current activism agenda, not the news agenda. Therefore, funded by foundations, the media tend to drift from the news agenda toward the activism agenda.

***

151

Invisible incentivizing for journalism to be pushed towards activism is not the only consequence of the growth of foundation funding of the media. The other consequence is a subtle incentivizing of the audience's divide and therefore polarization.

The efficiency of the news-media product funded by foundations is evaluated not by the market, but by specific forms of impact-assessment. The criteria can be different from foundation to foundation, but they generally relate to the resonance made by publication in the public sphere (often literally 'made-up' resonance). These criteria do not necessarily coincide with the traditional indicators of journalism success in the market, such as an increase in circulation, paid subscriptions or ad revenue.

For traditional journalism, particularly for journalism funded predominantly by advertising, the growth of the audience is an essential business goal. It increases both the sales of news to the audience and the sales of the audience to the advertisers. There are some secondary criteria, such as the affluence or loyalty of the audience, but its size is paramount.

The desire to increase circulation forced the media to address as broad an audience as possible, even within a selected stratum. Being an industrial enterprise, the media, particularly within the advertising model, sought to gather, generalize and standardize the audience. The audience might be split by consumer characteristics (income, demographics, etc.) but preferably not divided politically, as political division would diminish the audience reach of the media. Such were there technological requirements of the media business. With regard to the public service of journalism, this meant that media funded by ad money cohered, depoliticized and united people.

Under foundation funding, the defining factor that incentivizes the media is not the size of the audience but the impact of the message. The ability to reach a broader audience also matters, but the primary goal is the value-based purity, preciseness and proselytism of the message. One study quoted a director of a non-profit TV company who said, "impact goes beyond the classic journalistic mission of simply informing the public to asking: 'Did I change minds? Did I move legislation?'" (Benson, 2018, p. 1071). The audience gets selected and divided according to people's readiness to join the cause, meaning according to their ability to be civically and politically engaged.

Foundations want to direct the press towards urgent social issues. This is the whole point of fundraising for journalism and funding journalism. Foundations' agendas, even though not political, are ideologically charged and intended to make a difference, to make an impact; this results in the selection and division of people based on their receptiveness to civic ideas.

***

Under such conditions, the media are incentivized not to broaden the agenda in order to reach a wider and united audience, but rather to propagate the properly aligned message to a larger number of potential followers. The media do not marry the message to the audience; they marry the audience to the message. They engage in the selection of the audience, but not the message; the message has already been pre-selected. As Ben Smith from the *New York Times* put it, "nonprofit journalism can be boring, more attentive to its donors than its audience."[1]

The switch in the principles of agenda-setting from audience-driven factors to message-driven factors leads to the atomization, not the generalization, of the audience. The switch from advertising to philanthropy in funding the media means the change from consumer profiling to civic profiling of the audience. Consumer profiling was depoliticizing and uniting, while civic profiling is politicizing and dividing. By making the media focus on certain topics and divide people, foundation funding reverses the cohering effect of the advertising model. Foundation funding has the potential to contribute to polarization – not significantly, just slightly, but at the systemic level.

Perhaps foundation funding could have avoided such a downside if it had funded not ideas or formats but the profession of journalism itself. Some foundations, indeed, aim to support journalism (for example, local news). But this implies an underlying ideology anyway – it assumes some pre-selected and artificial vision of what journalism is and what ends it must serve. The formation of journalism standards abandons the newsrooms and goes to foundations. The only neutral way to support the profession of independent journalist is a market-funded paycheck; all the rest reflect the desires of someone from outside the newsroom regarding journalism.

***

The ways in which foundation funding reshapes mechanisms of agenda-setting in the media have started to attract the attention of media researchers. Rodney Benson of New York University conducted a study of foundation funding. He wrote that,

> ... Yet there has been too little critical analysis of the nonprofit alternative... We need better answers to questions like: Who exactly is in charge of these nonprofits, what are foundations asking in return for their support, and what

---

[1] Smith, Ben. (2020, March 29). "Bail out journalists. let newspaper chains die." *The New York Times.* https://www.nytimes.com/2020/03/29/business/coronavirus-journalists-newspapers.html

are the material and ideological limits to reform embodied in this new organizational model of journalism? In other words, we must acknowledge the possibility that foundations are just as capable of non-democratic "media capture" on behalf of their own interests as they are of fostering civic benefits for society as a whole. (Benson, 2018, p. 1060.)

Based on the analysis of the "close intertwining of elite management and boards between foundations, nonprofits, and commercial media" and having conducted a series of interviews with them, Benson stated that,

Despite the language of civic duty that surrounds the foundation world like a golden haze, there are also often specific strings and metrics attached to grants. Foundations increasingly prefer funding specific projects to general operations, increasing the possibility of some degree of "media capture" by foundation donors <...>. Certainly, such arrangements create the possibility of a conflict of interest, or appearance of such. (Benson, 2018, p. 1073.)

He concluded that,

Foundation project-based funding has also sometimes skewed media attention towards fashionable issues favored by philanthropic donors while ignoring a range of equally or even more urgent social problems. Philanthropic support mostly reinforces and extends an upper middleclass, pro-corporate orientation in mainstream American journalism. (Benson, 2018, p. 1060.)

***

As foundation-funded journalism is predestined to focus on pre-selected pressing social issues, it often reiterates the themes of the mainstream media but without the panoramic view the mainstream media are expected to offer due to their market-driven news coverage.

"Even if donors don't make clear their desire for a particular thesis or ideological slant, there are the potentials for self-censorship. Money talks," stated James Warren in *Poynter*, discussing the *New York Times'* plan to seek philanthropic funding. He quoted Alan Mutter, a former newspaper reporter and current industry analyst, who wrote to him that,

Third-party funding necessarily raises questions of (1) whether a topic would have been covered if the money were not available, and (2), whether the reporting and conclusions of the resulting stories were influenced by the need to please donors, especially if the publisher has a hope of obtaining future funding.[1]

---

[1] Warren, James. (2017, September 3). "The New York Times is looking for nonprofit

Since foundation funding incentivizes certain topics to be covered and certain approaches to be employed, newsrooms redirect their resources toward funded projects. Allocative control amplifies distortion in agendas in two ways: 1) it encourages certain topics and formats, and 2) it diverts limited newsroom resources away from other topics and formats.

***

It used to be the job of editors to define what social issues are pressing. Basically, this is like the job of a priest explaining the meaning of existence. To maintain this function and this institution, society paid the 'church tax', the institution maintenance fee, which in the case of media was buying news and ads. Castles, of course, often wanted to interfere in the practice of temples in order to get proper prophecies and interpretations, but a strong developed church could more likely than not withstand the will of the powerful and dictate its own will.

Now, the church of the media is in decline, and the parishioners are encouraged to save it by bringing their offerings to an intermediary institution that decides what themes the preacher must emphasize in order to sustain its parish. This intermediary supposedly knows better what the preacher should do and what the congregation wants.

Who are those people who are called upon for donations to support journalism? What is their social, cultural and political profile?

As they donate to the media, they most likely recognize its civic significance and would like to amplify its civic impact. So, they most likely belong to the highly 'mediatized' upper-middle class and/or the elite. They know what the media are there for, but among all the media functions, they most likely focus on the civic impact, not the panoramic cohering inherent to commercial journalism. They want to reinforce a message, not generalize the audience. With these motives, they must want to refine and reinforce particular topics, pre-selected from their and their mainstream media's already-existing agenda, but without the commercial/panoramic, background. Foundation funding is an invisible amplifier of the pre-selected fragments of agenda. This is where its polarization potential comes from.

Bensons stated that,

...Nonprofit media are not likely to do any better than mainstream media in connecting to the non-urban, non-cultural elite voters whose concerns about jobs, trade, and globalization tend to be ignored or dismissed in news coverage

funding. Will it succeed where others have failed?" *Poynter*. https://www.poynter.org/business-work/2017/the-new-york-times-is-looking-for-nonprofit-funding-will-it-succeed-where-others-have-failed/

and public policy, and who arguably as a result helped elect the "populist" Republican Donald Trump to the U.S. presidency. (Benson, 2018, p. 1067.)

***

Martin Scott, Mel Bunce and Kate Wright in "Foundation Funding and the Boundaries of Journalism" (2019) explored the foundation impact specifically on non-profit international news and came to similar conclusions. They found that,

> ... Foundations did not try to directly influence the content of the journalism they funded. However, their involvement did make a difference. It created requirements and incentives for journalists to do new, non-editorial tasks, as well as longer-form, off-agenda, "impactful" news coverage in specific thematic areas. As a result, foundations are ultimately changing the role and contribution of journalism in society. (Scott, Bunce & Wright, 2019, p. 2034.)

The authors stated that, "Foundation funding ultimately encourages journalists to focus on producing longer-form, off-agenda news coverage about topics that broadly aligned with the priorities of the most active foundations" (Scott, Bunce & Wright, 2019, p. 2035).

The pre-selected focusing of foundation-funded journalism on narrow topics at the expense of a more balanced panoramic view was also noticed. They stated that,

> In the case of non-profit international news, foundations direct journalism (both intentionally and unintentionally) towards outcome-oriented, explanatory journalism in a small number of niche subject areas. (Scott, Bunce & Wright, 2019, p. 2035.)

The findings support the hypothesis that foundation funding leads journalism to focus on the message and not on the audience (as commercial journalism would do). This setting pushes journalism toward pre-selected message delivery, which is closer to marketing and propaganda than to journalism.

The for-profit media can also experience a similar temptation. Or they can be pushed to promote the agendas of someone from the outside in order to accommodate advertisers and perhaps surrender to them some of their newsroom autonomy. But it is at least noticed and criticized there. No one will criticize non-profit media for pushing important topics because of foundation funding.

***

When foundation funding incentivizes certain themes and diverts resources from others, it leads to the pressing, in sponsors' opinion, social issues to be pressed even more by the journalists. The problem is that fundraising aims to solve pressing issues with financial contribution being just a means, not the goal; but for the contractor, contribution *is* the goal. The contractor is oftentimes more interested in the perpetuation of the funding than the solving of the issue, because there will be no funding without this issue. This risk is particularly obvious when the philanthropy contractor is a media outlet because the mass media are able to induce the reality via their coverage.

For journalism, foundation funding almost inevitably creates a conflict of interest. Journalists will subliminally overemphasize the significance of those topics that are well-funded by philanthropists. Charity money creates a demand for triggering media coverage. The agenda skews towards better-funded issues not because of newsrooms' autonomous view of what is newsworthy, but because of newsrooms' need for available funding. At some point, the pressing social issues reported on under such incentives become not just covered, but reproduced in the agenda and, through the agenda, in the media-induced reality.

The problem is more or less known in philanthropy. In foundations, special ethical committees are often commissioned to oversee the appropriateness of expenditures so that funding does not reproduce the issues it aims to fight against.

But when it comes to crowdsourced fundraising, exemplified in the media by the membership model, the problem only grows, as there is no such ethical supervision or even public understanding of the agenda risks related to philanthropy funding.

The *Guardian* and the genesis of the membership model

"Since you're here...
... we're asking readers like you to make a contribution in support of our open, independent journalism."

Such an appeal is shown to everyone accessing the archive articles on *The Guardian* website. The *Guardian* does not sell news. It sells journalism itself. On the Support Website[1], the *Guardian* asks:

---

[1] Support the *Guardian* web site. https://support.theguardian.com/us/contribute

> Support our journalism with a contribution of any size. Your support helps protect the Guardian's independence and it means we can keep delivering quality journalism that's open for everyone around the world.

Unlike other mainstream media that have closed their content by a paywall to try to squeeze any money they can out of readers accustomed to free content on the internet, the *Guardian* decided to keep its journalism open for all, regardless of where they live or what they can afford to pay. The request for contributions states that,

> We have upheld our editorial independence in the face of the disintegration of traditional media – with social platforms giving rise to misinformation, the seemingly unstoppable rise of big tech and independent voices being squashed by commercial ownership. The Guardian's independence means we can set our own agenda and voice our own opinions. Our journalism is free from commercial and political bias – never influenced by billionaire owners or shareholders. This makes us different. It means we can challenge the powerful without fear and give a voice to those less heard.

Demanding no cost from readers, the newsroom itself, however, has a cost to cover – the cost of production. Instead of selling news, the newspaper started asking for money to directly support independent journalism, which it aims to maintain.

***

The *Guardian* membership program originated from its event production activity. In 2012, the newspaper organized a festival, testing a new format of audience engagement and a new segment of business. As their traditional media business was faltering, the leadership sought new solutions.

The festival succeeded: 6000 readers attended it over the weekend. "The atmosphere was great. The debates were absorbing. The food, fringe conversations and music were incredibly relaxed and enjoyable," wrote Alan Rusbridger, then the editor-in-chief.

After the success, the *Guardian* started thinking about how to develop it further. Alan Rusbridger recollected in 2014:

> In various sessions we asked a number of questions of the readers and participants. Would they want something like this again? More generally, how did they feel about the issues newspapers around the world were – and are – kicking around: paying for content v free content, open v closed, and so on.[1]

So, they pondered both the event program and the issue of whether to introduce a paywall, as many others had done. Recalling discussions after the first inspirational engagement events, Rusbridger wrote that,

> The answers were revealing. Yes, the readers definitely wanted more – much more – of this. The prospect of being part of the debates, ideas and conversations we could start and host was immensely appealing. Most readers said they would happily contribute money to the "cause" of the Guardian – but an overwhelming majority also wanted the journalism to be free, so that it could reach the maximum possible audience. A fair number were happy to be subscribers, but the most hands shot up when asked if they would like to be "members".[1]

***

Announcing the launch of the membership program in 2014, Alan Rusbridger proclaimed:

> From today you can become a member of the Guardian. You can become a closer part of the community of journalists, readers and friends of an institution that has been around for well over 190 years. By joining you can be part of our journey of transformation into an open and global 21st-century media company.[2]

Building on the success of the festival, the first version of the *Guardian* membership program emphasized access to the *Guardian*'s events rather than the general support of the *Guardian*'s journalism. From the historical perspective, the collective search of the media industry for 'something else' to be sold instead of news went through the attempts at event organizing led by the *New Yorker* and *Texas Tribune* and resulted in the festival and subsequent membership program of the *Guardian*. Such was the genealogy of the membership model.

Within its membership program, the *Guardian* initially promoted access to a range of events and different newsroom-led activities, inviting readers to join their "three-tier membership scheme":

> Friends, which is free and gives access to events, news and bookings; Partners, which costs £15 per month and includes a range of discounts and

---

[1] Rusbridger, Alan. (2014, September 10). "Alan Rusbridger: welcome to Guardian Membership." *The Guardian*. https://www.theguardian.com/membership/2014/sep/10/-sp-guardian-editor-alan-rusbridger-welcome-to-guardian-membership

[1] Ibid.

[2] Ibid.

priority booking for events; and Patrons, which costs £60 a month and will include an extra level of access including a "backstage pass" to GNM operations, including newsroom tours, print site visits and insight into the editorial process.[1]

Thus, the model still looked transactional: it sold the product – the events, with a ranged access, akin to a freemium model. The events were expected to become that 'cute little monkey' the resort-beach photographer is forced to sell instead of photos.

To fill the membership program with activities, the *Guardian* launched Guardian Live, which would be,

> ...a rolling programme of events, discussions, debates, interviews, keynote speeches and festivals to bring the Guardian brand and experience to life in venues in the UK and internationally."[2] For that purposes, they also planned to renovate and open a special venue in a former 19th century passenger terminal, "a spectacular industrial space in Kings Cross, which is itself turning into one of the most vibrant and stimulating areas in London. [3]

***

Events still are part of the *Guardian* membership program but as an added bonus to membership rather than its main focus. At some point, the paper revealed that people would now be paying for their symbolic affiliation with the *Guardian*, not for the club-like service for socialites. The club-style membership engagement remains a pleasant addition of the offer. "Instead of using tote bags, tickets to live events, or other swag," the *Guardian* started asking for support, shifting "from a commercially focused plea to an emotional, service-based request."[4]

The newspaper has started soliciting direct financial support for its journalism. This is what has become the essence of the membership model,

---

[1] Sweney, Mark. (2014, September 10). "Guardian launches new three-tier membership scheme." *The Guardian*. https://www.theguardian.com/media/2014/sep/10/guardian-membership-scheme-patrons-kings-cross

[2] Ibid.

[3] Rusbridger, Alan. (2014, September 10). "Alan Rusbridger: welcome to Guardian Membership." *The Guardian*. https://www.theguardian.com/membership/2014/sep/10/-sp-guardian-editor-alan-rusbridger-welcome-to-guardian-membership

[4] Schmidt, Christine. (2017, November 17). "Asking members to support its journalism (no prizes, no swag), The Guardian raises more reader revenue than ad dollars." *NiemanLab*. https://www.niemanlab.org/2017/11/asking-members-to-support-its-journalism-no-prizes-no-swag-the-guardian-raises-more-reader-revenue-than-ad-dollars/

a new business model of journalism, now known to the media industry around the globe.

Thus, the classification of the program as 'membership' mutated into something a bit different from what was initially assumed. For now, the label 'membership program/membership model' has become the description of a new form of financial interaction with the audience, which is, primarily, opposite to a paywall. It keeps media content free to access but, in return, openly appeals to the audience for donations to support journalism offered by a respected media organization. In reality, this is a purified version of an institution maintenance fee for journalism being levied on a voluntarily basis and collected by a media outlet directly.

***

As business in general continued to decline, the new membership program became a challenging venture for the *Guardian*. The first period of the membership program brought in, by 2016, even bigger losses than expected. But the program was given carte blanche by the publisher for three years to prove that membership could work.[1] Judging by some circumstantial evidence, a reversion to the paywall had been a possibility if the new program had not succeeded.

A set of other radical measures was implemented. New editor-in-chief Katharine Viner took over from Alan Rusbridger. Expenses and jobs were significantly cut. The U.S.-based philanthropic arm was established in 2016 that reportedly secured $6 million "in multi-year funding commitments" in the first year.[2] The *Guardian* widened its news operations in Australia, the US, and worldwide.

The efforts appeared to pay off. In 2019, "*Guardian* performs remarkable comeback, but at cost of 450 jobs."[3] BBC reported that, "*The Guardian* recorded an operating profit of £0.8m for 2018-19: its first such profit in two decades and the culmination of one of the most significant turnarounds in recent British media history."[4]

---

[1] Martinson, Jane. (2016, January 25). "Publisher of the Guardian and Observer aims to break even within three years and launches a new strategy focusing on future growth." *The Guardian*. https://www.theguardian.com/media/2016/jan/25/guardian-news-media-to-cut-running-costs

[2] Bilton, Ricardo. (2017, August 28). "Could The Guardian's quest for philanthropic support squeeze out other news nonprofits?" *NiemanLab*. https://www.niemanlab.org/2017/08/could-the-guardians-quest-for-philanthropic-support-squeeze-out-other-news-nonprofits/

[3] Mayhew, Freddy. (2019, May 1). "Guardian performs remarkable comeback, but at cost of 450 jobs." PressGazette. https://www.pressgazette.co.uk/guardian-comeback-financial-but-at-cost-of-450-jobs/

The effectiveness of the membership model seemed to have been proven.

***

Curiously, the *Guardian* continues offering a subscription that is not based on a paywall and just offers some premium extra benefits such as access to a presumably fancy news app or ad-free reading on the website. Thus, it is not news trade but rather a sale of 'something else'. At the time of breaking even (May 2019), the *Guardian* was selling 190,000 of these premium subscriptions, which were seen by analysts as another form of readers' support.[1]

At the same time, the *Guardian* had "365,000 recurring financial contributors and members" and also "print subscriptions across the Guardian, Observer and Guardian Weekly at a record total of 110,000".[2] On top of this, more than 300,000 people had given one-off contributions in the previous year. In 2018, Statista put the *Guardian* in the 7th place among the world's leading mainstream newspapers in digital subscriptions, perhaps counting recurring memberships as subscriptions (Figure 8).

Number of digital-only subscribers to selected newspapers worldwide as of 1st quarter 2018 (in 1,000s)	
1. The New York Times (USA)	2800
2. The Wall Street Journal (USA)	1389
3. The Washington Post (USA)	1000
4. The Financial Times (UK)	720
5. Bild (Germany)	390
6. The Economist (UK)	350
7. The Guardian (UK)	300
8. Aftonbladet (Sweden)	250
9. Times of London (UK)	220
10. Le Monde (France)	160

Figure 8. Source: Statista[3]

---

[4] Rajan, Amol. (2019,1 May). "Guardian records first operating profit since 1998." *BBC*. https://www.bbc.com/news/entertainment-arts-48111464

[1] Benton, Joshua. (2019, May 1). "Want to see what one digital future for newspapers looks like? Look at The Guardian, which isn't losing money anymore." *NiemanLab*. https://www.niemanlab.org/2019/05/want-to-see-what-one-digital-future-looks-lik

[2] Tobitt, Charlotte. (2019, May 1). "Guardian group meets target to break even at end of three-year financial turnaround plan." *PressGazette*. https://www.pressgazette.co.uk/guardian-group-meets-target-to-break-even-at-end-of-three-year-financial-turnaround-plan/

In 2019, with 190,000 premium subscriptions and 365,000 recurring financial contributors and members, the *Guardian* would likely have taken the 5th place in the world in the rating of digital subscriptions.

Membership as a new business model

The membership model has become perhaps the brightest (or even the only) ray of light in the media market over the murky past two decades. Many other media organizations have started applying different elements or versions of membership in their business.

Most membership ideas revolved around selling a symbolic affiliation with quality (or local, or activist) journalism; programs of engagement with the brand are usually a supplement, ranging from seminars and festivals to readers' participation in the newsroom planning meetings and teleconferences.

The membership evangelists from the Membership Puzzle Project distinguish the "thin" model of membership, when members just donate money to their favourite media outlet and mostly resembles donors, and the "thick" model, when members also show up to events, offer advice and feedback and interact.[1]

There is also some merging area between "subscription plus" (or premium), when subscribers buy the product but also express their support, and "membership lite", (or "thin membership"), when members patronize and financially support journalism but otherwise rarely engage.[2]

***

The Membership Puzzle Project created a database of news orgs employing different forms of membership and had collected more than 160 names from around the world by 2020.[3] Each media outlet in this list has a 'mission statement' that is essentially an offer behind the membership pitch,

[3] Watson, Amy. (2018, November 14). "Number of solely digital newspaper subscribers worldwide 2018." *Statista.* https://www.statista.com/statistics/785919/worldwide-number-/

[1] Rosen, Jay, & Peon, Gonzalo del. (2017, October 4). "Introducing the Membership Models in News Database for your use and contributions." *The Membership Puzzle Project.* https://membershippuzzle.org/articles-overview/introducing-the-database

[2] Goligoski, Emily, & Myers, Kate. (2018, September 11). "Demystifying 'membership lite': Why membership and subscription serve different goals." *Poynter.* https://www.poynter.org/newsletters/2018/demystifying-membership-lite-why-membership-and-subscription-serve-different-goals/

[3] Membership in News Database. https://membershippuzzle.org/tools/database

with a range of areas of commitment – from investigative journalism to helping to find fun on the Internet.

The list contains many well-recognized and much spoken of names, such as *Charlotte Agenda, BuzzFeed News, Columbia Journalism Review, HuffPost, Intercept* and others. Some news brands are known for their specific journalist services, such as *PolitiFact*, which focuses on political fact checking; Russian dissident *Novaya Gazeta*; the German 'constructive journalism' *Perspective Daily*, which focuses on solutions; and *Positive News*, which has a similar idea. Perhaps the biggest names, along with the *Guardian*, on the list are *Texas Tribune* and the *Atlantic*.

***

But the worthiest of discussion is the Dutch *De Correspondent*. Starting with an idea similar to membership in 2013, even before it was called so in relation to the *Guardian*, *De Correspondent* managed to raise $1.7 million before its site had even published its first article.[1]

The success factors included the well-known names of its co-founders, prominent Dutch journalists, a well-managed campaign and a well-received journalism manifesto.[2] The manifesto claims that,

> We cover stories that tend to escape the mainstream media radar because they don't fit neatly into the drama of the 24-hour news cycle. De Correspondent provides an antidote to the daily news grind – shifting the focus from the sensational to the foundational and from the attention-grabbing headline to the constructive insight. We refuse to speculate about the latest scare or breaking story, but work instead to uncover the underlying forces that shape our world.[3]

Basically, the manifesto offered to slow down the 'Hamster Wheel', as described by Dean Starkman, which journalism happened to be trapped in

---

[1] Ingram, Mathew. (2013, Nov 29). "This online journalism startup raised $1.7M in crowdfunding and you've never heard of it." *GigaOm*. https://gigaom.com/2013/11/29/this-online-journalism-startup-raised-1-7m-in-crowdfunding-and-youve-never-heard-of-it/

[2] Pfauth, Ernst. (2013, November 27). "How we turned a world record in journalism crowd-funding into an actual publication." *Medium*. https://medium.com/de-correspondent/how-we-turned-a-world-record-in-journalism-crowd-funding-into-an-actual-publication-2a06e298afe1

[3] Filloux, Frederic. (November 30, 2017.) "De Correspondent's successful membership model." *Global Investigative Journalism Network*. https://gijn.org/2017/11/30/de-correspondents-successful-membership-model/ (A later version - Wijnberg, Rob. (2018, October 16). "Everyone is saying membership is the future of journalism. Here's how you can put it into practice." *Medium*. https://medium.com/de-correspondent/putting-membership-into-practice-2e980c025fc9)

because of the traffic race on the internet. As the manifesto's author and *De Correspondent* co-founder Rob Wijnberg later explained,

> We try to tell precisely those stories that aren't news, but news-worthy nevertheless. Or, as we often say, that reveal not the weather but the climate…. Our ultimate goal: to replace the sensational with the foundational and the recent with the relevant…
>
> It's no longer our correspondents' goal to be the first, get a scoop, or be picked up by other outlets. Their goal is to thoroughly ground themselves in the major developments of our time and, along the way, share their learning curve with a growing community of followers.[1]

This was the best ideological substantiation for so-called 'slow media', or the "antidote to the news", as Wijnberg called it.

It seems both Starkman and *De Correspondent* struck a nerve in fighting the 'hamsterization of journalism', as people reacted to the offer very well. By 2017, *De Correspondent* had 60,000 paying members. "If *De Correspondent* were published in the United States, it would have more than one million paid-for readers, more than half *The New York Times'* number. If it were in France, it would have 230,000 subscriptions, nearly twice that of *Le Monde*," commented *Global Investigative Journalism Network*.[2]

***

The comparison of the Dutch audience to its American or French counterparts made sense, and this sense finally trapped *De Correspondent* into an unpleasant situation.

For the membership model, as much as for subscription, the size of the audience matters. Unlike (some) generous donations within the foundation funding model, membership is based on a small contribution from many members. To convert the reader base into sufficient money and sustainable income, the scale of the audience outreach has to be significant.

That is why membership hardly fits local news orgs or the media of a limited language base. They would better rely on larger donations of more generous and bigger sponsors.

---

[1] Wijnberg, Rob. (2018, September 12). "The problem with real news – and what we can do about it." *Medium.* https://medium.com/de-correspondent/the-problem-with-real-news-and-what-we-can-do-about-it-f29aca95c2ea

[2] Filloux, Frederic. (November 30, 2017.) "De Correspondent's successful membership model." *Global Investigative Journalism Network.* https://gijn.org/2017/11/30/de-correspondents-successful-membership-model/.

Joshua Benton from *NiemanLab* called the *Guardian* "a weird newspaper" partly because it had "nearly two-thirds of their readers coming from outside the country they're based in."[1] Anglophone newspapers can have this luxury. Guardian News & Media deputy chief executive David Pemsel, when introducing the membership model in 2014, highlighted that this represented "new, meaningful ways to monetise our huge audience of over 100 million global users."[2]

The *Guardian* had the prospect both to monetize its already-existing 100 million readers and increase this number even more, as the English-reading audience on the Internet has reached 1.106 billion and constitutes the world's biggest online language population.

De Correspondent had a native language niche of only about 24 million; which is very limited for a media business model, based on small contributions, to be a viable prospective reality let alone even sustainable. They wanted and needed more.

***

In 2017, *De Correspondent*, with its proven successful ideology of 'unbreaking news' and membership, decided to expand into the English-reading online audience.

They started an extension campaign very wisely. *De Correspondent* established the Membership Puzzle Project in partnership with the New York University journalism program led by Jay Rosen, one of the world's most prominent media experts.

Having started studying "membership trials and membership errors"[3] in the media around the world, the Membership Puzzle Project found that membership know-how is in high demand. They managed to secure $700,000 in foundation funding to support membership projects in 17 countries[4] under the patronage of the Membership in News Fund.[5] While

---

[1] Benton, Joshua. (2019, May 1). "Want to see what one digital future for newspapers looks like? Look at The Guardian, which isn't losing money anymore." *NiemanLab.* https://www.niemanlab.org/2019/05/want-to-see-what-one-digital-future-for-newspapers-looks-like-look-at-the-guardian-which-isnt-losing-money-anymore/

[2] Sweney, Mark. (2014, September 10). "Guardian launches new three-tier membership scheme." *The Guardian.* https://www.theguardian.com/media/2014/sep/10/guardian-membership-scheme-patrons-kings-cross

[3] The Membership Puzzle Project. About. https://membershippuzzle.org/about

[4] Schmidt, Christine. (2018, October 22). "Here's how you can be part of a $700,000 experiment in building membership models around the world." *NiemanLab.* https://www.niemanlab.org/2018/10/heres-how-you-can-be-part-of-a-700000-experiment-in-building-membership-models-around-the-world/

studying membership cases and innovations, they also promoted the idea of membership in the audience.

The US/Anglophone-focused fundraising campaign for the *Correspondent* was launched at the end of 2018. They aimed to raise $2.5 million in a month. They got to $1 million in 9 days and then it stalled. Jay Rosen rushed for a final attack and pitched the idea on *The Daily Show* with Trevor Noah.[1] That show, by the way, was unusual because Noah had lost his voice and used his smartphone voice assistant to interview Rosen.

The goal was reached, and $2.6 million was raised, a fact that was very well-received by media folks, as it seemed to prove that "people formerly known as the audience" (the metaphor created by Jay Rosen back in 2006[2]) are willing to pay for quality journalism in the form of donation.

***

But soon after, the shocking-for-many news about the 'unbreaking news' project broke. As stunned media people on Twitter tweeted;

> After raising millions in donations based on very lofty, high-horsey talk about fixing the broken US news industry, *The Correspondent* says it won't open a US newsroom and never wanted to be a US national news org.[3]

Indeed, as *De Correspondent* stated on March 25, 2019:

> We've closed our campaign office in NYC, and we have decided that we won't open a newsroom in the US for now. We don't aim to be a national US news organization (we have founding members from more than 130 countries around the world!) but instead want to cover the greatest challenges of our time from a global perspective—in English. For that vision, Amsterdam is as a great place to start.[4]

Jay Rosen and other 'ambassadors' sounded confused. Rosen said in *NiemanLab*,

---

[5] Membership in News Fund. https://membershippuzzle.org/fund

[1] Benton, Joshua. (2018, December 7). "Jay Rosen pitches the English-language Correspondent on The Daily Show." *NiemanLab*. https://www.niemanlab.org/2018/12/jay-rosen-pitches-the-english-language-correspondent-on-the-daily-show/

[2] Rosen, Jay. (2006, June 27). "The people formerly known as the audience." *Press-Think*, Jay Rosen's blog. http://archive.pressthink.org/2006/06/27/ppl_frmr.html

[3] Tom Gara on Twitter. (2019, March 26). https://twitter.com/tomgara/status/1110540015157870594

[4] Pfauth, Ernst. (2019, March 25). "An update from Amsterdam: here's how we're building The Correspondent." *Medium*. https://medium.com/de-correspondent/an-update-from-amsterdam-heres-how-we-re-building-the-correspondent-f2c5012e6a9c

I think it's understandable why people had the impression that there would be a U.S. headquarters, because some of the signaling that *The Correspondent* did, especially earlier in 2017, first half of 2018, was suggesting that. So that's not anyone's fault but the *Correspondent*'s, because there was talk about a New York base... And there had been a lot of indications ... that a U.S. headquarters was in the deal.[1]

In his blog, Rosen stated that, "Yep. The *Correspondent* screwed up in its communications with members."[2] The scandal broke, and the *Correspondent* tried to explain and doctor the story, awkwardly, and finally admitted in an "unsigned unconditional apology" that, "We screwed up".[3]

The story cast a shadow over the membership model in the US. There were also talks that some earlier fundraised money had been used for later fundraising, not journalism, which raised questions about transparency.[4] As an old Russian saying regarding a delicate situation with guests goes, "The silverware has been found, yet an unpleasant aftertaste lingers."

As of March 2020, the *Correspondent* had 50,000 members.[5] This is not that impressive, being well below fundraising campaign expectations, and it did not even outperform its Dutch mothership (60,000).

Membership and the donating audience: paying for others to read

Apart from all the local factors, the American misplay of *De Correspondent* highlighted a significant pitfall of the membership model. The newsroom using this model cannot do what it wants. It must do what the members want.

---

[1] Owen, Laura Hazard. (2019, March 27). "The Correspondent's editor-in-chief talks about what U.S. expansion means (and doesn't — an office)." *NiemanLab*. https://www.niemanlab.org/2019/03/the-correspondents-editor-in-chief-talks-about-what-u-s-expansion-means-and-doesnt-an-office/

[2] Rosen, Jay. (2019, March 28). "Yep. The Correspondent screwed up in its communications with members. Here's how." *Press-Think*, Jay Rosen's blog. https://pressthink.org/2019/03/yep-the-correspondent-screwed-up-in-its-communications-with-members-heres-how-it-happened/

[3] Owen, Laura Hazard. (2019, April 30). "The Correspondent apologizes as Nate Silver, David Simon, and Baratunde Thurston speak out." *NiemanLab*. https://www.niemanlab.org/2019/04/the-correspondent-apologizes-as-nate-silver-david-simon-and-baratunde-thurston-speak-out/

[4] Ibid.

[5] *The Correspondent*. https://thecorrespondent.com/

The membership model married individual subscription to philanthropy foundation funding, eliminating the intermediaries (foundations). The media themselves accept the role of fundraiser for the cause of pressing social issues.

Within this model, incentives for news selection remain within the newsroom, but they are not market driven. They are driven by the editorial search for the most resonating pressing social issues that could justify fundraising and stimulate readers to donate. This change has led to transformations in the mechanisms of agenda-setting.

The impact of capital, advertisers, billionaires or authorities on agenda-setting through different forms of direct and indirect control has been known for a long time. The impact of philanthropy funding is only starting to be recognized. The impact of the membership model on agenda-setting remains uncharted territory.

***

In collecting the practices and know-how of membership from around the world, the Membership Puzzle Project emphasizes that listening to 'people formerly known as the audience' is one of the keys to success. This is not just listening. Basically, newsrooms must let the readers in, in any form that may please them. Not complying with the wishes of donors can put the continuation of funding at risk.

"Participation takes many forms in the more muscular models for membership," – reported Jay Rosen and Gonzalo del Peon. – "In the UK, The Bristol Cable's members have a say in everything from editorial to strategic and business decisions according to co-founder Adam Cantwell-Corn. The organization has monthly meetings at which members and staff vote on the topics they want to see covered that month."

When people from outside of the newsroom vote on the topic to be covered, this is not even allocative control; this is operational control.

Newsroom autonomy has been saved from advertisers (they are just not interested anymore). It is more or less protected from the rare species of billionaires concerned with the media's survival. But, under crowdfunding, newsroom autonomy is readily given away to the crowd. The crowd decides if all the news is "fit to print".

In *Public Opinion* (1922), Walter Lippmann called the newspaper audience the 'buying public'. The term characterized the audience as a commodity that is sold to advertisers. Long before Smythe, Lippmann wrote,

The real problem is that the readers of a newspaper, unaccustomed to paying the cost of newsgathering, can be capitalized only by turning them into circulation that can be sold to manufacturers and merchants. And those whom it is most important to capitalize are those who have the most money to spend. Such a press is bound to respect the point of view of the buying public. It is for this buying public that newspapers are edited and published, for without that support the newspaper cannot live. A newspaper can flout an advertiser, it can attack a powerful banking or traction interest, but if it alienates the buying public, it loses the one indispensable asset of its existence. (Lippmann, 1929 [1922], p. 324.)

Nowadays, the 'buying public' is the public buying journalism. When the audience donates to the cause of journalism, or any cause offered by journalism to promote, this audience de-facto acquires an influence and a say, thereby switching from being the customer to being the commissioner.

The public can buy journalism indirectly through supporting and reinforcing the declared mission (in the best-case scenario) or directly through dictating media themes and agendas.

***

When the donating audience obtains allocative and sometimes even operational control over newsroom autonomy, what exactly will this control be used for?

The key distinction between the donating audience and subscribers is that the donating audience does not consume news it pays for. This 'buying public' buys nothing. It is the paying public. At the same time, as the *Guardian*'s editor-in-chief Kath Viner insisted, "the newspaper is not a charity, despite offering very little incentive for readers to pay for its content beyond the altruistic desire to keep the news free for others to read."[1]

So, this is neither a charity nor commercial transaction. It is a direct institution maintenance fee. The paying public wants journalism to be maintained with its public service delivered to society in general, i.e. to others. That is the whole point of the membership model – not to buy news for oneself but to pay for others to read it.

Explaining the difference between subscription and membership, Jay Rosen emphasized the role of a *cause* for fundraising:

---

[1] Mayhew, Freddy. (2019, May 1). "Guardian performs remarkable comeback, but at cost of 450 jobs." *Press Gazette.* https://www.pressgazette.co.uk/guardian-comeback-financial-but-at-cost-of-450-jobs

Subscription is when you pay your money and receive a product, like The New Yorker magazine via snail mail or access to the Times of London website. It is fundamentally a transactional relationship.

Membership is when you join a cause because you believe in the importance of the work being done.[1]

The paying public not only buys journalism for others, it also joins some *noble cause*. Originally, this cause was supposed to be journalism itself, the institutional existence of a media brand and the public service provided by this brand. But it is not the only interpretation of a cause. The cause is also the existence of a certain type of journalism, such as the 'unbreaking news' of *De Correspondent* or the existence of a certain tradition of journalism, such as the one embodied by the 200-year-old brand of the *Guardian*. Eventually, a cause is also a theme, an approach, or a narrow topic to be covered, for which the 'members' of the *Bristol Cable* would vote, if they are allowed to make decisions in the newsroom.

Not only does the membership model subsidize content to be delivered for free to those who do not want to buy it, it also preselects this content in order to fit the idea of a cause chosen by the payers. It makes content ideologically charged and meant to be spread for free. These are, essentially, the technical characteristics of propaganda. The membership model incentivizes journalism to mutate into propaganda.

***

Membership is a sort of crowdfunded philanthropy propaganda and also a sort of slactivism, as members outsource their activism (support to a *cause*) through small donations.

Economically, membership is a hybrid model that combines the elements of payment *from above* and *from below*.

In terms of expected effect, which is paid for, membership resembles paying *from above* for agenda-spreading, in the same way as advertisers or political sponsors would do in order to spread a message.

In terms of a financial mechanism, membership resembles paying *from below*, as payers are 'people formerly known as the audience'. They used to buy news but now are solicited to pay for an agenda to be spread to others. Under the membership model, a part of the audience has turned into the paying public and taken the place that formerly belonged to advertisers and propagandists.

---

[1] Rosen, Jay, & Peon, Gonzalo del. (2017, October 4). "Introducing the Membership Models in News Database for your use and contributions." *The Membership Puzzle Project.* https://membershippuzzle.org/articles-overview/introducing-the-database

The impact of membership on journalism is probably even more profound. Being most likely the only relatively efficient business innovation in the dying industry, membership has impacted traditional subscription. Media organizations with paywalls have started to solicit subscription as a donation, adopting, along the way, other features of membership, such as dependence on the donating audience and selection of the most donatable topics and tones.

The membership model itself is presently practiced by a relatively few media organizations: there are only 162 names in the database of the Membership Puzzle Project as of June 2020. However, the ideology underpinning the membership model has already bridged foundation funding and subscription payments. Fundraising motives have infiltrated the subscription model. In its surrogate forms, the membership model has changed the nature of reader revenue and its impact on the mass media.

8. Why subscription mutates into membership

> Except on a few subjects where our own knowledge is great, we cannot choose between true and false accounts. So we choose between trustworthy and untrustworthy reporters.
>
> *Walter Lippmann. "Public Opinion", 1922.*

The media as a notary service: news validation instead of news production

In the media environment where content has become redundant, the only viable business model for the news business is to be paid *from above*. Increasingly, the product of journalism will be paid for not by those who consume it but by those who want it to be delivered to others.

In the media market in developed countries, a peculiar phenomenon has emerged, whereby paying for journalism is becoming more desirable than buying its product. The social demand for the news media to continue existing is stronger than the economic demand. "Respondents are more likely to donate $10 to a free news site than pay a fee of $10 to access news," says one study.[1]

***

An individual can't help but be bombarded by the news. To receive news only internet access is required, not access to the news media, as was the case just 20 years ago.

Everyone's personal media environment is configured in such a way that messengers and social networks automatically rain notifications onto smartphone screens. Social media notifications are designed to pop up, flash, vibrate and jingle. Online content attacks one's offline digressions via sensory seduction, as we are constantly called to re-immerse ourselves online. The (almost) five-sense notifications not only tease the curious mind with announcements, they can generate Pavlovian reflexes wherein the senses automatically react to those stimuli to consume more content.

---

[1] Van Duyn, Emily, Jennings, Jay, and Stroud, Natalie Jomini. (2018, January 18). "Chicago News Landscape." Moody College of Communication. The University of Texas at Austin. https://mediaengagement.org/research/chicago-news-landscape/

Human nature has its own reasons for surrendering to these sensory calls. Hormonal stimuli incentivize group communication through a sense of pleasure akin to the pleasure of social grooming. This is because being together is a key part of the survival code. However, digital communication and digital social grooming are surrogates. They are too easily available, with no physical and almost no psychological entry cost, which makes their hormonal pleasure easily achievable and irresistible. It is a drug, leading to an addiction at the level of hormonal pleasure.

For almost everyone, these compelling attractors make social networks their point of entry into the online world. As a result, before users make a rational choice and visit news media websites, they have already gone through the social media newsfeed and hence been briefed of the daily news agenda.

While people do not need the media to get the news, they still need the media to make sure the news resonates with others, with the group. People want to make sure the news they encounter in their newsfeed is officially accepted by society as valid.

***

This is what journalism is for now. The media are news notaries; they supply not the news but the service of news validation. Not for long, though, as the validation of significance by dissemination, the factor that made the media the officially recognized news supplier in the past, also works well on the internet. Some internet mechanisms, such as Twitter's trending hashtags, can already serve as a new form of news validation. The internet, no doubt, will learn how to extract socially sanctioned validation of the news from validation by dissemination. But before this happens, the media are still needed by readers to make sure the news is valid for others and for society in general.

With such a mode of news 'consumption', the media can hardly offer the news as a transactional commodity. What many subscribers pay is becoming, in fact, a validation fee, not a subscription payment. For example, for the *New York Times*, the very idea of reading the 'newspaper of record' is, essentially, the idea of news validation. This peculiar 'validation demand' gives the *New York Times* a significant advantage over its competitors. As the significance of the news is validated by the scale of its dissemination, a paper with a larger circulation and broader coverage is the better – the most authoritative – news validator.

Studies are increasingly revealing the phenomenon of so-called 'subscription fatigue' – people are tired of online-businesses' endless attempts to get them to subscribe to their services. Specifically in the news industry, studies also show that the majority will subscribe to only one news source, if at all; which suggests that this is a competition in which the "winner takes all." [1] This is good news for the *New York Times* (and a few like them) and bad news for all others. The more the validation function moves to the leader(s), the worse are the chances of all others. The demand for news validation causes the swarm effect: readers seeking to validate news join a larger swarm: significance is best validated by a larger quantity (larger dissemination). The news-validation function is a business factor that is driving media concentration.

***

The news-validation service is an important step of the media towards the membership model, as it makes people regard the media as a source of evaluation, not news.

Everything that has happened to journalism amid its decline supports this movement. The prevalence of opinion journalism over journalism of fact (due to the redundancy of news) makes the attitude towards events (not the news about events) the main use-value in news production and consumption. People want to see already-known news to be covered from the right angle; they also want others to see the news covered from the right angle. People want to make sure they have joined the right cause and, equally important, that many others have joined this cause, too. The news must be validated within a certain value system. This unavoidably pushes the news-notary service of the media towards political biases.

Thus, to a large extent this shift is not the fault of the news media. It is the digital environment, composed of both new and old media, that creates the conditions for the membership motives to infiltrate subscription, even though the transaction still looks like traditional subscription (a payment for the access to news). As the news is predominantly delivered through social media, the news media must guide and validate people's appropriate reception of the news. The news validation within a certain value system is the only remaining function of news business that might have relative use-value for readers.

The leading mainstream media 'got it'; maybe, intuitively. Increasingly, media outlets are soliciting subscription as a donation to a public service of checking news against values. The value checking needs a strong value

---

[1] Reuters Institute Digital News Report 2019.
https://reutersinstitute.politics.ox.ac.uk/sites/default/files/2019-06/DNR_2019_FINAL_0.pdf

foundation. The need for the business to survive forces the media to shift its operational emphasis from news to values.

As a result, the former transactional mechanism of subscription is mutating into a membership, i.e. supporting a *cause*. When subscribing to a newspaper or a magazine, people are not buying news as they already know the news. They are paying for the appraisal of the news' value, and therefore for the impact this news might have. They pay *from below* but with motives *from above*. They pay for the confirmation of the proper attitude toward the news and/or for this attitude to be delivered to others.

Thus, subscribers are gradually turning into two new categories of payers:

1) those who pay the validation fee for the news validation service of the media and

2) the donating audience contracting the media to influence others.

Both types pay the media not for news but rather for impact.

The paywall is increasingly becoming the mechanism for collecting the validation fee and soliciting subscription as donation.

Soliciting subscription as donation

"*Washington Post* sells itself to readership with new slogan," reported CBS News[1] in February 2017, a month after Trump's inauguration. This slogan was "Democracy Dies in Darkness", a phrase coined by legendary American investigative journalist Bob Woodward, whose name, of course, immediately invokes reporting on the Watergate scandal, when the *Post* brought the American president to account. Amid Trump's accusations of the media being "the enemy of the people", the slogan emphasized the role of the media as a pillar of democracy. Subscription marketing directly proclaimed ideological values as at the core of the commercial offer.

Watchdog journalism, accountability journalism and the like have represented important functions of the media since the beginning of the 20th century. However, there is some difference between then and now. Watchdog journalism of the past, predominantly journalism of fact, sought to reveal the facts for the public to judge. On the other hand, contemporary journalism, having become journalism of opinions, mostly offers an attitude towards 'already-known' facts. Or, more accurately, facts have turned into *worthy* and *unworthy* facts – something akin to the dichotomy of "worthy

[1] Bat, John. (2017, February 22). "Washington Post sells itself to readership with new slogan." *CBS News*. https://www.cbsnews.com/news/the-washington-post-introduces-its-new-slogan/

and unworthy victims" that Herman and Chomsky used when describing the Propaganda model (Herman & Chomsky, 2002 [1988], p. 37).

The growing role of news judgment can be interpreted in a way that suggests that the accountability (or ideological) function of journalism has simply evolved. However, news judgment has also become a key part of the subscription commercial offer. Journalism has openly started retailing its impact, which is certainly something new.

For this to happen, many factors in the media had to coincide: the drastic decline in advertising and subscription, the switch from journalism of fact to opinion journalism, the 'hamsterization of journalism', the oversupply of news, the quantization of content that led to articles being trimmed down to shrill news teasers, the relative success of the membership model, etc. All these factors have forced journalism to bet on the last available commodity: the commodity of political stance.

***

The line between membership and subscription is increasingly blurred. Behind what is called subscription, membership motives are most often invoked. In many cases, the membership model does not supplement subscription, but rather coalesces into it. The merging of philanthropy and transactional business corrupts them both.

In their search for a viable business model and being pushed by the general political agitation seen as a demand for journalism with a political slant, an increasingly larger number of media organizations have started moving towards the hybrid of membership and subscription. The hybrid is easy to recognize – the media 1) offer subscription to content and 2) simultaneously ask for support for a cause they aim to promote.

No longer can the media sell news to the audience or the audience to advertisers; so, they try to sell the audience to the public – to the donating audience with a civic consciousness that feels strongly enough to donate to a cause.

Subscription solicited as donation is donscription, a business chimera, the spread of which has politicized the media and introduced a completely new mode of journalism – postjournalism.

***

The hybrid of a transactional scheme with charity motives could not but come with consequences.

The membership model assumes that, through their donations, people join the cause of journalism. However, donations require the best possible triggers. The cause for donation to the media is inevitably shifting and will continue shifting to more triggering causes. The threat to democracy – or, taking also the conservative media into consideration, political outrage – is a better trigger than simply the maintenance of journalism.

The media must search for more triggering causes and, at some point, they must produce them. When the motives of the membership model (joining the cause) are inserted into the transactional subscription model (selling the attitude), it politicizes and radicalizes the news media.

Does donscription work without Trump?

The British public has been accustomed to institution maintenance fees: BBC has been maintained on public license fee since 1923. Perhaps the cause of the *Guardian* membership model has indeed been more of a journalism cause than a political one. However, the biggest increase in the *Guardian* membership happened during the polarizing Brexit upheaval and the Trump bump, which echoed in all the Western news media. In May 2019, when the *Guardian* broke even, Joshua Benton wrote in *NiemanLab*:

> Guardian digital traffic is rising; monthly pageviews are up 70 percent since 2016, some of which is I'm sure the result of the twin shocks of Trump and Brexit. (The Trump Bump and the Brexit...Jump? Pump?) But publishers know well that audience doesn't always translate to revenue. [1]

Unsettling news came from the *Guardian* a year later, in April 2020. Amid the COVID-19 pandemic,

> The Guardian Media Group has said it expects revenues to be down by £20m over the next six months as it announced new measures to cope with the financial impact of the coronavirus crisis.[2]

Of course, despite the incredible growth in news traffic, the pandemic hit all media as advertising practically vanished and subscription could not fill the void; as Benton noted, traffic is not always convertible into profit. Nevertheless, the *New York Times* reported the continuing growth of digital

---

[1] Benton, Joshua. (2019, May 1). "Want to see what one digital future for newspapers looks like? Look at The Guardian, which isn't losing money anymore." *NiemanLab*. https://www.niemanlab.org/2019/05/want-to-see-what-one-digital-future-for-newspapers-looks-like-look-at-the-guardian-which-isnt-losing-money-anymore/

[2] Mayhew, Freddy. (April 15, 2020). "Guardian group takes action to protect business in face of £20m half-year revenue shortfall." *PressGazette*. https://www.pressgazette.co.uk/guardian-group-takes-action-to-protect-business-in-face-of-20m-revenue-shortfall/

subscriptions in Q1 of 2020. The pandemic did not prevent it but rather helped. One of the obvious explanations was Trump. More precisely, Trump's impeachment and the coverage of Trump's response to the pandemic gave a new boost to the old Trump bump's momentum.

It looks like the membership success of the *Guardian* in 2016–2019 coincided with Brexit and the global media excitement about Trump. If so, then the *Guardian* membership success was based not on the cause of supporting journalism, but on the publics' agitation with Brexit and Trump. However, as this has now waned (in the UK at least), it looks like the cause of journalism itself cannot galvanize the membership model enough for people to join. In a report on expected budget cuts and other measures in the *Guardian* in 2020, not a word was said about its salvational membership business model.

If the negative prognosis regarding the *Guardian* will be confirmed, then the cause of quality journalism will prove not to be triggering enough for the membership model. In this case, a political cause will remain the only viable and triggering enough cause for the audience to join with membership contribution. And even the political trigger for donation to media outlets needs to be strong enough: it needs to possess the emotional power of an outrage equivalent to that produced by Trump. A question arises: Are the membership model and its subscription surrogates sustainable enough for the media outside the Trump bump and, specifically, outside selling the Trump scare?

***

Perhaps, due to historical media and political traditions, the functions of journalism and political stances merge more easily in the American media. A cause of journalism mutated into a political cause. The prominent media got the cue and started selling themselves as a means of political resistance (or resistance to resistance, in the case of the conservative media in the Trump era).

Just like in the membership model, the noble cause and the impact of media coverage on it was put at the forefront of the mainstream media subscription offer. The subscription slogans tried to sell impact, not content.

Symbolic or direct referrals to Donald Trump were sometimes used as subscription teasers, such as the figure of Trump in this subscription offer on Facebook (Figure 9).

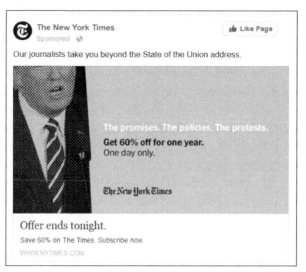

Figure 9. The *New York Times*' subscription commercial on Facebook.

Watching the success of flagships, other media also tried to sell the Trump scare, openly linking membership and the political cause. As *Slate* offered:

> We've been holding Trump to account all year. Help us keep going. Become a member.

The mélange of membership and subscription, on the one hand, and of political and journalism causes, on the other, amid the shrinking business, has produced some very odd combinations. In March 2020, *Slate*, for example, announced that its membership program, Slate Plus, would be combined with a paywall. But, all the same, "Becoming a member is also the best way to help us shape that journalism," hence the need to "Support our independent journalism."[1]

***

In the US, the ability to solicit support for a political cause under the guise of the cause of journalism marks out the difference between those media outlets profiting from the Trump bump and those struggling to sell mere content, particularly local content.

Two decades ago, the American local megapolis newspapers were thriving enterprises, and the local news agenda was a valued commodity.

---

[1] Hohlt, Jared. (2020, March 25). "Slate Is Starting a Metered Paywall." *Slate.* https://slate.com/briefing/2020/03/slate-metered-paywall.html

Now they are rapidly in decline. Only those who switched to selling the audience to the public, along with the successful commodification of the Trump scare, are thriving; which is clearly seen in the chart from Chapter 2, tracing the subscription dynamics of the leading American newspapers (Figure 10).

Newspaper	2002 print circ	2019 digital subs
The New York Times	1,113,000	2.7 million
Los Angeles Times	965,633	170,000
The Washington Post	746,724	1.7 million
New York Daily News	715,070	27,000
Chicago Tribune	613,429	100,000
Newsday	578,809	25,000
Houston Chronicle	552,052	37,000
The Dallas Morning News	521,956	72,000
San Francisco Chronicle	512,129	57,000

Figure 10. Source: NiemanLab[1]

This chart can be interpreted as a testimony to the success of soliciting subscription as donation, on the one hand, and offering a political cause in the guise of journalism, on the other. News isn't saleable, but agenda-setting still is (or is believed to be). Those media selling news to the audience are doomed. Those selling the audience to the public will survive, as long as Trump and Trumpism are in the spotlight (or as long as some other equally triggering things keep happening after Trump is gone).

For an assessment of the effect of the Trump bump on the mainstream media, it is important to look at not just the time period when the news media were selling Trump, but also at their business indicators before they realised the saleability of Trump and polarization. Here is another look at the dynamic of the *New York Times* digital subscription: before Trump, the growth curve of subscriptions was not very impressive (Figure 11). Basically,

[1] Benton, Joshua. (2019, July 31). "The L.A. Times' disappointing digital numbers show the game's not just about drawing in subscribers – it's about keeping them." *NiemanLab.* https://www.niemanlab.org/2019/07/the-l-a-times-disappointing-digital-numbers-show-the-games-not-just-about-drawing-in-subscribers-its-about-keeping-them/

it had been rather flat for five long years since the NYT paywall started in 2011, even though this was the early period of digital growth and the *New York Times* was the world leader in this new business format anyway (they performed better than others). There is a possibility that after Trump the dynamics will plateau, unless the news media find something as equally disturbing.

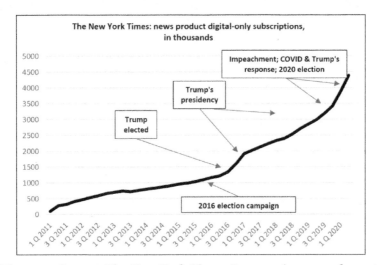

Figure 11. Source: The New York Times Company's press releases[1].

***

Four mainstream newspapers in the world have reached digital subscriptions exceeding one million: the *New York Times, Wall Street Journal, Washington Post* and *Financial Times*. The *Wall Street Journal* and *Financial Times* are business outlets. They work in a conservative professional niche, where the sanctioned validation of news remains an important tool of social regulation. This will keep the biggest business newspapers alive a bit longer than others. The *New York Times,* with its incredible achievement in digital subscription, also remains a national newspaper of record; the *Washington Post* plays the same card to some extent. At the same time, they both exploit certain elements of membership in soliciting subscription. In their subscription pitches, they both can be seen as focused on news validation and asking the audience to join the cause.[2]

---

[1] The New York Times Company's press releases. http://investors.nytco.com/press/press-releases/default.aspx.

[2] There were some differences in the degree of their devotion, as noted by Jay Rosen in 2018

The huge gap in the subscription figures for these two and all the rest also confirms the hypothesis that news validation and the pitching of a cause contribute to media concentration. Because of the effect of significance validation by dissemination, only the largest media brands can provide such a specific news service. In the crowdsourced model, when it is about the media, a sort of swarm behavior forms. Quantity generates quantity because news validation and cause-promotion look reliable and effective only when a large enough number of readers join the same source.

If the winners take all, then it remains for the losers to only rely on patrons or foundation funding of a limited scale. Crowdfunding potential simply does not have the capacity to support all. Both validation fees and donscription tend to swarm around a few competing leaders.

In the meantime, the media in the US and around the world are watching the *New York Times* record-breaking digital subscription figures and thinking that this is the way to go. They are copying the tone and the approach for soliciting support and merging the journalism cause with the political one. However, donscription really only works for the largest brands; for all the others, it is a kind of cargo cult. But, to catch up, they think they merely need to try harder and make their voices more radical, adding more radicalization and politicization to the media environment.

Those readers who still subscribe for news will be unlikely to subscribe to more than one outlet. Those who decide to support a political cause will support the biggest ones, as they will believe that those will be the ones with the most impact.

So, because readers want to validate the value of news for themselves or for others, they will choose the biggest news outlets. It appears the Trump scare is a premium commodity. Whilst it can be displayed in a corner store, people nevertheless prefer to buy it in the flagship superstores.

A paradoxical situation emerges: while resting on a political cause, donscription demonstrates outstanding results, but only for a limited number of the largest media brands. Their success cannot be replicated by others. Despite this the entire news industry follows the leading examples, desperately trying to profit from soliciting subscription as donation to a political cause. As for the most of media brands' excuse – they basically do not have any other options left to pursue.

– Rosen, Jay. (2018, October 21). "Next time you wonder why New York Times people get so defensive, read this." *PressThink*. https://pressthink.org/2018/10/next-time-you-wonder-why-new-york-times-people-get-so-defensive-read-this/. But the devotion of both outlets most likely has equally strengthened by 2020 under the pressure of the donating audience. Having a larger donating audience, the *New York Times* experienced stronger pressure on its newsroom autonomy.

***

The first evidence of the membership model may be found in the political press of the 19th century, as exemplified by *Neue Rheinische Zeitung*. To fund this paper, in 1848, Karl Marx asked comrades to join the cause and contribute. The membership model succeeded in Lenin's *Iskra*, having become the backbone of the revolutionary Bolshevik party. Now, in a lighter slacktivist form, the membership model substitutes declining commercial subscription for the legacy media.

Just a decade ago, the media used to sell the audience to advertisers. Within the membership model, they now try to sell Smythe's audience to Lippmann's "phantom public".

***

It is hard to say whether the donating audience receives the service it pays for within the membership model. Do the media really have the impact they promote – do they really protect democracy through their highly devoted coverage with a political stance? Without a real market response, meaning without payable commercial demand, the metrics used in membership can be deceiving.

Moreover, the expected impact can lead to unplanned and even opposite outcomes, such as growing polarization, which, in fact, damages democracy even more. However, this polarization effect increases the demand for journalism with a political stance. The media might claim to be pursuing democracy, but polarization works better for this business model. Amid the dying market, the goal is continuing donations, not the discontinuation of the cause. Donscription traps the media in a positive feedback loop, with a negative outcome for society.

This is one of the specificities of the media business: it induces what it sells. Drifting towards more donscription, the news media are incentivized to induce polarization, not democracy.

9. From making happy customers to making angry citizens: journalism follows money

> You become responsible, forever, for what you have tamed.
> *Antoine de Saint-Exupéry. "The Little Prince", 1943.*

Ad-driven media: merchants of happiness

Describing the relations between the media and advertisers at the end of the 20th century, Edward Herman wrote that the media "are funded largely by advertisers who are also profit-seeking entities, and who want their advertisements to appear in a supportive selling environment" (Herman, 2000, p. 102).

The ability of advertising to impact the content of the carrier has long been known. This is how allocative control works: not only do advertisers give money to the media that offer a proper context for the brand to be placed in, the media themselves compete for this money and adjust content in a way they think advertisers would like. As a result, the media system funded by ad money drifts towards content that would by no means have repelled this money but rather attracted it.

Graham Murdock gave an example of how the competition for ad money forced an entire culture industry to completely switch the tone of how it depicted the world. In the post-WWII period, American television drama was "dominated by anthologies of single plays, many of which dealt with working-class life," wrote Murdock. These dramas, obviously covering 'pressing social issues', were popular with audiences and regularly attracted high ratings. However, advertisers were not pleased with the lower-class characters in these dramas, which were seen "as damaging to the images of mobility and affluence they wanted to build up around their products" (Murdock, 1983, p. 143).

Around the mid-1950s, advertisers started to redirect their budgets toward "the action adventure series that were beginning to emerge from the old Hollywood studios." There were multiple business advantages of this genre. Adventures were put into extravagant and glamorous settings, while handsome heroes and heroines set the tone, within which the consumption of advertised goods became more desirable. Adventure and action dramas

185

also contained the minimum of dialogue and the maximum of action, which made them ideal material for export overseas.

Thus, allocative control of ad money changed the focus and tone of TV series. This shift, in its turn, defined the prevalent depiction of the world in mass TV and movie dramas in order to make it more ad-suitable. Ad money encouraged consumerism and suppressed politics in meaning production. The media and other mass culture industries were responsive. They created the culture of consumerism.

***

In his book *No Longer Newsworthy: How the Mainstream Media Abandoned the Working Class,* Christopher R. Martin came to a similar conclusion regarding the time period when culture industries switched from covering ordinary people's lives to chasing an affluent audience for the sake of better ad sales. Martin wrote that,

> By the late 1960s and early 1970s, newspaper companies, then becoming publicly-traded, bigger chains, moved to a new business trajectory that changed the target news audience from mass to upscale, and altered the actual news narratives about the working class in US journalism.[1]

As Graham Murdock pointed out, advertising also impacted the coverage of the 'quality' papers. They competed by offering advertisers a conducive "editorial environment" for their products. Specifically, he mentioned that personal investment advertising increased the media's tolerance, and even appetite, for a "misleading picture of modern capital and the corporate economy" (Murdock, 1983, p. 143).

"Personal finance news also began its ascendancy in the 1970s. The focus was on individualism...," confirmed Martin.[2] The middle-class audience learned that they have savings, and these savings should be invested in financial markets. Not only did this setting serve the development of financial capitalism, it also prevented the public from engaging in protests and secured political stability.

***

The structural impact of advertising was the focus of Herman and Chomsky's *Manufacturing Consent.* As they explained,

---

[1] Martin, Christopher R. (2019, August 27). "How writing off the working class has hurt the mainstream media." *NiemanLab.* https://niemanreports.org/articles/how-writing-off-the-working-class-has-hurt-the-mainstream-media/

[2] Ibid.

Before advertising became prominent, the price of a newspaper had to cover the costs of doing business. With the growth of advertising, papers that attracted ads could afford a copy price well below production costs. This put papers lacking in advertising at a serious disadvantage: their prices would tend to be higher, curtailing sales... For this reason, an advertising-based system will tend to drive out of existence or into marginality the media companies and types that depend on revenue from sales alone. (Herman and Chomsky, 2002 [1988], p. 14.)

As a result, "Working-class and radical media also suffer from the political discrimination of advertisers," concluded Herman and Chomsky. "Political discrimination is structured into advertising allocations by the stress on people with money to buy" (Ibid., p. 16).

The market force – the media's leaning toward advertising – had both political and economic impacts, as it changed the structure of the media market along with the structure of the social, demographic and political interests represented by and in the media. The ad-based media focused on creating content attractive to the buying audience needed by advertisers. The audience received a picture of the world in which controversies and social issues were suppressed and consumer ideals of a wealthier and happier life were emphasized. Thus, the allocative control of advertising over agenda-setting in the mass media beautified the reality.

The avoiding of controversies under the pressure of advertising is reminiscent of the work of a different propaganda model. As Soviet dissidents used to quip, the acuteness of an issue is judged by how diligently it was concealed in the Soviet newspapers. In general, the concealing of breaking news by the news media – a paradox, technically speaking, – always was, and still is, a direct sign of propaganda.

***

"Big brands fund terror through online adverts," claimed a London's *Times* investigation in February 2017. "Some of the world's biggest brands are unwittingly funding Islamic extremists, white supremacists and pornographers by advertising on their websites."

The *Times* revealed that the commercials of hundreds of large companies, universities and charities, including Mercedes-Benz, Waitrose and Marie Curie, appeared on "YouTube videos created by supporters of terrorist groups such as Islamic State and Combat 18, a violent pro-Nazi faction."[1] Via YouTube plugins, the brands also appeared on the respective

---

[1] Mostrous, Alexi. (2017, February 09). "Big brands fund terror through online adverts." *The Times.*

hate sites. For example, L'Oréal ads appeared in a video posted by preacher Steven Anderson. The *Guardian* found ads for its membership model on videos posted by Britain First.[1] The *Times* wrote,[2]

> The practice is likely to generate tens of thousands of pounds a month for extremists. An advert appearing alongside a YouTube video, for example, typically earns whoever posts the video $7.60 for every 1,000 views.

In the next month, more than 250 brands, including L'Oréal, McDonald's, Audi, Marks & Spencer, Lloyd's of London, HSBC, RBS and many others, suspended their campaigns on YouTube. The largest boycott in the modern history of advertisers began.

The British government pulled its ads from YouTube, too, as it did not want to spend taxpayer money on advertisements for military recruitment and blood donations, which sat next to extremist content. *Channel 4, BBC,* and the *Guardian* joined the action.[3] The boycott then spread to the US, with AT&T, Johnson & Johnson and Verizon pulling their ads from YouTube.[4]

***

YouTube reportedly started losing millions in ad revenue. *Forbes* wrote:

> Red-faced executives at Google and its property YouTube have been doing a lot of apologizing this week as major advertisers in the U.S. and Europe flee both the search engine and its video platform after discovering their ads were running alongside hate-filled, extremist content.[5]

https://www.thetimes.co.uk/article/big-brands-fund-terror-knnxfgb98

[1] Vizard, Sarah. (2017, March 17). "Google under fire as brands pull advertising and ad industry demands action." *Marketing Week.* https://www.marketingweek.com/google-ad-safety/

[2] Mostrous, Alexi. (2017, February 09). "Big brands fund terror through online adverts." *The Times.*
https://www.thetimes.co.uk/article/big-brands-fund-terror-knnxfgb98

[3] Grierson, Jamie. (2017, March 17). "Google summoned by ministers as government pulls ads over extremist content." *The Guardian.* https://www.theguardian.com/technology/2017/mar/17/google-ministers-quiz-placement-ads-extremist-content-youtube

[4] Hern, Alex. (2017, March 23). "YouTube and Google boycott spreads to US as AT&T and Verizon pull ads." *The Guardian.* https://www.theguardian.com/technology/2017/mar/23/youtube-google-boycott-att-verizon-pull-adverts-extremism

[5] Schrieberg, David. (2017, March 23). "U.S., U.K. boycott of Google and YouTube by major advertisers spreading over hate content." *Forbes.* https://www.forbes.com/sites/davidschrieberg1/2017/03/23/u-s-u-k-boycott-of-google-and-youtube-by-major-advertisers-spreading-over-hate-content

The root issue behind this brands' revolt against YouTube and Google was programmatic ad trading, an automatic auction-based system driven by algorithms and deciding what ads are put onto what videos according to price, outreach and some other parameters. While offering the most efficient and fastest ad placement, the system was generally blind to content; not to mention that video content is inherently difficult to classify. This was further exacerbated by the fact that the extremist and controversial videos might have also been popular, so the programmatic algorithm saw them as such and placed respectable brands alongside them.

After the scandal shook the ad world, Google implemented measures that gave advertisers more control and confidence that their reputation would not be compromised, and their ad budgets would not subsidize extremists and terrorists. Advertisers obtained the levers to choose narrower or broader types of content for their ads or to completely ban the placement of their ads alongside some types of content. Afterwards, Google undertook additional efforts to better classify types of content and mark those that might have been considered risky for brand safety.[1]

The notion of brand safety underwent a development that impacted not only programmatic ad placement but the entire industry of advertising and content production, including the media.

Eventually, Google introduced "Advertiser-friendly content guidelines"[2], the instruction that lists what types of content are "not suitable for ads and will result in a 'limited or no ads' monetization state." Among the categories of content that will not be included in the program of monetization on YouTube are "Controversial issues and sensitive events". Here is how Google defined them:

'Controversial issues' refers to topics that may be unsettling for our users and are often the result of human tragedy.

A sensitive event is usually an unforeseen event in which there has been a loss of life, typically as a result of a pre-planned malicious attack. Sensitive events can cause a mournful response from the public or, at times, an extreme or visceral reaction. An event must be relatively recent if it's going to be considered a sensitive event. Historical events are generally allowed to monetize if presented within the context of a documentary or historical debate.

[1] Shayon, Sheila. (2017, March 23). "Google increases YouTube brand safety controls following boycott." *Brandchannel*. https://www.brandchannel.com/2017/03/23/youtube-brand-safety-032317/

[2] Advertiser-friendly content guidelines. Google. https://support.google.com/youtube/answer/6162278

This policy applies even if the content is purely commentary or contains no graphic imagery. [1]

Basically, the news media covering all dramatic events must understand that their videos will most likely not be monetized on YouTube.

***

No one would have had objections if the system disincentivized and, better still, expelled extremist and terrorist content. However, advertisers have also always preferred to avoid any troubling content. In the meantime, reports about political troubles, catastrophes, crimes, tragedies, violence and the like are often what constitute the most important news. From the advertisers' point of view, the news is risky content.

On the internet, advertisers never know what dramatic headline will be placed next to their advertised brand. Therefore, ad money, when given a choice, would prefer not to deal with this content at all. Media buyers confirm that,

> Brands don't want to be near controversial issues or near any news. But the net of controversial issues has grown. The 24-hour news cycle means there's always some kind of drama. [2]

Buyers call this the 'fear of the screenshot': the fear that people will capture and start to share pictures of a brand in an inappropriate context. "All it takes is one letter from one person saying you were here. People are tweeting at advertisers. It's fear of the screenshot." [3]

In 2018, a *Digiday* survey of 400 media buyers "found that 43 percent of respondents said they explicitly avoid advertising next to the news and half of those say they're steering clear of news content more than they had before." If buyers choose to remain on news sites, "they must understand that doing so comes with a risk." [4]

One of the survey's findings is particularly interesting. When asked if they "avoid advertising next to Trump related content," 58% of marketers answered 'yes'. [5]

---

[1] Ibid.

[2] Pathak, Shareen. (2019, February 22). "'Fear of the screenshot': Candid thoughts of ad buyers at the Digiday Media Buying Summit." *Digiday.* https://digiday.com/marketing/candid-thoughts-ad-buyers-digiday-media-buying-summit/

[3] Ibid.

[4] Weiss, Mark. (2018, December 3). "Digiday Research: 43 percent of media buyers say they avoid news content." *Digiday.* https://digiday.com/marketing/digiday-research-43-percent-media-buyers-say-avoid-news-content/

Due to the advancement of ad-buying inventory, marketers obtained an opportunity to blacklist certain words in order to avoid unfavorable contexts for their ads to be placed in. As a result, "Ad buyers are also increasingly using keywords and sentiment analysis to create custom categories of content to avoid, with a focus on reducing their exposure to Trump."[1] One of them said that, "Believe it or not, our president is often not brand-safe."[2] Trump appeared to be not that universally good for media business.

In addition, more advertisers want to avoid controversial content at all. In June 2020, during the massive protests against racism and police brutality, a big advertiser,

> ...told a leading online news publisher not to run its ads in stories related to the Black Lives Matter movement. Articles mentioning police-brutality victims such as "Breonna Taylor" and "George Floyd" were off limits, as were those with the word "protests."[3]

Basically, advertisers have banned news as ad carriers for their brand.

Digital advertising tools have simply and candidly exposed what was known in the industry long ago: advertising does not like the news because the news is often bad news. It is not a beneficial context for displaying advertisements to the audience.

New advertising tools have merely allowed allocative control of advertising money to turn into operational control – the direct demand to the platforms and publishers regarding what content should be used to accompany brands. This obviously shall not be news content.

***

The new inventory of advertising allows for the preselection of not only content but also the emotional conditions of news consumers in order to accommodate advertisers' wishes.

Cable sports network *ESPN* has created an instrument that predicts viewers' mood during digital broadcasting of sports events. "About 80% of people who register with the ESPN app, for example, select their favorite

[5] Ibid.

[1] Benes, Ross. (2017, October 18). "'Our president is often not brand-safe': Why publishers struggle to monetize the Trump bump." *Digiday.* https://digiday.com/media/president-often-not-brand-safe-publishers-struggle-monetize-trump-bump/

[2] Ibid.

[3] Haggin, Patience. (2020, July 12). "Target, MTV blocked ads from news mentioning 'George Floyd' and 'Protests'." *The Wall Street Journal.* https://www.wsj.com/articles/target-mtv-blocked-ads-from-news-mentioning-george-floyd-and-protests-11594576272

sports and teams in exchange for a more tailored experience," reported Quartz. "ESPN pairs that information with what's happening in the game to predict what fans are feeling and serve them ads that cater to the moment." [1]

Travis Howe, *ESPN*'s senior vice president, said that, "Whether or not a sports fan is happy, sad, slightly anxious, or overjoyed, we have the ability to anticipate their emotion and deliver relevant ads to them that creates a personalized experience."[2] It is easy to assume that it is always more preferable for advertisers to have their ads exposed to fans of the winning team. The feeling of unity in joy and happiness is the best context for an ad message to sneak in.

This makes the channel of ad delivery interested in consumer happiness, and, if possible, in creating this happiness. A media channel with such an ability is incentivized to pursue their users' happiness for better advertising business.

***

The emotional personalization of ad delivery has become a trendy business tool in the media of general interest, too. In 2016, *USA Today* introduced a sort of emotional scoring of its content for better offers to advertisers. "The publisher is trying to show a link between the emotions a story is likely to evoke and ad performance," reported *Digiday*.[3] *USA Today* started "categorizing its content by topic and tone". A certain score calculated on that basis would presumably give advertisers a better sense of where to place their ads.

In 2018, the *New York Times*'s Advertising & Marketing division launched nytDEMO, an AI-driven product that aims to learn readers' demography and reactions for better engagement and ad targeting. One of the projects, called Project Feels, employed machine learning to identify "the most meaningful associations between content, keywords, and emotion using deep learning." The AI-driven model was reportedly able to predict "emotional response to any content." Based on this knowledge, "perspective targeting" would be offered as a new ad product. "Perspective targeting allows advertisers to target their media against content predicted to evoke

[1] Rodriguez, Ashley. (2018, May 3). "ESPN is selling ads based on sports fans' wildly changing emotions." *Quartz.* https://qz.com/1268657/espn-is-selling-ads-based-on-sports-fans-changing-emotions/

[2] Ibid.

[3] Moses, Lucia. (2018, September 19). "Project Feels: How USA Today, ESPN and The New York Times are targeting ads to mood." *Digiday.* https://digiday.com/media/project-feels-usa-today-espn-new-york-times-targeting-ads-mood/

reader sentiments like self-confidence or adventurousness," reported the *New York Times* press-release.[1]

Similar tools were worked on in *El Pais*. Pedro Ventura, director of technology on data and monetization at Prisa Media, said:

> News can't be happy all the time; that's the reality. <...> We're general news, so like the Guardian or Le Figaro, we cover a broad spectrum, and, of course, much of that is terrorist-related news or the Catalonia conflicts. Some advertisers just don't want to be near that.[2]

To accommodate advertisers, the publisher of *El Pais* has defined a set of 32 audience emotions and created "happiness" segments, among others, in order "to put advertisers at ease". Newspapers would charge a higher fee for advertisers who want this option on top of regular targeting.[3]

***

It is hard to overestimate the invisible harm that will be done to journalism by such tools. With mood-based targeting, the prioritization of content will gradually be outsourced to advertisers. Advertisers want users to be happy when seeing the brand. News rarely provides happiness.

The selling of emotions to advertisers inevitably leads to a temptation to induce only those emotions that suit advertising, with happiness being at the top. The ad-based media are merchants of happiness, now with the tools of precise emotional measurement.

The selling of emotions and the ability to induce emotions in order to accommodate the payer represent the ultimate degree of advertising's impact on news production. Those media relying on ad revenue are eventually incentivized to induce happiness, which in turn incentivizes positive news and leads to the creation of a more positive picture of the world.

***

[1] The New York Times Company press release. (2018, February 15). "The New York Times Advertising & Marketing Solutions Group Introduces 'nytDEMO': A Cross-Functional Team Focused on Bringing Insights and Data Solutions to Brands."
https://investors.nytco.com/press/press-releases/press-release-details/2018/The-New-York-Times-Advertising--Marketing-Solutions-Group-Introduces-nytDEMO-A-Cross-Functional-Team-Focused-on-Bringing-Insights-and-Data-Solutions-to-Brands/default.aspx

[2] Davies, Jessica. (2019, April 29). "El Pais owner Prisa Media built a brand-safety tool to reassure news-wary advertisers." *Digiday*. https://digiday.com/media/el-pais-owner-prisa-media-built-brand-safety-tool-reassure-news-wary-advertisers/

[3] Ibid.

The glamorized or otherwise positively doctored picture of the world in the ad-driven media, however, does not fit another view of the mass media, according to which the media are full of 'doom and gloom'.

Indeed, the inclination to report disturbing news has been a common trait of 'popular' newspapers and tabloids. This might look disproving the hypothesis that advertising incentivizes the embellishment of the picture of the world in the media.

The 'popular' papers bet on a larger audience. Larger circulation allowed larger revenue from copy sales and also attracted advertisers with mass-market products for the 'downscale' consumers. These advertisers tolerated the lower affluence of the audience and the lower quality of the channel for the sake of wider outreach.

Interestingly, the 'popular' papers and tabloids satisfied the mass audience's interest in disturbing content but at the same time accommodated, to some extent, the advertisers' need for embellishing the reality: those types of the media just did not dive too deep into political controversies. The pressure of advertising money on agenda-setting was not only reality-embellishing but also depoliticizing. As Graham Murdock noticed, advertisers' demand for a larger audience brought "a marked decline in overt partisanship... and a concentration on the non-contentious and consumer-oriented areas of leisure and personal life" (Murdock, 1983, p. 143). The 'mass' mass media might have not avoided disturbing content, but they nevertheless tended to avoid divisive political issues, as this could potentially split the audience and therefore diminish its size, the main business asset of the 'popular' media.

Thus, many pre-internet advertisers generally tolerated the negativity of the 'popular' mass media; but they incentivized their indifference to politics.

***

With the advent of the internet and social media, advertisers have moved to other, more efficient platforms and now dictate their will to them. Those advertising budgets that still remain in the news media do not dominate their business model anymore. Without sufficient funding support, the advertising demand for reality embellishment and manufacturing consent is no longer that influential in the media as it used to be.

Disturbing content in the media has become unchecked.

Reader-driven media: negativity bias

In a Russian comedy play, "The Radio Day", the chief editor asks his staff journalists to urgently find a new topic for a coming talk show. He says, "Hasn't something really, really bad happened? That would be really, really good." He knows what is needed for a successful talk show.

The negativity bias of the media can be explained through the ideas of behavioral economics.

In 1979, economists Daniel Kahneman and Amos Tversky published their seminal work "Prospect Theory: An Analysis of Decision under Risk". This was a study in cognitive psychology and behavioral economics that shed light on the subliminal evaluation of risks in decision making. (Kahneman won the Nobel Prize in economic sciences in 2002 for his and Tversky's insights into decision making; Tversky died in 1996 – the Prize is not awarded posthumously).

According to Kahneman and Tversky, people are not necessarily rational in their decision making, as was seen in the then-dominant 'expected utility theory' (the 1960–70s). Kahneman & Tversky developed an alternative theory of choice, according to which people irrationally weigh the probability of potential losses and potential gains. As they put it, "(T)he value function is defined on deviations from the reference point; generally concave for gains and commonly convex for losses; steeper for losses than for gains" (Kahneman & Tversky, 1979, p. 279).

This value function (Figure 12) illustrates that people would prefer to avoid losses rather than acquire equivalent gains. In other words, it is better not to lose \$5 than to find \$5. Thus, the human attitude toward potential losses and potential gains is asymmetrical. Losses outweigh gains. The probability of losses impacts decision making (risk taking) more heavily than the same probability of gains. "A salient characteristic of attitudes to changes in welfare is that losses loom larger than gains", as Kahneman and Tversky put it (1979, p. 279).

For those planning to make a purchase on Amazon, negative reviews are much more insightful and valuable than positive ones. Clay Shirky cited in his *Cognitive Surplus* an open source aphorism, "Good community plus bad code makes a good project" (Shirky, 2010, p. 144). Indeed, nothing attracts or unites people better than bad things. Bad news plus good crowd makes a good engagement.

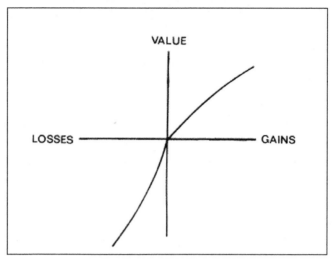

Figure 12. The value function on the scale of gains and losses, according to the Prospect Theory (Kahneman & Tversky, 1979, p. 279).

***

"Real news is bad news – bad news about somebody, or bad news for somebody," wrote McLuhan in *Understanding Media* 15 years before Kahneman and Tversky published their discovery (McLuhan, 1964. p. 222).

The inclination of people to value negative news more than positive news provides an interesting excuse for the yellow press, tabloids and the like. As journalists often say, they are not responsible for the negativity bias in the media; this is what people want. This is in the nature of humans. Behavioral economics implies that this might be true.

The media subliminally exploit people's inclination to pay more attention to negative news. "It leads if it bleeds", as an old reporters' saying goes. In their pursuit of reader attention, the media are naturally inclined toward negativity. The balancing of this natural predisposition requires some systemic counterweights or some artificial, conscious counter efforts.

Advertising that requires proper content is one of those natural counterweights. Another one is reputational – an editor's ambition to build a respectable media brand (though the brands of 'popular' papers and tabloids can be considered respectable, too, at least in terms of professional performance).

***

Some people in the media industry try to resist the negativity bias by controlling the forces pushing for negativity and other negative distortions of news reporting.

For example, so-called 'slow journalism' confronts the 'hamsterization of journalism'. The analogy to 'slow food' as opposed to 'fast food' is used; the idea presumes that one can enjoy food, or journalism, as a high-quality cooked product.

Similarly, the concept of 'constructive journalism' aims to confront the negativity bias in the media. 'Constructive journalism' covers the utmost pressing social issues, but with a focus on solutions, progress and positive tendencies.

A special professional educational project, the Solutions Journalism Network, was launched in 2012. The project aimed to "train and connect journalists to cover what's missing in today's news: how people are responding to problems." It stated that "We're working to bring solutions journalism to every newsroom worldwide."[1]

British magazine *Positive News* (daily online and print quarterly) focuses on "good journalism about the good things that are happening." The magazine's quasi-manifesto declares that,

> When much of the media is full of doom and gloom, instead *Positive News* is the first media organization in the world that is dedicated to quality, independent reporting about what's going right.
>
> We are pioneers of 'constructive journalism' – a new approach in the media, which is about rigorous and relevant journalism that is focused on progress, possibility, and solutions. [2]

Some other attempts to build media projects on 'constructive journalism' cause a buzz in the industry from time to time. In 2018, *Cornwall Live*, a local British news site, "invested in positive news" by launching the Happiness Project with a happiness correspondent.[3] *The Better India* started as a side-project blog in 2009 but turned into a foundation-funded full-size media outlet with 27 full-time staffers by 2018.[4]

---

[1] The Solutions Journalism Network. https://www.solutionsjournalism.org/

[2] *Positive News*. About. https://www.positive.news/about/

[3] Tobitt, Charlotte. (2018, March 13). "Cornwall Live invests in 'positive news' by introducing happiness correspondent." *PressGazette*. https://www.pressgazette.co.uk/cornwall-live-invests-in-positive-news-by-introducing-happiness-correspondent/

[4] Wang, Shan. (2018, March 7). "The Better India will show you all the positive news, on all the channels you might want it." *NiemanLab*. https://www.niemanlab.org/2018/03/the-better-india-will-show-you-all-the-positive-news-on-all-the-channels-you-might-want-it/

***

Constructive journalism is journalism with an agenda, and therefore the membership model fits it very well, as both assume that journalism sells impact. Under this premise, people do not buy information – they join a cause.

Positivity in journalism can exist, but only when paid *from above*, either by advertisers, unknowingly, or by sponsors, deliberately. These are artificial, unnatural conditions for news supply. If news supply is left to be driven by pure news demand, it will lean toward negativity.

In 2014, the Russian local news website *City Reporter* from Rostov-on-Don conducted an experiment. Journalists decided to publish only good news for one day. Even when they got a disturbing tip (such as an alert about a possible bomb at a local railroad station), they reworked it into a solution or positive outcome (a bomb was not confirmed).

According to deputy editor Victoria Nekrasova, "We looked at events, excluded homicides and catastrophes, and put positive headlines. Unfortunately, such news was not popular". As a result, their website traffic plummeted that day to 30% of its normal level.

Perhaps, with some constructive journalism techniques, they would have performed better. But what the case shows is clear: the mechanically introduced filter of positivity momentarily ruins the traffic. This 70% decline in traffic is an approximate price to pay for being positive in news supply.

The only way to compensate for the natural environmental negativity bias of the media is to proclaim a mission and sell it or to give the newsroom autonomy to an outside payer, such as advertisers, foundations or other sponsors. Otherwise, the natural 'behavior' of traffic is just to run away from a deliberately 'socially constructed' positive agenda.

Inducing demand, the news media reshape the audience

After the printing press liberated the literate man from tedious hours of copying, the recording of thoughts and events became the literate person's principal duty. The enhanced exchange of news and ideas created an environment for the further intensification of political, religious and intellectual life, with its ever-growing appetite for news and thoughts. Thus the cultural effect of self-induction in the media industry was revealed: the supply of news induces the demand for news.

This is a peculiar relationship between supply and demand wherein, unusually, supply comes first. Journalism became a technological prerequisite to news supply and a business response to news demand.

***

When capitalist production saturated the market with goods and services, the focus of production started shifting from material utility towards symbolic value. "For a long time, capital had only to produce goods; consumption ran by itself...," wrote Baudrillard in 1978. "Today it is necessary to produce consumers, to produce demand, and this production is infinitely more costly than that of goods." Baudrillard stated that this tendency also applied to the production of meaning. He wrote that,

> No longer is meaning in short supply, it is produced everywhere, in ever increasing quantities – it is demand which is weakening. And it is the production of this demand for meaning which has become crucial for the system. (Baudrillard, 1978, p. 27.)

Smythe stated that "the Consciousness Industry" made "monopoly capitalism function through demand management (advertising, marketing, and mass media)" (Smythe, 2012 [1981], p. 185). Advertising and marketing, the younger siblings of the media, do the job of inducing the demand for other goods. The media, since the very beginning, have also induced the demand for its own products. Readers of the 16th century bought the Venetian *avvisi* because they had read previous ones and liked the idea of the news. The symbolic value of news is always pre-conditioned by previous consumption.

The uniqueness of journalism, and possibly of all culture industries, is constituted by the capability of its product to induce the demand for the next round of consumption. Each act of news consumption is a promotional product trial of the next act of news consumption.

If, as Elisabeth Eisenstein suggested, printing itself was a "forerunner" of the industrial mode of production (Eisenstein, 1979, p. 31) and printed newspapers historically were the first instances of industrial capitalism, then journalism is a pure implementation of capitalism's ability to induce demand. There is no need in journalism for those who do not know what it is. News consumption is a conditioned reflex, a learned addiction. It is symbolic that historian Andreas Würgler called the owners of Italian *scrittorie*, the former scribes' workshops turned into the first newsrooms, "news dealers" (Würgler, 2012).

The producers of the media aim at stimulating appetite, not satisfying it. The marketing of journalism is embedded in the product of journalism. Each phase of the production process – from digging around for a scoop to composing a headline – is aimed at making the audience want more. Success in the media is measured not by informing the audience but by readers' increasing return for the next supply.

The media create their audiences and make readers crave pre-liked news and agendas. The induced demand means an induced agenda. The characteristics of induced agendas depend on a business model based on either ad revenue or reader revenue.

***

In terms of news coverage, ad revenue encourages blind spots, while reader revenue encourages spotlights.

According to the rule of allocative control, the origin of money impacts the mechanisms of selection in agenda-setting. If content production is controlled by ad money, news sections tend to be suppressed or news content tends to be corrected toward more neutral and positive news. If content production is determined by reader money (or traffic), disturbing content, including polarizing and triggering political news, tends to be emphasized.

Of course, many other general and specific factors defining the principles of agenda-setting in concrete media outlets may be at play. But reliance on either ad revenue or reader revenue incentivizes the media to create two different and even opposite pictures of the world. The media relying on ad revenue make the world look nicer. The media relying on reader revenue make the world look grimmer.

It is not just about how the world is seen. It is about how the audience feels and what the audience becomes. Media business that mostly relies on ad revenue requires an audience that consists of happy and economically able consumers. Media business that mostly relies on reader revenue requires an audience that consists of frustrated and politically strangulated citizens. The media not only address these audiences; they create and reproduce them.

Subscription solicited as donation: a new and unexplored cause of media bias

The decline in the media business caused by the internet has not distorted the picture of the world in the media. It has distorted the habitual distortion.

Over the last 10 to 15 years, both advertisers and audiences have fled to better platforms, where content is free and far more attractive and ad delivery is cheaper and far more efficient.

Not only did the media's revenue fall, its structure flipped. Ads used to bring in more revenue than readers, but ad revenue has slipped away the fastest. The media – and journalism – have found themselves in uncharted territory. First, earnings are not enough to survive. Second, reader revenue took over ad revenue in funding journalism. The news media have never faced such conditions before.

Media analysts have scrutinized the decline of media business and its impact on journalism. Much less attention has been paid to the reversal from ad revenue to reader revenue and its impact on journalism and agenda-setting.

***

Ad money incentivizes positivity, and reader money incentivizes negativity; but there has always been a third factor balancing the external impact – newsroom autonomy. To some degree, it can resist not only the push for negativity but also the pressure from both the political interests of the elites and the commercial interests of the media's own sales departments.

Normally, journalists are affiliated with but not assimilated by the elites. In terms of social demography, newsrooms are filled with highly educated and passionate people who are well-networked with the elites but remain a part of their own professional clique. In terms of psychology, those who get selected for this profession meet some specific criteria. They need to be very ambitious, often bordering on narcissism; have a proclivity, sometimes messianic, for public service; and a very specific professional ever-challenging innate need to dig for scoops 'at any cost', which is always spurred on by competitiveness. All these criteria create a caste with a high level of self-awareness and self-determination. Much like priests of a cult, journalists normally think they do not serve the ruling elites – they shepherd them.

The demographic and psychological characteristics of journalists force them to oppose the political pressure of the elites as well as the business pressure of the media as a commercial enterprise. Or it also can be said that newsroom autonomy creates economic value of a higher level than the routine trade of ads or copies. The *Washington Post* boosted its symbolic and real capital after the 1972–73 Watergate scandal. By promulgating the huge story worthy of a presidential resignation, the *Post* rose from local to national status; a shift that had, of course, some pleasant business outcomes. In the 1971–73 Pentagon Papers scandal, the *New York Times* and their fellow colleagues in the *Post* and other major outlets faced a serious legal risk, which any normal business would have steered away from. But not the news media. *Time Magazine* reported that applications to journalism schools in 1974 reached an all-time high.[1]

The search for all kinds of 'Pentagon Papers', 'Panama Papers' and other huge WikiLeaks' leaks that would smash the elites, is a fundamental professional standard, elaborated by journalism in the 20th century on the basis of the same capitalist mode of production that allegedly subjugated the media to the ruling elites.

"At news organizations the central organizing principle is usually to produce something with social impact first ahead of utility or profit," said Emily Bell, the director of the Tows Centre for Digital Journalism at the Columbia Journalism School, NY. She substantiated her statement with simple logical proof: by just doing their job, journalists are more likely to "end up being ostracized or imprisoned rather than ringing the opening bell at the New York stock exchange."[2]

Neither advertisers nor readers are able to make journalists muckrakers, watchdogs or the public moral's supervisors. These functions are the product purely of the self-imposed and jealously guarded journalist autonomy. In an environmental sense, this function of the media is a hygienic function of the social ecosystem that maintains the elites' healthy reproduction. From this point of view, the news media is the instrument of the environment aimed at the elites, not the instrument of the elites aimed at the environment.

The media priests are well-aware that the power of the pulpit has more value than all ad contracts combined. This mass is well worth Paris. When the status of priest is well-maintained, the tributes and offerings will be

---

[1] *Time Magazine.* (1974, July 08). "Coyer Story: Covering Watergate: success and backlash." http://content.time.com/time/magazine/article/0,9171,943934,00.html

[2] Bell, Emily. (2014, November 23). "What's the right relationship between technology companies and journalism?" *The Guardian.* https://www.theguardian.com/media/media-blog/2014/nov/23/silicon-valley-companies-journalism-news

brought in. Normally, journalists did not and did not need to bother with selling their product; they just got paid. The Vaisya, the people of the lower caste of merchants in ad sales and marketing departments, took care of it.

***

In the Golden Age of the media, the principles of agenda-setting were governed by the complex interplay of three factors: ad dependence, reader dependence and newsroom autonomy. However big the impact of advertising money was, the newsroom always had a say. Ad money might incentivize the beautifying of reality and a structural shift in the news agenda towards less disturbing content, but there also was a 'glass wall' between the newsroom and marketing department. Journalism, not paper space, has always been the main asset of newspapers; media CEOs generally understood this.

Newsroom autonomy used to mitigate the distortions induced by media business when the media business provided enough money for newsrooms to stay strong and self-confident. When media business failed its maintaining function, the skews induced by media business outweighed the resistance of newsroom autonomy. During hard times, newsroom autonomy loses its ability to fend off the encroachments of business factors.

With the switch from ad to reader revenue, even the principle of the editorial 'glass wall', which used to protect the newsroom from advertisers' wishes, disappeared. The marketing department now interacts with the audience, not advertisers; how is it possible for the newsroom to fence itself off from the wishes of subscribers? The wall between editorial and business dissolves when the business rests on readers.

All in all, not only have the media been rendered dependent on a declining revenue coming predominantly from readers, they have also thus become defenseless against readers. Newsroom autonomy has shrunk because of both the decrease in revenue and the increase in dependence on readers' support.

What advertisers and corporations wanted from the agenda-setting in the media was known. It remains to be explored – and experienced – what the donating audience might want from the news media.

***

Douglas Rushkoff, when assessing what has happened to the internet in the last twenty years, stated that the digital space was captured by corporations and commercialized. "The seemingly God-like abilities offered by the net were productized," he wrote. "The internet went from town hall to shopping mall."[1] This happened, of course, under the pressure of advertising money which had migrated onto the internet.

The ability to customize messages personally, but on such an enormous distributive scale, converted social media into profit extraction platforms. According to Maslow's hierarchy of needs, social media provide people with a service of the highest value. They allow for better, faster and broader self-actualization than any media in human history. In return for this service, social media collect the personal data exposed by the users in the process of self-actualization. Precise user profiling helps connect people better and increases the relevance of the newsfeed. But this same profiling also allows for better and, in fact, the most efficient commercial targeting in history. Revenue collected by platforms from advertisers is a platform fee that society pays to platform landlords for the service of users' self-actualization.

This is how the town hall has become a shopping mall. To develop a McLuhan dichotomy, an amazing personal service of platforms comes with a harmful social disservice. There is no evil plot behind this, even though some actors (actually, many actors) have managed to use social media settings to pursue their own interests. Such is an environmental effect of a new medium, enthusiastically met and used by both users and advertisers. Service's convenience enslaves and blinds users and amplifies disservice.

The traditional media, on the contrary, have disappeared from advertisers' radars. The subsequent loss of advertising unshackled the media from ad money's beautifying impact on agenda-setting. Therefore, rephrasing Rushkoff, the media went back "from shopping mall to town hall." However, due to the specifics of the new business model with a focus on reader revenue, this is a very peculiar town hall full of angry citizens.

***

Reader revenue for the media is now supplied by an odd source. It looks like subscription and is sold like subscription, but it has motives that are increasingly not commercial and transactional, but rather civic and philanthropic.

In part, the audience still believes that it buys news. But news is usually already known from the newsfeed on social media. The audience increasingly buys not news, but the validation of already-known news from a certain point of view.

---

[1] Rushkoff, Douglas. (2019, November 14). "Was Humanity Simply Not Ready for the Internet? A 1990s cyber enthusiast considers whether he's to blame for our digital woes". *Medium*. https://medium.com/team-human/was-humanity-simply-not-ready-for-the-internet-968ff564653c

In order to supply such a product, the media need to reorganize their agenda-setting to accommodate the expectations of readers, i.e. the donating audience. Readers pay to make sure 1) they receive the right agenda and 2) the right agenda is delivered to others. This blend of the validation fee and the membership surrogate of subscription encourages the sliding of journalism toward crowdfunded propaganda: the media must validate, justify and supply to others the picture of the world sought by the payer.

The observation is well-supported by similar processes occurring in social media that has been identified as 'participatory propaganda' (Wanless & Berk, 2017; Asmolov, 2019; and others). 'Participatory propaganda' signifies the phenomenon of ordinary users joining, subliminally or deliberately, the distribution and support of political ideas in efforts that traditionally were intrinsic to classical propaganda. Now, the blogosphere and particularly social media have given users an opportunity to be the propagandists in their own right.

In 'participatory propaganda' on social media, people contribute their participation. For 'crowdfunded propaganda' in the news media, people contribute their money to a cause. But for the latter, they need someone to do agenda-setting on their behalf, and this agenda-setting contractor is the news media. So, this is *crowdfunded and outsourced propaganda*.

***

Allocative control of advertising money made the media target a mostly affluent audience. In terms of political economy, the ultimate product of such a media system was neither the news nor agendas but the buying transactions that kept capitalism rolling. Informing was not the primary business goal of the ad-driven media. They made people buy; content was just a decoy.

This political economy schema has now made its way to social media, where self-actualization in the form of communication can be seen as a decoy, with the ultimate purpose to make people buy what is advertised.

What is the final purpose of funding in the traditional media then, if they have switched from ad to reader revenue?

The final purpose of the reader-driven media within the validation/membership subscription model is to make people donate. It is not news – readers already know all the news. It is even not agenda-setting, because the donating audience is already immersed in the agenda on social media. The work of the media is to refine and justify the agenda and inculcate it in others. But for the media themselves, the desired result is making people donate.

As always, the media induce the demand for their product. To that end, they induce the reality, in which the audience will stay constantly triggered and willing to donate. Within this new business model, the media commodify what they fight with. This is why the mainstream media in the US kept commodifighting Trumpism, even though everyone understood how beneficial it was for Trump.

*****

Under the advertising model, the characteristics of the target audience were well-known. The most important were income, education, job position, area of living, property cost, etc., – all revolving around the ability to buy advertised goods. As noted by Herman and Chomsky, the cultural power of marketing and advertising created a world of virtual communities based on consumer demographics and taste differences. They wrote:

> These consumption- and style-based clusters are at odds with physical communities that share a social life and common concerns and which participate in a democratic order. These virtual communities are organized to buy and sell goods, not to create or service a public sphere. (Herman & Chomsky, 2002 [1988], p. xviii).

If the characteristics and political impact of the ad-driven media's audience were known, then what are the characteristics of the audience of the reader-driven media? What is the political impact of this newly emerged cultural entity – the audience paying the media for news validation and donating to the media, considering the fact that the media targets this audience not just for its attention (as they did to the buying audience) but also for its donations?

This has yet to be identified by media sociologists and political scholars. But the main assumption could be made on the basis of etymological analysis. The core feature of the donating audience is that it consists of people who are able to donate. They are not just financially able – the amount of money donated to the media is not enormous – but rather that they are psychologically inclined to do this. They are a particular class of people, presumably educated enough, most likely old enough (they are the Last Newspaper Generation that remembers the role of the news media), and most likely belonging to the cultural, political and business elites, academia or other areas of meaning production and consumption. The most important characteristic of this class has to be their political involvement and empathy, at least at some level, along with their political or social awareness and citizen consciousness.

The closest synonym for 'donating audience' would be 'concerned citizens'. The psychological, educational, and social profile of the audience's members should relate to their ability to be concerned with social and political developments. They are the only demographic category that can be responsive to the news media's calls to join the cause. All other groups stay impervious to the subscription pitches.

***

'Concerns' are the key factor for why the media targets their audiences. The more concerned people are, the more likely they will donate. For media outlets with a subscription-membership model, people's concerns are not something that should be solved and eradicated. On the contrary, concerns should be cultivated and reproduced.

Happiness and peacefulness are disincentivized. The trendsetting emotional tone is easy to read even on the faces of TV hosts. In the 1970s, TV anchors had to wear smiles; now, they are obliged to wear an anxious grimace. Today's news anchors make a kind of 'basset face' that would have looked unprofessional on 1970s TV. In return, an anchor with a 'corgi face' from the 1970s would look like an idiot on today's news show.

Not only do the media have to address 'pressing social issues', they also have to support and amplify readers' irritation and frustration with those issues. Ideally, the media should not just exaggerate the menace but induce public concern themselves.

The history of the American media has seen a dramatic example of such a business attitude. At the very end of the 19th century, Pulitzer's and Hearst's media empires competed for readership by instigating a patriotic hysteria and hatred towards Spain. The media turned into what the U.S. Senator Elizabeth Warren called a "hate-for-profit machine" when characterizing *Fox News* 120 years later.[1] The public mood and the pressure on the politicians induced by the media for the sake of higher circulation contributed to the sparking of the 1898 Spanish-American War.

As the media have no other viable business options remaining, except attempting to earn through the subscription-membership hybrid, they are compelled to refine and push on concerns and, most importantly, to fire up polarization as the most triggering socio-psychological mechanism.

There is no evil plot, 'liberal bias', nor 'right-wing conspiracy' behind it. Such are the environmental settings of a media industry that has lost its ad

---

[1] Epstein, Jennifer. (2019, May 14). "Elizabeth Warren turns down Fox News, slamming 'hate-for-profit machine'." *Bloomberg.* https://www.bloomberg.com/news/articles/2019-05-14/warren-turns-down-fox-news-slamming-hate-for-profit-machine

and news business to the internet. The media based on the subscription-membership business model must push pressing political issues and therefore be polarizing. This is their survival mode. They will not extinguish social and political conflicts but rather fire them up. Without a polarized environment, the media are doomed today and more so tomorrow. Political polarization is their last resort. Using McChesney's metaphor of the 'rich media/poor democracy paradox', it can be said that democracy has not benefited from the reversal. Since the media has become poor, democracy has gone wild.

The ad-driven media produced happy customers. The reader-driven media produce angry citizens. The former served consumerism. The latter serves polarization.

10. Manufacturing anger. The post-'propaganda model'

> Our wicked enemies abroad say that we, Soviet writers, write by command of the Party. No, we write by command of our hearts. But our hearts belong to the Party.
>
> *Mikhail Sholokhov,*
> *the 1965 Nobel Laureate in Literature,*
> *the author of "And Quiet Flows the Don".*

The moral of Lippmann's elitism

The Herman-Chomsky Propaganda model (PM) explores "the interplay between economic power and communicative power" (Mullen & Klaehn, 2010, p. 217). As Herman recalled, "We had long been impressed by the regularity with which the media operate on the basis of a set of ideological premises, depend heavily and uncritically on elite information sources and participate in propaganda campaigns helpful to elite interests" (Herman, 2000, p. 101).

The Herman-Chomsky model is based on a critical reassessment of Lippmann's metaphor of "manufacturing consent" from his 1922 book *Public Opinion.*

Lippmann drew a line between "realism and romanticism" in the understanding of democracy. A romantic concept of democracy posits that the proper procedures of representation creates a government of the people, by the people, for the people. This view implies that people are "omnicompetent" and know what they want, what decisions are to be made and who can make these decisions. In fact, as Lippmann insisted, people rarely know anything beyond their daily routine. A picture of the world is available to people only in the form of the subjective judgment of "self-centered man". Left to their own devices, people with segmented and disparate views are not capable of elaborating a competent opinion regarding the optimal strategies of governance over common interests (hence the title of his next book – *The Phantom Public*, 1927).

Because public opinion is impacted by so many distorting factors but is "supposed to be the prime mover in democracies", the common interests "can be managed only by a specialized class whose personal interests reach beyond the locality" (Lippmann, 1929 [1922], p. 253). This class, the class of administrators and politicians – the decision-making elites – needs to both receive adequate information about social reality and spread useful information to the public. This task can be accomplished by a special cohort of educated and independent experts who know "how to create and operate public opinion" (Ibid., 255) and can advise the leadership competently and unbiasedly.

Thus, Lippmann described, in a positive way, a model of a deep state apparatus, with an expert machine, aimed at mitigating the distortions of personal and public information. No democratic procedure or institutions per se could refine common interests of so differently, shortsighted and biasedly informed people without special knowledge of how to forge public opinion and social coherence. And "wise leaders," Lippmann stated, always "seek a certain measure of consent" (Ibid., p. 245).

Being obviously a fan of Machiavelli, whom he often referred to, Lippmann underlined not just pragmatism but also the morality of pursuing public consent for political and administrative actions. "Coercion is the surd in almost all social theory, except the Machiavellian," he wrote (Ibid., p. 295). This thought implies that the manufacture of consent is a wholesome substitute to the otherwise inevitable, oftentimes violent, suppression of dissent.

Here is the context in which Lippmann used the idea of 'manufacturing consent' for the first time, a large piece worth citing:

> That the manufacture of consent is capable of great refinements no one, I think, denies. <...> The creation of consent is not a new art. It is a very old one which was supposed to have died out with the appearance of democracy. But it has not died out. It has, in fact, improved enormously in technic, because it is now based on analysis rather than on rule of thumb. And so, as a result of psychological research, coupled with the modern means of communication, the practice of democracy has turned a corner. A revolution is taking place, infinitely more significant than any shifting of economic power.
>
> Within the life of the generation now in control of affairs, persuasion has become a self-conscious art and a regular organ of popular government. None of us begins to understand the consequences, but it is no daring prophecy to say that the knowledge of how to create consent will alter every political calculation and modify every political premise. Under the impact of propaganda, not necessarily in the sinister meaning of the word alone, the old constants of our thinking have become variables. It is no longer possible, for example, to believe in the original dogma of democracy; that the knowledge needed for the management of human affairs comes up spontaneously from

the human heart. Where we act on that theory we expose ourselves to self-deception, and to forms of persuasion that we cannot verify. It has been demonstrated that we cannot rely upon intuition, conscience, or the accidents of casual opinion if we are to deal with the world beyond our reach. (Lippmann, 1929 [1922], p. 248.)

The Propaganda model: the basics

The manufacture of consent, which Lippmann saw as a steadily improving mechanism of coherence in a complex democratic society, evolved into the Propaganda model of the mass media described by Herman and Chomsky. What was aimed at better governing in Lippmann's theory became seen as a means of preserving the elites' control over the population in Herman and Chomsky's view. "Clearly, the manufacture of consent by a 'specialized class' that can override the short-sighted perspectives of the masses must entail media control by that class," clarified Herman (2000, p. 101).

Lippmann thought that consent can be managed by the endeavors of experts in mass communications and public relations. Herman and Chomsky revealed that the mass media play a propaganda role under the influence of structural political-economic forces. The media became a manufacturer of consent by their economic design. They called the Propaganda model a "guided market system" (Herman & Chomsky, 2002 [1988], p. lx). They wrote:

> In fact, our treatment is much closer to a "free market" analysis, with the results largely an outcome of the workings of market forces. Most biased choices in the media arise from the preselection of right-thinking people, internalized preconceptions, and the adaptation of personnel to the constraints of ownership, organization, market, and political power. Censorship is largely self-censorship, by reporters and commentators who adjust to the realities of source and media organizational requirements, and by people at higher levels within media organizations who are chosen to implement, and have usually internalized, the constraints imposed by proprietary and other market and governmental centers of power. (Herman & Chomsky, 2002 [1988], p. lx.)

The propaganda function and self-censorship in the media were not forced or directly ordered and paid for by the elites. When BBC journalist Andrew Marr, in a 1996 interview with Chomsky, stated that he never censored himself, Chomsky's replied, "I don't say you're self-censoring – I'm sure you believe everything you're saying; but what I'm saying is, if you believed something different, you wouldn't be sitting where you're sitting".[1]

The free-market nature of propaganda in the commercial media fits well with the idea Smythe expressed at about the same time in his paper "On the Audience Commodity and its Work" (1981). Smythe described a two-part function of media when the economic motives of advertisers in agenda-setting reinforce the political interests of the ruling elites. He wrote:

> The answer <...> to the question, what is the principal function which the commercial mass media perform for the capitalist system was essentially to set an agenda for the production of consciousness with two mutually reinforcing objectives: (1) to mass market the mass-produced consumer goods and services generated by monopoly capitalism by using audience power to accomplish this end; (2) to mass market legitimacy of the state and its strategic and tactical policies and actions, such as election of government officers, military thrusts against states which show signs of moving toward socialism (Vietnam, Korea, Cuba, Chile, Dominican Republic, etc.), and policies against youthful dissent (Smythe, 2012 [1981], p. 187.)

***

Herman and Chomsky introduced a propaganda model that "traces the routes by which money and power are able to filter out the news fit to print, marginalize dissent, and allow the government and dominant private interests to get their messages across to the public" (Herman & Chomsky, 2002 [1988], p. 2). They singled out five filters that "interact with and reinforce one another" (in the quote, I split the filters into different paragraphs for visual clarity – A.M.):

> The essential ingredients of our propaganda model, or set of news "filters," fall under the following headings:
> (1) the size, concentrated ownership, owner wealth, and profit orientation of the dominant mass-media firms;
> (2) advertising as the primary income source of the mass media;
> (3) the reliance of the media on information provided by government, business, and "experts" funded and approved by these primary sources and agents of power;
> (4) "flak" as a means of disciplining the media; and

---

[1] Chomsky, Noam. (1996, February 14). "Noam Chomsky on Propaganda." The Big Idea. Interview with Andrew Marr. *BBC*. Transcript.
http://scratchindog.blogspot.com/2015/07/transcript-of-interview-between-noam.html

(5) "anticommunism" as a national religion and control mechanism. These elements interact with and reinforce one another. (Herman & Chomsky, 2002 [1988], p. 2.)

The Propaganda model worked particularly well when it was used to analyze the conjoined stances of the mainstream media regarding American foreign policy. The applicability of the PM in this regard was fascinating. Herman and Chomsky used their filters to show, with meticulously calculated numbers of mentions and profound discourse analysis, how differently (but jointly) the media in 1970–80s treated seemingly similar events, such as wars, elections or assassination attempts, depending on whether the American ruling elites were friendly to the regimes or proprietors responsible for those events (or allegedly responsible).

Particularly fascinating was the description of how the mainstream media used the concept of 'worthy' and 'unworthy' victims for hiding or highlighting crimes in order to demonize unwelcomed political stances. Through calculating the mentions and the papers' space allocated for news coverage, Herman and Chomsky showed how killings by ideological enemies were deliberately placed at the forefront and center in the media space, further enhanced with prolonged detailed coverage, while similar or more terrifying murders by ideological allies were not given much attention, if noticed at all.

The significance of Herman and Chomsky's findings was not in pointing out the existence of the distortions, but in unveiling the regularities in media coverage. Certain events would produce certain types of coverage with a high level of predictability, which made the Propaganda model a tool of almost scientific precision. Even today, in a completely different media environment, the basic methodological idea of the PM – to examine the regularities of the media filters designed by the business of media – works very well.

Functions of media: an ongoing process of change

Herman and Chomsky's definition of the media, with which they opened their *Manufacturing Consent*, goes as follows:

The mass media serve as a system for communicating messages and symbols to the general populace. It is their function to amuse, entertain, and inform, and to inculcate individuals with the values, beliefs, and codes of behavior that will integrate them into the institutional structures of the larger society. (Herman & Chomsky, 2002 [1988], p. 1.)

It is noteworthy that they started their list of the mass media's functions with "amuse" and "entertain" before "inform." This, of course, exposes a critical political economy approach to the media, essentially a Marxist one, that was prevalent in the political economy of communications of the late 20th century.

The view that the capitalist mainstream media is 'infotainment' is still dominant in critical media theories. The idea of the media serving capital by means of distraction from pressing social issues and manufacturing consent is also a common ground for teaching and studying the media in universities. This common ground is steadily turning into a common fallacy. The disease of being stuck in the evidential base and critical judgements of the 1990s has afflicted many theoretical frameworks in cultural and media studies, while the praxis of studied objects has either drastically changed or ceased to exist.

***

The mainstream mass media do not amuse and entertain anymore.

New sources of amusement and entertainment have arisen in digital media. News from around the world and just around the corner now buzzes and blips in the cellphone notifications of social media. Political and economic news arrives directly in the user's newsfeed. Celebrities became the media and drew the audience away from glossy magazines to Instagram and similar platforms, where their personal fandom base far exceeds anything that even the best glossy magazines' readership ever could be. Sports and sport fans' engagement is much more attractive and vivid on social media and special websites with social features. All kinds of catastrophes, deaths, crushes, pranks and the like, traditionally attracting public interest, have found a better vehicle in YouTube, Twitter and other social platforms.

The newly emerged forms of media consumption have merged with, and continue to expand, the range of already-traditional digital forms of 'infotainment'. The COVID-19 lockdown boosted the development of peer-to-peer 'infotainment' platforms, such as text and video messengers, group video calls and webinar platforms. New digital media benefited from the quarantine tremendously. New media activities appeared, such as Zoom game nights or Zoom drinking parties, to replace the forbidden bar going during the pandemic. Some of them will stay in routine use.

Video games continue to evolve, adding increasingly more social features. Users gather to dance in multiplayer games like *Fortnite*. Inside the games, users acquire fancy outfits, gestures and dance moves for their in-

214

game personalities. The purpose of such new features is obviously to enhance the self-actualization service of the games. Pop-idols come into the game space to deliver their show. During the COVID-19 lockdown, US rapper Travis Scott performed a live concert inside the online shooter *Fortnite*. More than 12 million players took part in the spectacle.[1] They stopped shooting each other and gathered in a certain virtual space inside the game to enjoy the show: 12 million at the same time. This is three times larger than the primetime viewership of *Fox News*, the most-watched US cable network (reached a high of 4.4 million during the first weeks of the lockdown in March 2020)[2] or the *New York Times* news digital subscriptions (4.4 million in July 2020).[3]

New platforms and devices delivering digital amusement and entertainment are much more attractive than boring old media. They are in fact attractive to the level of physical addiction, as they appeal to the entire sensorium. They immerse users into the digital environment of information and entertainment with triggering sounds, vibration, flashing, and so on (Miroshnichenko, 2016). The metaphor of *Amusing Ourselves to Death*, Neil Postman's 1985 book title, which addresses the media environment with TV on top, is now more relevant for describing new rather than old media.

***

There is nothing left in the exclusive possession of old media to amuse the audience. For everything amusing and entertaining, new media offer better capabilities and capacities. Both advertisers and the audience have fled to better amusers and entertainers.

Out of 12 hours of daily media consumption, Americans spent 6:35 with digital media, 3:35 with TV, 1:20 with radio and 0:20 with newspapers and magazines in 2019.[4] Old media already have under half of the population's media-consumption time budget. This half rests predominantly on TV

[1] Stuart, Keith. (2020, April 24). "More than 12m players watch Travis Scott concert in Fortnite." *The Guardian*. https://www.theguardian.com/games/2020/apr/24/travis-scott-concert-fortnite-more-than-12m-players-watch

[2] Mir, Andrey. (2020, April 16). "Old media and COVID-19: news demand surges, business crumbles." *Human as media blog*. https://human-as-media.com/2020/04/16/old-media-and-covid-19-news-demand-surges-business-crumbles/

[3] "The New York Times Company reports 2020 first-quarter results." (2020, May 6). The New York Times Company press-release. https://investors.nytco.com/investors/investor-news/investor-news-details/2020/The-New-York-Times-Company-Reports-2020-First-Quarter-Results/default.aspx

[4] He, Amy. (2019, May 31). "Average time spent with media in 2019 has plateaued. Digital is making up losses by old media." *eMarketer*. https://www.emarketer.com/content/us-time-spent-with-media-in-2019-has-plateaued-with-digital-making-up-losses-by-old-media

watching by the older audience and radio listening by drivers in traffic. Radio will die soon after self-driving cars hit the roads. With the demise of the last newspaper generation, even the share of TV will decline. The time spent with newspapers by the general population is already insignificant, despite the huge impact mainstream newspapers have on discourse formation.

Criticizing the mass media for being entertaining instead of informative is no longer relevant. Entertaining has been stolen from the media by the internet, together with advertising money.

However, the idea that the media business relies on inducing some feelings still holds true. As the funding of the media has flipped to the opposite of its previous model (from advertising to reader revenue) so have the induced feelings. The media now induce not amusement and entertainment but frustration and anger.

***

Herman and Chomsky compiled their Propaganda model when journalism was funded by advertising. The media sold the audience to advertisers, and this economic setup predefined the way the media adjusted their mechanisms of agenda-setting.

Advertising as the main source of revenue for the media has gone. News retail as a sustainable business is fading, too. The reader money still coming to newspapers can be broken down into four categories:

1. Residual transactional news subscription.

2. Validation fee – paying for the validation of already-known news within a certain value system by a weighty media brand.

3. Donscription – subscription solicited as donation to support a cause promoted by a media outlet.

4. Membership – direct soliciting of donations to a noble cause; formally, the cause of journalism but, in fact, increasingly a political cause.

Other old media – radio and TV – exploit equivalent motives for consumption of their product, but they just monetize them differently, through cable subscription or advertising, though these are also declining.

As the funding of the media has been reversed from advertising to reader revenue, and new factors impacting agenda-setting in the media have appeared, the Herman-Chomsky Propaganda model should perhaps also be revised.

The Propaganda model revised

How does the Propaganda model work if the filter of advertising is replaced with the filter of readers' payment-for-impact? What form of social coherence is emerging instead of 'consent' when one of the main driving forces of the Propaganda model has been changed?

Methodologically, the Propaganda model can still be applied to the media, but the switch in their filters will lead to a reversal in the agenda-setting outcome. In the Propaganda model based on subscription-membership instead of advertising, the media create the coherence of anger, not consent.

***

Herman and Chomsky avoided the temptation to rank their filters by the level of their importance. As they commented on different occasions, "It varies from case to case" (Alford, 2018, p. 152).

Herman and Chomsky also admitted that the PM filters may have different manifestations in different political systems and clarified that they described the media system that existed in the USA. Similar observations ("We have several observations, but no rules" – Mullen, 2009, p.12) were said to be applicable in other countries with media systems integrated into free capitalist markets or even those without the latter. 20 years after the model was published, Herman and Chomsky said that,

> (a) Ownership and (b) advertising belong to straightforward institutional analysis – these are the kinds of institutional arrangements that predominate among US media firms and elsewhere. (c) Sourcing and (d) flak are two well-established processes to which any elite-serving media will adapt, whether we are talking about the elite US or British media or the elite media under Stalin and Hitler. On the other hand, (e) anti-communism, as a major theme of media production during the twentieth century, was reflective of the prevailing system of belief in the Western states, and has evolved with the collapse of the Soviet bloc since the first edition of Manufacturing Consent. (Mullen, 2009, p. 13-14.)

It is hard to say if the disciplining of the mass media in the Soviet Union can be called "flak"; I think the Nazi media were no different in this regard. There is no need for Herman-Chomsky's flak if a special Party official in the newsroom censures texts before publishing and editors and journalists can be fired simply through a Party committee direct decision (or even convicted and executed, in the darkest times). The best flak is the Gulag, the ultimate form of cancel culture.

But the approach is obvious: the impacts of different PM filters may vary in time and space.

As the political, cultural and economic conditions for the media have changed, so has the Propaganda model. Not only have some filters changed their content, their imaginary ranking can be arranged in a new way, too.

A reservation needs to be made: since Herman and Chomsky rejected ranking the filters, their original formal order is used, with simplified descriptions given by Herman in 2000:

> We noted that the five factors involved – ownership, advertising, sourcing, flak and anti-communist ideology – work as 'filters' through which information must pass, and that individually and often in cumulative fashion, they greatly influence media choices. (Herman, 2000, p. 102.)

Thus, in the new technological and economic conditions, a revised list of the PM's filters can appear as follows (Figure 13).

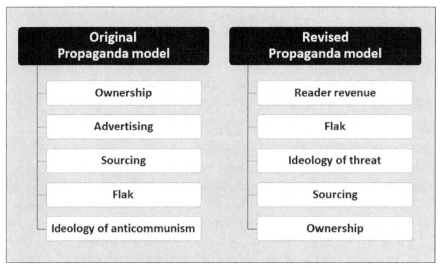

Figure 13. The Propaganda model revised.

A new and weird reader revenue

"Before advertising became prominent, the price of a newspaper had to cover the costs of doing business," wrote Herman and Chomsky in *Manufacturing Consent* (2002 [1988], p. 14).

Well, the same is true after advertising has become insignificant.

Herman and Chomsky titled the section about advertising "The advertising license to do business: the second filter." The metaphor implies that those media orgs who ingratiate themselves with advertisers get an opportunity to do better business. This used to be the case – ad money allowed the media to thrive in the 20th century. To win advertisers' favor, the media needed to gather a proper audience – both in quality and quantity – and provide a proper "supportive selling environment". Advertisers chose those media that attracted a better audience and had a better context. Those media not chosen by advertisers were "at a serious disadvantage" and eventually were marginalized and driven from the market. This happened to "working-class and radical papers," which were quite popular before ad money took command over the media market.

Besides the purely marketing choice of an appropriate audience and appropriate context, advertisers conformed to what we would now call brand safety considerations. Herman and Chomsky stated that advertisers generally preferred to avoid publications "with serious complexities and disturbing controversies that interfere with the 'buying mood'" (Herman & Chomsky, 2002 [1988], p. 17). For example, viewers would prefer TV programs about how Americans eat when they dine out over programs investigating the Pentagon's deeds.

The advertisers' preference for avoiding complex and troublesome contexts in favor of contexts that stimulated consumption had a statistically significant impact on the media industry. Risk-averse advertising money drove the media industry, in general, towards being more lifestyle- and celebrity-focused and less politically involved – compared to the 18th and 19th century media, which had a larger share of funding from political parties and readers.

It is also noteworthy that advertising money made the media industry, in general, more politically neutral and unbiased. This was not because of high standards of impartiality (though they, too, existed at the level of newsroom autonomy), but because political bias would have repelled readers with opposite views and diminished the audience. Advertising money, seeking a larger audience, depoliticized the media and protected society from political polarization in the media.

***

The switch from advertising money to readers' money can be described as a switch from advertisement licensing to donation licensing of the media. This is leading to a full turnaround in the licensing requirements. The donating audience and its demand for impact, not for a "supportive selling environment", will lead the media to push pressing social issues. Advertisers avoided them, but the donating audience wants them.

The reversal in conditions of licensing from advertising to donations puts depoliticized media "at a serious disadvantage" and favors media that politicize their content and their readership.

There is a possibility that the competition for donating money will make more successful those media whose tone is more passionate or even hysterical, regardless of what end of the political spectrum they are at. What is important is that they should drift towards the poles of the spectrum, where emotions are stronger and louder and where triggers for donations work better. Much like how the pursuing of ad money made the media industry impartial and politically disengaged, the pursuing of donation money is making the media industry partisan and politically split.

The ad-driven media drove society toward a Huxleyan amuse-yourself-to-death and socially blind consumerism. The donation-driven media will drive society toward hyper-politicized and hyperpolarized crazes of anxiety and anger, with media outlets becoming the competing Orwellian crowdfunded Ministries of post-truth setting the tone.

***

Herman and Chomsky metaphorically compared advertisers to the patrons of the media. They wrote:

> The choices of these patrons greatly affect the welfare of the media, and the patrons become what William Evan calls "normative reference organizations," whose requirements and demands the media must accommodate if they are to succeed. (Herman & Chomsky, 2002 [1988], p. 16.)

After ad money disappeared, the media found a new payer and patron and "normative reference organization" – the donating audience. It is the will and wish of the audience, picked up by the editors, that sets the filters of agenda now. If the editors are not properly in tune with the audience, they will quickly be caught out themselves. The backlash of the donating audience has become more powerful than ever because now it is increasingly the audience who pays, or is expected to pay, for newspapers (and forms a viewership that defines which TV shows will be paid for by remaining advertisers).

Flak

Here is how Herman and Chomsky defined flak in the past:

"Flak" refers to negative responses to a media statement or program. It may take the form of letters, telegrams, phone calls, petitions, lawsuits, speeches and bills before Congress, and other modes of complaint, threat, and punitive action. It may be organized centrally or locally, or it may consist of the entirely independent actions of individuals.

If flak is produced on a large scale, or by individuals or groups with substantial resources, it can be both uncomfortable and costly to the media. (Herman & Chomsky, 2002 [1988], p. 26.)

Flak is going to be the second most impactful filter of agenda-setting in the media that are predominantly paid by the donating audience. The reason is simple: in the mind of people in the news media, flak directly accompanies money donated by the audience for the media to properly validate news or peddle a *cause*.

***

According to Herman and Chomsky, flak could cause reputational harm, led to the withdrawal of advertising contracts or forced the media to spend a lot of money on remedial PR and legal defenses, sometimes including court cases. Therefore, flak was not just unpleasant negative feedback. It could lead to a decrease in revenue and an increase in expenses. Besides, because of flak, people in the media could lose their job. This factor forced them to censor themselves at the level of personal decisions.

In the modern media system, four types of flak can be singled out according to their sources, mechanisms and effects:

1. Legal flak
2. Organized flak
3. Meta-flak: the pressure on advertisers
4. Grassroots flak

***

Legal flak. The most devastating recent story about how a media outlet was literally destroyed by flak was the case "Hulk Hogan vs. *Gawker*". In 2012, *Gawker* published the sex-tape of Hogan, a professional wrestler and movie star. In 2016, Hogan won a $140-million lawsuit that ultimately bankrupted *Gawker*.[1] It became known during the process that Silicon Valley venture capitalist Peter Thiel helped finance Hogan's lawsuit. Theil had his own personal motive. Many years ago, in 2007, *Gawker* outed Theil

---

[1] "Hulk Hogan v. Gawker: Invasion of Privacy & Free Speech in a Digital World." First Amendment Watch at New York University. https://firstamendmentwatch.org/deep-dive/hulk-hogan-v-gawker-invasion-of-privacy-free-speech-in-a-digital-world/

as gay in the notorious tabloid manner of exposing someone's private live simply for the sake of better circulation; as Theil later commented, they ruined "people's lives for no reason."[1] He waited nine years, until an occasion presented itself and the revenge became a dish cold enough to be served.

Peter Thiel was later reported to have invested in a startup called Legalist, which aimed to legally support the victims of sexual harassment. Some commentators assumed that the startup might also take on potentially winnable cases about harassment in newsrooms purely to punish the media. This alarmed a number of journalists,[2] who, in the wake of the *Gawker* case, worried that "Thiel and others with deep pockets have an agenda to sponsor a systematic push-back against legitimate media outlets."[3]

The media carefully watch those who have harmed them, but the latter watch the media, too, because the media do harm as well. Interestingly, the very term 'flak', as Christian Fuchs explained, stems from German military jargon: the Germans used flak as an abbreviation for Fliegerabwehrkanone, anti-aircraft artillery (Fuchs, 2018, p. 80). Flak as intense anti-aircraft gunfire became a metaphor for intense criticism, barrage fire aimed at suppressing the enemy's offensive movement.

So, flak can also be seen as a defense – a defensive reaction of those vulnerable to airstrikes of the media (and who are willing to fight back). This 'defensive' connotation of the term does not particularly fit the debunking pathos of the Propaganda model. That is why some PM scholars have suggested using something like 'countermeasures to discipline the media' instead of 'flak', as recollected by Fuchs (Ibid, p. 80).

The Thiel-Hogan-*Gawker* case was a matter of private individuals being harmed by a popular online tabloid. In the area of politics, flak has become a powerful environmental force and sometimes a weapon purposely used by organizations.

***

---

[1] Sorkin, Andrew (May 25, 2016). "Peter Thiel, tech billionaire, reveals secret war with Gawker." *The New York Times.* https://www.nytimes.com/2016/05/26/business/dealbook/peter-thiel-tech-billionaire-reveals-secret-war-with-gawker.html

[2] Hunt, Joshua. (2016, September 1). "What Litigation Finance is really about." *The New Yorker.* https://www.newyorker.com/business/currency/what-litigation-finance-is-really-about

[3] Hayes, Dade. (2017, November 8). "Startup launches post-Harvey legal support hotline #MeToo tales." *Deadline.* https://deadline.com/2017/11/peter-thiel-startup-launches-legal-support-hotline-metoo-tales-1202204009/

Organized flak. The institutional flak machine has been long known in the form of different think tanks and institutions studying the media and the freedom of the press. Herman and Chomsky listed a number of such organizations at the time they introduced their model, such us the American Legal Foundation, the Capital Legal Foundation, the Media Institute, the Center for Media and Public Affairs, Accuracy in Media, Freedom House and others. These entities conducted media studies, provided judgment about media biases and sometimes filed libel suits to aid "media victims" or organize pressure on media outlets in some other way. Herman and Chomsky highlighted that these institutions had wealthy corporate sponsors and could be "regarded as institutions organized for the specific purpose of producing flak" (Herman & Chomsky, 2002 [1988], p. 27.)

However, technically speaking, a media environment had to have institutions studying the media and their impact and, technically speaking again, anything they produce is flak, i.e. some critical feedback that highlights flaws, biases and possible corruption in the media. Because of their power, which is socially sanctioned but privately executed, the media should be checked up on. Watchdogs must be watched over.

Interestingly, some modern flak machines not only research and expose the media's possible misdeeds but directly aim to retaliate against and harm unwelcome media outlets. They even set traps for such media outlets in order to get kompromat.

A story involving the *Washington Post* in 2017 can be counted as falling within a type of 'special operation' flak. A woman contacted reporters and accused Republican U.S. Senate candidate Roy Moore of sexual harassment when she was underage. It took the *Post* reporters two weeks to investigate the inconsistencies in the woman's account and reveal that she was affiliated with Project Veritas, "a group of conservative provocateurs that for a decade has run sting operations to embarrass left-leaning groups and seek evidence of political bias among top media organizations," as the *Washington Post* characterized it.[1] The *Post* nearly fell into the trap, but professional rigor guided them to safety. The provocation failed, and the reputation of *Washington Post* was saved.[2]

---

[1] Roig-Franzia, Manuel, and Ellison, Sarah. (2020, March 29). "A history of the Trump War on Media — the obsession not even coronavirus could stop." *The Washington Post.* https://www.washingtonpost.com/lifestyle/media/a-history-of-the-trump-war-on-media--the-obsession-not-even-coronavirus-could-stop/2020/03/28/71bb21d0-f433-11e9-8cf0-4cc99f74d127_story.html

[2] White, Jeremy. (2017, November 28). "Washington Post claims woman came to them with false Roy Moore abuse story in bizarre plot to discredit newspaper." *Independent.*

The case, however, exposed new prospects for contemporary flak. Now, not only can flak be reactive in regard to the media's failures, it can also be proactive and try to incite such failures.

***

The elites and power can produce flak, too. Trump's war on the media[1] was not limited to his attacks on journalists and media outlets; his invectives spearheaded backlash and sometimes real threats to mainstream media orgs from the alt-right.

Some of the initiatives of the right represented organized network activities. For example, a group of conservatives, including GOP consultant Arthur Schwartz, were reportedly setting out to find journalists' most deeply shameful social media posts, using algorithms and scanning posts back as far as the journalists' teenage or college years, according to the *Washington Post*[2]. They occasionally succeeded; after some inappropriate posts were found, several liberal media high-ranking employees resigned.

The group even tried to raise $2 million to investigate reporters and editors from "CNN, MSNBC, all broadcast networks, NY Times, Washington Post, BuzzFeed, Huffington Post, and all others that routinely incorporate bias and misinformation into their coverage. We will also track the reporters and editors of these organizations," as was stated in their pitch.[3]

***

Meta-flak: the pressure on advertisers. Advertisers remain a tool of flak as they were at the time when Herman and Chomsky introduced their model. The difference is that advertisers themselves are now afraid of flak. Not only might advertisers have their own ideological reasons for withdrawing contracts from media outlets, they also do not want to be associated with flak-sensitive content in the news media because of possible backlash on social media, a factor that did not exist at the time of the original Propaganda model.

https://www.independent.co.uk/news/world/americas/us-politics/roy-moore-washington-post-fake-story-woman-veritas-sting-plot-james-okeefe-alabama-a8079216.html

[1] Roig-Franzia, Manuel, and Ellison, Sarah. (2020, March 29). "A history of the Trump War on Media — the obsession not even coronavirus could stop." *The Washington Post*. https://www.washingtonpost.com/lifestyle/media/a-history-of-the-trump-war-on-media--the-obsession-not-even-coronavirus-could-stop/2020/03/28/71bb21d0-f433-11e9-8cf0-4cc99f74d127_story.html

[2] Ibid.

[3] Allen, Mike. (2019, September 3). "Trump allies raise money to target reporters." *Axious*. https://www.axios.com/2020-presidential-campaign-trump-allies-journalists-6733432f-b008-45d3-99c2-9dca7931faff.html

Thus, advertising flak in the mass media is now comprised of advertisers' own politically motivated decisions and a sort of meta-flak, as advertisers have become a conduit of the flak started not by them but by the public.

Within such meta-flak, advertisers withdraw their contracts not only from the mass media, but also from social media platforms. In fact, internet platforms suffer from advertising meta-flak even more than the mass media, simply because advertising, in general, has relocated to internet platforms.

In 2020, civic activists called on advertisers to boycott Facebook because Facebook did nothing, in their opinion, to clear out hate speech from users' newsfeeds. By July 2020,

> ...800 companies worldwide have pulled millions of dollars in advertising from the social network, with brands from Coca-Cola to Ford to global conglomerate Unilever demanding that Facebook monitor hate speech more aggressively.[1]

Despite the unprecedented scale of the boycott, Facebook denied the allegation and refused to change its policy[2], which was based on minimal interference in what the users express on the platform, except for obviously extremist and illegal content. Unlike Twitter, which decided to take the responsibility of judging and marking users' content,[3] Facebook insisted on being just a platform, not an editorial entity.

Watching the massive demand to boycott channels that do not comply with political or ethical agendas, which can impact even such giants as YouTube (the boycott of 2017) and Facebook, advertisers, of course, are cautious regarding advertising in the mass media, too. Polarization in the media can split advertisers in a way similar to how the poles of a magnet organize iron filings into two circles. For example, a number of advertisers pulled their commercials from Laura Ingraham's show on *Fox News,* despite its high ratings, after she mocked, as the media put it, "shooting survivor and activist David Hogg for being rejected by a handful of colleges."[4] In a

---

[1] Scola, Nancy. (2020, July 3). "Inside the ad boycott that has Facebook on the defensive." *Politico.* https://www.politico.com/news/magazine/2020/07/03/activists-advertising-boycott-facebook-348528

[2] Rushe, Dominic. (2020, July 2). "Mark Zuckerberg: advertisers' boycott of Facebook will end 'soon enough'." *The Guardian.* https://www.theguardian.com/technology/2020/jul/02/mark-zuckerberg-advertisers-boycott-facebook-back-soon-enough

[3] *The Verge.* (2020, June 18). "Trump vs. Twitter: The president takes on social media moderation." *The Verge.* https://www.theverge.com/21275532/trump-twitter-social-media-tweets

politicized environment, flak and the fear of flak become more powerful factors than ratings and outreach.

***

Grassroots flak. The power dynamics in meaning production are oftentimes seen through a Marxist lens, with the economic elites in control of agenda-setting, as was the case in the 1990s, the last decade of the classical capitalist institutionality. The internet and social media have changed the distribution of power in meaning production. New media platforms have empowered those previously voiceless, "the people formerly known as the audience" (Rosen[1]). In their turn, the news media became dependent on reader revenue. These two factors – the voicing of the formerly voiceless and the media's growing financial dependence on them – has resulted in a new way of disciplining the news media, the grassroots flak.

Arithmetically, the cancellation of 1000 subscriptions is both less probable and less painful for a media outlet than the withdrawal of 2 or 3 ad contracts. Massive subscription cancellation requires a truly significant wave of readers' withdrawal to financially match the loss of a few advertisers. In this instance, flak should seemingly have lost its effectiveness in the new business environment dominated by reader revenue.

However, thanks to the technological viral capacity of social media, flak has acquired significant additional influence in this new environment. The internet emancipated authorship, including that of flak. Flak is no longer the prerogative of the elites having access to opinion-making. Everyone has this access. Additionally, the internet and specifically social media have empowered flak with the reach and speed of viral distribution. In the past, no elite possessed the power of flak now held by the Twitter activist core.

***

Social media created an environment filled with people contributing their time, efforts and expertise for finding, editing and distributing content for the sake of self-actualization. These contributions cumulate into a collective-intelligence organism I call the Viral Editor (Miroshnichenko, 2014). Self-actualization depends on the response from others. Therefore, content shared within the Viral Editor has to trigger others' responses. In this environment of instantaneous communication, an unprecedented

---

[4] Schwartz, Jason. (2018, October 16). "Big advertisers still shunning Ingraham's Fox News show months after boycotts." *Politico.* https://www.politico.com/story/2018/10/16/ingraham-fox-news-advertising-902466

[1] Rosen, Jay. (2006, June 27). "The people formerly known as the audience." *PressThink.* http://archive.pressthink.org/2006/06/27/ppl_frmr.html

amount of free time is devoted to searching for something triggering: something remarkable, exciting, funny, terrifying, outrageous, insulting, etc.

As people are more sensitive to risks than to opportunities, negative information is generally more valuable. Allied to the thirst for response and hence the virality pursued on social media, the negativity bias of info consumption creates an environment that inevitably incentivizes the search for and sharing of outrageous and insulting content.

This environment has even spawned a new phenomenon: people who search for triggering content in order to share their outrage for better socialization have gradually become people looking to be insulted. Lolcats or travel photos are increasingly ceding their former suitability for response-triggering to expressing outrage. Being insulted and outraged is turning into social capital, and this is exclusively an effect of social media and their mechanisms of response triggering and harvesting.

If a sufficient amount of free time and passion is invested, especially with the help of algorithms, something negative can be found about everyone and everything: with an unlimited number of iterations, the possible becomes inevitable (Miroshnichenko 2014). The longer this goes on, the more it happens: as people and institutions leave more digital footprints, some of their footprints are bound to appear outrageous. As doctors joke, there are no healthy people – there are only incomplete diagnoses.

With limitless attempts, everything can and will be found; and if the Viral Editor deems a negative piece of information interesting (or if it is persuaded to deem it so), it will do what is needed to provide bad publicity, shaming and oftentimes even threats. The outrage regarding improper thoughts or opinions provides fuel that keeps the entire system running. In this case, the Viral Editor is the crowdsourced inquisitor of cancel culture. It merely remains for a potential target to be caught out by a bit of bad luck and somehow get on the radar of this new social-media flak machine.

***

Journalists and the media are among the best targets for this constant search for insulting and inappropriate content, principally because they are still one of the main sources of political discourse as well as pressing and polarizing issues. The media's publications are in the high-risk zone. Social media create ideal conditions for grassroots flak to thrive. No article or column that fails the purity test will go unnoticed by the Twitter progressives' or conservatives' politburo. Watchdogs have ended up being watched by a bigger and nastier collective Big Brother.

Multiplied by the tendency toward polarization in both old and social media and also by an incredible amount of free time spared for searching for triggering content, the new flak machine has achieved power that exceeds its old, advertising era's embodiment. Even though a per-unit price of new flak (the cost of one repelled reader) is much smaller than a per-unit price of old flak (the cost of one repelled advertiser), the power of flak has increased tenfold and will increase further as it impacts the symbolic and social capital of journalists and the media, which is comprised of the attitudes of others. Subsequently, this can be converted into career or monetary losses, the fear of which is the acting power of the grassroots flak.

***

Alongside that flak improvement, a new factor of flak emerged related to the new economic setting. In the ad-driven media system, flak was initiated by the elites, but the value of flak was formed separately by advertising (contract withdrawal) or by the cost of defense in court or the cost of reputational repair. In the reader-driven media system, the source of flak and the cost of flak are embedded in the same group – the donating audience. This flak can act directly and immediately; for example, when readers cancel subscription if they decide that a media outlet regularly fail to validate news in an expected manner, or if the cause of donation is not worthy or maintained improperly.

This is how Jay Rosen characterized this newly emerged relationship between the audience and the *New York Times*:

> The readers of the New York Times have more power now. <...> The Times depends on its readers' support more than it ever has. <...> One of the joys of having a subscription to the Times is threatening to cancel it. Which is simply to say that a Times loyalist is also a critic. It has always been that way — the Times gets a lot of criticism — but now the situation is growing more tense and anxious.[1]

This is not to say that this is the reader's money that talks. Flak often comes from those who are not even subscribers. Perhaps, the fear of readers being repelled by content that does not comply with their expectations impacts agenda-setting even more than actual subscription cancellation (which, by the way, at a statistically significant scale, rarely follows the outrage expressed by readers). It is the media's self-accepted dependence on

---

[1] Rosen, Jay. (2018, October 21). "Next time you wonder why New York Times people get so defensive, read this." *PressThink*. https://pressthink.org/2018/10/next-time-you-wonder-why-new-york-times-people-get-so-defensive-read-this/

the real and imaginary audience that made the media so unusually susceptible to the criticism of the public. The power of this new flak rests on the news media's own fear of the audience.

In terms of growing pressure on the media, donation-based business model is the path to the dark side. Donations lead to expectations, expectations lead to demands, demands lead to flak, flak leads to suffering.

***

On January 17, 2018, the *New York Times* published the letters of Trump supporters on its opinion page. Introducing the brave initiative, *NYT* wrote that,

> The Times editorial board has been sharply critical of the Trump presidency, on ground of policy and personal conduct. Not all readers have been persuaded. In the spirit of open debate, and in hopes of helping readers who agree with us better understand the views of those who don't, we wanted to let Mr. Trump's supporters make their best case for him as the first year of his presidency approaches its close.[1]

The fact that the leading American newspapers gave a pulpit to the president's supporters was met with outcry from its audience. Readers and the *Twitterati*, as *NYT* executive editor Dean Baquet called, obviously, a liberal faction of Twitter, were outraged. "The New York Times is in bed with Donald Trump!" sarcastically summed up the reaction Jim Warren from *Poynter*.[2] The *New York Times* was forced to defend its decision. Editorial page editor James Bennet took responsibility and said, "It's my fault".

When readers buy content for themselves, they can be judgy; the public is always judgy. But everyone understands that subscribers cannot impose their requirements upon concrete editorial decisions. Consumers can be unsatisfied, but they cannot dictate what the news media cover and how they cover it. Transactional news retail more or less protected newsroom autonomy from the audience's encroachment upon content control. But when the readers' motives are not to get news but to join a cause, the readers become the patrons. And the readers embrace this – they feel that they should have a say and can impose their will regarding the coverage of concrete topics. The audience, indeed, has accepted the role of "normative reference organization" instead of advertisers.

---

[1] *The New York Times*. (2018. January 17). "Vision, Chutzpah and Some Testosterone". https://www.nytimes.com/2018/01/17/opinion/trump-voters-supporters.html

[2] Warren, Jim. (2018, January 18). "Giving his backers a high-profile platform." *Poynter. Morning Media Wire.* https://bit.ly/35Aaei4

***

The discontent of readers regarding the content of the media outlet is now not expressed via consumerist behavior such as the refusal to consume a disliked product, but rather via the ideological diktat of readers' collective patronage over the media. The grassroots flak is articulated and cumulated by the passionate Twitterati, whose platform power now exceeds that of individual journalists, entire media organizations and the traditional elites. If, in the past, the media had to comply with the worldview of the ruling elites, now not just the media but the ruling elites themselves must behave with an eye to the Twitterati.

Grassroots flak has become the most powerful form of flak. The power of grassroots flak was handed to it by the news media themselves. They need to seek the audience's support amid the vanishing sustainability of the traditional business models and end up seeking the audience's approval, which they never receive. Flak does not work through approval.

***

In October 2018, in analyzing readers' power over the news media, Jay Rosen distinguished the *New York Times* from the *Washington Post*, implying that the *Times* tried to withstand the pressure of the audience. The pressure came from both political sides. Rosen quoted the *NYT*'s publisher, Arthur G. Sulzberger, who said that,

> We won't be baited into becoming 'the opposition.' And we won't be applauded into becoming 'the opposition.'[1]

As Rosen clarified, "By 'baited' he clearly meant the taunts of people like Steve Bannon and President Trump. By 'applauded' he meant, I think, the pressure coming from Times loyalists."

People who paid for *Times*' journalism were readers, not advertisers. And they were readers from a certain social stratum. As Rosen characterized the most demanding *NYT* readers,

> They want the Times to be tougher on his <Trump> supporters and more relentless in calling out his lies. They want Times journalists to see what they see — an assault on democratic institutions, the corruption of the American Republic — and to act accordingly.[2]

---

[1] Rosen, Jay. (2018, October 21). "Next time you wonder why New York Times people get so defensive, read this." *PressThink*. https://pressthink.org/2018/10/next-time-you-wonder-why-new-york-times-people-get-so-defensive-read-this/

[2] Ibid.

As of 2018, the *New York Times* had resisted. Rosen wrote:

> But these people are perceived as a threat by the Times newsroom. The fear is that they want to turn the Times into an opposition newspaper. This is not how the Times sees itself. The fear is that they want the Times to help save American democracy. This too is not how the Times sees itself.[1]

Rosen compared the stances of *NYT* and the *Washington Post*, bringing up the *WashPost*'s motto "Democracy Dies in Darkness". He quoted Dean Baquet, executive editor of the *Times*, who once made fun of the *WashPost* motto, saying that it "sounds like the next Batman movie."[2]

The *New York Times* tried to remain the national 'paper of record' and represent a spectrum of opinion, at least in op-ed. In a November 2019 interview with *BBC*[3], Dean Baquet said:

> I make it very clear when I hire, I make it very clear when I talk to the staff, I've said it repeatedly, that we are not supposed to be the leaders of the resistance to Donald Trump. That is an untenable, non-journalistic, immoral position for The New York Times."[4]

But the most demanding part of the readership thought differently. In 2018, op-ed editor James Bennet managed to defend his decision to publish the letters of Trump's supporters. In 2020, he was forced to resign[5] after picking the wrong columnist, Republican senator Tom Cotton, who said to "send in the troops" in a column on the op-ed page during the protests against police brutality and racism.

Interestingly, the publication of an opinion from a Taliban leader[6] just three months before (February 2020) on the same op-ed page did not cause

---

[1] Ibid.

[2] Ibid.

[3] Baquet, Dean. (2019, November 13). "New York Times: 'We're not supposed to be leaders of the resistance to Donald Trump'." *BBC*. https://www.bbc.co.uk/programmes/p07tvmjn

[4] As quoted in: Jones, Tom. (2020, June 8). "The controversy at The New York Times is over more than just one op-ed. The future of the Times could be at stake." Poynter. https://www.poynter.org/newsletters/2020/the-controversy-at-the-new-york-times-is-over-more-than-just-one-op-ed-the-future-of-the-times-could-be-at-stake/

[5] Darcy, Oliver. (2020, June 7). "James Bennet resigns from New York Times after Cotton op-ed backlash." *CNN*. https://www.cnn.com/2020/06/07/media/james-bennet-new-york-times-resigns/index.html

[6] Haqqani, Sirajuddin. (2020, February 20). "What we, the Taliban, want." *The New York Times*. https://www.nytimes.com/2020/02/20/opinion/taliban-afghanistan-war-haqqani.html. The byline contained clarification: "Mr. Haqqani is the deputy leader of the Taliban."

such a huge backlash as the publication of an opinion from a sitting US senator, despite the fact that the columnist from the Taliban, as CNN wrote, was acknowledged as a "specially designated global terrorist" by the FBI, which was offering $5 million for information leading directly to his arrest.[1] Justifying the op-ed appearance of an author from the Taliban, the *NYT*'s spokesperson told *CNN* that,

> ...our mission at Times Opinion is to tackle big ideas from a range of newsworthy viewpoints. We've actively solicited voices from all sides of the Afghanistan conflict...[2]

What happened to James Bennet is logical: in a polarized environment, it is possible for the American 'paper of record' to cover all sides of the Afghanistan conflict, but not the American one.

Amid Bennet's resignation, some media critics tried to carefully remind Baquet about "we are not the resistance", but polarization in the media has shifted much further, to the degree that the very concept of 'all sides' has become effectively banned by flak. "The spirit of open debate" and "better understanding of those who disagree" that *NYT* tried to promote as far back as in 2018 could not withstand flak in 2020.

***

Soon after James Bennet, another staff editor and *NYT* op-ed writer, Bari Weiss, resigned too, finally having had enough of the atmosphere and accusing some colleagues of bullying her in the company Slack channels and on Twitter for having different views. In her resignation letter, she recollected that the *Times* hired her and some other authors after the paper admitted its failure to anticipate the outcome of the 2016 election, which meant *NYT* "didn't have a firm grasp of the country it covers". The idea was to hear the voices of the centrists and conservatives on the opinion page and learn to understand "other Americans".

Epistemologically, this new approach might look sound. In the understanding of Trumpism, it was hard to find something more useless than the conventional and publicly approved take on Trump. Nobody knew which nonconventional understanding of Trumpism would work, but what

---

[1] Bergen, Peter. (2020, February 21). "What the New York Times didn't tell readers about its Taliban op-ed is shocking." *CNN*. https://www.cnn.com/2020/02/21/opinions/new-york-times-taliban-op-ed-haqqani-bergen/index.html

[2] Ibid.

was known exactly was that the mainstream view did not work at all. So, any alternative was worth a shot.

However, the lesson has not been learned, according to Weiss. She wrote:

> Instead, a new consensus has emerged in the press, but perhaps especially at this paper: that truth isn't a process of collective discovery, but an orthodoxy already known to an enlightened few whose job is to inform everyone else.[1]

"Twitter is not on the masthead of the New York Times," she concluded. "But Twitter has become its ultimate editor."[2]

NYT's publisher Sulzberger said in 2018 that the paper would be neither "baited" nor "applauded into becoming 'the opposition,'"[3] meaning, most likely, baited by Trumpists and applauded by the loyal audience. But it nevertheless started happening, though in a slightly different way – the paper was pushed by the audience and without much applause. Without any allocative control, which would be the intermediary of advertisers' influence in the past, the grassroots flak started directly impacting the newsroom's operational control over topics' and authors' selection.

Considering the significance of the *New York Times*, it can be said that the career cases of its opinion editors, whatever individual specificities they had, set an example for the industry, which is another effect of flak. At a systemic level, the chilling effect of these cases will narrow the spectrum of voices in the media, as everyone saw what might happen to them individually when flak takes over journalism.

***

The American mainstream media, as the media faction most rapidly moving toward the *donating-for-the-cause* business model of journalism, set a pattern of what flak now looks like in the new media environment. They received the utmost politicized flak from all possible angles.

- They were criticized by the right for liberal bias.

---

[1] Weiss, Bari. (2020, July 14). Resignation Letter. *Bari Weiss blog.* https://www.bariweiss.com/resignation-letter

[2] Ibid.

[3] Rosen, Jay. (2018, October 21). "Next time you wonder why New York Times people get so defensive, read this." PressThink. https://pressthink.org/2018/10/next-time-you-wonder-why-new-york-times-people-get-so-defensive-read-this/.

- They were attacked by Trump for being the 'fake news media' and the 'enemy of the people'.

- They were criticized by its core liberal audience and the Twitter politburo for serving Trump and being not ardent enough to the cause.

- Finally, the mainstream media were criticized from the classical left for serving capitalism and neoliberalism.

In the same way as the right's resentment is nostalgic of the great America of the past, the left's resentment longs for the great class struggle of the past.

As Pedro-Carañana et al. introduced this line of criticism, "The liberal media are ... attentive to issues of gender and racial equality, but inattentive to representing the interests of the working class" (Pedro-Carañana, Broudy, and Klaehn, 2018, p. 12). They referred to the idea of Nancy Fraser, who stated that the liberal media have adopted the position of 'progressive neoliberalism', "the late alliance of multiculturalist and pro-diversity social justice movements with the corporate forces of cognitive capitalism" (Ibid, p. 12).

As Nancy Fraser herself explained her criticism of new elites,

> In its U.S. form, progressive neoliberalism is an alliance of mainstream currents of new social movements (feminism, anti-racism, multiculturalism, and LGBTQ rights), on the one side, and high-end "symbolic" and service-based business sectors (Wall Street, Silicon Valley, and Hollywood), on the other. In this alliance, progressive forces are effectively joined with the forces of cognitive capitalism, especially financialization.[1]

Fraser held that that 'progressive neoliberalism' was ratified with Bill Clinton's election in 1992, continued by Barack Obama, and impersonated by Hillary Clinton in 2016. Having taken power, 'progressive neoliberalism' degraded the living conditions of working people, in whose eyes "feminists and Wall Street were birds of a feather, perfectly united in the person of Hillary Clinton."[2] This all contributed to the electoral potential for Trump, as she implied.

---

[1] Fraser, Nancy. (2017, January 2). "The end of progressive neoliberalism." *Dissent Magazine.* https://www.dissentmagazine.org/online_articles/progressive-neoliberalism-reactionary-populism-nancy-fraser

[2] Ibid.

The old left fought for the rights of the majority; the progressives switched to the minorities. The majority struck back in a way that neither liked, but the old left can now say "I told you so!"

The traditional left's media criticism, blaming vocal minorities for stealing and diverting the social justice agenda from the class struggle of the broader working masses, does not create impactful flak by itself. But it still represents a powerful intellectual tradition that is responsible for influential concepts and, most importantly, for the very language of media criticism. For example, the invective 'corporate media' produced by the old left back in the 1980–1990s is widely used by the Twitterati's progressives, despite the fact that the conditions that created this concept have ceased to exist and the former 'corporate media' have rather incorporated the progressives and are now as susceptible to their grassroots flak as to the corporate boards' discontent.

***

The public response to the content of the media defines whether the donating audience will continue to donate. The media funded under the motives of donation aim at having an impact. The impact is hard to measure. Whether it is the cause of democracy or saving the polar bears, how can whether the cause succeeds be measured? Basically, success never happens. Moreover, the media themselves are disinterested in this actually happening. If the cause succeeds and is resolved, they will lose their raison d'être for asking for donations. Therefore, they must eternally push the issue as the most pressing one.

Under these business circumstances, a positive resolution of issues pushed by the media is either not achievable or not desirable. In a technical sense, the cause to which the media invite to join is always a fake, as it is always a process, not a result, and a process through which the media profit.

The cause of democracy is the best candidate for this role. As democracy is a process, not a result, and as the media are affiliated with democracy historically, culturally and institutionally, switching from ad revenue to donation revenue will inevitably make the media politically involved and politicized. In the American mainstream media, democracy will surely continue to be threatened even after Trump is gone.

Here is where the role of flak appears. Flak is the servomechanism of allocative control, sometimes achieving the efficiency of operational control (the resignation of an editor because of an improper publication). As a servomechanism, flak 'helps' to maintain the triggering motive, which in turn keeps the audience alert and alive. Flak is the best indicator of whether the medium aligns with the expectations of the donating audience.

The price is the loss of newsroom autonomy. This pressure on autonomy cannot be compared to the relatively benign pressure the media endured under the advertising model of revenue.

***

Thus, what has changed since the Propaganda model appeared is:

1) the abilities to produce flak; they belong not only to the elites now, and

2) the working force of flak; now, it is not only costly defense and ad withdrawal but also, and increasingly so, the fear of subscription cancelation and career 'cancelation' – the pressure the donating audience puts on media professionals.

Flak, the negative and purposely suppressive feedback to the media's content, is always vocal and manifestative. Since it is now reinforced by social media watching the news media, with tons of human-hours contributed, criticisms always point out exactly which author, article or even phrasing deserves condemnation. This is why flak has much more impact as a content filter in the reader-driven media than in the ad-driven media.

Ideology of threat

Herman and Chomsky noticed that the mainstream media always aligned with the ideology of anti-communism in covering foreign conflicts, elections, and political crises. In reviewing the performance of their model 20 years after its introduction, they stated that, "Anti-communism was a staple that provided content, narratives, heroes and villains" (in: Mullen, 2009, p. 14).

However, at the pinnacle of the Cold War, the propaganda filter that Herman and Chomsky described as anti-communism was most likely based more on the Red Scare, the nuclear fear, than on the populace's fear of communist ideology.

When the Soviet Union ceased to exist, the communist ideology supposedly disproved itself, in the capitalist elites' opinion. But more important is the fact that the enemy threatening with the nuclear bomb vanished. Either way, as Herman and Chomsky admitted themselves,

> The force of anti-communist ideology has possibly weakened with the collapse of the Soviet Union and the virtual disappearance of socialist

movements across the globe, but this is easily offset by the greater ideological force of the belief in the "miracle of the market" (Reagan). The triumph of capitalism and the increasing power of those with an interest in privatization and market rule have strengthened the grip of market ideology, at least among the elite, so that regardless of evidence, markets are assumed to be benevolent ... (Herman & Chomsky, 2002 [1988], p. xvii.)

While the triumphal fanfares claiming the superiority of capitalism over communism surely had to start blowing after the victory in the Cold War, they would hardly be able to replace the anti-Soviet nuclear fear in the Propaganda model. The mobilizing and cohering power of positive stimuli is always weaker than that of negative stimuli.

Perhaps the ideological filter of the PM related not so much to ideologically meaningful content (anti-communism), but rather to the capacity of psychological mobilization, which is performed best of all by the image of the enemy.

Mobilization by the image of the enemy is 'ideologically agnostic': any enemy mobilizes, regardless of their ideological stances. The image of the enemy acts at the deepest level of collective biological survival. All the ideological coloring of the enemy is a propagandist trick: ideologies just transfer the biological fear of 'stranger danger' to the social level, trying to turn biological survival mobilization into social loyalty.

The core cohering force that led the mainstream media to speak jointly and align with the interests of the ruling elites was the fear of the dangerous and powerful enemy, not anti-communist faith. The anti-communism of the media in the 1970–80s can be considered just a local case of the fear of the enemy. When *this* enemy was gone, the ideological filter lost its power of cohering the media and mobilizing the audience.

***

The idea of mobilization through an enemy image was on the radars of PM scholars, too, among other attempts to re-evaluate the ideological filter.

In a 2009 interview with Andrew Mullen, after twenty years of the PM application, Herman and Chomsky admitted that,

> Since 1989, this staple has morphed into an array of substitutes. But the structural role that anti-communism and its successors have played, namely, the provision of an Enemy or the Face of Evil, remains as relevant as ever. <...> The 'war on terror' has provided a useful substitute for the Soviet Menace. (Mullen, 2009, p. 15.)

The search for a proper ideological filter formulation lasted for so long because there was not a satisfying enemy equal to the Soviet Menace. For twenty-five years (1991–2016), the Propaganda model had been incomplete.

Donald Trump finally solved the problem. He happened to be terrifying enough to match the former mobilizing power of the Soviet Menace. The Russians, by the way, also happened to be of use, evoking the good-old Cold War propaganda tradition with its well-elaborated repertoire.

**

The audience of the advertising-based media system was not politically split; at least not as significantly as it is today. The funding model played against political division. Advertising required a structuring of the audience according consumer-demographic profiling but incentivized political homogeneity, as this homogeneity was required in order to increase the media outreach. Therefore, it was enough to have one ideological threat for all. The anti-communist ideology filter may have been received with a different degree of zeal in different media outlets, but it was accepted, basically, unanimously and jointly.

The audience of the reader-driven media is sharply split ideologically and cannot jointly react to the same ideological threat. One threat does not fit all anymore. In a society with such a media system, the audience is pushed to congregate around the political poles of, roughly, the left and the right, or the progressive and the conservative. Their media, turned by reader funding into crowdfunded propaganda machines, should obviously exploit different threats to energize their audiences for better donations to the cause.

However, these different threats must reflect a binary split value system, where the opposites play the role of mobilizing enemies for each other. For a donscription-driven media system, the Cold War ceased to be an external mobilizing factor. The fear of enemy has to come inside the national media system for the better soliciting of readers' contribution on each side of the spectrum: the Cold War must become a Cold Civil War. Each side must fear what the other side sees as protection from the encroaching of the opposing side.

This setting must display itself in any reader-driven media market. In the US media market, the need for an ideology of threat was perfectly represented by the figure of Donald Trump. For conservatives, Donald Trump became a symbol of resistance against liberal and migrant threats to "Great America". For progressives, Trump himself became a threat to democracy. In a sense, Trump united American partisanship by increasing the charge and, therefore, interdependence of the opposite poles.

The process has been beneficial for politics and the mainstream media but extremely destructive for society. The ideology of threat as a filter of the Propaganda model leads, among other things, to the dehumanizing of the enemy. Being brought inside the national media system, it decreases the opportunities for civil dialogue, as the polarized media of opposite political camps must dehumanize each other's audiences. The binarity of threat, which is needed for the media system based on subscription soliciting as donation, makes the media competing 'hate-for-profit' machines.[1] Fear-mongering and enemy dehumanizing become systemic factors embedded in the business model.

For the American liberal media, the overlapping of threat ideology and business dependence on the very same threat created a schizophrenic exaltation. They wanted Trump out ideologically but needed him to stay economically. This exaltation deprived them of the choice to not cover Trump, despite many calls to do so.

The right-leaning media were most likely interested in Trump both politically and economically. Their authenticity stayed intact in this regard.

After Trump, the reader-driven media based on soliciting subscription as donation will need to find an equivalent binary threat to preserve the mobilizing power of the political cause they undertake to promote.

Sourcing: opinions' supply

According to Herman and Chomsky, "The mass media are drawn into a symbiotic relationship with powerful sources of information by economic necessity and reciprocity of interest" (Herman & Chomsky, 2002 [1988], p. 18).

The media cannot afford to have correspondents everywhere where something might happen. They need to rely on other networks through which important information circulates – the bureaucratic networks of government and corporations. Thus, the information supplied by the bureaucracies has economic value: it would cost the media a lot to obtain equivalent information, particularly from overseas, on their own.

---

[1] The metaphor was introduced by senator Democrat Elizabeth Warren to label *Fox News*. – Epstein, Jennifer. (2019, May 14). "Elizabeth Warren turns Down Fox News, slamming 'hate-for-profit machine'." *Bloomberg*. https://www.bloomberg.com/news/articles/2019-05-14/warren-turns-down-fox-news-slamming-hate-for-profit-machine

Besides, governmental and corporate sources are usually seen as recognizable and credible sources of information in their respective areas. If not from them, then from where would society have obtained vital information about the state and business affairs? Bureaucracies not only provide, they also produce information of high importance. That is why they were the primary and often exclusive sources of crucial information.

The recognizability of the source, credibility, expected trustworthiness and originality of information made the use of 'official' information a necessity for journalism not least because the media declared pursuing 'objectivity' and 'factuality' as use-value of their product.

***

Herman and Chomsky highlighted a scale on which the government and corporate bureaucracies produced public information, often specifically aimed at the media. By 1988, the Pentagon had the public-information service with many thousands of employees. The U.S. Air Force alone revealed that its public-information outreach included the following:

- 140 newspapers, 690,000 copies per week
- Airman magazine, monthly circulation 125,000
- 34 radio and 17 TV stations, primarily overseas
- 45,000 headquarters and unit news releases
- 615,000 hometown news releases
- 6,600 interviews with news media
- 3,200 news conferences
- 500 news media orientation flights
- 50 meetings with editorial boards
- 11,000 speeches. (Herman & Chomsky, 2002 [1988], p. 20.)

Herman and Chomsky emphasized that, "Only the corporate sector has the resources to produce public information and propaganda on the scale of the Pentagon and other government bodies" (Ibid., 21).

This governmental and corporate information mega-machine unavoidably became an important link in the supply chain of media production. Herman and Chomsky wrote that,

> In effect, the large bureaucracies of the powerful subsidize the mass media, and gain special access by their contribution to reducing the media's costs of acquiring the raw materials of, and producing, news. The large entities that provide this subsidy become "routine" news sources and have privileged access to the gates. Non-routine sources must struggle for access, and may be

ignored by the arbitrary decision of the gatekeepers. (Herman & Chomsky, 2002 [1988], p. 22.)

As a result, the media became affiliated with and dependent on the government and corporate sources and narratives they produced. If journalists bite the hand that feeds, they can be punished with a subsequent refusal of access, and their competitors will be given an advantage. As Herman and Chomsky stated,

> Because of their services, continuous contact on the beat, and mutual dependency, the powerful can use personal relationships, threats, and rewards to further influence and coerce the media. It is very difficult to call authorities on whom one depends for daily news liars, even if they tell whoppers. Critical sources may be avoided not only *because* of their lesser *availability* and higher cost of *establishing* credibility, but also because the primary sources may be offended and may even threaten the media using them. (Herman & Chomsky, 2002 [1988], p. 22.)

Press-releases release the media from the expense of obtaining this info, but at the cost of following the versions presented in press-releases. This service has the political price of acquiring the pre-adjusted narrative and the economic value of the bribe. The controlled sourcing is a structural factor that creates "economic necessity and reciprocity of interest" and makes the media dependent on governmental and corporate information.

***

Herman and Chomsky's view of the media and sources symbiosis was sometimes criticized, for example, for not taking newsroom autonomy into account. It is a matter of professional honor for many journalists not to rely solely on official sources and rather treat them critically. However, the contribution of the Herman-Chomsky Propaganda model in the understanding of source-media symbiosis is unassailable. The classical political economy of the media had mostly focused on economically manifested factors of power's influence on the media, such as ownership or advertising. To this, Herman and Chomsky added sourcing as an impactful environmental factor. They unveiled its systemic nature and political-economic mechanism.

Since Herman and Chomsky introduced their model, two important tectonic shifts have occurred in the media and have impacted the nature and structure of sourcing. First, the media switched from ad revenue to reader revenue. Second, the media swayed from journalism of fact toward opinion journalism. These shifts predefined three major changes in sourcing.

1) Decline of bureaucratic sourcing. The importance of 'raw materials' and bureaucracies as sources has decreased, while the importance of content curation and expertise has increased.

2) Rise of expert sourcing. The structure of the body of experts in the media has changed. In addition to experts in economics, politics, military, security, and foreign affairs, more academics in liberal studies and experts with a background in activism have joined the media as opinions have become required more than facts.

3) Polarization of sourcing. The growing polarization in the media, caused by the focus on reader revenue, has powered the formation of opposing expert filter bubbles, thus furthering polarization.

***

Decline of bureaucratic sourcing. When society becomes more polarized, the bureaucracy loses the status of objective and unbiased primary source. With higher polarization, the partisan attitude becomes all-pervading and extends to the bureaucracy. As the media participate in politicization and polarization, they express the same politically loaded criticism – or support, depending on their stances – towards the ruling party and their policies carried out by the bureaucratic apparatus.

The most obvious example: the attitude of the American liberal media toward Trump extended to Trump's administration. It was not the case that bureaucratic sources of the White House or the rest of Trump's key administrative institutions were considered as authoritative or beyond question for the media, as was implied in Herman and Chomsky's *Manufacturing Consent*. It was quite the opposite, as no matter what view was expressed by a Trump appointee, it would most likely be received critically. For the liberal media, this made sense: if an official was an appointee of Trump, it was already an indicative characteristic. But this reasonably critical attitude went beyond the personal and extended to institutions in general.

In a polarized society, the bureaucracy is most likely seen as impacted by partisanship. It can be discussed, if this is so, but the point is that the bureaucracy has ceased to be a source that Herman and Chomsky considered as the primary one in forming media narratives and agendas.

Another factor that weakened the sourcing role of the bureaucracy is the internet. It undermined the exclusivity of the bureaucracies over information from distant areas or closed structures. For example, in the time of Chomsky's criticism of the US military policy, almost the only way journalists could get information about overseas military operations was to collaborate with the military. Now, any journalist can reach out to locals, bypass official filters and get alternative information. Moreover, alternative information from locals will reach journalists on its own. The same is true for closed and secret structures: the internet has created an environment that facilitates leaks bypassing official filters. Just as any monopoly of old institutions over information has been destroyed by the emancipation of authorship, the same has happened to the monopoly of the bureaucracy over information exclusivity.

Herman and Chomsky thought that government and corporate bureaucracies subsidized the media by supplying news, as it was rather expensive to have correspondents everywhere. And they were right. But now it costs almost nothing to get evidence from wherever you need it using the internet and social media. As a result, the bureaucracies now subsidize spam.

Of course, the huge and ever-growing amount of content produced by governments and corporations can impact and frame the worldview of some media outlets or journalists, particularly those that are lazy or biased. But in general, this content is, for the media, either an object of criticism or white noise, not a source.

Thus, the bureaucracy, be it governmental or corporate, is not a highly valued primary source for the media anymore because all its value factors have diminished or are gone:

1) The bureaucracy is not seen as objective because of polarization.

2) The bureaucracy has lost exclusivity because it can be easily bypassed.

3) The bureaucracy does not subsidize newsgathering because newsgathering costs almost nothing in the era of the internet.

***

The divorce of the media from the bureaucracy as a news source has, however, a flip side for the media. The issue is that the bureaucracy also does not need the media as much as it used to. The internet emancipated authorship for everyone, including those in power. They can communicate with the public directly. They have all the technological means to be the media themselves.

This tendency was first detected in the US in the early 2010s. The media jealously pointed out that the White House had created its own "Obama's media machine, state run media 2.0".[1] Indeed, as the 2012 re-election

---

[1] Dwyer, Devin. (2011, 14 February). "Obama's media machine: state run media 2.0?" *ABC News.* https://abcnews.go.com/Politics/president-obama-white-house-media-operation-state-run/story?id=12913319

campaign was approaching, the White House started using all media formats, old and new, to cover the president. The media complained that the White House had replaced them with its own media capacity. As *ABC News* reported,

> Over the past few months, as White House cameras have been granted free reign behind the scenes, officials have blocked broadcast news outlets from events traditionally open to coverage and limited opportunities to publicly question the president himself.[1]

At the time, the White House had 1.9 million followers on Twitter, 900,000 fans on Facebook and an average of 250,000 visits to its YouTube channel per month. Its website had roughly 1.1 million unique monthly visitors in January 2011. By comparison, *ABC News* had 1.2 million followers on Twitter, 150,000 fans on Facebook, and averaged 21.7 million unique visitors per month, reported *ABC News*.[2]

The practice continued after Obama was re-elected. As journalists were accustomed to being gatekeepers and democracy watchdogs, they were not happy with the White House becoming a more successful medium in covering the president. In 2013, *CBS* wrote:

> It's all courtesy of the Obama image machine, serving up a stream of words, images and videos that invariably cast the president as commanding, compassionate and on the ball. In this world, Obama's family is always photogenic, first dog Bo is always well-behaved and the vegetables in the South Lawn kitchen garden always seem succulent.[3]

Having direct access to such a world-ranking celebrity as the president of the USA, his own media machine produced high-quality and highly demanded content that simply beat competitors covering the president in the media. Pictures, videos, jokes and all kinds of media products showing the president through the loving eyes and minds of his subordinates instantly reached the public and became popular.

"Barack Obama is the coolest president ever. Period," stated *The Indian Express* in 2016, featuring a gallery of the official White House photographer Pete Souza's amazing pictures.[4] Many of them were true chef-

---

[1] Ibid.

[2] Ibid.

[3] *The Associated Press.* (2013, April 2). "Flattering Obama images flourish as White House media access narrows." *CBS DC.* https://washington.cbslocal.com/2013/04/02/flattering-obama-images-flourish-as-white-house-media-access-narrows/

d'oeuvre, the best in the genre, capturing Obama with kids, staffers, politicians, family, etc. In these pictures, he looked the irreproachable 'People's President'. The masterpiece images of Obama candidly interacting with people became a powerful secret ingredient of his coolness recipe in addition to his truly nice personality. No president before, not to speak of after, could have had such a photo- and tele-genic portfolio.

The media rightfully worried that such content was always controlled and doctored. It always showed the president from the needed angle. "You'll have to look elsewhere for bloopers, bobbles or contrary points of view," pointed out an observer in *CBS*, stating that "Flattering Obama images flourish as White House media access narrows." [1]

No censorship, filtering or any of Herman-Chomsky's Propaganda machine systemic distortions were needed for manufacturing consent regarding Obama's coolness. It was still a recognizable and highly trusted (in Obama's time) bureaucratic primary source that supplied exclusive content and framed narratives, but absolutely not in a way Herman and Chomsky saw as sourcing. "Capitalizing on the possibilities of the digital age," [2] the bureaucratic source supplied exclusive and doctored content directly to the public. The source still worked, but not for the media. The filter still aimed at manufacturing consent, but not within the Propaganda model of the media.

***

As a first-class bureaucratic source, Barack Obama himself was also the first-ever president who literally replaced the media with bloggers in the production chain of news supply. In 2015, instead of a traditional interview with journalists after the State of the Union address, Obama invited to the White House three YouTube stars: GloZell (3 million followers), Bethany Mota (8 million followers) and Hank Green of Vlogbrothers (2.4 million followers).[3]

---

[4] *The Indian express*. (2016, November 13). "Barack Obama is the coolest president ever. Period." https://indianexpress.com/photos/trending-gallery/barack-obama-is-the-coolest-president-ever-period-2952012/4/

[1] *The Associated Press*. (2013, April 2). "Flattering Obama images flourish as White House media access narrows." *CBS DC*. https://washington.cbslocal.com/2013/04/02/flattering-obama-images-flourish-as-white-house-media-access-narrows/

[2] Ibid.

[3] The White House, President Barack Obama. (2015, January 23). "Watch President Obama's interview with YouTube stars." https://obamawhitehouse.archives.gov/blog/2015/01/22/watch-president-obamas-interview-youtube-stars

The media were confused and sounded slightly upset, even the liberal ones among them. "YouTube star who drinks cereal from a bathtub to interview President Obama," headlined *ABC News*, referring to GloZell, who, indeed, sometime before had posted a YouTube video of herself taking a cereal bath.[1] "YouTube stars interview Obama and things get weird," reported *CNN*.[2] One of YouTube's stars, Hank Green, fired back, "Legacy media isn't mocking us because we aren't a legitimate source of information; they're mocking us because they're terrified."[3]

The conservative *Washington Times* wrote,

> Howard Kurtz, Fox News' media critic, called the interview "beneath the dignity of the office" of the presidency, while other members of the press expressed unhappiness with Mr. Obama's seeming dodge of the tough questions they could fire in favor of a softball sit-down, question-answer session.[4]

***

Those were the salad days in the relationship between the president and the media corp. Then came Donald Trump. He completely broke the Herman-Chomsky Propaganda model. His media behavior, not to mention his presidential and personal behavior, opened a new era in media sourcing. There is no need to go deeper here, as Trump-media relations were one of the most covered topics from 2016 to 2020.

The point is that Trump became one of the most powerful sources for the American and world media, but totally not in a way described by the Propaganda model, because he was the source and the medium for himself at the same time. He was also the most valuable source for the mass media but, again, completely not in a way implied by the Propaganda model. For them, Trump did not supply news, he supplied triggers. He defined their agenda, but this agenda did not manufacture consent. The media used him

[1] Bruce, Mary. (2015, 22 January). "YouTube star who drinks cereal from a bathtub to interview President Obama." *ABC News*. https://abcnews.go.com/Politics/youtube-star-drinks-cereal-bathtub-interview-obama-today/story?id=28398889

[2] Sommers, Chloe. (2015, January 23). "YouTube stars interview Obama and things get weird." *CNN*. https://www.cnn.com/2015/01/23/politics/youtube-obama-interview/

[3] Ponder, Trish. (2015, January 26). "Hank Green says it's not ok for the mainstream media to snipe at YouTube stars." *Pensito Review*. https://www.pensito.com/2015/01/26/hank-green-says-its-not-ok-for-the-mainstream-media-to-snipe-at-youtube-stars/.

[4] Chumley, Cheryl K. (2015, January 23). "Obama slammed for YouTube talks with GloZell, a woman who ate cereal from tub." *The Washington Times*. https://www.washingtontimes.com/news/2015/jan/23/obama-slammed-for-youtube-talks-with-glozell-a-wom/#ixzz3Pf4uuixz%20

to commodify polarization on both sides of the political spectrum. They treated him depending on their polarized stances, but he was able to bypass them on Twitter extremely efficiently.

All in all, the digital emancipation of authorship, coupled with political polarization, changed the nature of bureaucratic sourcing for the media. In the US, the divorce of the media from official sourcing started with Obama and completed with Trump. "Misinformation from the Trump administration is the biggest challenge," said Laura Helmuth, the editor-in-chief of *Scientific American* and the former health and science editor at the *Washington Post*. "Really good reporters are wasting a ton of time refuting misinformation from the White House." In the time of the release of *Manufacturing Consent*, 1988, such a statement about the role of the White House as a source would have been unimaginable.

***

Corporations, if they need to manufacture something in the public opinion, can bypass the media, too. Brands have become media themselves. What is the point of subsidizing other media through news supply if you have your own?

If, according to Herman and Chomsky, "The mass media are drawn into a symbiotic relationship with powerful sources of information by economic necessity and reciprocity of interest" (2002 [1988], p. 18), then the weakening of the relationship with sourcing does not support the "reciprocity of interest" between the powerful and the media anymore. From the Propaganda model's perspective, the media happily broke away from the control over the agenda imposed via bureaucratic sourcing. This, however, would be a one-sided interpretation. In reality, official and corporate sources focus now more on their own platforms and therefore pay much less attention to the media. The media have broken free from the dependence on official and corporate sources, and this is not a good presage for the media.

The vanishing dependence of the media on government, military, corporate and other kinds of bureaucracy as a prevalent source also undermines the overall cohesion between the ruling elites and the meaning-producing elites. Besides all the other effects, the deepening gap between governance and meaning production aggravates the anti-establishment inclination of the new media ecosystem in general. As a result, the media will rather challenge the news and narratives of the powerful by all means, particularly if the media count on the donating support of the audience from the other end of the political spectrum.

The growing gap between governance and meaning production is not caused solely by political contradictions; rather, it is business-related. Under the unavoidably polarizing donscription business model, at least a part of the media system will always attack the ruling party and its bureaucracy in power. There is no longer any reason to see the media industry as a culture industry manufacturing consent; it now has strong 1) anti-establishment and 2) divisive environmental incentives.

***

Rise of expert sourcing. Since the introduction of the Propaganda model, the media has completed the reversal from journalism of fact to opinion journalism. The divorce from bureaucracies as the prevalent primary source, coupled with the move toward opinion journalism, has forced the media to search for a new sourcing mechanism. This new sourcing has to:

1) be an alternative to official sources – in terms of the status, but also often the stance, and

2) supply not news but rather curation, selection and interpretation, because facts are plentiful, but navigation is scarce.

The media cannot sell news *downwards*, because news almost always is already known via other channels, mostly from the newsfeed on social media. The media cannot sell agendas *upwards*, because payment *from above*, both in advertising and political forms, migrated to more efficient channels on the internet. So, the media sell agendas *downwards*, having implemented an unprecedented and weird business model, within which the audience join a cause and pay to support the media that validate the news or promote a cause. Raw facts are not in demand under this business model. The new model requires more opinions and expertise as the primary source for more or less saleable content in the media.

The focus of sourcing has moved from 'raw materials' for news toward the expertise around already-known news.

The growing demand for expertise was particularly noticeable amid the COVID-19 pandemic, where the media recruited a significant number of experts with a background in medicine and public health. The abundance of triggering and often ambivalent information about the coronavirus outbreak needed to be navigated and sorted out. The public wanted factual explanations, emotional guidance and moral validation or disapproval for government policies and public and personal behaviors. In the first month of the quarantine, the media propelled some pandemic experts to the status of national celebrities.

Similarly, the crisis of the 2016 US election, or Brexit, or any other dramatic election of recent times, propelled the fame of not reporters, as in the time of Watergate, but experts and commentators, who preach rather than inform. With this change in sourcing, columnists and commentators have become the central figures in the news media, having taken the throne from reporters and investigators.

***

Herman and Chomsky paid tribute to experts as well, though for another reason. They wrote that experts were supplied within the sourcing mechanisms provided by power and corporations.

Power tamed and used experts, they implied. Respectable alternative sources from among academics and intellectuals with authoritative but dissident opinions would have undermined the dominance and authority of official sources, noted Herman and Chomsky. The problem was solved by government and corporations through co-opting experts and putting "them on the payroll as consultants, funding their research, and organizing think tanks that will hire them directly and help disseminate their messages" (Herman & Chomsky, 2002 [1988], p. 23).

The process of forming the proper body of experts for the media was carried out on a deliberate basis and on a massive scale. Many hundreds of intellectuals were brought to sponsored expert institutions to study preselected issues. In reality, with their expertise and research findings, they propagandized the official or corporate viewpoints or neutralized dissident and undesired viewpoints. The affiliation of intellectuals with think tanks, funded by governments and corporations, institutionalized their expert status and "catapulted them into the press".

It is noteworthy that media appearances reinforced their expert status even more. This was the time when the very concept of the 'media appearance' appeared – appearances in the media became an important part of academics' and intellectuals' dossier, as if they were celebrities seeking fame. Before that, appearances at famous universities were what counted.

***

The institutional involvement of experts by corporations was in many cases used for 'manufacturing consent' as a deliberate strategy, sometimes even with a hint of conspiracy. The most well-known was the case of the Tobacco Industry Research Committee (TIRC), which was created in 1953 amid the growing public concern regarding the harm to health done by smoking. The TRIC was funded by tobacco companies and run by a PR firm. The purpose was to 'research' the causes of lung cancer and to show that those causes can vary. The ultimate goal lay in the area of PR, not public health – that is why the project was run by a PR firm. The idea was to cast doubt on scientific evidence on the connection between smoking and cancer. It was obviously not an initiative aimed at increasing expert knowledge, but a PR conspiracy against public awareness.

Lee McIntyre in his *Post-truth* regarded the story of the TIRC as the "blueprint for the science denial," developed in society afterwards as a prerequisite for post-truth. The TRIC sowed doubt in an independent scientific consensus by trying to convince the public that all possible hypotheses should be considered and weighed equally, as this is allegedly the truly scientific approach. Thereafter, it became possible "to capitalize on the resulting public confusion to question whatever scientific result you wish to dispute" (McIntyre, 2018, KL449).

The same pattern of science denial through using alternative expertise was traced later in the debates on global warming. Scientific and allegedly-scientific expertise has proven to be a good tool of distortion, diversion, and partisanship.

***

In a broader context, the influx of experts into the public sphere was also stimulated by the mutation of industrial capitalism into *soft* or *knowledgeable capitalism*, as characterized by Nigel Thrift in his 2005 book *The Rise of Soft Capitalism*.

The growing complexity of markets, the economy and the macro-economy forced capitalism to produce and adopt more knowledge and expertise, stated Thrift. Businesses started seeing the world in a scientific way, as something able to be understood and managed via information and knowledge. The scientific way of thinking and even vocabularies started being used not just to combat unfavorable science, as the tobacco barons tried to do, but in order to apply knowledge for better business organizing, market expansion and profit extraction.

The expansion of expertise into communication practices, caused by the growing amount and complexity of information, was a global process in the late 20th century, as electronic and then digital communications tied the entire world into a global market with instant signal-response. In the 21st century, with the rise of the digital economy, or the economy of knowledge, expertise and the ability to navigate the information surge became a crucial feature for individuals, organizations and society. Responding to the demand, expertise became a part of the media and even a genre of journalism along with traditional reporting. This is how experts sidelined celebrities and politicians in the ranks of special guests and columnists.

Herman and Chomsky distinguished the influence of the experts in international security, terrorism and defense issues at the time. Another cohort of experts was patronized by corporations interested in promoting consumerism and depoliticization. The structure of the body of experts affiliated with the media has changed since then.

Experts with a background in military and security have kept their positions but are concentrated mainly in the conservative media. The liberal media broadened the range of experts by recruiting intellectuals with a background in liberal and critical studies of all sorts. They were not in such a demand during the 'good old days' of *manufacturing consent*; now they are.

***

According to Herman and Chomsky, the promotion to the rank of experts used to be done through, in a sense, corrupting intellectuals by affiliating them with think tanks and other sorts of governmental and corporate research institutions. With such a profile, intellectuals could be propelled to experts in the media. But they had needed to have at least some prior intellectual record and expert verification, such as an academic background and a think tank affiliation.

Now, this promotional power undividedly belongs to the media. With this tendency, the promotion of columnists to the rank of experts was oftentimes made. The rule of the validation of significance by dissemination has worked out: someone who wrote a lot on something became an expert in what he or she wrote a lot about. At a certain level of fame (based on the factor of distribution: readership, followers, media appearances, etc.), some experts, particularly those recruited from columnists, had a broader area of expertise. They became a sort of expert 'without portfolio', a universal expert.

This is quite a postmodernist phenomenon. Some modern – postmodern – celebrities, for example, have not grown out of any area of preceding fame or success, such as arts, show business, sports or politics. They at once have become 'pure', self-induced celebrities, as exemplified by Paris Hilton or Kim Kardashian, persons famous solely for being celebrities. Social media with their mechanisms of virality, Instagram first of all, have made being a celebrity a professional occupancy.

The market value of celebrities is a function of celebrities' 'dissemination'. Since social significance is also a function of dissemination, celebrity-value is an expression of pure significance: in this case, a *significance without meaning.* Similar to how money represents an abstract pure value without a material application and therefore is useful for the measurement of any value, celebrities also represent the pure value of *significance without meaning*, the pure abstract value of virality.

The same mechanism of the validation of value/significance by dissemination entailed the formation of a body of experts, made by the media, in the media, for the media. They might or might not have some preceding academic or field expertise, but essential for the expert's status is their frequency of media appearances and a modicum of intellectual, writing or speaking skills, of course coupled with a proper demographic and political profile.

The most advanced experts of the postmodernist era become universal experts, the Kardashians of expertise. In fairness, it is noteworthy that some areas of expertise objectively favor the universalism of scope and vision (such as media expertise, for example, to which I must confess I luckily belong, or politics).

All in all, the media have managed to ride the wave of demand for expertise and have produced a required body of experts out of their columnists and frequent interviewees, in addition to those recruited in academia and practical fields.

***

Besides a wide range of columnists and commentators promoted to experts, one more rich and prospective niche of expert recruitment has appeared – activism.

Activism is a good way to bolster one's reputation and publicity; in many cases publicity is an important amplifier for activism, as it helps to raise awareness. These settings meet the principle of validation by dissemination. If an activist has gained some reputation, their publicity verifies their significance (in addition to the actual personal qualities that are required for succeeding in activism). Activists with a certain level of publicity can be propelled by the media to expert status. A part of today's expert body in the media have trodden this exact career path.

With the decline of general trust in institutions, the role and number of classical experts will decrease, and the role and number of expert-activists will grow. Experts-made-of-activists serve the needs for polarization in the media very well. Navigation in the turbulent news environment assumes not just the rational assessment (actually, the rational assessment least of all) but also the emotional evaluation and validation of what is right and what is not through forming an attitude. This sort of expertise is *moral expertise.*

People often need guidance to define which aspects of the current events are appealing and which are appalling, according to the shared system of values. To this end, experts with activist backgrounds are the best suited, as they are allowed to, nay even required to, impose moral guidelines.

In the conservative media, the moral expertise of events, actions, behaviors and persons will be judged based on whether they comply with the sense of nostalgia for the Great Past and fuel resentment. For this, experts are likely recruited from among activists with backgrounds in activities related to the Second Amendment, religion, the pro-life movement, the right conspiracies of all kinds and alike.

Resentment expertise in the conservative media is symmetrically mirrored by grievance expertise in the liberal media. Grievance expertise organically comes from civic, humanitarian and social justice activism.

**

Polarization of sourcing. With a higher stake in the media, the donating audience increases pressure on newsrooms in terms of what experts or columnists are inappropriate to be given the floor. The Twitterati furiously condemn newsrooms for the wrong choice of authors, commentators and experts.

Flak from the donating audience narrows the newsroom's choice of experts and commentators down to the carriers of 'politically correct' views (on both opposing sides). The necessity to spark the audience's feelings to join the cause (and better subscription) incentivizes the media to involve more 'ardent' experts.

Technically, experts cannot be 'ardent'. If they are, they are probably propagandists. Considering that the mechanisms of expert recruitment in the media shifted towards columnists and activists, it is possible to say that the tone of expertise has moved more towards political and moral judgment and less towards balanced consideration. This move is needed for the media to succeed in soliciting subscription as donation.

The switch of the media towards more opinion journalism, married with polarized flak, leads to the shaping of *expert filter bubbles*, the circles of regular experts around politicized media brands.

Expert polarization occurred not only in politically loaded developments such as, for example, the 2017–2019 Mueller investigation in the USA or the 2019–2020 impeachment, but also during the COVID-19 pandemic. With their ardently founded reasoning, the opposing expert bubbles set two completely different agendas, helping to polarize audiences and secure their loyalty to the media propounding competing worldviews. Even distant-from-politics topics, such as mask-wearing, were polarized and politically weaponized.

***

The cocooning of the media into their expert filter bubbles is invisibly but inevitably and powerfully reinforced by new technical opportunities of media measurement.

In the past, the editor packaged content in big parcels, including the set of experts, commentators and columnists selected for an issue. The audience, of course, could have individual preferences regarding certain authors and experts, but the reaction tended to be quite general and directed towards the entire package. The reaction was also deferred. It gave the editor some freedom and time for maneuvering and balancing. The editor had the luxury to think about an edition as a whole, as an assemblage of elements complementing and balancing each other.

This has been changed by the quantization of content on the internet and social media. Any quantum of content can be now counted individually and instantly; moreover, the reaction to this quantum can also be registered immediately. Clicks, likes, shares, comments and subsequent Twitter reactions became a tool of the audience's immediate pressure on newsroom autonomy.

The editor instantly sees what the audience likes or hates; hate is more visible, due to the higher value-factor of 'negativity bias'. The instant reaction to any tiny piece imposes pressure on the editor. With growing dependence on audience loyalty and donations, the temptation to eliminate and avoid those authors and commentators that carry the risk of a negative reaction begins to dominate. The editor's selection is restrained by the instant negative reaction. The editor is negatively incentivized not to deal with opinions not complying with the view of the most vocal part of the audience.

As Glenn Greenwald described it in regard to TV,

> ...cable news programs are constructed to feed their audiences only self-affirming narratives that vindicate partisan loyalties. One liberal cable host told me that they receive ratings not for each show but for each segment, and they can see the ratings drop off — the remotes clicking away — if they put on the air anyone who criticizes the party to which that outlet is devoted (Democrats in the case of MSNBC and CNN, the GOP in the case of Fox).[1]

---

[1] Greenwald, Glenn. (2020, May 18). "Ben Smith's NYT critique of Ronan Farrow describes a

***

Eli Pariser, the author of the term 'filter bubble', saw the instant and unmediated accommodation of the news supply to people's reaction as one of the prerequisites for the filter bubble. He compared the newsroom of *Gawker*, the then-skyrocketing tabloid-type new online media outlet (the late 2000s), and good-old the *New York Times*. In *Gawker*'s newsroom, there was a Big Board, a huge screen showing the top posts by page views. "Write an article that makes it onto the Big Board, and you're liable to get a raise," reported Pariser. "Stay off it for too long, and you may need to find a different job" (Pariser, 2011, p. 32).

The *New York Times* at the time held a completely opposite stance, disregarding the instant reactions of the audience. Pariser appraised this as an advantage and even the dignity of journalism. His account of it deserves a longer quote:

> At the New York Times, reporters and bloggers aren't allowed to see how many people click on their stories. This isn't just a rule, it's a philosophy that the Times lives by: The point of being the newspaper of record is to provide readers with the benefit of excellent, considered editorial judgment. "We don't let metrics dictate our assignments and play," New York Times editor Bill Keller said, "because we believe readers come to us for our judgment, not the judgment of the crowd. We're not 'American Idol.'" Readers can vote with their feet by subscribing to another paper if they like, but the Times doesn't pander. Younger Times writers who are concerned about such things have to essentially bribe the paper's system administrators to give them a peek at their stats. (The paper does use aggregate statistics to determine which online features to expand or cut.) (Pariser, 2011, p. 32.)

The editor whose newspaper is funded predominantly by advertising can allow themselves to say that "Readers can vote with their feet by subscribing to another paper if they like". The editor whose newspaper depends solely on reader revenue cannot.

After the reversal in the business model from ad revenue to reader revenue, the relations between "our judgement" and "the judgment of the crowd," as *NYT* editor Bill Keller called it in the quoted fragment, have reversed, too. In 2020, just 10 years later, "our judgment" can no longer allow the risk to be too different from "the judgment of the crowd" vocalized on Twitter. "We're not 'American Idol'" went the same way as "We are not

toxic, corrosive, and still-vibrant Trump-Era pathology: "Resistance Journalism"." *The Intercept*. https://theintercept.com/2020/05/18/ben-smiths-nyt-critique-of-ronan-farrow-describes-a-toxic-corrosive-and-still-vibrant-trump-era-pathology-resistance-journalism/

resistance". These are not the right mottos for the media business based on soliciting subscription as donation. Journalism surrenders each next "We are not...".

Some might be tempted to accuse the leadership of the *New York Times* of this surrender, as the 'paper of record' has suffered from it, perhaps, the most. But such are the environmental conditions, including those related to the fading business, not someone's individual fault. It has impacted journalism in general.

***

The instant and constant pressure of likes (rather 'hates') from those who pay or who can initiate powerful flak most likely makes editors very cautious about picking the 'wrong' authors and experts. This environmental and irresistible force insulates the media in their ideological filter bubbles when pitching for support, including their bubble of experts. The experts orbiting each media outlet gradually turn into a set of speakers pre-approved by the donating audience; actually, by the most vocal part of the donating audience. This is not even a stable state; it represents the progressing and escalating dynamics of the media moving towards extremes on the chosen side of the political spectrum. Polarization is not a final stage; it is an accelerating process.

With the expertise and opinion supply split into two opposing echo chambers, experts, authors and commentators whose opinion does not chime with the party line are unlikely to have access to pages or airtime.

The political cocooning of expert selection is just half of the problem. The other half relates to the amplification of extremes and the suppression of centrist views. Centrist experts can appear in the media, but they are not those who generate buzz, virality, and spin-off in the polarized media environment aimed at frustrating and engaging the donating audience. Moderateness does not work well in this market. The business model aggressively eliminates undesired opinions and passively disincentivizes modest and centrist opinions.

Sourcing in the media has not just switched from news to opinion supply; it has switched to the supply of opinions, preferably those more ardent and necessarily pre-approved by the most vocal part of the donating audience.

Ownership of the media: it is not what you think it must be

Under the idea of ownership as a filter of the Propaganda model, Herman and Chomsky grouped together three intertwined factors: "size, ownership, and profit orientation of the mass media" (Herman & Chomsky, 2002 [1988], p. 3).

Size related to the cost of capital investment needed to establish a newspaper. Early newspapers were industrial only in a technological sense: they printed many identical copies of the same product. But in terms of their economic and business organization, they remained workshops of a comparatively small-scale business.

The workshop-organized papers tended to be class-related because they were respectively funded – either by political patrons *from above* or by class-specific self-identified readers *from below*, such as merchants, the bourgeoisie, and, later, workers. These were the first identifiers of the media audiences when the audience of papers started taking structure from the unsegmented primeval soup in the 17th to 19th centuries.

When advertising became the dominant factor of the media business, the scale of distribution outvalued the social addressing of content. Profit-seeking became the leading motive for publishing newspapers (compared to party papers).

The papers with more ads obtained an advantage: they could cash in on copy sales and advertising. The significance of the class identifiers of the audiences diminished, and the audience started being structured within consumer profiling. The profit orientation with newly opened opportunities to increase profit on ads favored the papers with broader content and larger audiences. To achieve these conditions, large enterprises were required.

The capital cost for the media to enter the market became a restraint for startups. This secured the media market for rich owners and big media corporations. The process of concentration in the media began.

***

The size of operations required for a truly profitable business in this market made newspapers big corporations, but also incorporated them into the corporate world. Herman and Chomsky marked out the factor of social affiliation based on size and profit-seeking:

> In sum, the dominant media firms are quite large businesses; they are controlled by very wealthy people or by managers who are subject to sharp constraints by owners and other market-profit-oriented forces; and they are closely interlocked, and have important common interests, with other major corporations, banks, and government. This is the first powerful filter that will affect news choices. (Herman & Chomsky, 2002 [1988], p. 14.)

That is why Herman and Chomsky, even without admitting so formally, nevertheless listed ownership (size and profit-seeking) as the first and assumedly most important filter of their Propaganda model. The media depicted the world deprived of social controversies and class struggle because they themselves belonged to the big corporations' world and therefore propagated that respective worldview. The class structure got masked by consensus, and the audience was identified along consumerist-demographic, not political, differences. Upon this, the personal, professional, thematic, value and other audience affiliations and dependencies in the media and their agendas were built.

***

According to the Marxist understanding of social-economic relations, concentration and corporate control are the pillars of the political economy of the mass media. The concentration of media ownership has been permanently increasing since the late 19th century. Any political-economic analysis of the media in recent decades has contained a scrupulous count of an increasingly smaller number of big corporations controlling increasingly larger chunks of the market.

One of the last tendencies of the classical political economy of the mass media, before it started losing its subject, was the transfer of ownership control from the media orgs to telecom corporations. The deliverers of signals had generally seized the power over 'signal' production, particularly in the TV and radio segments. Newspapers have mostly avoided such a fate, but that is merely because investors have not seen a viable business there.

Concentrated ownership (along with size and profit-seeking) is still an important factor in defining the principles of agenda-setting. But its impact has significantly decreased for several reasons.

1) The political-economy power of ownership concentration moved to new media – social network platforms, whose size and outreach are simply incomparable with that of old media – and defines the principles of meaning production on the internet.

258

2) With emancipated authorship, the power of public opinion – now flak – has increased tremendously. Flak generally outperforms ownership in terms of their impact on agenda-setting.

***

Ownership is still an impactful force in the media industry, but it is not the ownership of the media. It is the ownership of platforms. The owners of platforms, mainly Google and Facebook, are those who determine the owners' power in the media system.

Media owners may still control the news media, but they no longer control the news. The media, the former monopolists of news production and delivery, have become a part of a bigger news ecosystem, within which the role of the media is shrinking. Consequently, the role of media ownership has also declined. In addition, new factors managing news production and delivery have appeared, such as sharing, or platforms, or algorithms, or virality, for which the classical political economy of the mass media (to which the Propaganda model belonged) did not even have a language. The entire Marx-Engels Galaxy, which contained the Herman-Chomsky Constellation, was swallowed by the McLuhan Universe.

According to Emily Bell, director at the Tow Centre for Digital Journalism at Columbia Journalism School,

> News spaces are no longer owned by newsmakers. The press is no longer in charge of the free press and has lost control of the main conduits through which stories reach audiences. The public sphere is now operated by a small number of private companies, based in Silicon Valley.[1]

Nowadays, news must fit not to print but to digital. At the fundamental, technological level, the settings of the digital environment are managed by completely different institutions and forces, over which neither media owners nor editors have any power whatsoever, and which they oftentimes do not even understand. Emily Bell brilliantly emphasized this redistribution of power,

> In creating these amazingly easy-to-use tools, in encouraging the world to publish, the platform technologies now have a social purpose and responsibility far beyond their original intent. Legacy media did not

---

[1] Bell, Emily. (2014, November 21). "Silicon Valley and Journalism: Make up or Break up?" The Reuters Memorial Lecture at St Anne's College. https://www.youtube.com/watch?v=XvM-MMgmFqA&feature=youtu.be&fbclid=IwAR1cf7GBQe8jv815ujK4Y6WGFRUdfLBb7djtStCsB26pFrEb8jsjrLS7HA0 A short transcript: https://reutersinstitute.politics.ox.ac.uk/risj-review/silicon-valley-and-journalism-make-or-break

understand what it was losing, Silicon Valley did not understand what it was creating.[1]

**

The factors of ownership, size and profit-seeking can now be applied to the digital platform, but they can hardly be seen as a content filter of the Propaganda model as it was defined by Herman and Chomsky. These factors impact content production but not towards consent; rather, the opposite. The platforms' profit depends on users' activity and therefore platforms' settings incentivize the radicalization of self-expression for the sake of a better response (the engagement of others). With respect to political content, this unavoidably leads to polarization, not consensus with the ruling elites. The digital platforms' ownership and profit-seeking environmentally entail anti-establishment, not pro-establishment, tendencies.

As for old media, classical ownership still matters to them themselves, but its influence on meaning production in society has dramatically decreased.

**

The other factor defining the decline of media ownership as a PM filter is flak.

Any media manager is now as much afraid of the audience as of the shareholders or the board. The media owners are under this pressure, too. With millions of users searching on the internet for something outrageous for their self-actualization, the new media environment can be extremely toxic to brand safety, including the safety of media brands. It is not without reason that companies are so concerned about this issue now. Meaning production is one of the most vulnerable areas of brand activity, be it advertising or media production.

Even some of the biggest brands have been ostracized and put at risk of losses after being caught with content that happened to be virally deemed inappropriate. Paradoxically, the executive power of cancel culture rests, for the most part, on the corporate culture of big capital. These are big corporations with their brand sensitivity and extra-cautious codes of conduct that most often execute the sentences of cancel culture. The media orgs are among them.

---

[1] Ibid.

This is something completely opposite to the classical filter of size and ownership as defined in the Propaganda model. The impact on a media brand that activists and the viral crowd have today, would have been unthinkable in the 1970–80s, when the only way for activists to spread their outrage regarding the media was through the media. The media were free to simply ignore criticism, which basically made them, their owners, editors and journalists immune to any general public's outrage. Without its own mechanisms of publicity, the only flak that mattered was the flak produced by the elites and the powerful, the classical Herman-Chomsky flak. They wrote:

> The public is not sovereign over the media—the owners and managers, seeking ads, decide what is to be offered, and the public must choose among these. (Herman & Chomsky, 2002 [1988], p. xix.)

This has changed since then. Now, because of the internet, the capacity to produce powerful flak has been 'democratized'. With polarization and the never-ending search for insulting and inappropriate content to be condemned, the media are much more vulnerable to flak from activists, the Twitterati and the general public than they used to be.

The technically enhanced flak has significantly increased business risks for the owners and career risks for the media professionals. Under such conditions, size and corporate ownership of the media may well be factors that are detrimentally affecting their arbitrary rights of agenda-setting.

11. Postjournalism: from the world-as-it-is to the world-as-it-should-be

Philosophers have hitherto only explained the world in various ways; the
point is to change it.

Karl Marx. The eleventh thesis on Feuerbach.

How did we get here?

By the end of the 20th century, the business model of the media took its
last and most optimal form: the media sold news *downwards* whilst
simultaneously selling the audience *upwards*, to advertisers, creating a
"supportive selling environment" or agenda. Advertising dominated the
business model, providing 70% of revenue and more. Ad revenue was so
plentiful that it made media organizations the largest and richest
corporations of the late capitalist period, on par with banks or oil
companies.

The business model, predominantly based on ad revenue and large
profits, predefined the method of agenda-setting. Generally, the mainstream
media's journalism facilitated consumerism, political stability and the
populace's alignment with the policies of the elites, as these were the
necessary conditions for the successful application of that business model.
Buoyed by this economic foundation, the media also carried out a public
service, supporting democracy as a political mode of capitalism.

***

Within the space of a mere 20 years, the internet completely broke the
idyll, which had taken about 500 years to build. The consequences have
gone far beyond just the switch of the material carrier and the ensuing death
of newspapers. As the social, economic and technological conditions that
brought about journalism are fading, so is journalism. What remains of it
has begun mutating.

Having lost business and fighting for survival, the news media need to
compete with new media. The competition imposes rules that damage the
news media's authenticity and integrity. The news media need to reduce
their linear and complete product, the qualities of which came from their
materiality and periodicity, to the snippets, blurbs and clickbait, the only
quanta of content that can fit in the new mode of delivery, the stream of the

262

newsfeed on social media. The quantization of content leads to the 'hamsterization of journalism' and erodes its unique content value. Paradoxically, by improving news-gathering and news-delivering capacities, the internet has adversely affected the quality of journalistic content.

Simultaneously, the new medium, the internet, has rapidly increased the amount of content that is seeking people's attention. Having become redundant, news ceased to be a valuable commodity. Journalism of fact has been replaced by opinion journalism.

***

The most significant change that has impacted journalism and caused its decline relates to the change in the business model. Advertisers are gone and will not return. Some residual subscription still remains, so reader revenue has become the dominant source of funding for journalism. However, this reader revenue is driven by a peculiar force. News consumers do not need news; they already know most news relevant to them, because content of all kinds, including news, is produced, sorted, personally customized and delivered first and foremost via social media and other digital platforms.

But due to their historical affiliation and morphological 'alignment' with the public sphere and politics, the news media still have a sanction and authority to validate news. The validation fee and subscription soliciting as donations are becoming a significant part of reader revenue. These payment motives have started impacting the principles of agenda setting.

Having lost the ability to commodify news *downwards* and agenda *upwards*, the media have found a last-ditch solution – selling agenda *downwards*. Under the validation fee, foundation funding, the membership model and its subscription-like surrogates, the media are paid seemingly *from below*; however, they are not paid for news, but for agenda-setting – for the reasons and motives normally coming *from above*.

This hybrid business model leads journalism to mutate into activism and the media to transform into the means of crowdfunded propaganda. Instead of manufacturing consumerism and consent, the media manufacture polarization and anger.

The hybrid and nevertheless continuously shrinking business model of the media has created a type of journalism never seen before. It has built itself upon the remains of classical journalism, appropriating its deviations and rejecting its standards. As a cultural phenomenon closing a significant epoch in historical development, simultaneously inheriting and rejecting the settings of the predecessor, this type of hybrid and decaying journalism can conveniently be called *postjournalism*.

***

Postjournalism is journalism that sells the audience to the public by soliciting donations in the form of subscription. Classical journalism pretended to be objective; it strived to depict the *world-as-it-is*. Postjournalism is openly normative; it imposes the *world-as-it-should-be*.

Similar to propaganda, postjournalism openly promotes an ideological view. What distinguishes it from propaganda, however, is that postjournalism mixes open ideological intentions with a hidden business imperative required for the media to survive. Postjournalism is not the product of a choice but is the consequence of the change in the media business model.

Postjournalism is a hyper-postmodernist entity. The value of its product is not comprised of use-value or symbolic value; its use-value *is* symbolic value. Postjournalism commodifies a good that nobody really consumes. The public – the donating audience – does not consume the agenda it pays for, because it pays for the agenda to be peddled to others. Ironically though, there are no 'others' willing to follow this agenda beyond the donating audience itself.

The media practicing postjournalism produce nothing else but the donating audience through the manufacture of its anger. Their agenda production entails no consumption. Nobody *learns* news from this agenda. It does not even have any impact on the assumed audience. Real propaganda involves the proliferation of ideas and values. However, postjournalism cannot do even that. Those whom it is supposed to reach and convert are already trapped in the same agenda bubble.

The only "others" for the agenda bubble, made of the donating audience and their media, are the inhabitants of the opposite agenda bubble on the other side of the political spectrum. Paradoxically, postjournalism supplies not so much content but, rather, the reason for the foes' existence and their motives, which justify their outrage and mobilization. However, there is also no expected agenda impact on opponents. The opponents do not consume 'opposing' content as information. They regard it as a source of energy to feed their anger. Polarization is the essential environmental condition and the only outcome of postjournalism (besides the earnings of the media that practice postjournalism).

Because of its self-containment and the need for energy input, postjournalism exists in a binary form in which the strength of the one side depends on the strength of the other. Their confrontation strengthens their audience-capturing power and maintains their business.

264

***

Postjournalism is a typically postmodernist phenomenon of simulation and self-referentiality. It follows in the footsteps of other cultural 'post-' phenomena, such as postmodernism and post-truth, having soaked up their essential features in applications to the media.

Postjournalism is characterized by the following essential features:

- Donscription: subscription solicited as donation
- Focus on impact, not news
- Negativity bias
- Activism
- Repudiation of professional standards
- Discourse concentration
- Post-truth
- Postmodernism

Donscription: subscription solicited as donation

As commercial sources of funding evaporated, 'nonprofit' funding appeared to be a solution. If people are willing to pay for a noble cause to be pursued, why not ask them to pay for such a noble cause as journalism itself?

Thus, the membership model was conceived and pioneered most prominently by the British *Guardian* and Dutch *De Correspondent*. The ability of the membership model to secure the sustainability of media business is yet to be proven. However, the first results have been impressive. The most persuasive (or lucky) news orgs have managed to solicit significant membership funding from readers, formerly known as subscribers.

Due to the structural collapse of transactional subscription based on news retail, the subscription model is increasingly moving towards adopting motives and arguments borrowed from the membership model. More and more news orgs are employing the techniques of soliciting membership. Even the most successful proponents of paywalls, such as the *New York Times* or the *Washington Post*, started promoting some of the motives based on a membership philosophy in their subscription offers. The previous transactional subscription is mutating into a membership-like subscription surrogate.

This tectonic shift in the media business has thus far remained unnoticed by the general public but may be considered at the core of many other processes in the media for which they are heavily criticized.

***

When agenda-setting in of the media was paid for by advertisers or readers indirectly and sufficiently, newsrooms held all the rights over defining the scope and spotlights of their editorial policies. Whilst these may well have occasionally been corrupted, deviant or maleficent, the decisions were exclusively theirs. When agenda-setting is sold directly to those who are willing to pay and want certain pressing issues to be covered and advocated for, the rule of external allocative control comes into play. Those topics and approaches that attract the most support and subscription-donations are the ones that become naturally selected.

Worse still, the media needs to amplify and dramatize those issues whose coverage is most likely to be paid for. This leads to the narrowing of the scope of agenda-setting to a limited number of the most worrisome and well-paying topics; and also to making those topics even more worrisome. This setting incentivizes not just the search for triggering issues but also triggering coverage. Only those news and opinions that meet the requirement of triggering donations will pass the filters of news budgeting in newsroom.

Similar to advertising's impact on agenda-setting, this new economic setting incentivizes the manufacture – however, not of consent but of anger in the media and by the media. Stimulated by the commercial needs of the media, anger and outrage produce growing political polarization in society.

Amid this transformation of the media industry, local and politically neutral media outlets become marginalized and are literally ceasing to exist because the old business models able to support them do not work anymore. They are too small to survive on donscription which requires a bigger scale of outreach. A direct consequence of the shift to postjournalism is that the media industry is losing local journalism.

Impact for sale

The public service of journalism used to be a by-product of the media business and was able to be delivered principally because newsroom autonomy was secured by the dispersed and plentiful funding (first, by readers in the era of the late penny press, then by advertisers). These were solely people in the media, the editors and journalists, the priests of public interest, who decided what to preach to the public, simply because the temple was rich, self-reliant and therefore powerful.

Starting with muckrakers such as Ida Tarbell, who exposed oil barons in the early 20th century and continuing with the *Washington Post* Watergate reporting or the *Boston Globe* Spotlight investigation, the great media of the past were able to keep those in power accountable. But never before have the media sold their public service function directly. They have never offered it to be directly funded from outside. Journalism's public service was not a commercial function. As Emily Bell characterized this detachment of the professional mindset from commercial tasks, "At news organisations the central organising principle is usually to produce something with *social impact* first ahead of utility or profit".[1]

But even the civic consciousness of journalists was hardly a leading motive for public service in the media. The function of public service could and must be cheered and honored in journalism, but it was rather a systemic, 'by-default' outcome of the profession of journalist itself.

In the faith of democracy, journalists, indeed, saw themselves as the priests, not the merchants or, let alone, followers. Maintaining democracy was their priestly professional duty, not a civic right or a commercial enterprise. Even when abused or corrupted, this was a specific professional mindset. The professional self-assertion, secured by financial well-being, protected by newsroom autonomy, and aimed at gaining reputational capital, incentivized the independent public service of the media. It wasn't for sale; it was spiritually far above any transactional motives.

As these conditions have now disappeared, public service is offered by the media for sale directly. Public service of journalism has become a part of the commercial offer of the news media.

***

Today, increasingly more media outlets are overtly selling their sacred function of public service, as if the priests had abandoned the Church and started selling rituals directly and in a pagan way. Actually, there was an exactly religious precedent for this. European bishops in the 15th and 16th centuries abused the power of rituals and, in the pursuit of money, started selling indulgences widely, wildly and greedily, without a connection to the spiritual meaning of redemption. They undermined the faith and caused the Reformation. (Interestingly, both the excessive sale of indulgences and the

---

[1] Bell, Emily. (2014, November 23). "What's the right relationship between technology companies and journalism?" *The Guardian*. https://www.theguardian.com/media/media-blog/2014/nov/23/silicon-valley-companies-journalism-news

subsequent Reformation were enabled by Gutenberg's invention – the printing press).

The newly emerging business model of the media, with prevalent reader revenue and increasing membership motives behind it, amid the insufficiency of funding, has put the media at the mercy of the donating audience. Those who donate to the media (or to a cause) most likely want to resolve some social issues. Basically, they assign this task to journalism and subsidize it for this purpose. The only newsroom autonomy remaining is to determine and formulate the most triggering and therefore most donatable issues. The media treading this path then need to stick to covering those issues; they have to continually shout them from the rooftops and redouble their activities, as there is always the fear that the motivation for donors to donate may otherwise weaken and disappear.

The sort of journalism which will most likely be donated to is one which makes selected issues more triggering, not one which unites the audience or keeps the powerful accountable. The determination to cause outrage as the most (or the only) visible proof of impact synergizes with the negativity bias, polarization, and amplification of triggers. The intermingling of these factors is inciting the increasingly hysterical tone in postjournalism.

Negativity bias

A teaser on the main page of the *New York Times'* website on May 14, 2020 read:

> Almost 3 million U.S. workers filed for unemployment last week. Although the weekly tally has been declining since late March, experts are warning of a long struggle ahead.

Technically, if one looks at the facts, the teaser says that the weekly index of unemployment has been in decline for more than a month. Which is – again, technically – not such bad news. But good news does not create a feeling that the public wellbeing is in danger. Within the reader-driven business model, a "supportive selling environment" (Herman, 2000, p. 102) needs to be negative. Readers must worry. A fact that is not even neutral but rather positive is nevertheless framed as bad news.

***

The negativity bias of the media may be explained through the Tversky-Kahneman Prospect Theory, according to which people are more sensitive to risks than to opportunities. Therefore, negative information is generally more attractive. Over their 500-year evolution, the media have naturally revealed this propensity and learned to use negativity in order to attract the audience.

In the ad-driven media, negativity bias is most likely balanced or outdone by the necessity to beautify reality in order to create a "supportive selling environment" for ads and to avoid content that can repel a bigger audience or pose risks to brand safety. In the reader-driven media, negativity bias has no such counterbalance as the advertisers' demand for sugarcoating reality. Therefore, the reader-paid media are inherently inclined towards *doom and gloom*.

However, postjournalism rides on a specific business model that does not sell news to readers. While the negativity bias of postjournalism can technologically and professionally inherit negativity gimmicks of the reader-driven media, in the donation-driven media, negativity bias has a different characteristic. It arises from the necessity to peddle pressing social issues and trigger the audience's emotions so they can be converted to joining the cause and donation. Postjournalism must scare the audience to make it donate. This is the role of negativity under this business model.

This imperative subliminally influences the professional attitude of editors and journalists on both poles of the polarized media environment. They all need to find the right things to terrify their audiences. Most importantly, polarization itself provides them with the material to incite fear. They need each other to terrorize their audiences with the dehumanized image of the enemy. The economic prerequisite of negativity bias leads to the political use of the ideology of threat, which reinforces polarization and is reinforced by polarization in return.

Negativity, a hysterical tone, threat ideology, polarization – all the driving forces of postjournalism – tend to feed off one another, putting the media environment, contaminated with postjournalism, at risk of spiraling into a vortex of self-perpetuating agitation.

Activism

When the media promote a certain cause for the audience to join through financial support, they risk becoming outsourced and crowdfunded press-offices for activist or political movements. Thereafter, their independence becomes compromised, while the regulative power of flak increases, leading to more polarization and cocooning the media into ideological filter bubbles.

269

Historically, journalism has always evolved towards more public involvement. Officially licensed and/or funded by authority the newspapers of the 17th century were used for propaganda. The revolutionary publicism of the 18th century enabled bourgeoise uprisings, social liberation and the emergence of the modern social order. Political journalism of the 19th century reflected the party system's evolution and the class struggle. The muckraking, watchdog and accountability journalism of the 20th century became the pillars of democracy.

However, except for cases of propaganda and party funding, the media's public involvement was always funded by *other* sources and for *other* purposes; namely, by readers buying news or by advertisers buying readers' attention. Those transactions represented an institution maintenance fee that allowed the media to provide a public service based on the commercial business model. Conversely, the media that were not paid by *other* than political sources for *other* than propaganda purposes were the political and propagandist media. They did not pretend to exercise either journalism or public service.

The wall between commercial funding and social function secured and was secured by newsroom autonomy. These settings maintained the independence of the media, an achievement that was crucial in enabling the media to provide a public service.

***

It is sometimes hard to distinguish between journalism and activism. As the media provided the public service of watching over the accountability of the powerful, journalism was close to activism. But they are not the same. Their tools, goals and philosophies are different. At the end of the day, activism itself, as a political exercise of (moral) power, also needs to be monitored. Activism can be corrupted by populism, crowd agitation, and a lack of educated expertise. Likewise, journalism needs to be monitored, too, hence the existence of flak which is exercised by activists, among others. Journalism's public service can be corrupted, too, by the abuse of people working in the media or by the business model, as was shown in Herman-Chomsky's Propaganda model.

Running side by side and sometimes sharing similar goals, activism and journalism are essentially separated by their social natures and institutional functions. The concomitance of their goals may happen when some sorts of activism share the same goal as journalism, such as supporting the freedom of expression, for example. However, when activism joins the goals of journalism, they remain separate. But when the opposite happens and journalism joins the goal of activism, it becomes a PR structure of activism.

270

In addition, their operational scope is different, even opposite. Activism narrows its focus on to selected issues, while journalism's focus of selection is always temporary, always moving from subject to subject and is exercised under the wider framework of the universal meta-activity of covering the entire spectrum of public interests.

Activism looks at some issues; journalism looks at all issues. Activism always emphasizes; journalism is expected to look for the spectrum and the balance, emphasizing something only if it is necessary for reflecting social significance. The ultimate goal of activism can normally only be a local topic for journalism because the strategic goal of journalism is always incomparably more global. Activism and journalism represent the narrow and the universal, the emphasized and the balanced – with consequences for their operational modes and outcomes.

***

Meanwhile, the motives of foundation funding and membership are inherently the same ones that underlie activism. Accepting these models, the media accept the risk of drifting towards surrendering their newsroom autonomy to external allocative control. Even if the goals of such funding are noble, it corrupts newsroom autonomy and, more importantly, leads to narrowing the media's scope, over-representing some topics and views while turning a blind eye to others.

Foundation funding, the membership model, and the membership-like subscription surrogates altogether represent a significant environmental force that is changing the media through activism's invasion of journalism.

The more subscription resembles membership, the more journalism behind a paywall is forced to adopt activism in order to satisfy the donating audience. At the end of the day, this journalism-activism hybrid needs not only to satisfy but also to trigger and terrify the donating audience in order to secure its loyalty for future payments. (For the TV news networks, these membership motives are represented through the loyalty of the viewership reflected in ratings that afterwards are monetized via cable subscription and residual advertising).

If the audience directly buys the public service, which has never been the case before, journalism unavoidably succumbs to activism under the pressure of allocative control, flak and other systemic factors.

The changes can be seen at the operational level. Just as the merging with marketing caused journalism to mutate into so-called 'native advertising' (advertising in the guise of editorial content), so its alignment with activism has made journalism drift towards 'native propaganda'.

Postjournalism has started to spurn the professional standards of classical journalism of the 20th century while successfully using its applied tools and methods.

Repudiation of standards

The professional standards and ethical norms of journalism aim to protect the public status of journalists and uphold the reputational capital of the media. The adherence to standards has a business dimension: journalists' independence and the reputation of the media organizations increase their influence and lead to a larger or more affluent audience and hence more advertising revenue.

Professional standards and ethical norms, therefore, are maintained by the 'subjective' moral resolve of professionals and by 'objective' systemic business incentives. History has witnessed many cases where adhering to standards would harm the business interests or even threatened the very existence of the media in the short run. However, media outlets that vehemently upheld and stuck to professional standards eventually improved their reputation and increased their capital value.

The symbiotic relationship between professional standards and business outcomes strengthens standards because it introduces a systemic factor into the equation. The impact of reputation on business is one of the regulators maintaining standards, in addition to people's moral predispositions. At the same time, the invisible ties between standards and business make standards susceptible to changes when business models change.

The switch of the media business model from ad revenue to the growing dependence on the donating audience, accompanied by the increasing politicization and polarization of the media environment, forms new conditions that impact both the moral and business rationales behind professional standards. Some of the established standards are increasingly often neglected, while others are openly rejected.

***

In the 20th century, journalism created and extolled a clear and well-articulated set of ethical norms and professional standards in free-market countries. The norms and standards were written in the codes widely accepted by practicing media organizations and professional media associations.

At the practical level, standards of journalism were meant to ensure the reliability and veracity of reporting, the main qualities that allowed the media to do business, wield respect and authority, and deliver a public service. Included within the fundamental standards of journalism were seeking truth, objectivity, independence, impartiality, accuracy, transparency, diligence in newsgathering, accountability and harm limitation.[1]

Some of these principles directly conflict with the changes that have occurred in the business and cultural environment in the last decade. Following those standards may now marginalize their proponents, while their repudiation may bring journalists and the media some reputational and business advantage.

One can argue that all of these standards have constantly been violated to a greater or lesser extent. This is true; however, the violation of standards did not remove their regulative power. Under the new conditions, the very nature of professional normative regulation is changing.

The growing dependence on membership motives and the donating audience makes the polarization of narratives a crucial factor for business success. Polarization means that journalists and the media need to take a stance. The professional standards of seeking truth, objectivity and impartiality are among the first to fall under the risk of being weakened or denied. The next to go are the standards of independence, accuracy, transparency, diligence in newsgathering, accountability and harm limitation.

***

One of the most profound changes in attitude towards standards concerns the professional norms of impartiality and objectivity. It is even possible to precisely point out the historical moment when this shift happened.

After the American establishment was traumatized by Trump's victory in 2016, the search for someone to blame began. Besides the usual suspects, the Russians, one of the theories claimed that it was the mainstream media that contributed to Trump's victory. Not only did the mainstream media generously cover Trump, seeing his campaign as entertainment, they also scrutinized Hillary Clinton rigorously, based on the professional premises of impartiality and neutrality. Basically, the media did not seriously analyze Trump's political agendas and promises to the electorate, as they did not really see him as a politician. Clinton, however, was treated as a politician,

---

[1] See, for example: Society of Professional Journalists Code of Ethics, https://www.spj.org/ethicscode.asp; or American Press Association Principle of journalism, https://americanpressassociation.com/principles-of-journalism/.

and therefore her background and policy statements were analyzed according to the standards of good-old watchdog journalism. The media exercised infotainment when covering Trump and political journalism when covering Clinton; this difference in the genres of coverage favored Trump and harmed Clinton. As was calculated by *Columbia Journalism Review*,

> Even more striking, the various Clinton-related email scandals – her use of a private email server while secretary of state, as well as the DNC and John Podesta hacks – accounted for more sentences than all of Trump's scandals combined (65,000 vs. 40,000) and more than twice as many as were devoted to all of her policy positions.[1]

Another study showed that, "the majority of mainstream media coverage was negative for both candidates, but largely followed Donald Trump's agenda: when reporting on Hillary Clinton, coverage primarily focused on the various scandals related to the Clinton Foundation and emails" (Faris et al., 2017).

"Don't blame the election on fake news. Blame it on the media," a headline in CJR stated.[2] Ultimately, a sort of 'abuse' of professional standards was declared responsible for the dramatic failure of Clinton and the shocking win of Trump.

From this point on, two flak responses arose, both censorial in nature.

1. A call to the media to ignore Trump's agenda, not to give him a floor, and, eventually, not cover him at all.

2. A demand to reconsider the norm of listening to both sides and giving equal consideration to all competing circumstances and opinions.

***

Being called out by the audience and by each other for propelling Trump to victory, the media and the public tried to articulate a justifiable thesis on why the president of the USA, the most newsworthy figure in the world, should not be covered. At first, the idea seemed to be too unconventional and overtly partisan. Some media did not hesitate; others tried to claim nonpartisan neutrality and resisted Trump in the name of democracy, not the Democrats.

Either way, the resistance to Trump's agenda was driven by the ultimate goal of ensuring that anyone other than Trump gets into the White House.

[1] Watts, Duncan J., and Rothschild, David M. (2017, December 5). "Don't blame the election on fake news. Blame it on the media." *Columbia Journalism Review*. https://www.cjr.org/analysis/fake-news-media-election-trump.php.

[2] Ibid.

The eventual purpose was political, not journalistic. Moreover, in fighting against Trump and yet simultaneously profiting from covering him, the media descended into politicization and polarization. (This development was specific to the USA, but it had common traits with many free-market media systems at the time. The political and media environment was and continues to be impacted by the growing influence of social media and the decline of the traditional media. This resulted in growing polarization that fueled both the uprise of the right in alternative media and the subsequent migration of the mainstream media to the left.)

***

Before 2016, the media in the USA might have expressed their endorsements in editorials; but when reporting, they tried to uphold standards of rigor and impartiality towards both political sides. The legacy of the transactional sale of news mandated adherence to the old standards of news as a commodity; the legacy of advertising sale prescribed the widening of the audience and impartiality was a part of this business code.

After 2016, this stance rapidly started changing. Journalists and the public began to openly demand a revision of journalism's standards towards more impact and involvement for the sake of democracy. For example, *CNN* White House correspondent Jim Acosta, known for his aggressive style of questioning Trump, claimed that, "Neutrality for the sake of neutrality doesn't really serve us in the age of Trump."[1]

Mark Lukasiewicz, a former executive at *NBC News*, recalled in *CJR* that, "A generation ago, television news was dominated by taped and edited reporting. TV journalism was mostly 'curated'." He called, essentially, for restoring this practice, referring to the Oscars ceremony aired with a 7-second delay to bleep out unexpected expletives. He suggested,

> Let truth-telling be a prerequisite for appearing on live TV. Repeat offenders who lie or obfuscate with abandon, no matter their position, should not be put on live again. Adjust the balance between "being first" and "being right."[2]

It is worth noting that the professional standard, which is supposed to regulate journalism here, is meant to be applied not to journalists' reporting but to a reported speech, namely the speech of the president of the US. This

---

[1] Ecarma, Caleb. (2019, May 28). "CNN's Acosta Rejects 'Neutrality for the Sake of Neutrality' during trump era in new book." *Mediaite*. https://www.mediaite.com/trump/cnns-jim-acosta-rejects-media-neutrality-during-trump-era-in-new-book/

[2] Lukasiewicz, Mark. (2020, April 1). "Can live TV become journalism again?" *Columbia Journalism Review*. https://www.cjr.org/analysis/journalism-needs-live-tv.php

tiny indistinguishable shift in standards of 'truth-telling' reflected the times well.

***

The idea to 'curate' reality and the statements of others in order to make things right was clearly expressed amid Trump's COVID press-briefings. It did not take him long to shock the public and the media with his statements regarding the pandemic. During the darkest days of the coronavirus spread in the USA, he either praised himself for doing "such a good job", sometimes obviously campaigning, or suggested exploring the potential of disinfectant injections.[1]

Amid such obviously nonsensical proclamations, the push back against neutrality and impartiality in reporting acquired an additional supportive argument: the live airing of Trump can be dangerous for people. Many media outlets even served the case up as if Trump really had called for disinfectants' to be injected and that some people might follow.[2]

After heated debates[3], *CNN* and *MSNBC* stopped airing what they considered to be unrelated parts of the briefings: for example, when a campaigning-style video[4] was run or when a success in border wall building[5] was discussed during a formal coronavirus task force briefing. The case is reminiscent of the story of Théophraste Renaudot, the editor of the French *La Gazette*, who reportedly cut the battlefield reportages of his king and war correspondent Louis XIII in 1633–1642. t This was most likely the only case in history in which an editor cut his king's writings. Renaudot knew better

---

[1] *NBC News.* (2020, April 24). "Trump suggests 'injection' of disinfectant to beat coronavirus and 'clean' the lungs." https://www.nbcnews.com/politics/donald-trump/trump-suggests-injection-disinfectant-beat-coronavirus-clean-lungs-n1191216

[2] *BBC.* (2020, 24 April). "Coronavirus: Outcry after Trump suggests injecting disinfectant as treatment." In the lead, BBC presented a slightly different version of the news: "US President Donald Trump has been lambasted by the medical community after suggesting research into whether coronavirus might be treated by injecting disinfectant into the body." https://www.bbc.com/news/world-us-canada-52407177

[3] Bauder, David. (2020, 17 April). "To air or not air Trump briefings? Pressure on at networks." *ABC News.* https://abcnews.go.com/Entertainment/wireStory/air-air-trump-briefings-pressure-networks-70210701

[4] Concha, Joe. (2020, April 13). "CNN cuts away from 'propaganda' briefing as Trump plays video hitting press." *The Hill.* https://thehill.com/homenews/media/492612-cnn-cuts-away-from-propaganda-briefing-as-trump-plays-video-hitting-press

[5] Da Silva, Chantal. (2020, April 4). "CNN, MSNBC cut away from Trump's coronavirus briefing as Americans call for end to continuous coverage." *Newsweek.* https://www.newsweek.com/cnn-msnbc-cut-away-trump-coronavirus-briefing-americans-call-end-continuous-coverage-1495754

what needed to be told. Trump could have comforted himself with the idea that he is king-like, at least in this instance.

With calls to the media to cut off Trump in order to protect the health of Trump's gullible followers, an interesting legal and logical case was created. Not only did the media insist on direct censorship, they also assumed the authority to decide that people legally capable of electing Trump were not intellectually capable of safely listening to him. The liberal media put themselves in the unusual position of patronizing Trump's followers.

***

The media got trapped into a sort of the *democrat's dilemma*, a metaphor made by Seva Gunitsky, professor of political science at the University of Toronto, out of the *dictator's dilemma*. The dictator's dilemma describes the paradox of controlling the spread of information. When the ruler allows the spread of more information needed for better governance and economy, the increase in information encourages the rise of alternative ideas and threatens the regime. More information is both needed by and dangerous to the dictator. The democrat's dilemma, Gunitsky suggested, is something similar but opposite: by forbidding information potentially harmful to democracy, democracy is thereby harmed; by allowing it, democracy allows antidemocratic ideas to spread.[1]

The issue here is that such reasoning is undertaken not by a ruler choosing an appropriate ratio of information spread, but by the media, who thereby openly accept the role of 'anti-dictator'. This is an overtly political role that reshapes all the principles of agenda-setting and standards of journalism.

The debate about the harm of neutrality in covering Trump and the calls for ignoring him has brought no visible results. The media could not allow themselves not to cover Trump, the last remaining source of their declining popularity and the main source of their residual business. But this debate has certainly changed the perception of journalist standards, having pushed journalists to take a side in the political fight.

***

Another post-election motive for reconsidering journalist impartiality, the idea of not giving equal consideration to both sides when it is obvious which side is right, appeared after the #MeToo movement. It has become acknowledged that there is no 'other side' when it comes to violence and

[1] Gunitsky, Seva. (2020, April 21). "Democracies can't blame Putin for their disinformation problem." *Foreign Policy*. https://foreignpolicy.com/2020/04/21/democracies-disinformation-russia-china-homegrown/

sexual abuse. This acknowledgment has been extended to other areas of reporting.

The rule of listening to both sides in any conflict and all-sided consideration of arguments was a common and simple norm of good journalism until very recently. Since 2016–2017, the active rejection of 'bothsidesism' has begun.

The Merriam-Webster Dictionary subtitled its article on bothsidesing "When equal coverage leads to uneven results." The definition says that,

> *Bothsidesing* and its related noun *bothsidesism* turn up in critiques of the news media when a journalist or pundit seems to give extra credence to a cause, action, or idea that on the surface seems objectionable, thereby establishing a sort of moral equivalence that allows said cause, action, or idea to be weighed seriously.
>
> By giving credence to the other side, the media gives an impression of being fair to its subject, but in doing so often provides credibility to an idea that most might view as unmerited.[1]

***

After Donald Trump suggested that it may be worthwhile doing some research into whether injecting disinfectants can cure COVID-19, the *New York Times* wrote that Trump's theorizing was dangerous, "in the view of some experts". Then, *NYT* retracted the phrase with the statement:

> We've deleted an earlier tweet and updated a sentence in our article that implied that only "some experts" view the ingestion of household disinfectants as dangerous. To be clear, there is no debate on the danger.[2]

Some Twitterati saw this as further proof of the professional failure of bothsidesism, implying that *NYT* published nonsense because of having to mechanically follow the principle of giving consideration to both sides.[3]

---

[1] The Merriam-Webster Dictionary. Looking at 'Bothsidesing' When equal coverage leads to uneven results. https://www.merriam-webster.com/words-at-play/bothsidesing-bothsidesism-new-words-were-watching

[2] New York Times Twitter. (2020, April 24). https://webcache.googleusercontent.com/search?q=cache:67AYKkE4HyQJ:https://twitter.com/nytimes/status/1253719616603541504%3Flang%3Den+&cd=1&hl=en&ct=clnk&gl=ca&client=firefox-b-d

[3] See, for example, critical notes on NYT's *bothsidesing* regarding this case: Mike Wagner – https://twitter.com/Garossino/status/1253729285065465856, or Sandy Garossino – https://twitter.com/prowag/status/1253676629429301248

"'Bothsidesism' is poisoning America," wrote media outlets.[1] The very pejorative 'bothsidesism' was meant to disprove and reject the old standard of reporting contentious issues from both sides. As journalist Wesley Lowery summed it up,

> American view-from-nowhere, "objectivity"-obsessed, both-sides journalism is a failed experiment. We need to fundamentally reset the norms of our field. The old way must go. We need to rebuild our industry as one that operates from a place of moral clarity.[2]

Noticeably, there were not many debates on bothsidesism in the conservative media. This perhaps indicates that 'journalism' on the political right has either never bothered with this standard or is not bothered about changing it now. Therefore, the revision of professional standards is an issue for liberal journalism, the former bastion of classical journalist standards. As Faris et al. noted in 2017 when studying asymmetric polarization in the American media,

> The leading media on the right and left are rooted in different traditions and journalistic practices. On the conservative side, more attention was paid to pro-Trump, highly partisan media outlets. On the liberal side, by contrast, the center of gravity was made up largely of long-standing media organizations steeped in the traditions and practices of objective journalism.[3]

***

Calls for the prohibition of inappropriate views might appear to be an outcome of ideological polarization. However, media determinism allows another viewpoint. Both polarization and the desire to prohibit opposite views are the result of a third factor, an environmental one – the emancipation of authorship.

Freedom of speech was an unconditional democratic value in the environment with limited access to publication. This access meant power, and it was protected by a high entry cost and authority licensing, either direct or hidden. The emancipation of authorship handed this access to everyone. However, without technical limitations, the value reverses into an

---

[1] Lalami, Laila. (2019, December 17). "'Bothsidesism' Is Poisoning America." *The Nation.* https://www.thenation.com/article/archive/trump-impeachment-journalism/

[2] Rosen, Jay. (2020, June 8). "Battleship Newspaper." *Pressthink.* https://pressthink.org/2020/06/battleship-newspaper/

[3] Faris et al. (2017, August 16). "Partisanship, propaganda, and disinformation: online media and the 2016 U.S. Presidential Election." The Berkman Klein Center for Internet & Society at Harvard University. https://cyber.harvard.edu/publications/2017/08/mediacloud

anti-value. It is the same as with the money supply: increased monetary emission leads to depreciation.

Freedom of speech has become technically guaranteed to everyone and as a result has lost its universal paramount value; moreover, the overproduction of free speech resulted in the necessity for society to find other filtering mechanisms than those that had previously been attached to the power control of the means of publication. From being technically (power-) conditioned, free speech, because of overproduction, is becoming socially (morally) conditioned.

***

When free speech is guaranteed to everyone, a new question arises: Does everyone really deserve the right to free speech? Should Hitler have enjoyed freedom of speech? It appears that universal free speech empowers bad actors, too, when everyone is allowed to speak and the impact of one's speech – the *effective* free speech – depends exclusively on one's intensity, talent and also – still – money/power (as these factors now underpin not access but the outreach of platforms).

A characteristic of this new environment, though, is that money/power no longer form a monopoly over freedom of speech. This former monopoly has been degraded to a privilege. With others having access to freedom of speech but without the privilege of money/power, the privilege of *effective* free speech is seen as an inequality of opportunities. Hence was born the idea to regulate *effective* free speech on the basis of morality. The factor of morality replaced the factor of access in the role of speech filtering amid free speech overproduction.

***

Morality-filtering of speech instead of access-filtering has become a new environmental force created by the digital media. The inequality of opportunities in free speech had not existed before the internet because there were no opportunities, except for those possessed by the powerful.

When the non-powerful gained access to free speech but not the ability of *effective* free speech, platform inequality appeared. Free speech lost its binary measurement and became a stepwise phenomenon with varying degrees of realization. Amid the universal technical access to free speech, the ability of someone to make more or less impact becomes seen as different degrees of free speech, often regardless of the talent or effort contributed.

The difference in outcome became interpreted as the inequality of rights: if someone produces less impact, it is because they have a lesser right (i.e. less platform power). The lack of effect is interpreted as the lack of rights.

So, these are not efforts or talents that define effective speech but rights that must be restored (or suppressed – for those whose capacity to produce an effect through speech is seen as 'unjust').

As often happens to postmodernist phenomena, the critical became the normative. 'Because' of the variability and conditionality of *effective* free speech, the right of free speech also became seen as variable and conditional.

When everyone is fully immersed in the media environment, media inequality is social inequality. Those deprived of their fair share of *effective* voice must have their rights restored. Socialism becomes media-socialism. It demands the socialization of the means of effective-speech production; it advances the progressive class, the social-media cognitariat, insisting, through its revolutionary party, the Twitterati, on the expropriation of the property of *effective* free speech from media exploiters.

***

The conditionality of free speech prescribes that bad people – trolls, extremists, foreign operatives, the rich, the powerful, the right, the left and, generally, all sorts of media-Hitlers – shall not be allowed to enjoy universal free speech. Their exercise of free speech is the abuse of the right.

Bad actors should be de-platformed. How can one tell good people from bad? It is easy: the good people are our people. Thus, before any political fuel is added, the media environment splits users into 'them' and 'us' with respect to the use of free speech because of its overproduction, acquired variability, and conditionality. These environmental settings unavoidably invoke questions about media inequality, platform abuse, and affirmative censorship.

The technical media emancipation of authorship laid the foundation both for polarization and for the invisible reconsidering of the fundamental principles of democracy, as the previous version of the democracy software was built on the previous version of the media hardware. Considering the tectonic scale of this shift, the re-evaluation of journalists' professional standards appears somewhat less dramatic.

***

Watchdog journalism and accountability journalism aimed to control the powerful in general, most likely regardless of their political affiliation. Holding the powerful accountable could be a risky venture. Impartiality and other qualities of good media practice strengthened the power of journalism. To protect the media against legal flak, this job required rigorous procedures and flawless arguments. Thus, one of the functions of professional standards is to protect journalists from flak. Journalists have special rights, even in court, as long as they are journalists, meaning as long as they follow their professional standards. Another example of the protective function of standards is one of the main principles of war correspondents – they do not touch weapons. Those carrying guns are not journalists and cannot count on special treatment; they will be treated as combatants.

With the change in the business model (from ad to reader revenue) the nature of flak has changed. The most powerful flak is now the grassroots flak of the donating audience, whose will is voiced by the Twitterati, the ideological warbands of both political camps. The protective function of standards has also become redirected. Now, the professional standards need to protect journalists not from legal flak or flak from elites, but from the grassroots flak of the Twitterati, whose platform power is now equal to, or even exceeds, the platform power of the elites and the media themselves. Therefore, the standards have to protect what this flak can harm the most; the standards must comply with this flak. The shift in the protective function of standards additionally makes them less professional and more ideological.

***

This shift in standards has accompanied the mutation of watchdog journalism and accountability journalism into *advocacy journalism* and *activist journalism*. Most recently, a new term, *resistance journalism*, emerged. The *New York Times* media critic Ben Smith coined the term in a column about one of the most celebrated journalists, Ronan Farrow of the *New Yorker*, whose reporting on Harvey Weinstein and other powerful persons won him a Pulitzer and contributed to the tectonic shift in the cultural landscape.

In his May 2020 article "Is Ronan Farrow Too Good to Be True?", Smith questioned the reporting methods of "a highly visible, generational star". He wrote,

> Mr. Farrow, 32, is not a fabulist. His reporting can be misleading but he does not make things up. His work, though, reveals the weakness of a kind of resistance journalism that has thrived in the age of Donald Trump: That if reporters swim ably along with the tides of social media and produce damaging reporting about public figures most disliked by the loudest voices, the old rules of fairness and open-mindedness can seem more like impediments than essential journalistic imperatives.
>
> That can be a dangerous approach, particularly in a moment when the idea of truth and a shared set of facts is under assault.[1]

[1] Smith, Ben. (2020, May 17). "Is Ronan Farrow too good to be true?" *The New York Times*.

"It appears Mr. Farrow was making a narrative virtue of a reporting liability, and the results were ultimately damaging," suggested Smith. He scrutinized some episodes in Farrow's writing that, he believed, were not always properly fact-checked because they were *too good*, and this was enough to put them into an accusatory narrative, as is implied in the title "...Too Good to Be True". He continued:

> We are living in an era of conspiracies and dangerous untruths – many pushed by President Trump, but others hyped by his enemies – that have lured ordinary Americans into passionately believing wild and unfounded theories and fiercely rejecting evidence to the contrary. The best reporting tries to capture the most attainable version of the truth, with clarity and humility about what we don't know. Instead, Mr. Farrow told us what we wanted to believe about the way power works, and now, it seems, he and his publicity team are not even pretending to know if it's true.[1]

The article caused a Tweetstorm. The balance between the necessity to resist evil and adherence to the standards of journalist rigor was debated by all registered and unregistered media critics.

"The most menacing attribute of what Smith calls 'Resistance Journalism' is that it permits and tolerates no dissent and questioning: perhaps the single most destructive path journalism can take," wrote Glenn Greenwald. He supported Smith's observation by stating that,

> With young journalists watching jobs disappearing en masse, the last thing they are going to want to do is question or challenge prevailing orthodoxies within their news outlet or, using Smith's "Resistance Journalism" formulation, to "swim against the tides of social media" or question the evidence amassed against those "most disliked by the loudest voices." <...>
> Affirming those orthodoxies can be career-promoting, while questioning them can be job-destroying. <...>
> When journalists know they will thrive by affirming pleasing falsehoods, and suffer when they insist on unpopular truths, journalism not only loses its societal value but becomes just another instrument for societal manipulation, deceit, and coercion.[2]

---

https://www.nytimes.com/2020/05/17/business/media/ronan-farrow.html

[1] Ibid.

[2] Greenwald, Glenn. (2020, May 18). "Ben Smith's NYT critique of Ronan Farrow describes a toxic, corrosive, and still-vibrant Trump-Era pathology: 'Resistance Journalism'." *The Intercept.* https://theintercept.com/2020/05/18/ben-smiths-nyt-critique-of-ronan-farrow-describes-a-toxic-corrosive-and-still-vibrant-trump-era-pathology-resistance-journalism/

In the subsequent debates, Farrow won the support of many. The *New Yorker* stood by its star reporter. Michael Luo, editor of newyorker.com, wrote on Twitter that "In his column on @ronanfarrow, @benyt, whom I have respect for, does the same thing he accuses Ronan of – sanding the inconvenient edges off of facts in order to suit the narrative he wants to deliver."[1]

Slate turned Smith's accusations on himself, scrutinizing his arguments in the same way as he did to Farrow. *Slate* concluded that, "Smith chose to perform broad-mindedness, sacrificing accuracy for some vague, centrist perception of fairness."[2]

In this quote, interesting is the very implication that the "centrist perception of fairness" is something reprehensible, a sort of bias. This says a lot about how the professional attitude toward standards in journalism has changed. From the point of view of activist journalism or, more so, resistance journalism, centrism is the same sin as the 'false equivalency' of both sides.

***

When Vladimir Nabokov compared the Tsar's censorship in Russia with the Stalin era's mind control, he wrote that Tsarism wanted writers not to voice the forbidden, but Stalinism demanded writers to ardently express the approved. Tsarism wanted writers' political noninvolvement; Stalinism demanded writers' political active engagement. The same parallel can be drawn for journalism under different business models. Advertising money wanted journalists to be politically detached; the donating audience requires them to be politically engaged. Within this axiological paradigm, neutrality is suspicious, centrism is a crime, and bothsidesism is treason.

***

As Emily Bell noted regarding the debates on Farrow and resistance journalism, "...there hasn't been a week like this in media criticism since the days of Dewey and Lippmann."[3] She referred to the debates of the 1920s, when contemporary understanding of the functions and standards of

---

[1] Michael Luo on Twitter. (2020, May 18). @michaelluo. https://twitter.com/michaelluo/status/1262388538412347392

[2] Feinberg, Ashley. (2020. May 21). "Is Ben Smith's column about Ronan Farrow too good to be true?" Slate. https://slate.com/news-and-politics/2020/05/is-ben-smiths-column-about-ronan-farrow-too-good-to-be-true.html

[3] Emily Bell on Twitter. (2020. May 18). @emilybell https://twitter.com/emilybell/status/1262531463926427658

journalism was established. A hundred years later, the standards seem to have fallen under a global revision.

To complete the historical parallel, the beginning of the 20th century was the time when advertising started taking over the media business. Walter Lippmann was perhaps the first who noticed that the media sold readers in the form of circulation to "manufacturers and merchants" (Lippmann, 1929 [1922], p. 324). So, the formation of the classical professional standards of journalism coincided with the formation of the classical advertising model of media business.

In the same way, the re-formation of standards now coincides with the tectonic shift in media business from advertising to reader revenue. The media are now soliciting money from surfeited readers with 'subscription fatigue'.

The difference is that the formation of the advertising model lasted until the 1960s, evolved gradually, as did standards along with it, while the collapse of this model happened in 10 years or less, historically instantly. The switch to reader revenue with its odd demands on professional standards has not been fully comprehended yet. This is not even to mention that the shocks of Trumpism and polarization made the changes in journalist standards particularly dramatic and distorted by the politicization of supposedly professional debates.

***

Postjournalism has devoured the standards of impartiality and objectivity first. The media that still hold on to those standards have least chance of success in the competition for the donating audience. Other standards will most likely follow. For example, one of the standards of classical journalism was harm limitation. Postjournalism, on the contrary, *must* harm opponents, there is no question about it; but it also harms public sanity through the search for efficient donscription triggers.

It is also becoming evident how the culture of questioning in interviews and at press-briefings is changing. The decline of impartiality and the politicization of the media logically lead to the use of questions as statements. Journalism advances questions, propaganda advances statements; postjournalism advances statements in the guise of questions.

What was formerly protected and required by media autonomy, the right and duty of a journalist to push for truth no matter what, now depends on how much a speaker or a source complies with the donating audience's prevalent views.

On the one hand, the hard and inconvenient questions will unlikely be asked if a person is generally approved of by the donating audience. On the other hand, if a person is disliked by the donating audience, the interview is more likely to take the form of an interrogation, with the questions aimed to accuse or expose, not to learn. A press-briefing may turn into a rally and an exchange of punches.

One of the typical signs of postjournalism is the rephrasing of the speaker's opinion into a form convenient for debunking: it begins with "Are you saying that..." and continues with what needs to be condemned. Modern media Don Quixotes fight not monstrous windmills but convenient strawmen they make of their opponents. With these and similar gimmicks, the term 'ambush journalism' has taken on a new sense. In postjournalism, the questions come from the attitude, not from meaning.

***

Postjournalism does not create completely new standards. As with any 'post-' phenomenon, first of all, it repudiates the old ones.

Standards are meant to protect journalists from flak – legal and elite flak in the past and grassroots social media flak in the present. Legal flak was predominantly based on catching journalists out on inaccurate facts and biases. Therefore, the standards of accuracy and impartiality were what was most needed in order to protect journalists from accusations.

With opinion journalism taking command, the risk of legal flak has diminished. For a crafty professional, it is much easier to avoid legal risks when operating with opinions as opposed to facts. Moreover, in the media market with prevailing opinion journalism, factual accuracy is less relevant because it will not protect journalists from flak. Quite the opposite – accurately reported but unwanted facts will cause accusations and may have career consequences. And vice versa: no one will judge a journalist too harshly for a lack of accuracy or rigor if a journalist covers things rightly in substance. The phrase "fake but accurate" from the *New York Times* headline about the 2004 Rathergate unauthenticated documents regarding George W. Bush's military service[1] may be said in a new way now: 'fake but right'.

The media are realigning their standards. From the point of view of the previous professional ethics, this realignment is turning journalism into postjournalism. Postjournalism values ideological purity above factual

[1] Balleza, Maureen, and Zernike, Kate. (2004, September 15). "The 2004 Campaign: National Guard; memos on Bush are fake but accurate, typist says." *The New York Times.* https://www.nytimes.com/2004/09/15/us/the-2004-campaign-national-guard-memos-on-bush-are-fake-but-accurate.html

impartiality. More accurately, precisely in the spirit of postmodernism, purity has become the new accuracy: one must be accurate and diligent in expressing their purity. The prevalence of ideological accuracy over factual accuracy is market-driven, and its violation has professional consequences for people's careers and commercial consequences for the media orgs' profits on both sides of the spectrum. New standards are not being created by the guild. Rather they are borrowed from journalism, activism and propaganda under the pressure of the dying business, formerly known as media, and the uprising Twitterati, formerly known as the audience.

Discourse concentration

The polarization of stances requires the commonality of topics, in which the stances have to be polarized. In Swift's *Gulliver's Travels* (1726), the deadly clash within the great Lilliput nation was caused by irreconcilable discord regarding which end of an egg should be cracked before eating it. But what united them was the egg.

The classical political economy of the mass media focused on ownership concentration. What is more pertinent for the understanding of postjournalism is discourse concentration.

Media with more diverse local or non-political agendas cannot sustain an ability to survive, and they are dying out. The remaining media are those who accept the drift towards politicization promulgated by the donscription model. To adhere to the model, they need to polarize themselves and their audiences. As technical prerequisites for polarization, not only is a two-part environment needed, but also a common battleground wherein the opposing parties can clash. In order to fight, they simply need to come into contact within common topics.

Some discourses serve as magnets that align all the previously chaotic iron fillings along the lines of the force field. The presence of the opposite pole is "sensed" only if a common force field is induced. There must be common discourses that are able to accommodate the diametrically opposite readings of one and the same story.

***

In the short period of post-Stalin liberation in the 1960s' USSR, there was a discussion about whether collective farms were an effective format for the socialist economy. At the Writers' Congress, the regime's darling poet Yevgeny Yevtushenko delivered an ardent speech calling to reform collective farms. The poet and later Nobel laureate Iosif Brodsky reacted, "If

Yevtushenko is against collective farms, then I'm for them." It is hard to imagine something more distant from Brodsky than a discussion about socialist forms of agricultural management. But he was a nonconformist and dissident, and he just wanted to troll his counterpart. Collective farms meant nothing to this duo whatsoever. But if one was for something, the other turned against it right away.

The need to always oppose the opponent, no matter what, sometimes leads to some curiously odd marriages. If Trump is for collective farms, then the mainstream media are against them. When Trump banned travel to China in January 2020, some commentators in the mainstream media jointly downplayed the epidemic danger in China.[1] They justified it by raising a concern that the travel ban could stimulate racism. The travel ban on Brazil[2] at the end of May 2020 raised no such concerns in the media regarding racism, because the main topic of the polarized standoff had already moved in the opposite direction: Trump supported faster reopening and downplayed the pandemic, while the mainstream media urged not to hurry. The travel ban on Brazil did not fit the picture that Trump has scant regard for people's safety; therefore, the news about the Brazil travel ban was reported neutrally and soon forgotten. It did not make such a polarizing issue as the same decision regarding China.

Some other discourses made huge and long-lasting waves in the American media environment, feeding polarization for months, sometimes even years. Among them were Trump's campaign and election, the alt-right uprising, the Russian meddling, judge Brett Kavanaugh's appointment, the Mueller Report, Trump's impeachment, Trump's response to COVID-19, and all their byproducts. They all involve nearly the same polarizing scenario: something happened to Trump (or was done by Trump), the liberal media reacted to it, and the conservative media reacted to their reaction.

Discourse concertation has become one of the factors of natural selection in the media market. Those media that join the dominant polarized discourses – join the common hype from the opposite sides of it – could also

---

[1] See, for example: Manjoo, Farhad. (2020, January 29). "Beware the pandemic panic." *The New York Times*. https://www.nytimes.com/2020/01/29/opinion/coronavirus-panic.html; Spinks, Rosie. (2020, February 5). "Who Says It's Not Safe to Travel to China?" *The New York Times*. https://www.nytimes.com/2020/02/05/opinion/china-travel-coronavirus.html; Parmet, Wendy, and Sinha, Michael. (2020, February 3). "Why we should be wary of an aggressive government response to coronavirus." *The Washington Post*. https://www.washingtonpost.com/outlook/2020/02/03/why-we-should-be-wary-an-aggressive-government-response-coronavirus/.

[2] Carvajal, Nikki. (2020, May 25). "The White House's travel ban for Brazil starts tomorrow." *CNN*. https://www.cnn.com/world/live-news/coronavirus-pandemic-05-26-20-intl/h_6045ecb37c3fe76d8faedb4e106e069e

join the understandable and accepted-by-the-audience paradigm of donation soliciting; those who did not, were excluded. As the donation resources of the politicized public are quite limited, they were allocated to the several largest news organizations that were most successful in donscription. Only a few media orgs in the USA financially profited from the Trump bump. Discourse concentration results in media concentration almost as efficiently as the concentration of media ownership did.

***

The validation of significance by dissemination means justification by quantity: the hype is a virtual hive for social swarming. Sensationalism has long been a well-known feature of the mass media: big scoops come and go. The specificity of media polarization caused by the donscription business model is that it dis-incentivizes small topics that do not suit the general discourses with the most polarizing potential. Old sensationalism encouraged journalists to search for tips and scoops everywhere; donscription forces the media to focus on the most triggering political topics. This is the difference between journalism and activism in the practice of news coverage: activism narrows the focus. And so does postjournalism: it narrows the field for searching for scoops to the most donatable causes. For the sake of soliciting a larger audience in the conditions of polarization, each news organization needs to join the general debate. Journalists then search for tips and scoops within a very limited number of polarization-tested narratives. They all stick to the same magnet of the day from its opposite poles.

The connection between polarization and discourse concentration was most visible in the US mainstream media, due in no small part to the media "obsession"[1] with Trump. In this environment of mutually induced polarization with regard to Trump, there was but a narrow set of major topics circulated in any given period across all the media.

However, similar regularities should exist in any developed democracy at the same stage of media development. According to the concept of asymmetric polarization (Benkler, Faris & Roberts, 2018), the liberal and progressive pole of polarization is most likely to be presented by the mainstream old media, while the right conservative radical forces are most likely to be present in new media and on social media, and to a lesser extent on TV and radio.

---

[1] LaFrance, Adrienne. (2016, September 1). "The media's obsession with Donald Trump," *The Atlantic.* https://www.theatlantic.com/technology/archive/2016/09/trumps-media-saturation-quantified/498389/.

The initial trigger and main topic supplier is always a figure on the right side of the political spectrum: Trump in the US, Bolsonaro in Brazil, Morrison in Australia, Modi in India, etc. (More rarely it can be a political party; the German AfD is an example). The same processes, with specific national political and media characteristics, can be observed in France, Hungary, Austria, Italy and even Sweden. A salient political figure (or a force) from the right throws into the fray some ideas or statements, which cause outrage in the mainstream media, which are predominantly liberal (due to their traditions, institutional affiliations, education of journalists and editors, and their belonging to certain social circles). In response, the critical attitude – liberal bias – of the mainstream media should cause a backlash in the conservative media and grassroots media platforms on the internet and social media.

The momentum engendered has begun to concentrate this polarization. The polarization feeds off discourses that both sides can diametrically oppose and thereby maintain its momentum. Hence topics and discourses that do not support polarization will not circulate for long or will be completely ignored. All the energy potential of the media industry will focus on the topics that fit polarization. Neutrality is an unfit asset for the donscription business model, as it has no potency for triggering donations.

The topics that provide polarization are promoted, while others are neglected. As a result, the diversity of coverage suffers, and marginal, local and positive news suffer; after all who can trigger polarization through positive news?

In fact, the focus on polarizing themes to the detriment of small and diverse topics negatively impacts the quality of public service that the media are now seeking to sell. The public service of the comparatively successful media becomes corrupted; the media that struggle to stick with less polarized and more diverse coverage become disadvantaged and marginalized. Postjournalism downgrades the public service of the media to a mere propaganda service.

***

Discourse concentration is a technical prerequisite of media polarization which can also have a set of cultural and even psychological consequences. Apart from the reduction in coverage and the deterioration of public service, the media's obsession with topics most suited to polarization leads to an emotional surge. When everybody runs one and the same story, every ensuing account has to be louder than the previous one in order to be heard. New and more radical arguments and statements need to be made.

Discourse concentration contributes to hysteria, a devoted companion of polarization.

Lastly, discourse concentration herds all participants into a sort of *format bubble*. Locked in a restricted set of discourses, the meaning producers get trapped in self-absorption and are not capable of catching up with the changes in the media environment, particularly those that integrate new media technologies with new formats of meaning production. When the best minds and most gifted authors become obsessed with snapping at each other, they principally focus on achieving a stronger bite, tending to overlook the events and trends outside their coterie of vipers. They are too engrossed to notice if their rhetorical fight is resonating at all beyond the confines of their battles.

The 500-year old classical formats of discourse production are becoming technically obsolete. Journalists producing political discourse produce it for the users of literate media. But literate media themselves already do not cover all the areas of political activity. Twitter and other social media were based on a different sort of literacy – shorter, faster, more affordable and more democratic. New media with shorter and simpler literacy have triggered and spearheaded the political rebellion against the old establishment in the same way that pamphlets and newspapers did four centuries ago. Being shorter, simpler and more mobile forms of literacy than manuscripts, they triggered and spearheaded the bourgeois and Protestant rebellion against the old elites in the 16th through to 18th centuries.

***

By the mid-2010s, shorter, faster and simpler forms of literacy in new media had gained sufficient critical mass to challenge the political order of old establishments and prove that the news media are no longer in command of the political. As a significant part of news and ads left the media, so did politics – it started moving on to better platforms.

Now, new-new media have appeared that generally tend to be more sensorial and less literate. Classical political discourses appealed to those who were literate in the old Gutenberg sense: those who were able to read and write comparatively long linear narratives and understand the cultural codes behind letters. One needs to stop and sit to read journalism. There is no need to sit when diving into new media platforms. One can scroll TikTok on the go. TikTok, Telegram, Spotify, socially interactive videogames, and other platforms and messengers are creating a completely new environment capable of non-narrative, or even non-literate, meaning production and proliferation. Memes, gifs, vines, dance moves, and manifestative nicknames in games are becoming means of socializing.

New-new media are visual technically, but they induce an audile-tactile – a sensory perception, in the McLuhanesque sense. Unlike literate media that involved users in a cognitive connection with ideas and other people, new-new media are creating a panoramic-sensorial and therefore emotional perception of reality.

Beginning with electronic media, literacy started losing its lead in shaping the political. What was facilitated by the first wave of social media, such as Twitter, Facebook and Instagram, is now regressing further, from more literacy to less literacy. New-new media may contain utterances but not text. They do not care about linear clarity and the elaboration of narrative. New-new media seek to involve users and give them a sense of socialization at every given moment. There is no time for deep thinking; and no need either. They focus is on the expression of mood and feeling, not ideas.

New-new media do not represent reality through text – they induce it immediately (Miroshnichenko, 2016). In new-new media, social reality is given as if it is the physical surroundings of the user. Just like physical reality, the digital social reality comes with diverse sensory signals simultaneously from all around, not as a linear text with its successive input of thoughts into the receiver's consciousness.

The media and old political establishments were shocked by Trump's victory and the global rise of the 'silent majority', baffled as to how this different type of thinking became so powerful. But this was not only a different type of thinking, it is a different media type of sensory perception of social reality, as if it were a physical reality. It was facilitated by the first waves of social media which began rejecting old media's literacy. But those early social media platforms were at least partly literacy-based. Now we are surrounded by types of emotional social media able to directly transmit social emotions, completely unmediated by literacy, where words are just one of the input signals, whose meanings are reduced to the level of exclamations and interjections.

***

Those obsessed with a limited number of very energy-consuming discourses in a closed circuit of the classical format of meaning production may think they run the entire public sphere. And they do, considering the inherent authenticity of journalism to the public sphere. But social and political activity gradually emerges on alternative non-narrative platforms and in non-narrative formats. Discourse concentration for better polarization in the media leads to the dominance of some themes over others and also to a concentration on discursive formats of meaning production and blindness towards other, newly emerged formats.

The new wave of social media formats, principally non-narrative and even non-literate ones, also represents a generational gap, where old discourses are, by and large, unable to penetrate these new-generation formats. Non-narrative meaning production will further empower both the radical right and the radical left, whose main characteristic will be neither 'right' nor 'left', but 'radical'. They understand and accept neither the format, nor the language that the old discourse-mongers believed to cover all political activity.

However much the old media may have boosted their polarized emotionality, they could never mimic the immediate emotionality of non-literate media, simply because of the innate limitations in the literate format of old media. In old media, polarization incites outrage, which contributes to the general emotional tone of society but without a significant impact on meanings' turnover outside the media. Discourse concentration is accompanied by the cocooning of the political discourses within literate media formats. This makes discourse producers and consumers blind to what is going on in the alternative media formats of political manifestation, which are rapidly growing. Many shocks are yet to come.

Post-truth: too good to be true

Journalism wants its picture to match the world. Postjournalism wants the world to match its picture.

The world seen through the prism of the media was always distorted; sometimes by the deliberate efforts of meaning producers, but principally by the systemic settings of the mode of production, including the technological (print, telegraph, radio, etc.) and political-economic (reader revenue, ad revenue, power licensing, party funding, etc.).

However, under each mode of production, there were professional standards that declared the value of objective truth and were able to mitigate (or hide) the distortions to some extent.

News retail, meaning the selling of news *downwards*, to the audience, had always employed the best fact-checker – the market demand. If readers wanted guidance for their social and business activity and safety, they buy news that is real. They would stop buying errors and fakes (unless they want fakes). The media based on news retail sought to grasp the *world-as-it-is*. At the systemic level, the invisible hand of market-driven fact-checking could be distorted only by negativity bias (the attraction of readers to terrifying news) or by the malpractice of journalists.

Audience wholesaling, the selling of agenda *upwards*, to advertisers or political sponsors, required a significant doctoring of the world picture. The focus on sponsored topics, politicizing or depoliticizing, avoiding unwanted pressing issues and the manufacture of consent were the systemic outcomes. However, the success of this model depended on circulation and audience outreach. Since the media were paid for gathering the audience by means of content, they could not afford to repel the audience through unduly false news. The adequacy and relevance of the picture of the world was still a business factor.

Unlike propaganda, commercially maintained journalism sought, or at least pretended, to be an adequate reflection of objective reality. Journalism referred to the *world-as-it-is*, even if it applied negative or positive filtering for better sales. The distortions were inevitable but reflected upon, studied and usually condemned.

***

The picture of the *world-as-it-is* relies on truth. Truth can be distorted or manipulated, but the demand for the news assumes that truth is at the core, and this truth is potentially verified by evidence, authority, knowledge, expertise, regularities and other ways to align as closely as possible with the truth. Truth is needed as a form of guidance that matches the objective reality. Individuals, communities and society need it for successful or secure functioning. Truth must match reality, not ideology; ideology oftentimes intervenes, but it is admitted as abuse and condemned.

In depicting the world, the truth might never be achieved in practice, but it is assumed as an ideal to be cherished and striven for. The critical thinking of what is objective truth and how much it is impacted by social (class, ideological, etc.) constructing is included and does not revoke the regulative power of truth.

The picture of the *world-as-it-should-be* always has post-truth built into it. Truth as a regulator is irrelevant, as it is replaced with justice (in the best-case scenario) or appropriateness. A reflected reality must match the intent, not the world. The picture of the *world-as-it-should-be* serves its creator, not its user.

This is an important hallmark of post-truth. The picture of the world that one wishes to *receive*, most likely refers to truth, even when deceiving or distorted. The picture of the world that is *meant to be imposed* more likely reflects post-truth. It reflects the preferences of its social engineer, not its user.

***

Today's news consumers start their daily online routine most often with the social media newsfeed on their smartphones. By the time (and if at all) users come to look at news media websites, they generally know all the news relevant to them. If the news is important but not verified by the repetitions of multiple headlines in the newsfeed, it needs to be validated by the media. Value validation of what is already known is the only news job left for the media. When facts are already known but are worrisome, factual reporting is no longer needed, and it must turn into evaluative commenting.

Within this media environment, the audience generally wants the media to validate or invalidate what it already knows and to scare readers with what they are already scared by. The media must confirm that the scare is legitimate. The connotation meaning of information prevails over the referential meaning: attitude prevails over content. This 'attitudinal' news-validation function of news media based on the donscription model is at the core of the definition of post-truth.

In the conditions of news redundancy, the need for attitude is much more pressing than the need for news. Attitude precedes meaning in the 'use-value' of news supply by the media. The supremacy of attitude over meaning is an interesting postmodernist phenomenon: post-truth, actually, is pre-truth. The picture of the *world-as-it-should-be* always appears before the *world-as-it-should-be* comes into existence because its existence is the dissemination of its picture. Post-truth is a 'post-'phenomenon historically, but, semantically, it is a 'pre-'phenomenon. The *world-as-it-should-be* firstly belongs to its creator-observer, with observation turning into creation.

This semantic reversal was noticed by Ruth Marcus from the *Washington Post*. In 2017, she suggested to forget about the "post-truth presidency," because that of Trump was the "pre-truth presidency." Trump made statements ahead of them being true, and then they became true, at least in the reality he created for them. "In this way, Trump serves as a human Heisenberg principle, changing a measurable phenomenon by observing it," wrote Marcus.[1]

Besides the Heisenberg principle, the reflection's precession of what is to be reflected is, of course, reminiscent of the Baudrillardian concept of

---

[1] Marcus, Ruth. (2017, March 23). "Forget the post-truth presidency. Welcome to the pre-truth presidency." *The Washington Post.* https://www.washingtonpost.com/opinions/welcome-to-the-pre-truth-presidency/2017/03/23/b35856ca-1007-11e7-9b0d-d27c98455440_story.html

simulacrum (Baudrillard, 2012 [1981]). Also worthy of noting is the fact that creation by vision or pronouncing is a common religious idea of cosmogony.

***

In 1995, Nicholas Negroponte, the founder of MIT's Media Lab, introduced the concept of the *Daily Me*, a customized news service that would tailor the newsfeed according to the tastes and needs of an individual.[1] Thus, the digital quantization of media content began. In the digital reality, it became possible to disassemble any newspaper into pieces and reassemble it for everyone personally. The principle of assemblage on this assembly line was thereby transferred from the media producer's end to the media consumer's end.

There was one large flaw in the idea: it required a user to recognize and declare their tastes and needs in information, which is an unnatural and unbearable task for a regular person. However, this 'innovative' view of news-service customization was popular at the time. The idea of creating a news ATM was even mooted, a machine that would allow a user to pick news categories, topics, authors, genres, etc., and print an individually customized newspaper.

As Marshall McLuhan would characterize this type of thinking, it represents rearview-mirror logic: "We look at the present through a rearview mirror. We march backwards into the future" (McLuhan & Fiore, 1967, p. 77). The idea revolutionized the mode of delivery for the obsolete product.

The really customized delivery of the news to everyone was realized 10 years later by social networks, without the necessity for users to reflect upon how and what they consume or to choose authors and topics. Algorithms do the job, learning people's preferences exposed by their previous online behavior.

Not only did social media put Negroponte's idea into practice, they also reversed its passive voice. By the *Daily Me*, Negroponte meant the *Daily-For-Me*. Social media did that, but they also made it the *Daily-By-Me*.

In a sense, the *Daily-For-Me* already hinted at the Barthesian 'death of the author'. The reader was supposed to take upon themselves a part of the author's authority over content by choosing topics, genres, authors, and so on. The original author would become just a supplier of the raw product, while the reader would complete the assembly of the end product.

At the next stage, in social media's *Daily-By-Me*, readers have become the full-fledged author of their agenda in many senses. They display their

---

[1] Harper, Christopher. (1997, April). "The Daily Me." *American Journalism Review*. https://web.archive.org/web/20090328114708/http://www.ajr.org/Article.asp?id=268

likes and choices for algorithms to learn their preferences and adjust their newsfeed accordingly (the *Daily-For-Me*); they also produce content for the newsfeed and therefore for others to see (the *Daily-By-Me*).

The combined product, the *Daily-Of-Me*, has become an authorial picture of the world, centered not in reality or even the educated editor's view of reality but in the user. The receiver has become the message or, to be precise, the pre-message – pre-truth.

***

In fact, the role of the reader in shaping media agendas has grown very slowly over 500 years of journalism, rapidly accelerating in the last couple of decades.

The first newspapers were audience-agnostic. The inner structure of the audience, even its feedback, was indistinguishable and even insignificant for the first mass media (which were, in reality, the elite media). The audience was comprised of those who could read and buy newspapers.

The first sign that newspapers started acknowledging the existence of the audience appeared when party newspapers emerged (circa late 18th century). They were not "newspapers for all who can read". Even though their audience specification originated from its owners, not readers, the characteristics of the audience, for the first time, began to matter.

The audience started being distinguishable for the media when thematically-focused newspapers appeared – for the bourgeois, workers, merchants, scientists, women, children, etc. The role of the audience increased even more when readers started writing letters to editors and editors started publishing them. The audience gained a voice. The genre of the interview appeared, which allowed even an ordinary passerby to become a co-author of the agenda.

What a shock it must have been for the guild when a reader filed a lawsuit against a newspaper for the first time. Punishment from the powerful was not unfamiliar to editors and publishers, but an ordinary reader had never been seen as legally equal to a newspaper before that.

Technologies significantly accelerated the audience's interference with the media. User-managed interactivity came to the media from video games. Douglas Rushkoff gave an account of the very first interference of the user with media in his 1994 book *Media Virus!* He cited his interview with Timothy Leary, who recalls that the video game Pong from the early 1970s allowed kids to "move things on a screen". As Leary said to Rushkoff,

The importance of the Nintendo phenomenon is about equal to that of the Gutenberg printing press. Here you had a new generation of kids who grew up knowing that they could change what's on the screen... The ability to change what's on the screen is the tremendous empowerment. (Rushkoff, 1994, p. 30.)

***

When users become able not only to consume media but also to input content into media, they get active and they get connected. From this interactivity, the participatory intervention of the audience into the media started. It has ended up, thus far, in user-generated content. The people formerly known as the audience now set the agenda, and they do it not only *in* the news media, but also *without* the news media at all.

What has happened in a cultural sense is that the audience has turned from a passive object to an active subject of agenda-setting. The worldview mentally and psychologically has become not world-centered, but user-centered. The world is now not some packaged object that is delivered to a user in the news. The world surrounds the users immediately, as a physical reality is extended (or induced) by the digital reality in the form of a digital interface's cocoons, with the users being the enslaved masters of their cocoons. The Universe – the Multiverse, to be precise – has become user-centric.

This is an important prerequisite of post-truth. Content becomes increasingly obliged to match not the world (whatever it is), but the user, with all their needs (tastes, opinions, fallacies, etc.). At the beginning of the evolution of the mass media, indistinguishable readers were given the content of the first newspapers in complete ignorance of who the readers were. At the end of the evolution of the mass media, content now revolves around the user, personally distinguishing them and their needs.

This evolutionary mechanism eventually facilitates bettering users' self-actualization on social media. It has completed the cultural shift in people's attitudes towards truth. With the transfer of content-centering from the producer's end to the consumer's end, truth has become detached from reality and attached to the user. The objectivity of the literate era's truth has flipped to the subjectivity of the digital era's post-truth.

A prosumer becomes the master of the reality. This makes the reality multiple and originating from many sources; basically, from all users and their content activity. Truth was universal; post-truth is multiversal. As Martin Gurri noted, "We aim to impose *our* facts and annihilate *theirs*, a process closer to intellectual holy war than to critical thinking."[1] Making facts one's own property is not solely Trump's prerogative. When Nancy Pelosi stated, "I reject your facts!"[1] she demonstrated, essentially, the same attitude. To be true means to be good enough for *me and those like me*. If it is good in our personal parts of the Multiverse, who cares if it is the truth or not in the Universe.

***

The physical world would verify truth by methods related to sensorial experience, the most reliable of which is death. One cannot cheat death (so far), so people need to respect physical ways of truth verification. Among them, the scientific laws of regularity appeared, first physical then logical, which were able to postulate truth without a constant need to hit one's forehead against solid objects in order to verify their solidness.

Post-truth is truth in the digital environment, where the physical risks of 'wrong' interactions do not exist. If the physical reality is made of objects, the digital reality is made of subjects – of others. The sensorial feedback of wrongdoing, the pain of hitting against objects, has turned into the pain of hitting against subjects, against others.

People are training to resettle into the digitally induced environment, where the spatial dimension is replaced by the temporal dimension. Instead of physical risks, social risks become absolutized. Digital is pure social. In the digital world, death is ostracism and cancellation. Cancel culture is apologetics and the practicing of a tribe's death penalty, similar to execution by stoning, where legitimacy is maintained by the collectivity of others. The numbers matter. This new regulator of wrongdoing is replacing the old criteria of truth: instead of the complying with the laws of the physical Universe, one now needs to comply with the values of the social Multiverse – or the part of it to which a person wants or needs to belong.

In the physical reality, the concept of irrefutable truth, ultimately verified by death, ended up being written in the Book: the *Torah*, the *Bhagavad-Gita*, the *Bible*, the *Quran* and some others. The irrefutability of physical principles, naturally maintained by the sensorium and the fear of pain and death, evolved into the same unquestioned set of moral rules and then scientific laws. The irrefutability is what is (was) truth.

---

[1] Gurri, Martin. (2020, May 26). "The way out of post-truth." *The Bridge*. Merkatus Center at George Mason University. https://www.mercatus.org/bridge/commentary/way-out-post-truth

[1] Mikelionis, Lukas. (2019, January 5). "Pelosi, Nielsen clashed during border-security meeting: 'I reject your facts,' House speaker said, according to report." *Fox News*. https://www.foxnews.com/politics/pelosi-interrupted-dhs-boss-nielsen-during-presentation-on-illegal-immigrants-saying-i-reject-your-facts

The idea of unified supreme knowledge, considered to be a source of truth and, later, also of hegemony and oppression, naturally dissolves as humans resettle into the digital environment.

There is no highest universal truth anchored in irrefutable laws anymore. In the participatory environment, the sole center of absolute power is replaced by the distributed authority. The Cloud has swallowed the Pyramid.[1] Vertical gravity disperses into multidirectional gravitations. As the objective world in the digital environment is not verified physically, significance is validated by distribution. That is why the number matters: the universal gets replaced by the multiversal. It is not without reason that Donald Trump, a pure media being, always referred, for proof, to something published in newspapers, or said by others, or proved by TV ratings, or that "everyone knows it". Interactions are verified by others – by as many others as are needed to be enough. Verification gets reduced to approval by others, often even imaginary others. In the digital reality, approval by others opposes cancellation by others, like life opposes death in the physical reality. This is not exclusively Trump's peculiarity; it is just his candid expression of the emerging new common principles of truth verification in the digital reality.

Verified by distribution, pre-digital post-truth becomes digital truth. It belongs not to the outer world, but to the users accumulating their subjective truths into a large enough collective amount of truth. Objectivity is replaced with collective massivity, which makes complete sense in the participatory digital environment.

***

The mass media emerged at the beginning of the Gutenberg era, with the highest universal truth written in the Book. Being the mass medium, they themselves started to corrupt the truth by distribution. Factoids, the mass media's phenomenon, make facts of what was pushed to public knowledge by dissemination. Factoids were facts in the reality induced by the media.

But factoids belonged exclusively to the mass media and did not cause much outcry in either the media industry or among consumers who generally were accustomed to tolerating media factoids, because factoids were not multiversal. Factoids in old media used to come from a superior, unitarian and authoritarian source, not from many peers. Those factoids

---

[1] Mir, Andrey. (2019, December 25). "The Pyramid against the Cloud: Institutions' perplexity regarding the Net." *Human as Media blog.* https://human-as-media.com/2019/12/25/the-pyramid-against-the-cloud-institutions-perplexity-regarding-the-net/

morphologically suited the Gutenberg pyramidal culture with vertical gravity and a solitary source of truth.

With the digital decomposition of truth into post-truth, factoids have ceased to be in the monopolistic possession of the media and have turned into fake news made by whoever has the means to make them. Now, the media fight fake-news and manifest this fight as part of their public service. Basically, the competition between old media and new media is the battle between factoids and fake news.

Fact-checking emerged in old media from investigative journalism in order to hold the powerful accountable. Amid the increase in media polarization, presently, the media's fact-checking is aimed not just at politicians but also at other media. With this retargeting, fact-checking mutates into factoid-checking, which is nonsense.

Moreover, nothing can be reality-checked against either facts or factoids in the digital reality. For factoids and post-truth, the scale of dissemination is the main and only method of verification. There is no ultimate verifying authority to refer to anymore. There is no longer the Book, nor the physically retaliating failure of interaction that would serve as the ultimate criteria of truth. The only viable way to fact-check something in the digital reality is to check the quantity and quality of its dissemination, which means looking at how many people join the distribution, why, and how many of them are influential – authoritative nodes of social networks (yet again meaning simply how many followers those disseminating the news have).

If the Universe was recorded in the Book, the Multiverse is recorded in the newsfeeds. The newsfeeds are taking over. At the end of their evolutionary path, the news media have to comply and compete with the newsfeeds, not the Book.

Post-truth is neither a gift by postmodernists nor an evil plot by the alt-right. They are developers, not inventors. Post-truth adjusts the regulative power of truth for humans to resettle into the induced environment, where the gravity of the Pyramid is replaced by the gravitation in the Cloud. The gravitation in the Cloud is maintained by the cumulative *gravitases* of users.

Adaptation to the gravitation in the Cloud instead of the gravity of the Pyramid is causing pain to the social body. No cure will help, hence the fever induced during this transition period is inevitable and will last until immunity is acquired.

Postmodernism unbound

Postmodernism traded truth for justice; postjournalism joined the cause.

301

Postjournalism has emerged from the technological and related business changes caused by the migration of the news and ads to the internet. Technological and economic circumstances created the hardware of postjournalism. Its software consists of the cultural presetting that has provided postjournalism with vibe, value, and zeitgeist. The software of postjournalism came from postmodernism, which itself is an umbrella concept that includes all the respective cultural phenomena, such as post-structuralism, post-positivism, post-industrialism, and alike. Post-truth carries on the business of the 'post-' phenomena; so, too, does postjournalism.

What is common to all 'post-' things is their structural and historical inheritance of the preceding phenomena with ideological and often manifestative repudiation of their norms and standards. For a 'post-' phenomenon, the past self is always the 'significant other', the reference point, regarding which the meaning and significance of the 'post-' are defined. A 'post-' phenomenon is not something self-sufficient. It is rather a final and dead-end mutation of what existed before, a transcending growth coupled with a rebellious rejection of origins. Any postmodernist phenomenon, including postjournalism, is the end rejecting the beginning of itself.

As postjournalism originated in the domain of meaning production, it could not help but absorb all the relevant gains of postmodernism. Because of their synergy, many values, settings, and predispositions of postmodernism are shared, deliberately or unconsciously, by the creative elites involved in journalism and therefore postjournalism production.

So, theoretically, it is possible to define the kinship between postmodernism and postjournalism by marriage (or affinity) and by descent (or blood), so to speak. This means that postjournalism can inherit some postmodernist features from people carrying on postmodernist cultural mindsets into postjournalism - which is affinity; but postjournalism has also inherited some postmodernist features directly - which is descent - due to its structural and systemic similarity to postmodernism.

***

Postmodernist affinity with postjournalism reveals itself in a wide range of concepts and notions that projected zeitgeist into journalist practices. Among the postmodernist conditions aligning with postjournalism, the following can be outlined:

- Incredulity toward metanarratives (Lyotard) and a sense of loss of universal coherence

- The replacement of reality with simulacra (Baudrillard)
- Pastiche (Jameson) and, in a broader sense, the rejection of the principle of originality
- The death of the author (Barthes) and putting the meaning at the mercy of the reader
- Commodification of the symbolical (Baudrillard)
- "Flatness or depthlessness" (Jameson) and the simplification of discourses
- Anti-historism, 'presentism' and an emphasis on synchronicity in lieu of diachronicity
- Valorization of authenticity over adequacy and relevance

Additionally, the post-structuralist influence on postjournalism can be seen in the following:

- A shift from structure to praxis
- A shift from the search for coherence to deconstruction as an epistemological principle
- Self-referentiality and the detachment of sign from reality
- Putting connotation over denotation (Derrida)
- "Breakdown in the signifying chain" (Jameson): the signifier relates not to the signified but rather to another signifier, a state Jameson labeled as 'schizophrenia'
- Myth as a sort of semantic parasitism (Barthes)

To complete the postmodernist pedigree of postjournalism, some post-positivist concepts can be listed, too. Among them:

- Emphasis on subjectivity
- Divorce of rhetoric from logic
- Valorization of phenomenology and experience as epistemological principles
- Dismissal of logocentrism
- Rejection of objective knowledge and absolute truth
- Conditioning of truth: relativism and the explanatory power of social constructivism

All these and many other postmodernist concepts contributed to postjournalism. They were not direct guidelines for postjournalists, but they predefined some cultural consensus, or the culturally dominant, as Jameson called postmodernism, within which cultural industries, including the media, work.

***

Many postmodernist concepts emerged as critical deconstructions. They unveiled the modernist structures underlying both progress and hegemony. For example, in order to challenge the absolutism of truth, the idea of the relativity of truth implied that knowledge is constructed to represent the dominant view, eventually making knowledge nothing but a means of hegemony.

But then, what was told was legitimized by telling. A common postmodernist flip has occurred: what was, in the original theoretical thinking, a critical deconstruction, has reversed into usualization, a sort of legitimation by practice, of what was debunked. The unveiled became admitted, and the admitted became legitimate.

Regarding the example of absolute truth as an agent of hegemony: the initially critical and revolutionary view of truth as a class construct has turned into the legitimate relativity of truth in principle. From this point onwards, there was no other direction except that leading to post-truth. In a truly postmodernist sense, structure surrendered to praxis. If truth was declared to be a social construct, then everyone has an excuse to do with truth whatever they want.

The postmodernist modus of mixing everything – styles, text and context, real and surreal, high and low – made the routinization of postmodernism unstoppable. The phenomenon of *usualization by criticism* transferred many (if not all) postmodernist concepts well into the lives of the masses, and far beyond the circles of intellectuals responsible for the origin and development of postmodernism. Postmodernism was unshackled.

***

One of the byproducts of postmodernism's usualization was that the political left's intellectual criticism unleashed postmodernism into the grassroots practices of their counterparts, the political right.

As Lee McIntyre noted in his analysis of the origin of science denial,

> Even if right-wing politicians and other science deniers were not reading Derrida and Foucault, the germ of the idea made its way to them: science does not have a monopoly on the truth. It is therefore not unreasonable to think that right-wingers are using some of the same arguments and techniques of postmodernism to attack the truth of other scientific claims that clash with their conservative ideology. (McIntyre, 2018, KL2128.)

After the 2016 US presidential election, it did not take long for explanations to appear, describing Donald Trump as a practicing postmodernist (though being hardly aware of it). An article in the conservative media pointed out that, "Donald Trump is the first president to turn postmodernism against itself."[1] In contrast, an article in the liberal news media defended postmodernism against associations with Trump.[2] Some others rather neutrally stated that Trump's ascendance was no accident and represented "the culmination of our epoch of unreality."[3]

Besides all of its paradoxicality, the debate signaled how the fallout from postmodernism had spread far beyond the domain of its origin. The usualization of the postmodernist mindset has permeated deep into society.

***

French postmodernists disseminated their ideas in the 1950–1970s, and the American academia assimilated it into the intellectual mainstream by the 1990s. Those generations were educated in the modernist traditions and still remembered that postmodernism critically related to modernism. The original postmodernism needed a cultural educational foundation. To disprove and repudiate the principle of absolute truth or that of historism, one needed to understand what it is (was).

When the students of the 1990s became professors themselves, their students started absorbing the purified version of postmodernism, refined from any footprints of the modernist fundamentals. The antibody became the body, not having the capacity to be it. The parasite forfeited the host and started 'parasiting' itself; which is, by the way, a postmodernist phenomenon in itself. This is something similar to what Jameson called the "breakdown in the signifying chain," when the signifier loses its signified and attaches itself to another signifier (Jameson, 2012 [1984], p. 419). According to Jameson, this was a symptom of schizophrenia; such has become the postmodernist criticism deprived of modernist fundamentals.

For example, in classical history, the continuity of historical time maintained a view of history as a homogeneous process with linear causality and the accumulation of progress. Such were the views of Hegel, Marx and Weber. This temporal framework with its "totalitarian periodization"

---

[1] Ernst, David. (2017, January 23), "Donald Trump is the first president to turn postmodernism against itself." *The Federalist.* http://thefederalist.com/2017/01/23/donald-trump-first-president-turn-postmodernism/

[2] Edsall, Thomas B. (2018, January 25), "Is President Trump a Stealth Postmodernist or Just a Liar?" *The New York Times.* https://www.nytimes.com/2018/01/25/opinion/trump-postmodernism-lies.html

[3] Heer, Jeet (2017, July 8). "America's First Postmodern President. Trump's ascendance is no accident. He's the culmination of our epoch of unreality. What does that herald for the resistance?" *The New Republic.* https://newrepublic.com/article/143730/americas-first-postmodern-president

(Foucault) put the accumulation of mainstream tradition and the growth of social organization at the front and center of historical knowledge. From the perspective of critical theory, this linear and homogenizing methodology of seeing the past helped legitimize the authority and hegemony and accompanied their oppression in the present. When Foucault suggested turning attention "away from vast unities like 'periods' or 'centuries' to the phenomena of rupture, of discontinuity" (Foucault, 2002 [1969], p. 4) and to use an archeological approach to reveal "several pasts," he was aware of the linear view of history, without which his concept would have lost its value. The Foucauldian *Archeology of Knowledge,* which advocated the interruption to the history of knowledge, makes no Foucauldian sense without knowing the history of knowledge.

***

Several student generations later, the part that followed the 'post-' – the basic part – has been dropped and forgotten. The method became a subject without an object. Archeology in place of history, with isolated excavations into the past, established the discontinuity of historical time. History ceased to be linear and became fragmented; it became centered not in time but in 'users', in people living now. The individual sense of history replaced historical knowledge. The re-centering of knowledge into a person's perception rooted out common objective knowledge and favored polarization, as history was disassembled and then reassembled into *nothing-but-glory* and *nothing-but-shame.* Resentments rooted in the great past and grievances regarding the oppressive past have turned history into a political battlefield of memory wars in the present.

Such cultural software has become a perfect energy source for postjournalism. Historical fragments are easy to select in any needed combination. People with a fragmented history easily accept the reassembling of the historical shards into any new discourse by any crafty mind.

Hamlet's "The time is out of joint" sat alongside "Something is rotten in the state" for Marcellus, a king guard officer. But both were heirs and guardians of the old order, of the order per se. Disrupted time and order are desired, nay, even relished, conditions for postmodernism.

The disruption of any signs of the absolute is an essential liberation tool used against institutions. Sadly for the media, they belong to the ranks of those institutions. By participating in the rebellion against institutions, the media edge ever closer to their own demise. Unlike the modernist revolution, the postmodernist revolution devours its parents before eating its children.

306

Lyotard's question "Who decides the conditions of truth?" (Lyotard, 1984 [1979], p. 30), which was posed to a society based on the hegemony of mainstream knowledge, not only remains in place but has grown ever more prescient. Postmodernism undermines the established hegemony by making hegemony the prize in a cultural struggle that eventually and inevitably invades politics. Basically, it has come down to the attempts to intercept hegemony, not to eliminate it. This framework is susceptible to even larger manipulation and leads to populism, division and polarization, the very phenomena that has spread in the 21st century.

The respective processes endured by arts and culture in general culminated sometime in the 2010s, when the media environment (coincidentally?) had matured enough to usualize the principles of postmodernism into the everyday life of everyone.

***

In *Public Opinion*, Lippmann noticed that Darwinian ideas of evolution coincided with "the spectacle of mechanical progress" (Lippmann, 1929 [1922], p. 108). The commonality of progress and evolution made them very popular and universal social concepts. It becomes obvious that nature, technology and society live under the universal law of progress and development from simple to complex.

Lippman predicted that the notion of relativity, which was being developed by Einstein at the time, might become the next popular cultural dominant, too. As he wrote,

> Relativity, like Evolution, after receiving a number of intelligible but somewhat inaccurate popular expositions in its scientific aspect, will be launched on a world-conquering career. (Lippmann, 1929 [1922], p. 106.)

Indeed, the concept of relativity soon permeated deep into social theories and social morality, where it shattered the seemingly irrefutable laws of the previous paradigm.

Now the anti-hegemonic spirit of postmodernism has coincided with, and been reinforced by, the changes in media. The internet ended the hegemony of the news media over agenda-setting which facilitated the new media environment to become the most suitable hardware infrastructure for the rapid and easy dissemination of postmodernism's software to the masses.

The concept of simulation is familiar to teenagers who have watched "The Matrix" or created alternative selves online. The self-referentiality of post-truth became common, even if unspoken, knowledge, as everyone is

307

assured that there is no such thing as objective truth. During the COVID-19 quarantine, Foucauldian ideas of bio-politics became known far beyond the usual narrow circles of academia, even if people could not formulate them precisely. TV series have become high art, and memes express philosophical and political thoughts. And so on.

What would traditionally be narrowly viewed as a revolutionary, fancy theory or intellectual movement during early postmodernism, has become common knowledge, or perhaps even a common feeling, of social reality. Grand narratives were discontinued, deconstructed and quantized in order to fit into the flows of newsfeeds, the continuity of which requires a user's participation, not content, as the content of newsfeeds is fragmented. In a sense, postmodernism was historically predestined to train people for settling into the nascent digital world, centered in the subjectivity of the user, not the objectivity of some abstract ideals.

***

As one of the consciousness industries, the media, of course, are marching in the avant-garde of the usualization of postmodernism. This is not because they fell in love with Derrida or Baudrillard, but because the entire cultural environment has become saturated with postmodernist views, expressed or implied. Most importantly, the morphology of the digital environment is perfectly set up for new media, including the news media, to become a playground for postmodernist ideas and practices.

However, being itself a genuinely postmodernist phenomenon, postjournalism has also had something to contribute to postmodernist culture, over and above merely reinforcing post-truth. The main integral postmodernist features of postjournalism can be listed as follows:

- Subjective modality of reality's representation in the guise of objective modality
- The pivot from the disruption of authorities to just disruption
- Identity signaling through dividual 'intensities' instead of individual feelings
- Commodification of ideology

***

Subjective modality in the guise of objective modality is one of the constituting features of postjournalism.

The hallmark of postjournalism lies in its radically different semiotic modality. By separating facts and opinions, classical journalism distinguishes *objective modality* (the utterances refer to aspects of reality as existing, non-existing, possible, probable, etc.) from *subjective modality* (the speaker's attitude toward the utterance's referent as to desirable – undesirable, proper – improper, just – unjust, etc.). At the level of good practice, this distinction was always committed to by the demarcation of facts from opinions.

Journalism of fact was believed to refer to reality. Opinion journalism emphasized the opinionated navigation of facts but still referred to reality. Postjournalism validates the significance of current events seemingly under the objective modality of *existing/non-existing* or *possible/non-possible*, but within the subjective modality of *right/wrong* and *good/bad*. To put it simply, in postjournalism, reporting is commenting.

To blame this on the personal propagandist intentions of journalists would be an easy call to make. However, this is a systemic environmental setting: the redundancy of news has decreased the value of fact reporting and increased the value of opinion and expertise. So, journalists have learnt to compress facts and opinions together and sell 'two for the price of one'. And on top of this, the business need for politicization has had its corrupting final touch. The deliberate intentions of journalists can only come into play after that, filling already polarized molds with concrete content.

Postjournalism passes off the opinion as the fact, the connotation as the denotation, the attitude as the referent. Subjective modality in place of objective modality can be referred to as the notion of "enunciative modality" that Foucault used in *The Archaeology of Knowledge*. Enunciative modality reflects the view of the speaking subject at the moment of speaking, though formally it represents a picture of the world. Analyzing discursive formations, Foucault referred to a 19th-century doctor who would observe and gather documents, data, correlations and methods, solely for the purpose of making an arbitrary use of them, modifying "his position as an observing subject in relation to the patient" (Foucault, 2002 [1969], p. 37).

Objective reality itself is not the final interest of such reality representation; the final interest is a useful application of a constructed picture of reality. Within 'enunciative modalities', the representation of reality is concerned "less with the formation of conceptual systems, or the formation of theoretical choices, than with the status, the institutional siting, the situation, and the modes of insertion used by the discoursing subject" (Ibid., 72).

Postjournalism disregards truth not in favor of lies (lies are a byproduct) but because truth is useless. Truth just is not needed when 'enunciative modalities' are at play. Instead of truth, other forms of verification take command, such as relevance, adequacy, authenticity, justice, usefulness and, most critically, dissemination. Meaning production needs to comply with what is useful – or demanded. In postjournalism, even fact-checking is used as a rhetorical gimmick.

***

Subjective modality in place of objective modality does not distort the picture of the world – it creates the world. With the merging of the subjective and objective, the signified collapses into the signifier, causing the post-truth effect of self-referentiality. The picture absorbs the world and starts preceding it exactly in the way Baudrillard saw it in *The Precession of Simulacra*, where he wrote:

> Simulation is no longer that of territory, a referential being, or a substance. It is the generation by models of a real without origin or reality: a hyperreal. The territory no longer precedes the map, nor does it survive it. It is nevertheless the map that precedes the territory – *precession of simulacra* – that engenders the territory. (Baudrillard, 2012 [1981], p. 388.)

The capacity of the subjective modality to create the world can also be illustrated by the linguistic category of performativity: an ability of *some* utterances to become actions. The performative are, for example, promises or the figures of politeness: we do what we say by saying it. As Roland Barthes noted in *The Death of the Author*, writing is no longer "recording, notation, representation"; rather, it is "a performative, a rare verbal form (exclusively given in the first person and in the present tense) in which the enunciation has no other content than the act by which it is uttered – something like the *I declare* of kings or the *I sing* of the early bards" (Barthes, 1977 [1967], p.145).

The performative power of utterance involved in agenda-setting is even more evident as its significance is established by its distribution. Dissemination on a sufficient scale can make any utterance in the media or on social media divinely performative, as if it is the Word of Biblical God that was 'in the beginning' and from which everything commenced.

The *enunciative modalities*, the *precession of simulacra* and other theoretical *critical* deconstructions became reversed into the colloquial *usus* within postjournalism, allowing the picture of the world to actually replace the world, not just in a post-structuralist sense of this phenomenon but on behalf of the audience. The ability of journalism to induce the demand for news blends nicely with the 'ability' of simulacrum to precede reality and induce Baudrillard's "hyperreality", or, in the news media, a needed agenda, which becomes social reality for adherers of these or those views.

The donating audience wants the picture of the world to comply with the audience's view of the cause, not with the actual world. If the truly subscription-based media, say, Venetian *avvisi*, had taken such an approach, they would have failed. When readers pay for information, they want world reflection, not creation. For the donscription-based media, subjective modality is a survival mode. Postjournalism is not descriptive; it is normative.

***

The pivotal shift from the disruption of authorities to just disruption is a postmodernist trend within postjournalism that embodies the negativity bias of the reader-driven mass media, unique to the donscription-based business model. Postjournalism must exploit nostalgia and resentment on the political right and guilt and grievance on the political left in order to incite the audience to join the fight. Therefore, culpable figures and institutions must be called out – not for debates and correction, but rather for disempowering and de-platforming, which must lead, in the induced reality, to elimination.

The disruption of power plays an important part in postmodernist thought. It is not just a declaration of the death of the author and the dismissal of any form of absolute; it has deeper epistemological roots.

"The history of ideas usually credits the discourse that it analyses with coherence," wrote Foucault in *The Archaeology of Knowledge* (2002 [1969], p. 149). Coherence was seen by many postmodernists as a prerequisite for homogeneity and therefore the hegemony of the center towards marginalia. Coherence is also one of the cultural byproducts of classical journalism. Coherence was needed for the manufacture of consent, which was seen in a positive sense by Lippmann and in a negative sense by Herman and Chomsky. According to Horkheimer and Adorno, coherence is produced when the media work as a cultural industry, since any industry produces a standardized product and therefore requires standardized consumers.

But the media aimed at subscription solicited as donation are incentivized to manufacture anger, not consent. The postmodernist theoretical condemnation of coherence as a display of oppressive homogeneity has found independent practical application in postjournalism. This is another original contribution of postjournalism to postmodernism.

Postjournalism sows discord not because it has something against homogeneity but because of profit-seeking. In Herman-Chomsky's Propaganda model, the image of the enemy was needed for the mobilization of the ideological loyalty of the masses to the elites. In postjournalism, the image of the enemy helps to mobilize support and subscription. The enemy is required for conducting business, which is otherwise dying anyway. Donation solicitation is simply more successful under the conditions of polarization, and polarization requires division, not coherence; or, one might say, polarization requires division, cohered into two opposite camps.

A disruptive mode of postmodernism has discovered new motives in postjournalism. Disruption produces a negative feedback in a homogeneous environment but positive feedback loop in a polarized environment. Two opposite "sectarian war bands"[1] in the media feed off one another for endless mutual disruption. Disruption enters the spiral agitation, demolishing everything else around. On the postmodernist side of the process, it has become a logical outcome: disruption was unleashed and swallowed the disruptors.

***

Identity signaling through flat dividual 'intensities' instead of complex individual feelings is a concept representing the emotional fuel of postjournalism.

In his analysis of postmodernist conditions, Frederic Jameson noted that, "The end of the bourgeois ego, or monad, no doubt brings with it the end of the psychopathologies of that ego – what I have been calling the waning of affect" (Jameson, 2012 [1984], p. 414). Deep feelings of modernity were replaced by *intensities* as Jameson called it, following Lyotard, with a peculiar kind of euphoria (Ibid., p. 414). The 'shared with others' emotional *intensities* instead of personal deep feelings became one of the defining features of postmodernism.

The machinery of modernism would throw a sensitive or artistic person into alienation as something opposite to urban and industrial standardization. In postmodernist culture, Jameson suggested, the very nature of "pathology" shifted: "the alienation of subject is displaced by the fragmentation of the subject" (Ibid., p. 414).

Jameson declared that the "autonomous bourgeois monad or ego or individual" got fragmented. The "*decentering* of that formerly centered subject or psyche" became the factor that eroded personal feelings, as there is no longer a whole self to experience feelings, or alienation, or Van Gogh's madness.

---

[1] Gurri, Martin. (2020, February 18). "Sectarian networks and big personalities will decide the presidential election." *The Bridge*. Merkatus Center at George Mason University. https://www.mercatus.org/bridge/commentary/sectarian-networks-and-big-personalities-will-decide-presidential-election

Jameson's fragmentation that leads to impersonal intensities instead of personal feelings plays well with Deleuze's concept of *dividual* as opposed to *individual* (Deleuze, 1992). The individual is the smallest and indivisible unit of society and is well-suited for both social control and self-expression. But for the purpose of better control, society makes individuals *dividuals*, fragmented entities, which are represented, for example, by an electronic code at a factory gate, a password at an ATM, or profiling characteristics in databases.

The idea of personality fragmentation also dovetails perfectly with the concept of identity formation and conceptualization. The modernist integrity of individuals became deconstructed by postmodernism and disintegrated into smaller features that represent the markers of identity, such as being black or white, native or migrant, straight or gay, a gun owner or a Mac owner, etc. Unlike individuality, identity markers are not personal. They always represent belonging with a group; they are selectively shared features. But, from the postmodernist point of view, they may constitute the core of personality.

Identity markers began to usurp the larger political or class identifiers of the past, which signified belonging with the social strata without signaling about a person's identity. Identity markers identify and prescribe individual behavior in the same way as class affiliation defined and prescribed the role of the individual in society. Both class identifiers and identity markers oversimplify and maroon multifaceted human nature in order to tie individuals to a side in the class struggle or in the identity struggle within a structure of society, pre-ordained by an ideology.

*** *

It is easy to notice that similar processes of identity fragmentation in individuals are taking place in marketing and particularly in social media psychographic profiling, which can count dozens if not hundreds of *dividual* features.

Postmodernist society emphasized not holistic personality but its welcomed or condemned (in marketing – useful) fragments, which were turned into identities for identification. The possession and most importantly displaying of proper identity markers forms an important part of socialization in postmodernist society.

Not only is *dividual* a new basis for identity formation and conceptualization, it also brings with it a new framework for both social unity and personal expression. But the expression of identity, paradoxically, is not individual. It is *identic,* shared on the basis of identity with others who overtly stress the fact of having the same identity. The disintegration of individuality into *dividuals* for the purpose of identification also aligns well with McLuhan's idea of tribalization.

***

The Russian national-religious ethos incited capitalizing on *collective suffering*, which helped socialism to spread there particularly well. The Protestant religious ethos prescribed capitalizing on *individual success*, which underlay Western democracies with their focus on human rights grown out of the bourgeois struggle for individual freedoms. Postmodernism and affiliated progressive movements have fused the Marxist postulation of social struggle with the bourgeois dogma of human rights into a new ethical hybrid that urges capitalizing on *individual suffering*.

More precisely, postmodernist progressivism encouraged capitalizing on *dividual suffering, or identity suffering*. Reason being that what is displayed for identification and socialization (tribalization) in the conditions of late capitalism is a group-attested suffering identity, not the intrinsically controversial multifaceted individuality.

The valorization of *collective suffering* or *individual success* reflected modernist ethics of socialism and capitalism and underlay the homogenization of society, creating room for oppression or inequality as by-products of socialism and capitalism respectively. In contrast, the valorization of *identity suffering* reverses homogenization and disintegrates the modernist societal structures at the cost of polarization and rage.

***

When the complex and contradictory *individuality* becomes reduced to the identity-based *dividuality*, former feelings become intensities, whose function is signaling rather than expressing.

The individual used to have a self and connect with others through self-expression. The identity is just an emphasized facet of the self. The identity gets expressed in prioritized displaying – signaling. Identity signaling becomes a dominant emotional function for identity recognition and acknowledgment.

As occurs within any environment flooded with signals, the overcoming of noise is the crucial factor in signal efficiency. Signals have to compete with each other and the noise. In modernist emotionality, feelings can allow themselves to be quiet and even silent. They are able to stay powerful regardless of the volume they are able to produce. Postmodernist emotionality cannot afford silent or quiet emotional signaling – it must scream. Perhaps this is the way to tell feelings from intensities: feelings can be powerful without being loud, but intensities cannot. Intensities are destined for the signaling of expected features to others, not expressing the complexity of self.

Exaggerated emotional signaling – Jameson-Lyotard's "intensities" – is one of the defining features of postmodernism.

***

The fragmentation of individuality down to identity markers caused a change in the kind of energy that fuels political activity. When the individual was at the center of the political sphere, rational ideas used to shape ideologies and ideologies were the foundation of political activity. In the postmodernist environment, ideologies are marginalized and emotions command the expression of the political.

It is becoming harder to define what ideology underlies the political stances of the left and the right in the postmodernist environment. But the stances of the left and the right can be sufficiently described through the senses of grievance and resentment respectively. Thus, intensities become a means of political struggle. Political activity has moved from debate towards rituals, the main form of which is signaling about opposing or endorsing a matter.

Fredric Jameson foresaw this move from rationality to emotionality and from feelings to intensities when he observed "a peculiar kind of euphoria", "something like a camp or 'hysterical' sublime" (Ibid., p. 423) as essential manifestations of postmodernism.

***

Intensities and intensities' signaling are important features of a connected and polarized environment with users' permanent response-seeking. Social media fit this postmodernist setting the most readily. Jameson explored the phenomenon of intensities instead of feelings mostly in the field of the arts. Social media emerged just at the right historical moment. They create a perfect environment for the usualization of postmodernist features, including intensities and intensities' signaling. Connected and polarized people display their identity markers as a form of currency for earning social capital; and since many compete in signaling, the overt noise makes them signal louder.

Another factor in intensities intensification on social media is the fact that social media allow people to freely express what is suppressed in the mainstream media intensities. Suppressed intensity is released with additional force into the less pressurized atmosphere of social media. The pressure difference amplifies agenda-setting polarization between old media and new media.

Polarized agendas make their way onto social media for further circulation and additionally increase rage and political polarization. For the majority on social media, as Martin Gurri noticed, "rage really is a rhetorical convention, like sonnet-writing for Elizabethan gentlemen." He wrote:

> Does the digital environment incentivize the rant? It would appear to do so. Amid the infernal howl of hundreds of millions of voices, you need to scream just to be heard. If you can also arouse a primal emotion like anger, you will attract more attention and so rise above other screamers.
>
> Yes, in a crowded information environment, potent emotions are needed to give traction to any message. But why is rage the default? Ranters in their virtual war-bands are nothing like factory workers in Victorian England or black civil rights militants in the 1960s. They aren't oppressed or marginalized. On the contrary, as a class they tend to be affluent, hyper-educated, and savvy in the ways of the web. They have few obvious reasons to be angry and can exploit different emotive techniques for their purposes.[1]

Gurri's search for the motives behind rage on social media was not without reason. These motives are obviously not social or economic. They are predefined by the postmodernist fragmentation of individuality right down to the identity markers and then by the necessity to communicate identity markers through intensities' signaling for the sake of better socializing. Paradoxically, the social media environment has built-in settings that encourage socializing through rage. This is something normally unacceptable and strategically disadvantageous in offline social communication. Offline, rage would result, among other things, in physical consequences that correct behavior through the sensorium. But on social media, particularly those with a short form of literacy, like Twitter, rage is not risky and can be beneficial.

These social networks' settings pose a bigger danger than social media's usual suspects, such as trolls, bots, disinformation or fake news, to which people are either hardly susceptible or able to eventually develop immunity. The environmental demand for the amplification of intensities' signaling is not received as a negative factor on social media. It entails neither repelling nor immunity; on the contrary, it stimulates engagement. For platform owners, it is a good thing, the bread and butter of business. The

---

[1] Gurri, Martin. (2020, May 26). "The way out of post-truth." *The Bridge*. Merkatus Center at George Mason University. https://www.mercatus.org/bridge/commentary/way-out-post-truth

amplification of intensities' signaling can only be condemned at the level of rational analysis. This is as if the air was both needed for breathing and toxic at the same time. The social media settings of signal intensification are both virally productive and socially toxic, as they enhance engagement but amplify rage and polarization.

***

Postjournalism has its own reason to join the shift from rationality to emotionality and peddling intensities' signaling up to the hysterical sublime. If the media solicit for donation, they need to promote a donatable cause. Not only do they seek engagement and loyalty from the audience, they themselves also need to demonstrate loyalty and engagement. Impartiality will not succeed in soliciting for donations. The media have to proactively and intensively signal their endorsing or opposing stances. Emotional signaling becomes an important feature of the business plan, gradually suppressing the rational substantiations of why the cause endorsed is noble. Soliciting should be persuasive and provable.

Technically, the rationale behind the cause is no longer needed if the media is savvy enough to merely find the right donatable cause and the right donating audience. Rationality is not in the compulsory program of journalism – intensities' signaling is.

Another intensifier of intensities' signaling in the media is competition, which, again, creates noise and the necessity for this noise to be overcome. The news media have joined the same noise race that social media are in.

Intensities' signaling is maintained even more so by the fear of negative feedback from the donating audience. Herman and Chomsky identified flak also as an emotional regulator of their Propaganda model. "Flak will tend to press the media to greater hysteria in the face of enemy evil," they wrote (2002 [1988], p. 34).

Indeed, the flak of the donating audience does not bother as much with fact-checking as it does with purity-testing. Orwell's *Two Minutes Hate* was a daily rite not so much for informing about the enemy, but for checking the fidelity of followers through observing whether they express their hate loudly enough.

Postjournalism, therefore, makes its own specific contribution to hyping postmodernist *intensities* and the *hysterical sublime*. Different aspects of postjournalism reinforce each other: the commodification of intensities aligns its 'efforts' with the work of negativity bias, flak, polarization, and activism of the media.

***

Commodification of culture and specifically ideology has long been a trend in postmodernist culture, having blatantly exposed itself in postjournalism.

According to Karl Marx, "Philosophers have hitherto only explained the world in various ways; the point is to change it" (The eleventh thesis on Feuerbach, 1845). Postmodernism inherited this mindset; not only did it switch from structure to praxis in the areas of semiotic and cultural analysis, it also brought its theory to social practice. Foucault was called "the militant intellectual" for a good reason.

Postjournalism, however, is distinct from Marxism or postmodernism in terms of their focus on social effect. In postjournalism, impact-seeking is not predefined by the ideological goal of changing the world. Impact-seeking is rather a derivative of profit-seeking. Ideology is a secondary task. Ideologically, the cause, which the media pitch for donscription, can be different: liberal, conservative, or even apolitical, if the cause for donation-subscription is chosen in non-political areas (in which case, however, it is unlikely be very donatable to). For postjournalism, existentially important is the business mechanism of soliciting for an ideological cause, not a color of ideology.

For classical journalism, social impact was a byproduct of its business model based on attracting the audience for better news retail and ad sales. Postjournalism seeks impact because soliciting donations is at the very core of its business strategy.

With this evolution, a truly postmodernist reversal happened. In the modernist era, ideology used to serve the economic interests of the ruling class. Postmodernism, being a product of late capitalism, made ideas profitable on their own. Ideology ceased to act as the servant of big business and instead became a big business in its own right. McLuhan's prophecy has been fulfilled, according to which,

> We are swiftly moving at present from an era where business was our culture into an era when culture will be our business. (McLuhan & Carson, 2011, p. 384.)

***

When analyzing consumerism in the late 1960s, Baudrillard came to the conclusion that value is created more and more on the side of consumption, not production. As markets developed, marketing became more crucial to business than production. Therefore, the formation of demand turned out to be more important than the production itself. Baudrillard suggested that the classical value theory with use-value and exchange-value must be

318

complemented with symbolic value and sign-value. These values were created by marketing, which was able to induce demand on the side of consumption, a process that Baudrillard called the "ideological genesis of needs" (Baudrillard, 1981 [1972], p. 63).

This sophisticated concept is reflected in layman terms in a marketing maxim, which says that a good marketer can sell anything, regardless of whether buyers really need it or not. Indeed, people have natural needs for very few things they buy. For the most part, the need for things (or the need for those peculiar qualities and quantities of things) is ideologically, or culturally, induced.

Jameson observed the change in value formation, too. He highlighted that nobody actually remembers what constitutes the use-value of things. This statement, seemingly quite metaphorical, can be easily understood by everyone who buys new clothes before their old ones are worn out, or by those who buy a new smartphone not because the old one does not work, but because the old one has become 'outdated' or 'out of fashion'. The original use-value of things becomes assimilated in other forms of value, symbolical most of all. Or, as Jameson put it, "(T)he culture of the simulacrum comes to life in a society where exchange-value has been generalized to the point at which the very memory of use-value is effaced..." (Jameson, 2012 [1984], p. 415.).

Jameson highlighted the economic foundation of postmodernism as the "expansion of capital into hitherto uncommodified areas" (Ibid., p. 424). That is why postmodernism is "the cultural logic of late capitalism," according to him.

***

For Herman and Chomsky, the ideological propagandist function was a derivative of the economic media system. Postjournalism, as with any 'post-' phenomenon, has reversed these political-economic relations. When the media solicit for donations, the ideological propagandist function becomes not the licensing condition but the business of the media. Any 'join-the-cause' subscription pitch means that the media outlet is going to sell itself as an ideological tool to those who are willing to pay for the discourse mongering.

The donscription-driven media grasp the nettle of the task to induce and maintain the demand for donatable ideology. Many see an ideological bias behind it (liberal or conservative). It also exists – at the level of people's choice. But behind the political choices there is also an existential necessity for the media to sell news validation and ideological impact. This necessity has been importuned because all other business models are vanishing or have already vanished. The news media have to drive toward this model in order to survive. Only then can the deliberate political choices of people in the newsrooms become relevant, coupling business necessity with a newsroom's traditions and demographics.

In many cases, of course, news organizations were predisposed to liberal or conservative biases. There is no question about *Fox News*, for example, which has always leaned toward conservatism. But even then, political biases tended to be denied or masked behind declarations of journalism's professional values and standards, which were superior to ideological values. The proclivity of many mainstream media to a predisposed liberal view was even less noticeable; anyway, journalism standards were honored or displayed much more firmly and visibly because open ideological stances did not comply with the advertising model and could even damage business interests.

Now, ideological stances are becoming business interests. Not only are formerly hidden biases now openly expressed, but they must also be aggressively displayed and marketed, both for efficient donation soliciting and in order to avoid flak from the donating audience, a powerful negative regulator.

Soliciting subscription as donation either incites ideological stances in the media, forcing them to make a choice, or reveals and amplifies their pre-existing ideological predilections. The American media market gives a clear example of this ideological impact of the new business model. However, this principle will work in any media market in which the media are deprived of news retail and ad sales, leading to their inevitable susceptibility to the pressure of the audience due to the shift in the business model. These conditions are universal, though with some national specificities, of course. The consequences are also common; namely increasing polarization, wherein political discords are overtly amplified by the business interests of old media and the environmental settings (and business interests) of new media.

***

Though its existence might have been in question, there was an overtly declared boundary between the ad sales departments and newsrooms in the classical media. Nowadays no one will even attempt to insist that there should be a boundary between what the donating audience wants and what the newsroom should write about. "Culture is our business": marketing and editorial policy are merging. The former impacts and predefines the latter, and vice versa.

Most of the contemporary criticism of the liberal mainstream media, not to mention the conservative media, usually rests on the presumption of their political bias. The economic factors are less visible, but they are more fundamental. The vanishing or lack of other business models is merely exacerbating an already desperate situation. The media are trapped into pitching a cause to solicit financial support (or loyalty/viewership – for TV), without which they would not be able to survive.

According to the rule of asymmetric polarization, this dramatic shift has impacted the liberal media to the largest extent. Their drift from journalism to postjournalism caused by their need to seek donations is more prominent because their journalism used to be more prominent. In the liberal media, therefore, the dynamics of politicization and polarization have to be specifically more overtly and forcefully exhibited.

On the other hand, the conservative media, in that sense, do still try to be as authentic as they always were, so to speak. The main change for them is the intensification of their activity in the polarization race. But they do also need the opposite side as it still takes two to dance the polarization tango.

12. Polarization: dividing, electrifying and uniting

Public consciousness has not yet assimilated the point that technology is ideology.

Neil Postman. "Amusing Ourselves to Death", 1985.

The Devil emerges from the foam at the mouth of an Angel fighting for a sacred, just cause. Everything turns to ash – people, systems, but eternal is the spirit of hatred in a fight for a just cause. Because of that, evil on Earth knows no end. Ever since I understood that, I believe that the style of polemic is more important than its subject. The subjects change but the styles form civilizations.

Grigory Pomerants, a Soviet philosopher and dissident. "The dogmata of polemics" (opposing to Aleksandr Solzhenitsyn, the author of "The Gulag Archipelago"), 1971.

Polarization is a media effect

The literature on polarization distinguishes between affective polarization and ideological polarization (Iyengar et al., 2019). Ideological polarization operates at the level of ideas and results in political polarization, which manifests in personal and social behavior, such as voting or political debates. Political polarization is a surficial dimension of the multilayered phenomenon of polarization.

Affective polarization, on the other hand, lies deep within the polarization mechanism. Affective polarization relates to animosity – people's confrontational inclination. A search for the roots of political and social conflicts should start with the mechanisms of affective polarization.

Research has shown that the growth of polarization has been seen in many western societies in recent decades, but most significantly in the US (Boxell et al., 2020). Scholars have examined different possible explanations and found correlations between the growth of affective polarization and such factors as increasing immigration, the deepening of racial and ethnic divisions, the growing role of ideological affiliation in socialization due to the political restructuring of society, the rise of partisan cable TV news, the proliferation of the internet and social media, the growing gap between the cultural elites and the masses, growing economic inequality, etc.

While all these factors certainly exist and impact polarization, they also represent a global cultural transformation, the changing of eras, the main characteristic of which is the rapid growth of communication exchange. People become aware of the "other" much more frequently and much faster than in any previous epoch. The information awareness underlies, among other things, growing globalization and accelerating migration. Not only have the electronic and digital media changed the cultural environment, they have also contributed to the physical spread of humankind over the Earth. They have done this in many ways – from amplifying conflicts to informing about opportunities overseas. Enhancements in communication have always led to surges in migration. Now, it is safe to assume that there have never before been so many people living in places other than those they were born in.

However, the largest-ever migration that media have facilitated is the resettling of people into the digital environment.

***

Media are often seen as an *instrument* facilitating or otherwise impacting cultural, political and social processes. Media surely do this, but rather as an uncontrollable *environmental force* than as a manageable instrument.

With digital media proliferation, the environmental impact of media has *imploded*. Media are no longer an external environmental force that impacts cultural and other forms of human life; cultural life itself happens to be completely immersed into the media environment.

The digital is not a part of the culture; it is its space, its environment in a very literal and physical sense. The old physical space of culture has only held onto some residual forms of cultural activities. Politics, social life and the economy operate now almost entirely inside the digital environment. The materiality of human life artifacts has become digital. This is not just a growing mediatization of culture, this is culture's complete resettling into the media environment.

The settings of culture are now media settings. Start-ups and algorithms created in Silicon Valley shape culture in a way Lévi-Strauss's kinship structures and myths used to (which is reminiscent of Neil Postman's *Technopoly* (1992) subtitle: "The surrender of culture to technology").

As human activity has moved almost entirely into the digital, the socialization of people also now occurs in the digital environment. Therefore, the conditions of socialization are predefined by the media settings of the digital environment. People now socialize not under the conditions of physical communication, but with their digital selves fully immersed into the digital media environment.

Polarization is one of the aspects of a person's socialization. Therefore, polarization also has media roots, or even predominantly media roots. These are the media settings of the digital realm that need to be explored in order to understand polarization. Polarization studies are the studies of media; more precisely, it is a subdiscipline of media ecology.

***

In the pre-digital environment, polarization had well-known capacities and limitations imposed by the physical forms of socialization. Social rigidity, resistance of the established order and the risks of physical personal and social interaction helped to keep polarization at bay.

Those restraints do not work in the digital environment. Not only have the physical restraints of polarization become irrelevant in the digital environment, the digital environment has imposed its own features that directly incentivize polarization. As a result, instead of the former 'physically' maintained restraints of polarization, society has acquired the digital amplifiers of polarization.

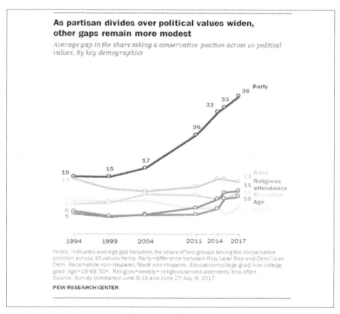

Figure 14. The Partisan Divide on Political Values Grows Even Wider.
Source: Pew Research Center.[1]

---

[1] Pew Research Center. October 5, 2017. https://www.pewresearch.org/politics/2017/

Studies show that political polarization in the US reached a low point in the 1950s (Pew Research Center, 2017; Napoli & Dwyer, 2018) and started skyrocketing in the late 2000s, which coincided with the spread of social media and the decline of the advertising in the news media (Figure 14).

***

Different media effects can be held accountable for four different dimensions of polarization.

1) Affective polarization. On social media, the 'struggle for recognition' amid increasing noise incentivizes extremes and radical views because they have a higher potential for response and, therefore, virality. The effect: people's animosity.

2) Agenda-setting polarization. On social media, the emancipated authorship allows for the crowdsourced formation of agendas, which particularly empowers evidence and opinions that are underrepresented and suppressed in the mainstream mass media. The effect: new media oppose the old establishment.

3) Rebound agenda-setting polarization. Competing with social media for the audience's attention, the mass media are forced to amplify or oppose (and amplify) topics that are preselected by the Viral Editor[1] on social media, which are already inherently polarized and polarizing. The effect: old media oppose new media and each other.

4) Ideological polarization. In the mass media, soliciting for subscription as donation incentivizes the selection of the topics that are most donatable, which are most likely politically polarizing topics, as they are the most triggering. The effect: irreconcilable partisanship.

Affective polarization

Social media are designed to encourage user engagement. Because of 'the thirst for response' (Miroshnichenko, 2014, p. 12), which can be referred to as the Hegelian 'struggle for recognition', emancipated authors (all of us) get involved in self-actualization through others – through their likes, comments, shares and other forms of automated and accelerated social exchange. Compared to offline social practices, social media have powerfully facilitated socialization.

10/05/the-partisan-divide-on-political-values-grows-even-wider/takeaways_fix1/

[1] The collective mechanism of news selection and micro-editing during viral distribution (Miroshnichenko, 2014).

But this service comes with a disservice. The increase in the speed of socialization has a price. The best mechanisms for gaining a response are simultaneously the most harmful for human relations. The fight for likes turns into just a fight. Automated social grooming inevitably rises to hysterical levels and turns into its opposite – a brawl, in full accordance with McLuhan's Fourth Law of Media (a medium reverses its effect when pushed to an extreme – McLuhan & McLuhan, 1988).

***

Two communication stunts are the most efficient at attracting reaction: *the oddity push* and *the extremity push*. They are interconnected: the push for oddity, when taken to its extreme, becomes the push for extremity.

The attractiveness of oddity has always accompanied mass communication. Elizabeth Eisenstein wrote about medieval chroniclers readily reporting about "comets and monsters":

> The news value of the odd as opposed to the ordinary event is still rated high even in these impious days. Insofar as they viewed dog-biting men as more newsworthy than man-eating dogs, monkish chroniclers had more in common with modern journalists than with medieval natural philosophers. (Eisenstein, 1979, KL14566.)

As Yuri Lotman put it in *Unpredictable mechanisms of culture*, "Habitual is invisible; turning habitual into unusual makes it tangible" (Lotman, 2010, p. 102). Objects that are aligned with the environment are less visible. The same goes for action: odd actions are more noticeable.

Normally, distinctions and oddities in actions tend to be eliminated in regular performance due to their effort cost. But their negative value for regular actions reverses into a positive value for attention seeking. An action-for-self tends to be regular and therefore preferably non-deviating because of the economy of efforts. But an action-for-others must be distinguishable in the same way as a signal must be different from the environment and other signals in order to be recognized.

Oddity is the most noticeable distinction. People tend to avoid oddity in physical action, labor performance and social interaction, but they willingly use it in the arts, where oddity becomes deliberately instrumentalized in styles, genres and performances. The use of oddity has become a beneficial strategy on social media, pushed by the thirst for response.

People have not started liking oddity in regular life, and they are most likely as averse to it as they were before. But the environmental settings of social media encourage the push for oddity on a scale previously unknown.

The environmental push for oddity amid the personal repulsion of it may be one of the psychological reasons why so many people become frustrated with social media.

***

If alignment is invisible and oddity is noticeable, then confrontment is salient. Confrontment is not just distinctive because it relies on being different; it directly attacks the initially presented point or environment. Therefore, confrontment has the highest potential of provoking reactive engagement. In terms of visibility and triggering a response – if all other restraints are put aside, just technically – confrontment is the best strategy for fast self-actualization.

On social media, the same features that provide an amazing service of self-actualization – rapid responsiveness, engagement, virality – simultaneously propel the extremization of expression. If the great Nero burned down Rome for inspiration, the miserable Herostratus burned down the Temple of Artemis to be noticed.

As many studies have shown, social media posts that express odd or radical views and ideas have a higher potential of being liked, commented on and shared. Robert Kozinets from Annenberg School for Communication and Journalism at University of Southern California studied the "sharing of images of food" on social media. The research indicated that people tend to share "images of food that look less and less like what regular people eat every day." The reason was that,

> ...the algorithms that drive participation and attention-getting in social media, the addictive "gamification" aspects such as likes and shares, invariably favored the odd and unusual. When someone wanted to broaden out beyond his or her immediate social networks, one of the most effective ways to achieve mass appeal turned out to be by turning to the extreme.[1]

As a result of such an environmental setting, "the most popular food porn images depicted massive hamburgers that were impossible to eat."[2]

Indeed, regular food (and regular whatever) cannot trigger a strong response. Modesty is a lost cause on social media.

The social media setting of extremes' amplification for better responses perfectly matches intensities' signaling as the postmodernist expression of

---

[1] Kozinets, Robert. (2017, November 13). "How social media fires people's passions – and builds extremist divisions." *The Conversation.* https://theconversation.com/how-social-media-fires-peoples-passions-and-builds-extremist-divisions-86909.

[2] Ibid.

identity markers, because both phenomena put the communicative task of efficient signalization at the forefront. Intensities' signaling and extremes' amplification reflect, respectively, the sociality and materiality of social media communication. They conjointly force users to communicate the utmost possibly distinguishable signals.

People try to resist the excessive power of amplifiers, of course – as much as they try to resist the environmental power of money, for example. The metaphor is not accidental: the response from others is the currency of social capital. The suppression of distinguishability in expression leads to losses in social capital.

***

The same amplifying setups work, of course, for political content. Brady et al. studied pre-election tweets of politicians and found "a 'moral contagion' effect: elites' use of moral-emotional language was robustly associated with increases in message diffusion." They concluded that,

> Specific moral emotion expressions related to moral outrage – namely, moral anger and disgust – were particularly impactful for elites across the political spectrum, whereas moral emotion expression related to religion and patriotism were more impactful for conservative elites. (Brady et al., 2018).

The research suggested that, "if politicians want to maximize their impact on Twitter, they need to resort to more moral and emotive vocabulary."[1]

A study by Pew Research found that the Facebook audience was 21% to 22% more likely to share congressional posts containing news links from partisan outlets than when the link came from a news source that fell in the middle.[2] In terms of response and the desired virality of a politician's presence on social media, people react 'better' to what gravitates to the extremes of the spectrum. Therefore, politicians, as with any other influencers and ordinary users seeking a response, must post more radical views and links in order to be better noticed and gain more engagement.

Whether it be the views of endorsement or opposition, the most radical of them have a higher response potential. Centrist or moderate views simply

---

[1] de-Wit, Lee, Brick, Cameron, and van der Linden, Sander. (2019, January 16). "Are Social Media Driving Political Polarization?" *Greater Good Magazine.*
https://greatergood.berkeley.edu/article/item/is_social_media_driving_political_polarization

[2] Messing, Solomon, van Kessel, Patrick, and Hughes, Adam. (2017). "Sharing the News in a Polarized Congress," *Pew Research Center.* http://www.people-press.org/2017/12/18/sharing-the-news-in-a-polarized-congress/.

have a lower prospect of being shared. Those expressing radical views on social media have more of a chance to gain a response in the form of comments, likes and shares. The amplification of extremes inevitably leads to polarization in the public sphere. The more the public sphere adopts social media, the more polarized people become.

***

The algorithms have learnt this tendency from human psychology and peddle content that will most likely be reacted to. Extremes are environmentally promoted by social platform settings on both levels: human and algorithmic.

Godwin's Law, which states that the likelihood of a conversation's participants being compared to Hitler increases in the course of online conversation, perfectly illustrates the principle of affective polarization. Affective polarization both eliminates the center and amplifies the extremes.

Print, with its delayed reactions to linear thought, started the Age of Reason; social media with their instant service of accelerated self-actualization has turned the Age of Reason into the Age of Rage.

Intensities' signaling and the amplification of extremes empower the impulses and emotions of the crowd to the detriment of moderate reasoning and inevitably lead to digital ochlocracy. Digital ochlocracy and digital platforms are bound together. In their symbiosis, the masses acquire power and contribute engagement, while the platforms monetize engagement and enable the self-actualization of users in the most satisfying way – through the tribalistic exercise of collective power.

This mechanism of polarization is not political in itself. It is purely a media-environmental mechanism driven by the thirst for response, with social media being the best spring found by humankind so far for quenching this thirst. Social media accumulate and release an incredible potential of affective polarization simply by offering people an opportunity to socialize.

The main value of social networks is tied to their biggest harm. Those who figure out how to adjust social media settings so that they enable engagement without producing affective polarization will deserve the Nobel Peace Prize.

Agenda-setting polarization

Social media were not always seen in a negative light. Before becoming a supplier of fake news and disinformation and before being an efficient tool of discord in the savvy hands of Russian operatives, social media were praised for spreading democracy during the time of the Arab spring and other Twitter revolutions. How did they turn from good to evil in less than 10 years?

The emancipation of authorship (Miroshnichenko, 2014) in the new media environment deprived the traditional media of their historical monopoly over agenda-setting. Thus, social media challenged the dominant worldviews established by the mainstream media. As Martin Gurri put it, "[t]he mediators lose their legitimacy". This was a factor that contributes to a "crisis of authority" (Gurri, 2018, p. 396).

The conflict between traditional and new media can be interpreted as a struggle between two modes of agenda-setting.

The broadcasting mode of agenda-setting is inherent to the legacy media. It is pyramidal – the agenda spreads along the force lines of vertical social gravity, top-to-bottom, center-to-periphery. It is economically and/or politically controlled by the elites and based on established institutions. The broadcasted agenda is created before distribution by news media editors according to their educated and class-affiliated preferences.

The engaging mode of agenda-setting was introduced by social media. It is dispersed and cloud-shaped – the agenda spreads in all directions within overlapped social graphs. It is controlled by participants through their natural (or artfully crafted) propensity to gather around the coagulating centers of social gravitas. The engaging agenda is created in the process of distribution by the Viral Editor (Miroshnichenko, 2014) or by the newsfeed algorithms of relevance (Pariser, 2011).

The agenda produced by old media with predominant broadcasting always conflicts with the agenda produced by new media with increasing engagement. Historically, any new media enhanced engagement: demotic script and particularly the phonetic alphabet emancipated writing from the monopoly of palaces and temples, the Guttenberg press emancipated reading, and, finally, the internet emancipated authorship. Each time, new social strata joined the process of meaning production/consumption. They acquired technical access to agenda-setting, which is a function of power, and thereby they challenged the old power. Each new medium undermined the old broadcasted agenda with a new engaging agenda. New media are always anti-establishment.

The conflict of agendas is always content-agnostic in its origin. A class struggle, economic formation, or ideological revolution tends to appear after new and old media clash. The conflict of agendas is predefined not by their content but by the principles of their formation, namely broadcasting and engagement. The conflict between two modes of agenda-setting is not political in nature; it is a morphological incongruity, a clash between the Pyramid and the Cloud.[1]

***

It is not new media that solely drive changes in the media environment. The presence of old media is equally crucial. The tension between the broadcasting and engaging modes of agenda-setting, between Pyramidal social gravity and Cloud social gravitation is required for significant cultural change and social upheaval to happen. There always must be two poles made into a circuit to reveal the difference of potentials. Polarization is an intrinsic morphological condition in an environment where new media are displacing old ones.

These conditions appeared in the late 2000s, when social media proliferated enough for their mode of agenda-setting to start challenging the agendas propelled by old media. Before social media, the internet performed functions of old media (McLuhan's principle of the rearview mirror) – web 1.0 was a library, a diary, a post service and a tool of personal and mass communication: telegraph/radio/TV/telephone. Social media and smartphones unleashed the true environmental power of the internet. The Pyramid lost its monopoly and the Cloud charged forward.

Street riots and electoral upheavals were created not by social media but as a resolution of the tension between the broadcasting and engaging modes of agenda-setting. The inclusive agenda of social media with users' self-made 'truth' (actually, post-truth) overlapped and clashed with the exclusive agenda of the mainstream media with its broadcasted and impenetrable 'absolute truth', which turned out to be a lie. When people see how significantly the agenda imposed upon them by the mainstream media differs from what they and their peers want to discuss online, they get galvanized. Further, social media provides the space and tools for this galvanization to be expressed, verified, amplified and coordinated.

***

This conflict of the agenda-setting modes took place in every society where social media interfered in the media landscape. It first occurred in the late 2000s, when educated and progressive urban youth around the world became the pioneers of digitalization and embraced the opportunity to collectively express their views, which initially were non-political.

---

[1] Mir, Andrey. (2019, December 25). "The Pyramid against the Cloud: Institutions' perplexity regarding the Net." *Human as Media blog.* https://human-as-media.com/2019/12/25/the-pyramid-against-the-cloud-institutions-perplexity-regarding-the-net/

Soon, the discrepancy between the 'official' and 'unofficial' agendas became apparent. Suppressed in the mainstream, the displaced views found alternative release in the low-pressure atmosphere of free expression on social media. This 'meteorological' mechanism of storm creation was not initially political; it was purely media environmental in nature. But empowering of the alternative agendas leads unavoidably to the question about agenda control, which is a political question. The competition between two modes of agenda-setting evolves into the questioning of power. Sooner or later, the media battle of agendas recruits political content (Gurri, 2018, p. 50; Miroshnichenko, 2014, p. 51).

This is something akin to the classic "no taxation without representation," but re-tooled for the digital era. "You do not represent us!" was the slogan of the rebellions of digitized youth everywhere. Numerous protests and revolutions broke out across the globe in the early 2010s including the Arab Spring (2009–11), Occupy Wall Street (2011), the 'social justice' protests in Israel (2011), the Indignados protests in Spain (2011), the student protests in Greece (2010–11), the anti-Putin protests in Moscow (2011–12), the Taksim Square Protests in Turkey (2013), among others.

***

However, by 2016, social media had spread widely and permeated society deeply enough to allow other social strata to participate in agenda-setting. No longer was it just the educated, urban and progressive youth who were emancipated and empowered by social media. Everyone had obtained access. The second wave of social media-driven protests started in the West.

In the countries with more or less established electoral democracy, this conservative (often labeled right-wing) backlash has manifested itself in unexpected (by the mainstream media) electoral outcomes. Such were the electoral results in

- Germany – 2017: the right-wing AfD took third place, having sprung out of nowhere
- Brazil – 2018: the 'Trump of the Tropics' Jair Bolsonaro won the presidential election
- Australia – 2019: the center-right Scott Morrison was unexpectedly re-elected
- India – 2019: the right-leaning nationalist Narendra Modi unexpectedly increased its tally in the parliament
- UK – 2019: Boris Johnson demolished his opponents; thus Brexit, however shocking it was in 2016, struck again

Many other countries have seen similar 'unexpected' electoral outcomes.

In developing countries, the second, conservative wave of social media-related protests led to grassroots nativist or religious extremist movements, which were anti-establishment in their nature, too.

Thus, at the early stage of social media proliferation, the protests represented a progressive backlash against the elites. Later, in the second wave, the protests represent a conservative backlash against the elites. It remained anti-establishment in its target, but this time it was conservative, not progressive, due to the demography of social media use and, hence, the demography of the views and values unleashed. A closer look at the US demographics of social media use in 2011 (the Occupy Wall Street protests) and 2016 (Trump's presidential victory) clearly shows this dynamic (Figure 15).

Age				
	18-29	30-49	50-64	65+
2011	79%	61%	38%	14%
2016	86%	80%	64%	34%

Community			
	Urban	Suburban	Rural
2011	53%	52%	44%
2016	69%	71%	60%

Education			
	High school or less	Some college	College graduate
2011	39%	58%	63%
2016	59%	73%	78%

Figure 15. Percentage of US adults who use at least one social media site (by age, education and community). Pew Research Center.[1]

The data indicate that the proportion of social media users in older groups increased 2 to 3 times more significantly than the proportion of users in the youngest category between the years 2011 and 2016. The growth was 20 p.p. (percentage points) in the '65+' group, 16 p.p. in the '50–64' group, and only 7 p.p. in '18–29' group.

---

[1] Pew Research Center. (2019, June 12). 'Social media fact sheet', Pew Research Center. https://www.pewinternet.org/fact-sheet/social-media/.

In the same period, the proportion of social media users among the most educated people increased by 15 p.p., while the proportion of users among the least educated people increased by 20 p.p. This means that by 2016, social media had a larger share of less-educated people than in 2011.

But the most significant conclusion is that the share of people using social media among rural dwellers in 2016 exceeded that of urban dwellers in 2011. Similar correlations apply for education and age: in 2016, the proportions of older and less educated people on social media reached almost the same range as that of younger people and the most educated in 2011.

If there is a social-demographic 'awareness threshold' (Gurri, 2018, p. 53) for political activation through social media, then younger, urban and more educated people reached this threshold by 2011, while older, rural and less educated people approached it circa 2016. Roughly, according to these data, the voice and stance of a social group (more educated or less educated, urban or rural) may be converted into a political effect when about 60% of the group start using social media. (This was, of course, a feature of the transitional period, when social media were still proliferating. Now, it will forever be seen as a specific historical feature of the early 2010s, when social media captured the youth, and the late 2010s, when social media attracted the elders. In the future, such regularities and the idea of a 'conversion threshold' might apply to the proliferation of new types of new media into social strata.)

The data illustrate the general dynamics: social media permeated deeper and broader into society, involving those strata that were far from the elites and therefore whose cultural values and political views were underrepresented in the mainstream media; first, they were the younger and more progressive, then the elders and more conservative.

***

When the masses are offered participation in agenda-setting and can validate their opinions only through peers and not through the mainstream agenda, their mainstream media underrepresentation starts bothering them. They do not just feel but also see that the elites and the media do not reflect their values. "You do not represent us!" spreads from youth deeper down through the population. And they see that their peers see and feel things the same way. Social media offer a compensatory form of online actualization and mobilization for those neglected and disdained by the mainstream media.

The new media's capacity to empower agendas that are suppressed by old media facilitated the progressive youth's rebellion against the establishment in the early 2010s and the conservative rebellion against the establishment in the second half of the 2010s. Trump's victory was the successful completion of the Occupy Wall Street movement. Those anti-establishment movements mutated in their demographics and ideology, but what united them and has only grown was the polarizing effect of the clash between the modes of agenda-setting. It is the polarization of the media environment, not fake news, that poses the crucial threat to democracy.

The establishment's way of agenda-setting continues to reside in old media, where educated and affluent elites, affiliated with the corporate capital and culture industries, represent their views. All the views that do not fit into print are squeezed out and forcefully surface in the low-pressure atmosphere of social media, where they additionally go through the filters of extremes' amplification.

When two differently-shaped agendas cover the same topic and the topic is significant enough for the difference to become a trigger, a clash between agendas is inevitable. Once again, this is not solely a product of new media; for two types of agenda to clash, old media are also required.

Now, the third wave of political effects caused by social media is on its way. This time, these are media that empower the instant emotional perception of reality, based on video fragments, such as TikTok and respective formats on Twitter, Facebook and Instagram. This is going to shape agendas in a completely new way, with no requirements for literacy, rationality or fact-checking. This new mode of agenda-setting will most likely bring a new wave of upheavals, this time more radical. Starting, againg, with the younger demographics who are completely out of touch with traditional political parties' agendas, and extremely anti-institutional – with a respective degree of polarization.

Rebound agenda-setting polarization

The engaging mode of agenda-setting on social media empowers agendas that are underrepresented in the mainstream media. When the difference between the engaging agendas of new media and the broadcasted agenda of old media becomes critically significant, social disturbances begin.

However, old media now exist in the same information space as new media – the digital space. They both compete for the audience's attention and time spent. The old media need to engage in competition. The alternative agenda of social media challenges the mainstream agenda of old media, so they strike back, reacting to, fact-checking and disseminating what was disseminated on social media. The content of new media shapes and reshapes the content of old media.

As the space for the agendas' encounter is digital, old media need to compete with new media by the rules of new media. In addition to the fact that this worsens the chances of old media, the competition further plunges old media into the escalation of polarization in two ways:

1) the news media join affective polarization

2) the news media deploy rebound agenda-setting polarization – they re-broadcast initially engaging, participatory agendas and amplify or oppose (and amplify) topics that are preselected by the Viral Editor on social media.

***

Affective polarization is based on the incentivizing of extremes and disincentivizing of moderates on social media.

The extremes' amplification has been known to the mass media, too. An entire type of old journalism, sensationalism, was based on it. However, the media editor, though being prone to sensations and odd news for the sake of circulation and profit, still had some filtering policies that incorporated the idea of the public good into news selection. Newsroom autonomy was a stabilizing force, more or less powerful, that was able to mitigate extremities and overreaching, be it ad money's excessive influence, overwhelming flak or excessive sensationalism. The media editor was also constrained, at least to some extent, by their contract or reputation.

The Viral Editor or social media algorithms do not have a reputation and do not care about the public good; they do not have any other filtering principles except the fitness of content for better and faster sharing. They are driven by statistics on people's choices of what is more attractive in terms of generating response and engagement. Being aimed at a fast and broad response, preferably a viral one, the social media environment incentivizes more radical expression.

To keep up in this race, the mass media have to play by the same rules. The mass media try to harness the same forces of attention-grabbing that drive social media. The amplification of extremes is one of these key forces. In old media, this is becoming reflected not only in headline choices, but also in the choice of topics, experts, pictures, etc.

Many of the technological, professional and ethical disruptions in journalism practice have come from the impact social media have had on old media: clickbait, traffic race, churnalism, hamsterization, and others. The radicalization of expression to the extent that would have been seen as

336

excessive even for propaganda is becoming the new normal in postjournalism. The audience of old media is getting used to engaging with media content with the same behavioral patterns that work on social media.

***

The economy of both old media and new media is based on audience engagement. New media want users to reveal more preferences and spend more time on the platform for the sake of better exposure to advertising. Old media want users to join the cause they promote and spare some money on subscription for support (or time and cable fees – in the case of TV).

The competition for the limited audience's time, coupled with content interdependence and mutual flak, tied old and new media into a united media environment. All the polarizing forces enclosed in old and new media trigger a multistrand polarizing vortex that sucks up everything around it.

The polarization of the joint media environment is growing even stronger because of the morphological asymmetry in media consumption. Deprived of representation in the most mainstream media, the conservatives resort to their own online platforms and networks, winning followers with the new weaponry of memes, bot-farming and trolling. Having monopolized most of the mainstream media, the progressives dominate in traditional political discursive formats.

The fact that traditional political discourses led by the progressives do not intersect with the new media weaponry employed by the conservatives, except for the scoreboards of the election outcomes, makes them even more estranged and reinforces polarization even further.

Ideological polarization

Ideological polarization is based on the confrontation of different value systems. Value systems compete for people; therefore, the polarizing effect of ideologies is inevitable. The mass media are one of the best conduits for values. They can be involved in ideological polarization due to either their ideological biases or the influence of their business models.

Open ideological biases and political endorsements of the media are defined by their deliberate choice and usually are well-noticed by the audience and the public. A political stance of a publisher or the party funding of a media outlet usually raises no questions. The open political involvement of the media is what allowed the public sphere to emerge. Political funding obviously makes the media biased and therefore contributes to the 'common', political type of ideological polarization.

The ideological biases induced by business models are harder to notice.

Media driven by news retail are more likely to be free from ideological biases because news retail incentivizes political impartiality. The balance of cohering and the divisive power of news retail ends up structuring the audiences according to readers' social and professional interests in the news. Readers from demographic groups with predominantly conservative values buy conservative news, while those from progressive strata buy progressive news; biases, if they exist, are transparent and 'authentic'. Thus, if news retail media are politically biased, the bias is the effect of the audience social structuring. Reader revenue coming from news retail does not contribute much either to ideological bias or to the polarization of the media.

Media driven by ad revenue focus on the consumer properties of the audience and tend to make the audience politically ignorant. However, as Herman and Chomsky showed, ad-driven media have built-in systemic settings that lead them to promote the agendas of the financial elites and corporate state. So, the ad-driven media are ideologically biased but do not amplify ideological polarization because they tend to not focus much on politics. They rather manufacture consent and therefore depoliticize society. As McChesney pointed out in his 1999 book *Rich Media, Poor Democracy: Communication Politics in Dubious Times*, in the Golden Age of the ad-based media, the political (electoral) involvement of the masses decreased tremendously. And so did polarization.

These two basic business models were disempowered by the internet, which won over readers and advertisers. A new model appeared that is based on soliciting subscription as donation and selling agendas *downwards* to the audience, not *upwards* to the elites and advertisers.

The soliciting of support from readers for propelling a certain agenda (ideas, values) has drastically changed the political and polarizing impact of the media. Donation in the form of subscription is based on the willingness of the audience to donate to the cause. The cause itself is a filter dividing the audiences along with their cultural and political value systems. The very ability to donate to the cause reflects readers' readiness for ideological involvement. Thus, transactional prerequisites themselves preselect those who are open, possibly subconsciously, to ideological polarization.

Besides, the soliciting of subscription as donation incentivizes the selection of those topics that are most donatable, which are most likely polarizing topics, as they are the most triggering. This media business model is highly divisive.

Essentially, the donscription-based media commodify polarization. Therefore, in order for them to continue business, polarization needs to be re-supplied. This business model of the media is the most polarizing one. Even the politically-funded media did not contribute to polarization that much; they just participated in ideological polarization in the course of 'normal' political competition. The donscription-based media do not reflect polarization; they reproduce it under the pressure of worsening business conditions.

While all other forms of the media's engagement in politics and polarization have been well-researched, the capacity of this last iteration (last in many senses) of the media business to induce polarization has remained below the radars of experts and the public.

**

In a media market based on ad revenue, the media must maintain political stability and social coherence, a media function Lippmann referred to as "the manufacture of consent" (and Herman and Chomsky after him).

In a media market with large and growing significance of soliciting subscription as a donation to the cause, the media must maintain political trauma and social disarray, a function that can be referred to as the manufacture of anger.

Thus, the media profiting from ad revenue unite the public; the media profiting from donscription revenue divide the public.

At the same time, the work of the news media as the first and iconic industrial enterprise remains the same: the media validate significance through standardization that tends to lead to coherence and homogeneity of the public (Adorno & Horkheimer, 1947).

However, under business conditions that require appealing to divisive issues, media standardization cannot be universally inclusive. The unity produced by the donscription media is divisively exclusive. They unite the public not *across the aisle*, but on the sides of the aisle. The news media maintain the split in the public, which is one of the most important formal prerequisites for polarization.

13. Understanding media effects: instrumental vs. environmental

Of course, there is an anti-Russian conspiracy. The point is that the entire adult population of Russia is involved in it.

Victor Pelevin. "Generation 'П'", 1999.

A new technology does not add or subtract something. It changes everything. In the year 1500, fifty years after the printing press was invented, we did not have old Europe plus the printing press. We had a different Europe.

Neil Postman.
"Technopoly: The Surrender of Culture to Technology", 1992.

McLuhan's Figure/Ground Analysis

The striking personality of Donald Trump was so captivating that it distracted the media, the public and pundits from the exploration of what made Trumpism happen. Whatever negative characteristics Trumpism can be (dis)credited with, this negativity only highlights the peculiarity of the fact that almost 63 million Americans voted for him in 2016. It is easy to condemn Trumpism; it is much harder to deal with the number of 63 million – and respective numbers in other countries supporting similar ideas. Sixty-three million people are hard to cancel; apparently, some form of cohabitation is unavoidable.

Trump was like a tree, behind which the public and the media could not see the forest. Since an environment is not visible to its inhabitants (the fish is not aware 'of the water it swims in' – McLuhan, *Playboy* interview, 1969), an *anti-environment* is needed in order to recognize substantial characteristics of the environment. McLuhan thought it was the task of artists to expose environments to us through creating anti-environments. Perhaps it is not only artists who possess the power to knock us off track so that we can notice the world we live in. Trumpism, a set of conditions emblemized by Trump, may be seen as an anti-environment that disrupts the invisibility of the new media/cultural/social environment. Trumpism allowed us to see media polarization and post-truth at work.

Figure/ground analysis calls for focusing on hidden *ground* and not being blinded by obvious *figures*. As McLuhan wrote, "The figure is what appears and the ground is always subliminal. Changes occur in the ground before they occur in the figure" (as quoted in Pruska-Oldenhof & Logan, 2017, p. 9).

Figure/ground analysis is fundamental to the environmental approach to media. As Robert Logan stated,

> He [McLuhan] believed that to understand the meaning of a figure one must take into account the ground in which it operates and in which it is situated. The true meaning of any 'figure,' whether it is a person, a social movement, a technology, an institution, a communication event, a text, or a body of ideas, cannot be determined if one does not take into account the ground or environment in which that figure operates. (Logan, 2011, p. 2.)

According to this approach, focusing on Trump's personality brings little understanding of the conditions that favor Trumpism. As Douglas Rushkoff put it, "Donald Trump is a media virus, but we're the ones spreading him."[1] So, the question is not 'What is Trump?' The question is 'Why has the public fallen susceptible to Trumpism?'

To better understand the phenomenon of Trumpism, the focus must be moved from the salient figure to the invisible ground. Donald Trump was not just an isolated phenomenon; he was the figure that represented a tectonic shift in the media and cultural environment. Trump was not a cause of this shift but rather its effect. From this angle, Trumpism is not a disease; it is an allergic reaction to the changes in the environment. It is an unavoidable cataclysm that signals the advent of a new era.

***

Shifting the focus to the environment allows not only the enchantment of Trump to be shaken off, but also the limitations of the instrumental approach that often prevails in a discussion about Trump can be overcome.

The shockingly unexpected presidency of Donald Trump plunged the public into a desperate search for a suitable explanation. Similar events have happened in many countries, where the rise of right-wing political movements happened in spite of agendas and expectations propelled in the mainstream media and by the elites. Since this search for an explanation was led predominantly by those directly impacted by the rise of the right and

---

[1] Rushkoff, Douglas. (2016, December 17). "Donald Trump is a media virus, but we're the ones spreading him." *Digital Trends*. https://www.digitaltrends.com/opinion/why-donald-trump-is-a-media-virus/.

conservative populism – by the media and the elites – an explanation was sought to provide a sort of moral and psychological compensation.

With reference to the USA, the desire to find someone or something accountable for such a frustrating electoral outcome inevitably led to singling out the most visible or most irritating factors behind Trump's victory. Among them, Facebook (the role of social media), Russian trolls/hackers (foreign meddling) and Cambridge Analytica (big data manipulation) became the most popular. Similar to the personality of Trump himself, these motifs happened to be turned into the figures that obscured the ground from view.

When a search for an explanation is meant to become a search for those accountable, 'prosecutorial bias' is unavoidable. For a 'blamable' explanation (and symbolic execution), an agency behind the causes is required. Environmental forces have no agency and therefore cannot be blamed. On the other hand, Trump himself, Facebook, the Russians, and Cambridge Analytica have agency. They meet the requirement of a 'blamable' explanation demanded by the media and the elites.

This is not to say that Trump, Facebook, the Russians, or Cambridge Analytic did not play a part. They not only did, they had to, because they could. The environment made some sorts of actions available, and the actors stepped in, as water takes the shape of a vessel. However, the 'blamable' explanation of actors' roles provides no understanding of the settings that made this role playable. Actors can and will be different; what predefines the range of their actions is the environmental settings. Figure/ground analysis helps bring the environment, not the figure (of Trump) or the figures (of Twitter, the Russians, Cambridge Analytica) front and center.

A similar approach needs to be taken in the analysis of the role of the media in the rise of postjournalism. It is not *Fox News* or *MSNBC* who shape the condition of polarization in the media environment. *Fox, Breitbart,* the *New York Times*, or *CNN* are the *figures* that overshadow the *ground*. They play their parts, too, but they need to do it, because the environment requires them to do so. Focusing on the performance of a concrete medium is convenient for blaming and traffic churning but useless for understanding and fixing the environment (if the latter is possible at all).

From instrumental to environmental

In explanations of media effects, two approaches can be singled out.

1. The instrumental approach assumes that a medium works as a tool used by a user for a purpose.

2. The environmental approach focuses on the capacity of a medium to become an environmental force that reshapes both the habitat and inhabitants.

The instrumental approach prevails due to the long tradition of communication studies with its famous Lasswell model *'Who says what, in which channel, to whom, with what effect?'* (Lasswell, 1948, p. 37). This model with all its later reiterations has been intrinsically instrumental. As McQuail and Windahl wrote,

> The Lasswell Formula shows a typical trait of early communication models: it more or less takes for granted that the communicator has some intention of influencing the receiver and, hence, that communication should be treated mainly as persuasive process. It is also assumed that messages always have effects. Models such as this have surely contributed to the tendency to exaggerate the effects of, especially, mass communication. On the other hand, this is not surprising when we know that Lasswell's interest at the time was political communication and propaganda. For analyzing political propaganda, the formula is well suited. (McQuail and Windahl, 1993 [1982], p. 14-15.)

Indeed, the Lasswellian instrumental view has dominated communication and media studies, especially when it comes to political communications. Human agency (often elevated to institutional agency) is central to the instrumental approach. That is why this approach is agent-centered, not media-centered. Media are seen as the instrument of someone's will, which is aimed at affecting someone else's will.

With the idea of media as the enhancement/extension of human physical or mental faculties, Marshall McLuhan laid out a prospective path for the environmental approach to the exploration of media effects. Perhaps the key distinction of media ecology from communication studies is that, in media ecology, media are not seen as mere instruments of communication or influence, but rather regarded as an environmental interface that modifies both the user and the environment regardless of what is communicated by whom to whom with what intent (hence 'the medium is the message').

The emergence of an environmental force from the use of an instrument can be described by John Culkin's famous paraphrase, "We shape our tools, and thereafter our tools shape us", which is often attributed to McLuhan.[1] The environmental approach is also well-explained through McLuhan's

---

[1] McLuhan Galaxy blog. (2013, April 1). "We shape our tools and thereafter our tools shape us." https://mcluhangalaxy.wordpress.com/2013/04/01/we-shape-our-tools-and-thereafter-our-tools-shape-us/

ideas of 'spaces' – acoustic space, visual space – shaped by the medium that dominates in a certain culture/era. What seemed to be just the instrumental use of a medium in a communication act (or a series of acts) becomes an environmental force when the user is not an individual but an entire culture. As McLuhan noted in *The Medium Is the Massage*,

> All media work us over completely. They are so pervasive in their personal, political, economic, aesthetic, psychological, moral, ethical, and social consequences that they leave no part of us untouched, unaffected, unaltered. The medium is the message. Any understanding of social and cultural change is impossible without a knowledge of the way media work as environments. (McLuhan and Fiore, 1967, p. 26.)

Another metaphor for describing the environmental approach to media effects belongs to Lance Strate, one of the founders of the Media Ecology Association. He wrote,

> A medium is not like a billiard ball, producing its effects by striking another ball. Rather, it is more like the table on which the game is played. Put another way, a medium is not an actor, it is a stage on which human agents play their parts. As environments, media do not determine our actions, but they define the range of possible actions we can take, and facilitate certain actions while discouraging others. [...] In other words, as Neil Postman (2000) has explained, cultures are formed within media, rather than media simply being produced by cultures. (Strate, 2008, p. 135.)

***

An example of switching from an instrumental to an environmental understanding of media was also given by media theorist Jeff Jarvis through a practical case. On 17 March 2011, the *Guardian* revealed that "The US military is developing software that will let it secretly manipulate social media sites by using fake online personas to influence internet conversations and spread pro-American propaganda."[1] An "online persona management service" would allow one US operator "to control up to 10 separate identities based all over the world." This was perhaps the first media mention of troll farms and the use of fake accounts by intelligence operatives to exert influence abroad. Reacting in the *Guardian* with a column, Jeff Jarvis, in essence, predicted the environmental consequence of such instrumental use:

---

[1] Fielding, Nick, and Cobain, Ian. (2011, March 17). "Revealed: US spy operation that manipulates social media." *The Guardian*. https://www.theguardian.com/technology/2011/mar/17/us-spy-operation-social-networks.

The US government's plan to use technology to create and manage fake identities for social interaction with terrorists is as appalling as it is amusing. It's appalling that in this era of greater transparency and accountability brought on by the internet, the US of all countries would try to systematise sock puppetry. It's appallingly stupid, for there's little doubt that the fakes will be unmasked. [...] But the effort is amusing as well, for there is absolutely no need to spend millions of dollars to create fake identities online. Any child or troll can do it for free. Millions do.[1]

What Jarvis highlighted, and history has proved, was a sort of media deterministic inevitability for a tool (fake account) to become an environmental force that is not used by humans but rather uses humans as its operators (resembling McLuhan's "Man becomes... the sex organs of the machine world, as the bee of the plant world" – McLuhan, 1994 [1964], p. 46).

Before the internet, the capacity to fake an identity had belonged to artists, spies and criminals almost exclusively. For ordinary people, there were neither needs nor occasions to fake selves, except for rare ritual events such as Carnevale or Halloween. The internet emancipated the fake identity, which subsequently was used for fun by millions and as a weapon by some. Fake accounts, indeed, "do not determine our actions, but they define the range of possible actions we can take" (Strate, 2008). In a sense, any account on social media is a fake, as it is constructed for the purpose of exerting our personal influence on others. Some do this professionally.

An instrument creates a range of possibilities of its use, from which an environment appears that changes the way people use an instrument and act in general. The way of acting predefines social developments and the evolution of entire cultures.

Media literacy: against instrumental relativism

The instrumental view of media effects often ends up in a sort of media relativism when the same operations or same tools are seen as benevolent or malevolent depending on who manages them. The seemingly logical dependence of media effects on good or bad actors, in fact, means that there are not any media effects; all outcomes are defined by the qualities of an actor, not a medium.

---

[1] Jarvis, Jeff. (2011, March 17). "America's absurd stab at systematising sock puppetry." *The Guardian.* https://www.theguardian.com/commentisfree/cifamerica/2011/mar/17/us-internet-morals-clumsy-spammer.

For example, it is commonly recognized that Twitter helped Donald Trump bypass the mainstream media and highjack the agenda (Owen, 2019; Enli, 2017). Within the instrumental approach, Twitter in hands of Trump seems to be responsible for the radicalization of discourse. Thus, Twitter (and similar platforms) is seen as a potentially dangerous tool (Manjoo[1]; Usher et al., 2018), when used by an evil agent.

However, Twitter has not always been seen in such a gloomy light. While doing the same job, Twitter was considered a progressive tool in the US 2008 election, when a presidential candidate, Barack Obama, for the first time, was widely praised for the use of Twitter as a way to reach out to voters directly and personally, bypassing the mass media (Owen, 2019).

The capacity of the same tool to be used either for good or for bad depending on who is employing it is reminiscent of the saying "guns don't kill people, people do", an argument of media neutrality that is normally rejected by any media ecologist. This is a typical case of instrumental relativism, as it focuses on a user and a purpose and not on a medium. If an outcome solely depends on who uses a medium, then it makes no sense to discuss a medium; only the user's intent/behavior matters.

Historical comparisons are good for debunking *figures*. The 'Twitter explanation' of Trump's victory elicits an even bigger discrepancy when compared with the context of the Twitter revolutions of 2009–2012, when Twitter was seen as an agent of democratization, not radicalization. When the *figure* of the viciously and victoriously tweeting Trump is removed, it becomes clear that Twitter-related democratization during the Arab Spring was at the same time the radicalization of the pre-existing environment. And, respectively, Twitter-related radicalization in Western democracies is, in fact, democratization (that paradoxically threatens the established institutions of democracy; the keyword here being 'established').

Twitter and Facebook allowed the bypassing of the established sources of agenda-setting (the elites, the legacy media), be it in the East or in the West (Levinson, 2013; Gurri, 2018; Miroshnichenko, 2014). This 'instrumental' function of the new medium was used by Barack Obama, by the activists of the Occupy Wall Street movements and the Arab Spring, by Donald Trump and by many others. The medium extended a political voice circumventing the mainstream media and the elites who controlled the agenda. This engendered an environmental force that came to serve,

---

[1] Manjoo, Farhad. (2017, May 31). "How Twitter is being gamed to feed misinformation." *New York Times*. https://www.nytimes.com/2017/05/31/technology/how-Twitter-is-being-gamed-to-feed-misinformation.html.

depending on other circumstances, democratization or radicalization (which are most likely two sides of the same coin).

When the essence of an instrument is looked at from the environmental perspective, the *figure* of an actor using a medium loses its screening effect and exposes the *ground*. Within the environmental approach, the work of the media environment and not Barack Obama or Donald Trump is what matters.

***

Another example of the limitations of the instrumental approach relates to focusing on such a salient figure as Cambridge Analytica, or, more broadly, psychographic algorithms on social media.

The manipulation of personal data collected on social media and used for the precisely customized delivery of politically charged content was a popular instrumental explanation for Trump's victory. While the effectiveness of this tool can be enormous and has been less than fully investigated, the instrumental relativism of this version exposes itself immediately. Before Trump, Cambridge Analytica was used by Ted Cruz's team and did not help him.[1]

Therefore, the role of the figure (Cambridge Analytica in this case) could be exaggerated. There was something else in the ground that had worked out for Trump and had not for Cruz.

A historical parallel with the use of similar digital tools in Barack Obama's campaign is also interesting. "Barack Obama's re-election team are building a vast digital data operation that for the first time combines a unified database on millions of Americans with the power of Facebook to target individual voters to a degree never achieved before", reported the *Guardian* in 2012.[2] The media cheered the efforts with naïve admiration:

> [...] a crack team of some of America's top data wonks <...> draws much of its style and inspiration from the corporate sector, with its driving ambition to create a vote-garnering machine that is smooth, unobtrusive and ruthlessly efficient. <...> If 2008 was all about social media, 2012 is destined to become the 'data election'.[3]

---

[1] Timmons, Heather. (2018, March 21). "If Cambridge Analytica is so smart, why isn't Ted Cruz president?" Quartz. https://qz.com/1234364/cambridgeanalytica-worked-for-mercer-backed-ted-cruz-before-trump/.

[2] Pilkington, Ed, and Michel, Amanda. (2012, February 17). "Obama, Facebook and the power of friendship: The 2012 data election." *The Guardian.* https://www.theguardian.com/world/2012/feb/17/obama-digital-data-machine-facebook-election.

The people developing the technology were called "The digital wizards behind Obama's tech-heavy re-election strategy".[1]

As this issue is seen from today's context, similar technologies that were used by the Obama team eventually ended up in the hands of Cambridge Analytica through its alliance with Facebook, which allowed it to compile and use the data of millions for the massive customization of a political message. Of course, the messages put forth by Obama and by Trump were completely different in tone and content. However, the media effect was the same: personalized grassroots mobilization.

The development of a tool for massive political message customization on a scale never seen before inevitably leads to creating an environment vulnerable to populism and polarization, regardless of who uses it. The tool might be introduced by an advanced (meaning progressive) politician, but will best serve a populist.

There is also another way to see this: the entire environment with massive, big data-driven message customization will lead politics and political styles towards more competitive forms of populism and more extreme polarization. It can be either Obama or Trump who uses the tool, but the environment created by this tool will favor Trump more than Obama.

The instrumental approach encourages one to be distracted by the *figure* of a beneficiary, Obama or Trump, from the *ground* that is created by the introduction of this technology. Whilst on the other hand, the environmental approach focuses on why this technology worked so well on Trump supporters and had such a profound environmental effect.

***

It is interesting to observe the 'instrumental vs. environmental' struggle in Herman and Chomsky's analysis of the Propaganda model. The idea of propaganda per se is very instrumental. It assumes that a propagandist aims to influence a receiving audience with a message to get a desired result – all the elements of Lasswell's formula. However, Herman and Chomsky underlined, on multiple occasions, that they focused on systemic and structural factors. They declared that they described "the forces that cause the mass media to play a propaganda role" (Herman & Chomsky, 2002 [1988], p. lix). Nevertheless, the instrumental character of the idea of

---

[3] Pilkington, Ed. (2012, February 17.). "The digital wizards behind Obama's tech-heavy re-election strategy." *The Guardian*, https://www.theguardian.com/world/2012/feb/17/obama-campaign-digital-team.

[1] Ibid.

propaganda often takes over and Herman and Chomsky describe how, for example, sourcing is 'used' by the elites, or what are the intents of the elites in dictating the agenda. The 'instrumental bias' sometimes pulls them back to Lasswellian reductionism.

This instrumental-environmental confusion is oftentimes reproduced by PM scholars. For example, Christian Fuchs stated that,

> Critical communication and media approaches such as the PM differ from bourgeois approaches in that the latter take the instrumental character of communication and power structures for granted and neutrally describe who communicates what to whom in which medium with what effect, whereas critical approaches show what role communication plays in power structures and into what contradictions of society it is embedded. (Jeffery et al., 2018, p. 168)

Fuchs noticed the connection of the formal "bourgeois approach" with the Lasswellian tradition. On other occasions, he himself, however, follows the instrumental approach when assuming the rational intent of elites behind flak: "In respect to 'flak', dominant interest groups use social media as 'soft power' tools for trying to influence the public sphere" (Ibid., p. 183).

The idea of someone's agency behind collective media use can limit the understanding of media. There is no doubt that anyone might try to use social media for whatever benefit they desire. But if any effect whatsoever is achieved, it is rather the effect of media that permit and shape certain forms of activity than the impact of a savvy propagandist on naïve users. The media behavior of both allegedly crafty propagandists and allegedly receptive users is the product of a medium (social media in the given case). A medium precedes and predefines the media behavior of a user, not the other way around. This is one of the basic readings of "The medium is the message".

As a result of such and similar critical theories that struggle between instrumental and environmental views, the mainstream media are often seen by the public and lay experts as an instrument deliberately used by corporations for reality distortion, as if there is some other media reality – a 'natural' one that is not distorted. The instrumental approach leads to a teleological inclination in the analysis. Therefore, if the media are run by the wrong actors for the wrong purposes, the point is to make it so that media are run by the right actors for the right purposes.

***

Interestingly, Walter Lippmann noticed this inconsistency in the instrumental criticism of the mass media when he argued with Upton Sinclair, who was, perhaps, the first among those debunking the media's service to "Big Business". Lippmann wrote about Sinclair's criticism:

> He cannot convince anybody, not even himself, that the anti-capitalist press is the remedy for the capitalist press. <…> If you are going to blame "capitalism" for the faults of the press, you are compelled to prove that those faults do not exist except where capitalism controls. (Lippmann, 1929 [1922], p. 336.)

Thus, Lippmann approximated the idea that this is not a fault or a merit of the user that the medium – newspapers – 'constructs' the reality; it is the effect of newspapers themselves. The replacement of the user, if it happens, does not cancel the distorting nature of the media's constructivism. Such a replacement will merely pass the Propaganda model to the hands of other propagandists, who, by the way, might not be constrained by anything, even market forces. The North Korean mass media, for example, create a truly parallel Universe for its inhabitants without any influence of capitalism.

The user may harness the instrumental power of a medium, but he or she becomes a slave to its environmental power if he or she cannot recognize it. Any seemingly self-reliant media Universe based on controlled, i.e. broadcasting media, even if they are in the 'right hands', will be smashed as soon as a new medium, which is always more engaging in the beginning, interferes. The environmental power of media always outweighs their instrumental use. The instrumental view of media assigns the effect to the good or bad intent of an actor. But the environmental power unleashed by a medium is able to change or replace the actors themselves.

The critical instrumental approach, however, is epistemologically well-suited for turning journalism to postjournalism, a form of crowdfunded polarizing propaganda. They both treat media as instruments of impact that need to be in 'good' hands, without digging deeper into what media do to those hands.

The instrumental reading of the media environment is always a misreading. As a result, observers always come to the same conclusion that media – be it the news media or social media – are always in the wrong hands. The instrumental approach has never reported the right instrumental use of a medium. For some mystical reasons, bad actors, or worse, conspirators, always take over any medium. If a medium is seen as an instrument, the detection of a conspiracy behind its use won't take long.

The instrumental view might help to explore mediated human behavior, but it does not go deep enough to explore the media conditions that induced this behavior. As Marshall McLuhan quite graphically highlighted in his *Playboy* interview,

> [...] and yet we still cannot free ourselves of the delusion that it is how a medium is used that counts rather than what it does to us and with us. This is the zombie stance of the technological idiot. (McLuhan, 1969.)

The instrumental explanations expose the figure(s) and neglect the ground. The focus on Trump's personality obscures the reasons for Trumpism. The focus on debunking *Fox News* or *CNN* obscures the origin of polarization. A medium as an instrument is to a medium as an environmental force what the figure is to the ground.

The instrumental view of the media tends to ascribe media effects to operational control. It is seen as if someone behind the curtain makes all the decisions, conspires on the plot, pushes the buttons, and finances the agents of influence. This all happens, too; this simply must happen, because the environment allows and therefore imposes it. There must be someone who wants to command the media. But no cultural process has the governability of a mechanical device. Besides, the multiplicity of operational initiatives behind media degrades the already illusive impact of each one of them even more. As media scholar Alicia Wanless put it, "The evidence of activity is not the proof of effect."[1]

Media can be seen, indeed, as tools used for certain effects. Within this view, humans control media. But this view is not able to explain the effect that media have *on* humans. Media as tools produce effects *for* people and do it in a more or less controllable way. Media as an environment have effects *on* people, and this occurs in uncontrollable and often unrecognizable ways. When a tool is used widely enough, it activates its specific environmental features that are no longer controllable by humans. Having lost instrumental control over a medium, humans have to endure and, if they are lucky, adjust to the environment created by this medium.

When applied to certain practical cases, the instrumental explanations of media effects might not be wrong. But it is important to remember that, because they are carrying on Lasswell's legacy, they are limited by rationalizing and emphasizing human agency.

[1] Alicia Wanless on Twitter. (2020, March 2). @lageneralista
https://twitter.com/lageneralista/status/1234464994848378880

The environmental explanation of media effects has to start with skepticism towards the instrumental explanations. To see the ground, it is necessary to dethrone the figure. It is necessary to show that this media effect does not solely belong to this situation of this media's use by this user.

The conspiracy of the alt-rights using social media for distorting democracy exists to the very extent that exists the conspiracy of neoliberal elites using the corporate media to distract the public. If there is a conspiracy in which the media is used against something, then all the users are conspirators. The instrumental approach to media effects is useful for blaming whoever is most suitable. The environmental approach is useful for raising people's awareness about their 'involvement in a conspiracy' and, most importantly, for developing immunity to media disservice, if it is still possible.

***

The distinction between the instrumental and environmental views is important not only for media analysis but also, and even more so, for media literacy. When one sees enraged users on social media or journalists very selectively covering news in the mass media, it must be understood that these users and journalists are under the influence of media.

Being subdued to the environmental force of media does not release anyone from the personal responsibility for what is done on social media or in the news media, but at least this explains that people are pushed towards more polarization and rage by the environmental settings of this particular media environment. The environmental understanding of people's media behavior can have a therapeutic effect on the perception of media reality, which generally looks unexplainably insane and frustrating within the commonly applied instrumental view.

The environmental approach to understanding media effects is even more important not only for the explanation of the behavior of others but for managing one's own media behavior. The awareness of what media do to people may help one avoid falling victim to a media disservice. Media create a convenience that always enslaves a user, making a user an agent of the malicious environmental side effects. Knowing that, one can practice a little bit of media hygiene in personal media use and in reacting to the media use of others.

14. The residual needs for journalism and the desperate needs of journalism

You can judge the likelihood of the survival of democracy by the survival
of the printed page.
Marshall McLuhan, 1962.

You cannot use smoke to do philosophy. Its form excludes the content...
You cannot do political philosophy on television. Its form works against the
content.
Neil Postman. "Amusing Ourselves to Death", 1985.

Newspapers as a discourse Holy Grail

The news media have suffered severe losses in business terms but
remain of substantial importance to maintaining the public sphere.
Newspapers are particularly indispensable for politics.

The public sphere has developed together with newspapers since their
very origins. They allowed the bourgeoisie to advance its agenda and foisted
debates about political and economic rights on the nobles and the clergy.
The bourgeoisie did not have birthrights or divine power over populations
and congregations, but it had class consciousness, political demands and
some money, which was used to buy the needed news and maintain needed
discourses in print.

The instrumental political use of newspapers was certainly a common
practice, as publicism was obviously employed in revolutions deliberately as
an instrument of persuasion. However, the creation of the space for
ideological debates was rather a by-product of covering business and
politics. Newly emerged economic relations required information exchange.
The nature of capital is networking, as capital flows between markets and
industries, linking them into a living ecosystem. For its flow to be efficient, it
needs information about prospects and risks, both economic and political.
This is how the handwritten Venetian *avvisi* and then the first printed
German newspapers appeared in the 16th and 17th centuries.

Capital became the first social network, the 'content' of which circulated
on the physical platform of newspapers. Seeking money, the nobles and the

353

clergy joined in this activity. Concurrently, the bourgeoisie emerged out of it and became a third power in the political-economic environment, where the circulation of information enabled the competition of ideas.

The environmental cultural effect of the circulation of 'technical' information about goods, prices and risks can be described through the *dictator's dilemma*. The dictator needs better information technologies for better governing and economic development. But the improvement of communications enhances the exchange of ideas, including those regarding better alternatives. The growing information exchange inevitably increases the freedom of choice and results in ideological challenges.

Newspapers were a technological improvement of communications that initially happened to enhance trade and governing. But the enhanced information exchange created new social and economic conditions with the unprecedented built-in diversity of personal and, most importantly, *practical* choices regarding political and commercial news. Merchants and burghers needed to autonomously decide what goods to buy, what enterprise to invest in, and what places or events to avoid. An unseen intellectual space of individual micro-attitudes and micro-decisions emerged with full individual and *practical* responsibility for the decisions made. This involvement was verified by economic return and oftentimes even by sensory feedback, as life, safety and wellbeing were not guaranteed in a turbulent time and were dependent on right and well-informed individual decisions.

The opportunities provided by a successful medium turn into the inevitability of their use. The new medium, newspapers, unleashed a new environmental force that enabled the public sphere and capitalism. Capitalism would not have been possible without the exchange of information about markets' and industries' prospects and risks. The same is true for the public sphere – it would not have appeared without the emancipated and enhanced exchange of ideas. Democracy, capitalism and journalism are substantially important to each other. They are, respectively, political, economic and communication dimensions of the same historical process.

***

The very materiality of newspapers is also tied to the needs of the democratic public sphere.

Autocracy and direct democracy can rest on oral culture. But representative democracy needs the alienation of will and thought. Representative democracy needs a proceeding pause between stimulus and action, between subject and object. It needs meaning to be divorced from its source and disseminated. It needs productive mediation.

As Jürgen Habermas pointed out, the modern public sphere emerged as a result of the disintegration of the feudal authorities (the church, princes and nobility). Once authorities became separated from the 'private matter' of citizens, the need for mediation between authorities and citizens appeared. Authorities needed to represent their power to the people as much as people needed to represent their will to the authorities. This is, essentially, the public sphere.

The process can also be seen as being predetermined from the other side, from the side of media development. It was not the feudal authorities' disintegration that led to the detachment of the 'private matter' and the necessity for two-way representation; it was a new medium, technically and financially available to a new class. Political pamphlets, trade newssheets and eventually newspapers allowed the bourgeoisie to print and distribute its 'private matter' that led to the feudal authorities' disintegration into the public sphere.

***

Mediation needs a medium. Representative democracy needs texts. The newspaper text possesses the perfect quality of a representative agency delegated in time and space; its physical capacities suit the public sphere just fine. This quality was provided by newspaper texts' length, regularity, genres and specific 'enunciative modality', a tone of appealing to readers, which assumes the creation of a certain social reality by describing it.

Non-democratic regimes, technically, can avoid textual publication and be content with oral and visual messages. Unlike literacy media, oral and visual media do not necessarily correlate with democracy. This is particularly true for radio, which McLuhan referred to as a "tribal drum". With its soundwaves, it turns diverse personal moves into a unified collective movement. The audially (or audile-tactile, as McLuhan characterized the sensory impact of electronic media) induced ecstatic unity does not assume reflective thinking; excessive thinking would even have destroyed it.

Also, due to the specificity of technological production, radio and TV broadcasting better fit centralization and control. In authoritarian regimes, broadcasting towers are easily controlled and make entry costs too high, a factor that helps maintain the monopoly over the agenda. Text distribution is a much more affordable way for alternative sources to appear.

Moreover, newspapers, i.e. literacy media, are even potentially dangerous for authoritarian regimes, as text intrinsically possesses the quality to leave readers alone with their thoughts. Authoritarian regimes technically do not need newspapers for inner use at all.

Thus, the Soviet Union fell precisely into the trap of the dictator's dilemma. As a huge modernist project, the Bolsheviks' socialist utopia required a large quantity of competent specialists. 'Likbez', the unprecedented project of the liquidation of illiteracy ('likvidatcia bezgramotnosty' – 'likbez', classical revolutionary newspeak) increased literacy in Soviet Russia from 30–40% in the early 1920s to 87% in 1939. More than 50 million adults (more than a third of the population) learned to read and write in just 15 years.[1] By 1959, 99% of the population over the age of 9 were literate. No national culture in history has seen such an instantaneous and massive boost in literacy. This provided the Soviet regime with a technological breakthrough by the 1960s, resulting in the first Sputnik and the first man in space, having made the USSR one of the two greatest world powers. But this also created a vast layer of the Soviet intelligentsia that eventually betrayed the communist ideals due to the increased ability to individually think and compare.

Radio and TV may seduce the audience through the images of happy consumerism or terrify them through images of unbearable suffering, but they cannot offer people the luxury of alienated abstract thinking, which is lonely but at the same time aligned with many others. They capture the recipient's consciousness entirely. As Neil Postman pointed out, "You cannot do political philosophy on television. Its form works against the content" (Postman, 1985, p. 7).

Print text, on the other hand, requires thought labor both from the author and the reader. However, the thought labor demanded by books is too heavy for the time-space requirements of the fluid public discourse. The thought labor admeasured by newspaper text fits just fine. Its regularity, responsiveness and breadth of coverage are more important than the depth of thought elaboration. This balance of the depth and breadth of the newspaper text is even reflected in journalists' professional mindset: for journalists, the lack of depth is compensated for by the breadth of vision and speed of thinking.

***

---

[1] Literacy. The pedagogical encyclopedia. (1964). Грамотность. Педагогическая энциклопедия. Под редакцией Каирова А.И. и Петрова Ф. Н. 1964. М., «Советская Энциклопедия». Том 1. http://pedagogic.ru/pedenc/item/f00/s00/e0000587/index.shtml.

Literacy made the exchange of abstract and universal ideas imperative. Newspapers, the lightest, fastest and most primitive medium of the literate culture, compensated for their primitivity with the speed and outreach of delivery. In a McLuhanist sense, newspapers delivered not the message, they delivered the literacy state of mind to the masses. This process underlay the political and economic modernization of society started in the Age of Reason. Without the proliferation of the 'literacy attitude' towards ideas among the masses, provided by the press, neither representative democracy nor industrialization, accompanied by the historically instantaneous growth of living standards, would have been possible. Ortega y Gasset pointed out in *The Revolt of the Masses* that the 'mass-man' of the early 20th century took the security of his political and economic wellbeing for granted, whereas this level of social security was not guaranteed even to the "rich and powerful" just a hundred years before (Ortega y Gasset, 1985 [1930], p. 46). Indeed, just one or two generations separated, and still separate, in some countries, 'ordinary people' of sudden modernity from famine, scarcity and political insecurity.

The chief medium of the era of modernity, newspapers, proliferated the literacy mindset, which process enabled the public sphere and emancipated people from personal subjection to princely authority by creating the mediating political institutions of representative democracy. Instead of former personal subjugation to the divine and unquestioned power of princes and clergy, mass literacy, in its print form, brought to the masses the belief in universal ideas, the cornerstone of Modernity. Social coherence had switched from the principles of personal subjugation to the principles of ideological submission, the foundation of which was later challenged, deconstructed and rejected by postmodernism.

***

Electronic media, as McLuhan noted, retribalized society and therefore diminished the significance and influence of literacy. This shift is not only about the ability to read and quantity of reading. The way people learn the news impacts the way social coherence is shaped – through ideas or through emotions. Reading of news, however sensational it might be, just because of its linear and semantic representation of the world, appeals to cognitive perception, whilst the delivery of information via radio, TV and now the digital media seeks to simulate the natural, sensory perception of the surroundings. Digital media do not represent reality, as writing and print used to do; they put the user into the induced reality, shaping along the way a new kind of sensorium – the digital sensorium (Miroshnichenko, 2016).

357

Retribalization of culture by the switch from literacy media to digital-sensory media reverses social communication from literacy not just back to orality, but even to the early stages of the origin of language. The early speech had to be a sort of vocal-dance performance, in which pointing gestures and emotional exclamations served a hunter or a gatherer to deliver meaning to their fellow tribesmen. At the early-speech stage, human communication was rather more persuasion than informing.

Interjections and exclamations, the first human words, combined emotions with the first attempts at semiotic replacement of objects by signs. The oldest part of speech, interjections, remains bound by context up to today. Along with demonstrative pronouns, which are obviously the substitutes for pointing gestures, interjections are tied to the situations of their use; their semiotic (the presence of absent object through a substitutive symbolic representation) is 'weak'.

The divide between reality and its representation in the human mind is intrinsically semiotic; it is the split between the signified and the signifier. Speech is a semiotic entity and a faculty of mind that allows operations with reality in its absence – the operation with reality through its representation in signs and thoughts. (The ultimate detachment of signifier from signified by the phonetic alphabet, as McLuhan noted, incited a kind of schizophrenic state of mind: "Schizophrenia and alienation may be the inevitable consequences of phonetic literacy." – McLuhan, 1969).

Radio and television returned vocal signals and gestures into communicating socially significant content. Interjections, in which the 'lack of semiotics' is compensated for by an emotional charge, became the main means of meaning expression on TV shows. The participants of "The Ellen DeGeneres Show" whom she starts talking to begin screaming interjections immediately. Of course, they are taught to do so; but they are taught to do so because this reflects and recreates the pattern of public behaviour assigned to this kind of media. It is needed to overcome the emotional fatigue of the replete audience; but by promoting emotional exaggeration, television maintains and reinforces this pattern for public behaviour, including public speeches and any behaviour 'addressed' to the audience.

If theatrical actors exaggerate their performance to ensure they can deliver their acting to spectators on the back rows, TV-shows' participants exaggerate their emotions because TV is a 'cool' medium, in McLuhan's terms, and it needs additional measures to be applied in order to heat up its effect on the audience, blasé about infotainment, for better reception. Exaggerated emotions of the people in the TV studio (or people delivering public speech) are expected to enhance the receptiveness of the indifferent passive audience through transmitting the emotional charge; it is something similar to establishing rapport in neuro-linguistic programming.

Considering the passivity-massiveness and physical 'absence' of TV audience (whose absent reaction is often substituted by recorded laughing and applauses), the simulated and transmitted emotions must be exceedingly intensive. This kind of emotional exaggeration represents not feelings but intensities, exactly as described by Lyotard and Jameson. The postmodernist replacement of feelings with intensities goes hand in hand with the replacement of literacy by orality and the retribalization of culture by electronic media.

The interjections' creeping revolution has proliferated into news and political TV-shows, as they are mostly filled with experts, not reporters, due to the dominance of opinion journalism; i.e. these shows are increasingly often conversational, which mode creates an additional opportunity for interjections to supplant other parts of speech in conveying message. The growth of the public use of interjections, the most 'non-semiotic' of verbal means, is a clear indication of the reversal of culture from literate to oral. And this reversal is media-determined, as interjections are not needed in literate speech (unless it quotes or simulates oral speech).

✳✳✳

Digital media took the retribalization of speech and mind even further, reversing not just literacy but language itself.

Any behaviour on social media is 'addressed' to the audience by default; everyone has become a broadcaster facing the audience's fatigue. The emancipation of authorship has delivered to the millions the necessity to overcome the unresponsiveness of the audience by means of intensities. In digital orality, the media evolution of the intensities' transmission has come down to the semantic structures of communication.

Interjections are partly symbolic, partly indexical signs, according to Pierce's classification. They directly indicate emotions and feeling (primary interjections) but may also convey residual abstract meanings related to those emotions (mostly secondary, or derivative, interjections). In digital communication, verbal interjections have turned into or are complemented by graphical abbreviations ('lol, 'omg', etc.) and emojis. Emojis are purely iconic, not symbolic or indexical signs. Emoji's signifier invokes emoji's signified by depicting emotions. In the digital media, the schizophrenic detachment of signifier from signified shrinks.

Digital media reverse the semiotics of reality's representation back to immediate interaction with the objects of reality – of the digital reality. The means of digital social communication in the newest media, such as Twitter or TikTok, resemble the vocal-dance communicative performance of the primeval humans in our pre-speech era. Digital orality is based on exclamations and digital gestures (many of which are pointing digital gestures). It aims to persuade rather than inform, it operates with emotions and objects (memes, pictures, videos, etc.) directly, rather than with information that represent objects in their absence.

Not only a post-literate era – a post-speech era is coming. McLuhan's retribalization of society by electronic media is being accelerated with the de-semiotization of culture by digital media. This is only logical, considering the forthcoming resettlement of humans *into* the medium, into the digital world, the induced reality of which will require direct operations with objects, mediated by the digital sensorium 'immediately', with no 'replacing' semiotics needed. To comprehend the oddity of this event and the trajectory of media evolution, just imagine the resettling of a caveman *into* a stone axe.

Media evolution will end up in quitting mediation, when the instrument itself becomes the environment. Media will extend human faculties to the point of the full merging with the environment, when media are no longer needed, which event can be called the Media Singularity, because the role of media in terraforming goes far beyond terraforming. The so-called Technological Singularity is, in fact, the final event, or, to use the language of Teilhard de Chardin, the Omega point, of media evolution.

***

Due to its technical specificity and its ingrained relation with the public sphere, journalism remains the supplier of the public discourses needed for politics. Text-based journalism, i.e. predominantly newspaper journalism, is at the core of the discourse making. TV and radio-journalism exercise public service as long as they simulate the text structure or supply evidence and emotions to support text-based discourses. In a broader sense, they perform a public service as long as their product requires literacy – if not in a literal sense, then in the sense of a text-based cultural context. Otherwise, TV and radio are purely infotainment entities.

Journalism is either text-based or text-biased, and newspapers are its Holy Grail.

The newspaper text, the weakest and most superficial among the texts of written culture, as with any transitional phenomenon, paradoxically was the last resort for the societal expectations of objective truth and, at the same time, a precursor of post-truth. The paradox of being the last resort of truth and a precursor of post-truth may also well be applied to journalism in general, as journalism appeared in the form of text, gave birth to the factoid and industrialized the principle of significance validation by dissemination.

Texts on the internet are not the main carrier, and even when used, they are not of the same nature as printed texts. They are hyperlinked; their linearity is weak. The length of reading on the internet is shrinking. Texts on the internet do not immerse a reader in themselves; rather, readers themselves are immersed in the networked panoramic digital environment.

The newspaper or journal article was the last text of modernity, the last text of the literate era, the last text of the Gutenberg Galaxy and, in fact, simply the last text.

The really immortal qualities of good-old journalism

The rivalry between journalism and the blogosphere has spawned a very interesting effect. In contrast to social media, journalism is now often credited by many with such qualities as responsibility, trust, professionalism, aiming to serve the public good, etc. Journalists have never before been praised with such honorable epithets.

Such a sudden admiration of professional journalism can be explained by people's demand for authority in news navigation and validation. In the environment of many self-appointed news sources with unknown status, the burden of selection of what is true falls upon the consumer, not the supplier of the news. As Mathew Ingram once paraphrased Dan Gillmor, "You are your own gatekeeper, and you now get to decide whom you trust for information."[1]

This is too hard to do in respect to the endless flow of news; it is much easier to follow an avowed authority. This is why people are seeking arguments in favor of the superiority of journalism over the blogosphere and social media, though the acknowledgment of journalists' outstanding responsibility or trustworthiness would have been deemed sarcastic 25 years ago.

If there were an imaginary professional contest between a journalist and a blogger, we might, no doubt, have handed the winning prize to a journalist. But in reality, it is not a "one-to-one" contest. It is the rivalry between institutional media and guerilla media activity, between the institution and the environment. Not only the nodes but also the connections between the nodes constitute the network environment. The qualities of the entire system depend much more on the qualities of connections between nodes

---

[1] Ingram, Mathew. (2011, September 7). "No, licensing journalists isn't the answer." *Gigaom.* https://gigaom.com/2011/09/07/no-licensing-journalists-isnt-the-answer/

than on the characteristics of the nodes themselves. It is not a matter of whether a certain blogger is good or bad at news production. What really matters is how the entire system gathers news, copyedits it in the process of distribution and shapes agendas.

***

In old media, the news is filtered before it is published. On the internet, the news is filtered after publishing, through the process of distribution. Every user for whom the topic is relevant contributes their time, passion, expertise, and evidence into the collective process of the selection and editing of the news. I call this process of collective editing the Viral Editor,[1] as this is basically the same job that traditional print editors used to do: searching for interesting stories; selecting topics, sources and materials most relevant to the user; and editing, copyediting and publishing. But the Viral Editor does this by the collective efforts of every user's close and distant connections – by 'other' users, preselected into everyone's social graphs.

The Viral Editor is able to supply news no worse than a professional journalist organization. This collective entity is relevant to its audience with 100% accuracy because it consists of this very audience. The Viral Editor possesses all the evidence, all the expertise, and all the styles that people, including the best journalists themselves, contribute to it for the sake of garnering response; the Viral Editor selects and distributes what is the best and most relevant to each involved. Therefore, it is able to investigate everything that is of people's interest. The Viral Editor embodies the shift from 'representative democracy' to 'direct democracy' in news mediation.

The algorithms of relevance that filter content in everyone's newsfeed and elevate topics to the top have learnt from the Viral Editor and now amplify the impact of this mechanism (often distorting significance by excessive amplification for the sake of better user engagement).

Possessing any possible media skills, the Viral Editor poses a threat not just to the mass media but to institutional journalism itself. Old media can improve the professional quality of its product as much as they wish or can, but they will nevertheless share the fate of the phaeton – to use a McLuhan metaphor – the most technologically and aesthetically advanced version of a chariot, but its very last version, because it appeared at the time when the first automobiles hit the roads. So, the phaeton did not survive; it only passed on to the new medium of transportation some technological features,

---

[1] Mir, Andrey. (2013, November 13). "The Viral Editor as a distributed being of the Internet. The Manifesto of the Viral Editor." *Human as Media.* https://human-as-media.com/2013/11/13/manifesto-of-the-viral-editor/

such as soft cushions and leaf springs. The Viral Editor took what is useful from journalism, too, but it does the same job better, adding its own environmental features along the way and changing the news environment.

New media do not deliver news; they immerse users into an environment where relevant news already awaits to be served to everyone personally, just as a side effect of the digital immersive existence – a new state of social existence. The Viral Editor is the best, fastest and most relevant-to-everyone supplier of news, comments, facts, opinions, expertise and whatever may be used for informing, amusing and spending time – with the best filtering and editing system of personal customization by friends and algorithms, with the best delivery system, connecting the environment directly to the user's sensorium increasingly more effectively.

Are there any real advantages of good-old journalism over the Viral Editor? Yes, but not many. They are not usually listed among those epithets with which people now praise journalism. What is in journalism's arsenal for its last stand?

- Completeness of the story
- Compressed panoramic agenda
- Professional status of the news media
- The effect of limited edition

***

Completeness of the story. The main advantage of old journalism relates not to the professional skills or ethical superiority of its priests but to the technology of its material manufacturing. Physical production demands placing the news into packages by the time of printing or airing, and that is why periodicals are periodic. Physically predefined periodicity, in turn, predefines the most important quality of journalistic content – the completeness of each piece.

As every story should be completed by the time of airing or printing, the journalist has to put the period in a narrative, no matter whether the real story is over or not. Thus, journalism cuts reality into parcels. A journalist must be able to put in a period. Period.

But reality is not sliced; it is streaming and arriving continuously. Cutting reality into slices is a form of professional violence over the nature of events. And this professional violence creates convenience for readers.

The internet destroys the technologically predetermined parceling of news content. On the internet, the news flows exactly in the same way as events occur in reality. The streaming content of the internet suits the streaming flow of events and does not suit humans' *literate* habit of parceled perceptions.

People get annoyed with this flow of what had earlier been in parcels. What is the 'story' on the internet? Where are the beginning and the denouement? What, finally, happened exactly? There are no clues or cues as to where to stop reading. Stories have turned to 'buzzing' and 'trending'. The flow of the newsfeed supplies only endless waves of climaxes and oblivions with no chance of putting in a period logically. This reality is never complete. It annoys or even frightens those accustomed to written culture with its magical power to cut reality into parcels and to turn the flow of events into completed stories.

The completeness of the reality in digestible parcels is both the customer service and the social function that a human editor can do and the Viral Editor cannot.

The next generations will most likely be more receptive to flow. With this switch, the transfer from logocentric consideration to intensities' amplification will be completed. Consumers of the content flow must be much more hysterical than consumers of the textual parcels. But this is the view from the past. For the generations accustomed to complete stories, being immersed in the environment of the ever-streaming flow of multimedia content quantized down to flashing snippets must be exhausting.

***

Compressed panoramic agenda. Every media outlet packs a picture of the world into a compressed panoramic agenda within the typical template of "breaking news – politics – business – social issues – cultural life – sports". Different media apply different variants of this pattern, but what is important is the regulative power of the pattern itself and the obligation of an editor to find relevant news and fill in all the appointed thematic sections with something significant, even when nothing significant has happened. This obligation to fill in the pre-structured agenda creates an all-in-one panoramic view of the world.

To get such a rounded view from the newsfeed requires reading the entire newsfeed, which is reminiscent of that "Borges fable in which the cartographers of the Empire draw up a map so detailed that it ends up covering the territory exactly", as Baudrillard recollected in *Simulacra and Simulation* (Baudrillard, 2012 [1981], p. 388). The Viral Editor filters reality, but it focuses on the news that is most interesting and relevant to a concrete user and is quite indifferent to the other parts of the panoramic agenda. The

Viral Editor makes no panoramic view. It sees the prominent peaks, but the valleys are hidden under a haze.

Meanwhile, it is enough to flip through the newspaper pages or watch a 15-minute newscast on TV to get an entire compressed agenda. It is exactly that structural pattern of the agenda in newspapers, which appeared, again, because of the physical limitations of the paper square, which enabled journalism to compress the world into the panoramic agenda that can be scaled down to a 30-second review. (The principles of this compression also contain opportunities for manipulation, but that is another issue.) This service will never be provided by the freely flowing stream of guerilla journalism managed by the Viral Editor.

***

The professional status of the news media. The professional skills of journalists, of course, still matter; while others are learning how to be media, journalists already know how. But, again, the high quality of the Viral Editor's product is predefined not only by the qualities of the nodes but by the settings of the connections between them. The investigative, watchdog, entertaining and other functions of journalism, along with the qualities of the best reporting or style may be provided by the random or collective efforts of the Viral Editor. As all the experts and all the witnesses, seeking better socialization in response to their expertise and evidence, are engaged with the Viral Editor, it supplies everything and selects the best. To each user, the Viral Editor delivers what is most relevant to them and what they 'deserve' through their digital behavior and friend selection (as it is judged by algorithms, increasingly).

The professional status of journalist is important not because of professional quality but for another reason. The status of the journalist works as a marker that shows: this piece is written not by whomever but by a special professional entitled to do this job. A label 'made by journalist' narrows the possible range of our presumptions about the origin and purpose of a text. The status of journalist, as well as the reputation of a concrete news outlet, serves to maintain the economy of efforts for people receiving news.

Most importantly, the professional status of the news media is the marker of their social validity. When a story is told by a journalist in a media outlet, a reader understands that this is a professional and institutional product from a profession and an institution *sanctioned* to supply this product on behalf of society. The status entitles journalists and the media to validate the news (that basically are already pre-delivered by the Viral Editor to the readers during their morning in bed while surfing on smartphones).

365

Since its function is now validation, not informing, that is the last viable and more or less demanded function of the mass media, the professional status of journalists and the media is important: validators must have a sanctioned status, just as a notary must have a license to operate.

Considering the huge volumes and multitude of the content flow, this small job of the professional status turns, in fact, to an effective psychological factor preserving the significance of journalism. This is also the real meaning behind people's beliefs in journalist professionalism. Professional status is just a signal of the news-validation credentials.

This circumstance underlines the significance of professional ethics in journalism, or more precisely, the significance of the talk about ethics. Journalists and their associations should vociferously proclaim and extol far and wide that they are special, avowed, sanctioned and commissioned; talk about professional ethics is the best way to proclaim the exclusivity of credentials. The concept of ethics and particularly talk about ethics beneficially singles journalists out from the crowd of self-propelled reporters of the Viral Editor.

***

The effect of limited edition. Because of the limitations of physical manufacturing, it is impossible to endlessly print on paper (as well as to broadcast on TV or radio). The very fact of limited physical capacity determines the selection of what to publish. This is why editorial policy in the media appeared. Basically, the physical limits of media created the most useful and yet underrated features of journalism: selection, parcellation, completeness, compression, and panoramic view. The effect of the limited edition is among them.

The value of the 'limited edition' is well-known in marketing. The product is valued more highly if it is known (and promoted) that the supply is limited. In the media, the effect of limited edition turns into a wow-effect. When a newspaper prints news about someone (or a TV program airs this news) – this still induces a 'wow!' Nobody says 'wow' when their name ends up on the internet; this is not a big deal (unless the name is propelled to fame or shame by distribution – 'significance by dissemination'). Everyone knows that the internet is notoriously limitless for posting whatever anyone wants. But on the contrary, to get on a newspaper page or on TV or radio, one needs to pass some selection process and must deserve to be cast. Appearances on the internet matter only under some conditions and after some distribution. Media appearances matter unconditionally and at once.

By default, everything published on a limited carrier will always be more valuable than whatever is published on an unlimited carrier. Something published on an unlimited carrier acquires value only after distribution if distribution happens. This is one more intrinsic advantage of old media that the internet will not be able to take over or take away.

All other features of journalism can be reproduced and appropriated by the internet, if not completely then to some significant extent.

– 30 –

The symbol "-30-" allegedly came from the telegraph code, where it meant "the end of message". The symbol was used in the old newsroom to signify the end of the story in typewritten manuscripts submitted to editors. In recent years, some old Canadian newspapers have used the '-30-' symbol on the front page of their last print issues (Figure 16).[1] They used the code for "the end of the story" to symbolize the end of their history.

Figure 16. The last front pages of some Canadian newspapers.

***

Traditional institutional politics still need political discourses, the best supplier of which has always been newspapers. For a riot to start, there is no need for discourse, so the discursive-making media are not essential for it. Unlike the classical revolution, a riot rests on the amplification of intensities, not on public discourse.

The progressive movements of the early 2010s and the conservative movements of the late 2010s were angered by mainstream agendas. Based

---

[1] Mir, Andrey. (2016, June 8). "End of story and history. Mysterious symbol '-30-': how the end of a newspaper story ends the history of newspapers." *Human as media.* https://human-as-media.com/2016/06/08/end-of-story-and-history/.

on the conflicts of agendas, those anti-establishment movements often regarded old media as the significant 'other', as representatives of the institutional world.

The political movements of the 2020s will be indifferent to old media. The old media discourses are too heavy and too logocentric to be bothered with when a tweet or a Facebook or TikTok video deliver a powerful emotional message the best. New political activity is increasingly based on identity markers' signaling and intensities' amplification, so the media of this political reality are social media, whose format fits this reality the best because this format creates this reality.

These new political movements might not have a need for old media at all. They have enough energy and hardware support from social media. Hence their very articulated emotions aimed at concrete institutions directly, not against just institutional discourses, as it was in 2011 and 2016. New protests do not need text-centered media; they work well with intensities-centered media. Therefore, they are losing interest in representative politics and representative media. They are the movements of direct action and are principally destructive for the old institutions, not just for institutional discourses.

There were no revolutions before newspapers, and there will be none after; only riots (yet, maybe, coups).

***

Just as the bourgeoise, Reformation and workers' movements of the 17th through the 19th centuries were coupled to the rise of print media with their representative discourse-making, the new political activity is coupled to social media with their direct democracy without any discourse mediation. The political demand for discourse-making is vanishing; or, more accurately, new media can serve political activity without discourse-making and, therefore, they can shape political activity that has no need for discourse-making.

The media-affiliated pundits and old-school activists try to cater to this new type of politics, but they overestimate their role and the role of their main weaponry, discourses, in new politics. The old media's need to support or condemn the new political movements is much more acute than the need of these movements to have any dealings with old media.

This asymmetric dependence makes business prospects of the news media even more flimsy, on top of what the internet has already taken away from them. Now the last resort, the function of news validation, is challenged. The news media offer the service of legitimizing or delegitimizing to the political forces that do not need this service. The only consumer of this service will be the old donating audience.

Perhaps the switch of the media hardware of society from old to new media will lead to the collapse of not just old media and journalism but the public sphere as we knew it in general. Political activity based on social media intensities, with no news media and no mediating elites, with no representative and elaborated discourse-mongering, will be hard to refer to as the public sphere. Its multidimensional Cloud gravitation will probably coagulate into some new forms of political meaning production.

The relations between this new mode of political activity and the electoral process remain mysterious. The electoral process as the base for power formation no doubt belongs to the old institutional world, to the Pyramid. Enabled by social media, the political activity of the Cloud incites direct actions, compared to which voting as power formation looks too slow, bulky, and yet deceiving. Most outrageous is the fact that voting gives the right of voice to those who do not deserve it, according to the polarized opinion of both parts of social media inhabitants regarding each other.

It can be predicted that relations between the social media 'post-public' sphere and the traditionally mediated public sphere will be full of discrepancies and disturbances. Most likely, the results of elections will drastically mismatch the 'trending on Twitter' and buzzing on other platforms of intensities' signaling.

The mass media will not have a decisive say in this conflict. But striving for survival, they will intensify their engagement with processes to which they do not belong. This will cause their journalism to mutate into postjournalism even more rapidly.

For those closed local newspapers with the symbol '-30-' on the front page of the last issue, their death was honorable.

Conclusion: an ascent from the maelstrom

> Is not the essence of education civil defense against media fallout?
>
> *Marshall McLuhan. "The Gutenberg Galaxy", 1962.*

The media is a specific sort of business that is able to induce demand for its product by supplying it. To succeed in this, the media modify their audiences to better fit a current business model.

Different business models have had different impacts on the audiences.

1) The media that focused on news retail made the audience buy news.

2) The media that profited from advertising made the audience buy advertised goods.

3) The media that have lost all the above models and started soliciting subscription as donation are struggling to make the audience donate.

The media are a sort of self-contained entity, whose business product became looped into a reproduction of the conditions of its reproduction. The residues of the public sphere are locked in a bubble comprised of the donating audience, the political elites and the mass media mediating them. Competing in the narrowing business niche of news validation and subscription solicited as support for a cause, the media are forced to amplify their promotion of a cause, which is increasingly a political cause.

Meanwhile, the majority of political activities have transferred to other media carriers. Old media try to contribute by competing with new media's intensities' signaling and polarization, but they no longer control political messaging and agenda-setting. Their broadcasting of the principles of agenda-setting tends to serve as an additional amplifier of polarization. As a result, the core business models of both new and old media effectively incite an extremes' race.

This effect of new and old media is neither instrumental nor politically managed; it is purely environmental. The effect is caused by the profit-seeking in new media and the desperate struggle for survival in old media. The media environment is set up for better performance, but the better performance of this combination of media, old and new, with their current business models, has brought uncontrolled side effects: polarization and societal disintegration.

Amid shrinking earnings, the newsroom autonomy that normally would have helped the news media withstand the negative pressure of the business model does not protect news organizations from sliding into postjournalism.

***

Postjournalism is journalism that is economically forced to take a political side and produce polarization and anger in order to trigger the audience's loyalty and donations in the form of subscription. Seeking social issues that are able to incite anger in the audience, the mass media amplify and sometimes make up those issues, thereby increasing polarization for the next round of selling the cause for better audience support and donscription.

The polarization loop is positively reinforced by donations and also by flak, the guiding feedback of the audience, which, under this business model, is garnering more power over newsrooms' decisions in choosing topics and authors.

It can be predicted, though, that the spiral of agitation in the media may reach a critical level, after which the donating audience will cease to be triggered by whatever the media can offer. The audience's eventual deafness to the media calling for donations may become the natural limit for this business model (if society does not disintegrate completely before that happens). After that, either new and even more terrifying events will be needed for the donscription model to be sustainable or this last iteration of journalism will cease to exist, ending the 500-year history of journalism.

***

Journalism is descriptive, while postjournalism is normative; journalism navigates, while postjournalism steers. In a sense, through postjournalism, the news media are returning to the times of bourgeois revolutions, when political newspapers promoted the rights of the class that emerged with this new type of media. The difference is that the early newspapers that sold the political agenda of the bourgeoise and then workers' movements had political goals; the goal of today's media that are slipping into postjournalism is their economic survival. They are run by the struggle for money, not the class struggle.

There is simply no such political goal for the media to achieve, which might make them abandon the polarizing donscription business model. The model is the goal itself, as it remains the only viable model for the leading news media (all others follow in the leaders' footsteps, succeeding much less, if at all). Or, as Marxist-revisionist Eduard Bernstein would say, "The goal is nothing; the movement is everything."

In the final period of their history, the mass media are doomed to sow polarization. They will not return to the manufacture of consent, a sin they were accused of in their Golden Age in the late 20th century, as there are no and will be no systemic conditions for it. Any other models are not sustainable. All attempts to support independent journalism through philanthropy initiatives will have a minor and temporary effect. The structural business conditions for independent journalism disappeared after news and ads migrated to the internet.

As newspapers have always been the base of journalism, they have suffered from the transition to postjournalism the most. They have been the main discursive platform for the public sphere. Their texts fit politics the best in terms of length, genre and 'enunciation modalities'. But newspapers happened to be the most susceptible to the donscription model: they have lost ad revenue and have been forced to switch to subscription in circumstances under which the news is not a commodity anymore; therefore, readers' money must be solicited for a different reason.

News validation and promoting political causes happened to be the last commodified newspapers' value instead of news retail. Thus, newspapers were forced to drift towards soliciting subscription as donation. They started forming discourses and attitudes that fit this model. Radio and TV have joined the trend, partly to seek converted forms of donscription (cable subscription, membership, donations, foundation funding, etc.), and partly because postjournalism, with its capacity for igniting anger, appeared to be effective at attracting the viewers' time and loyalty, which, on TV, still can be monetized through residual advertising revenue. As a result, the entire mass media ecosystem is increasingly growing contaminated by postjournalism.

***

Being engrossed in the same agitation they offer their audience, media professionals are too busy to reflect upon these structural changes in the media environment. Terrified by the messages they convey, they overlook the message the medium itself has become. The figure has overshadowed the ground. This is explainable: the worrisome decline in the business model, the annoying growth of social media and astonishing political events readily divert attention away from much less salient but nevertheless much more fundamental consequences of the systemic shift from ad revenue to reader revenue.

Meanwhile, this is a shift of a century scale: the last time an event of comparable magnitude happened was in the first half of the 20th century, when the media industry gradually turned away from reader revenue to ad revenue. Moreover, because that turn coincided with the rise of movies, radio and TV, it was not even noticed as an independent business process. The mid-20th century's shift in the media was rather reflected upon in terms of its cultural influence (Adorno and Horkheimer's *culture industries*, McLuhan's *global village*, Postman's *amusement-to-death*, etc.). And that shift lasted about 50 years, having shaped the economy of the media by the 1960s.

So, not only have today's media professionals been distracted by new media technologies and political events, none of them have ever dealt with a structural shift of such magnitude. The prevalent consensus still holds that the media sell the audience to corporations for ad revenue. In fact, however, the news media increasingly sell imaginary Smythe's audience to Lippmann's phantom public for donation, a business model that is completely reshaping the principles of agenda-setting.

Thus, behind the polarizing effect of postjournalism, there is a systemic economic factor, and nothing can change, reverse or overturn it.

***

There are two parallel and intertwining processes defining the conditions of agenda-setting. First, journalism is mutating into postjournalism, and the largest news media orgs are turning into the crowdfunded 'Ministries of post-truth'. Second, old media in general are becoming a part of the digital media environment dominated by social media with their own intrinsic polarization bias. As a result, old and new media are conjointly and interdependently contributing to polarization. The mechanisms and motives, however, are different. Social media polarization is a side effect of better user engagement for better ad targeting. Old media polarize the audience for better soliciting of support. But both produce polarization because of the very design of their business models.

Fake news is not the principal problem in this new media environment. The impact of fake news is already mitigated by the users' growing immunity and also by the growing noise that diminishes the potency of fake news' impact. The critical issue of the new media environment is polarization. It is systemic and profound; no ecosystem factor is seen on the horizon that might limit or counteract the polarizing effect of new and old media. Even the ongoing decline of old media will not solve the problem, as they will remain the discursive platform for the public sphere for another 5–10 years. This is sufficiently long enough to cause significant damage in the area where the affective and agenda-setting polarization of social media gets articulated and transferred into political discourses that shape the public sphere, politics, policies and electoral outcomes.

373

***

Polarization studies are media studies, and media ecology is the discipline that allows the environmental causes behind polarization to be seen.

In ecology, pollution is an outcome, and it is essential to look at the systemic forces producing pollution. In the media environment, fake news is the pollutant, but the systemic force producing the pollution is polarization, and underlying it are media settings. In order to fight against the cause of media pollution one must fight against polarization, not fake news.

A search for solutions that will reduce polarization can be conducted in two areas.

1) Media education: the raising of people's awareness of how old and new media incite polarization.

2) Media engineering: the search for settings that will encourage news coverage (in the news media) and socialization (on social media) without stimulating polarization.

***

Media education and, in a narrower sense, media literacy have inherited the classical concepts of education, which were based on the idea of *how to use* media technologies (writing, books, computers, etc.). This is completely logical when media are seen as instruments. The goal of education was to integrate individuals into the physical and social environment via the use of respective techniques and tools.

No one would teach an individual how to integrate into natural, biological conditions of living; how to breathe, for instance. On the other hand, some techniques of self-control, such as yoga, for example, teach one how to interfere with the natural way of breathing. Some schools of yoga, in a sense, teach *how not to breathe*.

The digital reality is becoming a natural environment for people resettling there. There is no need to teach anyone how to use social media or the internet, just as there is no need to teach *how to breathe*. These skills come naturally. Media education must focus on withstanding the power of natural forces. Techniques for control of the digital body should teach users *how not to breathe*.

When media are an environment, not instruments, and a fully immersive environment, such as the digital one, media education must be *anti-environmental*. Marshall McLuhan expressed a related idea when he stated in *The Gutenberg Galaxy*, "Is not the essence of education civil defence against media fallout?" (1962, p. 246).

In the digital reality, media literacy is not about *how to use*. Digital media literacy should be about *how not to use*. Media literacy is the ability to mindfully switch between media and, ultimately, to willingly turn off any medium however emotionally attractive and sensory pleasing it may be.

In the physical reality, education mostly meant teaching the operation of material objects, i.e. spatially. In the social reality, operating in time has been growing in significance. The digital reality is purely social; it is space-ignorant and time-biased. In the digital reality, media literacy is time management in the professional occupation and time hygiene in the personal life (with the gradual and accelerating merging of these two).

***

The first step to finding a cure is recognizing the disease. Media education starts with the awareness of the natural distorting forces of the media environment.

The anti-environmental character of media education means exposing the settings of the environment and attributing them to media, not to humans. What we are dealing with in the digital reality is not people. These are people's proxies that are processed by media. Media turn living humans into users with certain profiles and types of behavior.

People's digital copies are the results of two main environmental processes:

1) the embellishing and faking of one's own personality by themselves for better representation on social media, and

2) the intensities' signaling and extremes' amplification in people's behavior, enforced by social media.

Purified confrontation, animosity and rage are media conditions, not human conditions. Human nature is more complex than that. Confrontation, animosity and rage are extracted and refined from human behavior by the media environment for the media platforms' better performance. It is a byproduct of the environmental settings aimed at higher user engagement for more efficient commercial targeting. Polarization based on extremes' amplification is a disservice of social media, which unavoidably, unfortunately, accompanies the greatest service of socialization and self-actualization that people have ever had.

Media polarization leads to the dehumanizing of opponents, which is, actually, a propagandist prerequisite for the physical neutralization of the enemy in conditions of war. Physical neutralization now even has its virtual equivalent in the digital reality. This equivalent has become easily demanded and applied. Technically speaking, polarization ends up in the implicit or explicit calls for the 'digitally-physical' neutralization of opponents, as they are not worthy humans. This would have been deemed as a war crime or an example of totalitarian terror in the physical reality, but it has become a daily Two-Minutes-Hate routine on social media, often exercised by educated and polite people who would otherwise never allow themselves to engage in it in real in-person communication. This is, no doubt, a media effect. They do it under the influence of media.

The same is true for the news media: they evolve towards postjournalism because of the change in their business model. Recognizing it, primarily by professionals in the media but also by the audience, will help in understanding the roots of polarization. Environmental awareness does not release actors from responsibility for what they so routinely do, but it helps to see how people are pushed by the environment and that they might deserve some compassion and sometimes even some forgiveness.

By exposing the fact that animosity and polarization are not solely human features but media-environmental effects, media education can rehumanize people: it can reverse the dehumanizing effect of polarization. These are not people from the left or the right that would like to annihilate each other; this is a systemic design that makes people lean to extremes in order for the system to capitalize on polarization. Acknowledgment of these environmental forces and understanding its mechanisms and power will help people avoid the dehumanizing of opponents and tolerate, at least to some degree, the otherness of others on the internet, social media and in the news media.

***

Increasing the awareness of media polarization may help to cope with its effects, but it will not eliminate its settings. Is it possible to re-engineer the systemic settings of social media and the news media that incite polarization?

Any media engineering solution should focus on social-economic fundamentals, such as dealing with the impact of ads or subscription on agenda-setting, the economy of attention, digital capitalism, etc. As Jan Krasni defined 'digital capitalism' (accumulating the definition from many scholars), it is "a media monetisation system which rewards attracting attention regardless of the posted content" (Krasni, 2020). So, the rewards for attracting attention need to be re-engineered in order to divert them from producing polarization.

In a paradoxical way, digital ochlocracy depends on digital capitalism. These two forms of power have shaped their symbiotic relations in a similar way as representative democracy depended on industrial capitalism, with old media being a communicative platform. Now, digital platforms give the crowds on the right and on the left power that they otherwise would have never had access to; the mass media reinforce and articulate this power into political discourses. In return, the crowds provide platforms and the media with a degree of engagement that allows for monetization. Populism and polarization are structurally embedded into this social-economic symbiosis. *This* hardware can and must work only with *this* software.

Is it possible to rearrange the economic and behavioral rewards for media use in such a manner that they incentivize people's engagement based if not on consensus, then at the very least on tolerance instead of polarization? This is a million-dollar question, literally; though, considering the capitalization of Google and Facebook, it is more like a billion-dollar question.

***

At first glance, a way to decrease polarization is to bridge the gap, bringing opposites together in order to eliminate misunderstanding, on the assumption that animosity is built on a misunderstanding. "Can we build social-media bridges?" asked de-Wit et al. in their review of studies on polarization.[1] Building bridges, or a cultural space for opposites to meet face to face meaningfully and without rage, looks like a desirable and potentially efficient solution.

Indeed, the negotiating of differences and building consensus out of irreconcilable conflicts is a fundamental need and quality of politics and everyday human communication. A vast arsenal of logical, rhetorical and political tools of negotiation and compromising has been developed by humanity. Rhetoric and the culture of debate are taught or used to be taught in schools and universities.

The issue is that all those frames and tools were linked to physical, predominantly in-person communication. The limits and deterrents of the physical reality made people polite and receptive; or at least their receptiveness remained generally within tolerated levels. The settings of physical communication made the ability to listen to the other side and others' arguments an advantage in politics and negotiations. Society has learned to disincentivize escalation by immediate negative responses and also by postponed losses. Under such environmental conditions, the

---

[1] de-Wit, Lee, Brick, Cameron, and van der Linden, Sander. (2019, January 16). "Are Social Media Driving Political Polarization?" *Greater Good Magazine.* https://greatergood.berkeley.edu/article/item/is_social_media_driving_political_polarization

bridging of opposites did not harm the public health but increased diversity, tolerance and inclusiveness.

The same was true for the written communication between opposites on the physical carriers – it was linear, delayed, stepwise, and moderated by the rules to levels of desirable compromise or acceptable tolerance.

Physical communication invokes politeness and tolerance, but digital communication does not. Building 'better' bridges between opposites will not curtail polarization in the digital environment, where the settings inherently incentivize engagement by response, with extremes getting responded to the best. On the contrary, any common space for the opposites to come into contact will most likely turn this contact into a clash. Left to their own devices, without physical or some other artificial deterrents and inhibitors, opposites in the digital environment will ignite and escalate polarization after any contact.

***

The fact that the expression of extremes is encouraged in the pursuit of response is only a part of the problem. This is perhaps not even the main problem of digital media polarization. The core problem is that the moderate / middle-ground is disincentivized. Moreover, when polarization achieves the levels of purity testing in the form of the Two Minutes Hate and a subsequent ideological purge, the middle-ground, actually, becomes suppressed. One cannot stay neutral and silent when the highest sacred values are at stake.

Most likely, any attempts to connect the opposites and extremes in the digital world will be fruitless and needless. They will only reinforce what is touched upon and articulated. Perhaps one of the potentially more fruitful searches for depolarization could be in the field of reinforcing the center. If one side of the spectrum thinks the past represents nothing but shame and the other side thinks the past represents nothing but glory, the only way to mitigate polarization is not to bring those sides together but to empower the voice of the center. It is the center who might assume, for example, that the past is much more complex than shame or glory, both of which are, actually, political tools of the present but not conditions of the past.

Anti-polarizing efforts by no means relate to the balancing of the opposites. They relate to silencing the extremes and vocalizing the center. How can the center become better responded to, better liked, shared, more popular, and more profitable for social capital and commercial monetization at the level of the very design of social media and the news media? The answer to this question is surely worthy of the Nobel Peace Prize.

***

The media settings that work for polarization are known. The service they provide is so convenient, attractive and self-reinforcing that no one can resist them at the systemic level, despite any rational past and future attempts. The question is whether it is possible to find settings that work for moderate and balanced self-actualization that would lean towards the center rather than the extremes?

The task of beneficially reversing malicious environmental forces is titanic, if feasible at all. The practical goal may be to find environmental forces of different effects and use them. For example, in the digital reality, there might be something equivalent to how newsroom autonomy worked in the legacy media – it was able to mitigate the negative environmental impacts of advertising or reader revenue. Theoretically, monopolistic social media platforms could implement this by introducing artificial restraints, similar to the news media, which could afford the balancing domination of newsroom autonomy when they were plentifully paid for by advertising in their Golden Age. The problem is that a media system with a thousand filtering entities is more diverse and less risky, in terms of ideological monopoly, than a media system with two or three monopolistic platforms.

Even a relatively weak factor of reversing polarization would help if it could at least slow down the self-reinforcing surge of polarization. As for the polarizing effect of old media, the spread of awareness regarding their forced descent into postjournalism caused by the decline and reversal of their business model might neutralize at least a part of their polarizing impact.

Ultimately, "How to get rid of polarization?" might be the wrong question. The correct question is more likely to be "How are we going to live with it?"

***

In *The Mechanical Bride* (1951), Marshall McLuhan offered a metaphor of escape from a deadly environment that was borrowed from Edgar Allan Poe's short story *A Descent into the Maelstrom* (1841). The sailor in Poe's story got sucked into a mile-wide maelstrom. Being captured by the horror, he, nevertheless, realized how wonderful was "a manifestation of God's power" and "became possessed with the keenest curiosity about the whirl itself". Revolving deeper into the vortex, the sailor noticed that some objects descended slower than others. He abandoned the boat and held on to a barrel. The boat, along with his brother, who was paralyzed with horror, went down and was swallowed by the abyss. Sometime after, the vortex disappeared, and the sailor found himself on the surface of the sea, where he was later picked up by a fishing boat.

Thus, the sailor managed to escape the maelstrom by understanding its forces and using the whirlpool's patterns. Or, as McLuhan put it, the "Sailor saved himself by studying the action of the whirlpool and by co-operating with it. <...> It was this amusement born of his rational detachment as a spectator of his own situation that gave him the thread which led him out of the Labyrinth" (McLuhan, 2005 [1951], p. 18).

Eighteen years later, McLuhan returned to his maelstrom metaphor in the *Playboy* interview (1969). Answering the question of whether he is "essentially optimistic about the future" amid "the upheavals induced by the new electric technology", he said:

> Cataclysmic environmental changes such as these are, in and of themselves, morally neutral; it is how we perceive them and react to them that will determine their ultimate psychic and social consequences. If we refuse to see them at all, we will become their servants. It's inevitable that the world-pool of electronic information movement will toss us all about like corks on a stormy sea, but if we keep our cool during the descent into the maelstrom, studying the process as it happens to us and what we can do about it, we can come through.

- 30 -

Bibliography

Alford, Matthew. (2018). "A Screen Entertainment Propaganda Model." In: Pedro-Carañana, J., Broudy, D., and Klaehn, J. (eds.), *The Propaganda Model Today: Filtering Perception and Awareness*. London: University of Westminster Press. Pp. 145–158.

Asmolov, Gregory. (2019). "The Effects of Participatory Propaganda: From Socialization to Internalization of Conflicts." *Journal of Design and Science*, (6). https://doi.org/10.21428/7808da6b.833c9940

Barthes, Roland. (1977 [1967]). "The Death of Author." In: *Image Music Text*. Essays selected and translated by Stephen Heath. Pp. 142–148. FontanaPress.

Baudrillard, Jean. (2000 [1969]). "Ideological Genesis of Needs." In J. Schor, D. B. Holt, & D. Holt. *The Consumer Society Reader*. US: New Press. Pp. 57–81.

Baudrillard, Jean. (1981 [1972]). *For a Critique of the Political Economy of the Sign*. St Louis: Telos Press.

Baudrillard, Jean. (1983). *In the Shadow of the Silent Majorities, Or, the End of the Social*. New York: Semiotext(e).

Baudrillard, Jean. (2012 [1981]). *The Precession of Simulacra*. In Meenakshi Gigi Durham and Douglas M. Kellner (Eds.): *Media and Cultural Studies: KeyWorks* (2nd ed., pp.388–407). Oxford: Wiley-Blackwell.

Baughman, James. (2001 [1987]). *Henry R. Luce and the Rise of the American News Media*. Johns Hopkins University Press. https://www.amazon.com/Henry-Luce-Rise-American-Media/9

Benkler, Yochai, Faris, Robert, and Roberts, Hal. (2018). *Network Propaganda: Manipulation, disinformation, and radicalization in American politics*. New York, NY: Oxford University Press.

Benson, Rodney, Neff, Timothy, and Hessérus, Mattias. (2018). "Media Ownership and Public Service News: How Strong Are Institutional Logics?" *The International Journal of Press/Politics*. 2018, Volume 23(3), pp. 275–298.

Benson, Rodney. (2018). "Can foundations solve the journalism crisis?" *Journalism*, 2018, Vol. 19(8), 1059–1077.

Blair, Ann, and Fitzgerald, Devin (2015). "A revolution in information?" In: Hamish, Scott (Ed.), *The Oxford Handbook of Early Modern European History, 1350–1750: Volume I: Peoples and Place*. Oxford University Press.

Boxell, Levi, Gentzkow, Matthew, and Shapiro, Jesse M. (2020). "Cross-Country Trends in Affective Polarization." Working Paper. The Stanford Institute for Economic Policy Research (SIEPR). https://siepr.stanford.edu/research/publications/cross-country-trends-affective-polarization-0

Brady, William, Van Bavel, Jay, Jost, John, and Wills, Julian. (2018). "An ideological asymmetry in the diffusion of moralized content among political elites." *Journal of Experimental Psychology: General*, 148(10), 1802–1813. https://doi.org/10.1037/xge0000532

Carey, James. (2009 [1989]). "Technology and Ideology: The case of the Telegraph." In: *Communication as Culture, Revised Edition. Essays on Media and Society*. New York, London: Routledge. Pp.155–178.

Crawford, Jarret T. (2017). "Are conservatives more sensitive to threat than liberals? It depends on how we define threat and conservatism." *Social Cognition*, Vol. 35, No. 4, 2017, pp. 354–373. https://guilfordjournals.com/doi/pdfplus/10.1521/soco.2017.35.4.354

Dearborn, Mary (1999). *Mailer: a Biography*. New York: Houghton Mifflin Company.

Deleuze, Gilles. (1992). "Postscript on the Societies of Control." *October*. Vol. 59 (Winter, 1992), pp. 3–7. The MIT Press. https://www.jstor.org/stable/778828

Disraeli, Isaac (1835/1859). "Curiosities of Literature." In: *The works of Isaac Disraeli* (ed. by B. Disraeli). Vol. I.

Eisenstein, Elizabeth L. (1979). *The Printing Press as an Agent of Change: Communications and Cultural Transformations in Early-Modern Europe*. Cambridge and New York: Cambridge University Press.

Enli, Gunn. (2017). "Twitter as arena for the authentic outsider: Exploring the social media campaigns of Trump and Clinton in the 2016 US presidential election." *European Journal of Communication*, 32:1, pp. 50–61.

Faris et al. (2017). "Partisanship, Propaganda, and Disinformation: Online Media and the 2016 U.S. Presidential Election." Berkman Klein Center for Internet & Society at Harvard University. https://cyber.harvard.edu/publications/2017/08/mediacloud

Foucault, Michel. (1972 [1969]). *The Archaeology of Knowledge and the discourse on language*. Trans. A. M. Sheridan Smith. NY: Pantheon Books.

Friedman, Barbara G. (2005). "The Penny Press: The Origins of the Modern News Media, 1833–1861." *Journalism History*, Volume 31, No. 1, Spring.

Fuchs, Christian. (2011). "The Contemporary World Wide Web. Social medium or new space of accumulation?" In: Winseck, Dwayne, and Jin, Dal Yong (Eds.), *The Political Economies of Media. The Transformation of the Global Media Industries.* Bloomsbury Academic

Fuchs, Christian. (2012). "Dallas Smythe today – the audience commodity, the digital labour debate, Marxist political economy and critical theory." *Triple C.* Vol 10, No 2, pp. 692–740. https://www.triple-c.at/index.php/tripleC/article/view/443

Fuchs, Christian. (2018). "Propaganda 2.0: Herman and Chomsky's Propaganda Model in the Age of the Internet, Big Data and Social Media." In: Pedro-Carañana, J., Broudy, D. and Klaehn, J. (Eds.), *The Propaganda Model Today: Filtering Perception and Awareness.* Pp. 71–92. London: University of Westminster Press.

Goss, Brian Michael. (2013). *Rebooting the Herman and Chomsky Propaganda Model in the Twenty-First Century.* New York: Peter Lang.

Gurri, Martin. (2018). *The Revolt of the Public and the Crisis of Authority in the New Millennium.* San Francisco, CA: Stripe Press.

Habermas, Jürgen. (1974 [1964]). "The Public Sphere: An Encyclopedia Article." *New German Critique,* No. 3 (Autumn), pp. 49–55.

Herman, Edward S. (2000). "The Propaganda Model: a retrospective." *Journalism Studies,* Volume 1, Number 1, pp. 101–112.

Herman, Edward S., Chomsky, Noam. (2002 [1988]). *Manufacturing Consent: The Political Economy of the Mass Media.* Pantheon Books.

Horkheimer, Max, and Adorno, Theodor. (1947). "The Culture Industry: Enlightenment as Mass Deception." In: *Dialectic of Enlightenment.*

Hotten, John Camden. (1874). Introduction to *An Early News-Sheet: The Russian Invasion of Poland on 1563.* An exact facsimile of a contemporary account in Latin, published at Douay. London: Chatto and Windus, Publishers. https://archive.org/details/earlynewssheetru00hott/page/n1/mode/2up

Infelise, Mario. (2002). "Roman Avvisi: Information and Politics in the Seventeenth Century." In: *Court and Politics in Papal Rome, 1492–1700.* Cambridge: Cambridge University Press.

Infelise, Mario. (2016). "The History of a word: Gazzetta / Gazette." In: Raymond, J., Moxham, N. (eds), *News Network in Early Modern Europe.* Leiden Boston, Brill.

Innis, Harold. (1950). *Empire and Communications.* Oxford: Clarendon Press.

Innis, Harold. (1951). *The Bias of Communication*. Toronto: University of Toronto Press.

Iyengar, Shanto, Lelkes, Yphtach, Levendusky, Matthew, Malhotra, Neil, and Sean J. Westwood. (2019). "The origins and consequences of affective polarization in the United States." *Annual Review of Political Science*, Volume 22, pp. 129–146.

Jameson, Frederic. (2012 [1984]). "Postmodernism, or the cultural logic of late capitalism." In: Meenakshi Gigi Durham and Douglas M. Kellner (Eds.), *Media and Cultural Studies: KeyWorks*, 2nd ed. Pp. 407–432. Oxford: Wiley-Blackwell.

Kahneman, Daniel, and Tversky, Amos. (1979). "Prospect theory: An analysis of decision under risk." *Econometrica*, 47(2), pp. 263–291. https://www.econometricsociety.org/publications/econometrica/1979/03/01/prospect-theory-analysis-decision-under-riskb

Kaplan, Richard. (2013). "Journalism History: North America." In: Nerone, John (Ed.), *Media History and foundations of Media Studies*. Volume I of: Angharad N. Valdivia (Ed.), *The International Encyclopedia of Media Studies*, First Edition. Blackwell Publishing Ltd.

Kilbourne, Jean. (1999). *Can't by my love. How advertising changes the way we think and feel*. New York: Touchstone.

Klaehn, Jeffery, et al. (2018). "Media Theory, Public Relevance and the Propaganda Model Today – Discussion. Jeffery Klaehn, Daniel Broudy, Christian Fuchs, Yigal Godler, Florian Zollmann, Noam Chomsky, Joan Pedro-Carañana, Tom Mills, and Oliver Boyd-Barrett." *Media Theory*, Vol. 2, No. 2, pp.164–191.

Krasni, Jan. How to hijack a discourse? Reflections on the concepts of post-truth and fake news. Humanities and Social Sciences Communications, volume 7, article number: 32 (2020). https://doi.org/10.1057/s41599-020-0527-z

Lasswell, Harold. (1948). "The structure and function of communication in society." In: L. Bryson (ed.), *The Communication of Ideas*. New York: Institute for Religious and Social Studies. Pp. 37–51.

Lenin, Vladimir I. (1961 [1901]). "Where to Begin?" In: *Lenin Collected Works, Foreign Languages Publishing House*, Moscow, Volume 5, pages 13–24. First published in *Iskra*, No. 4, May 1901.

Levinson, Paul. (2015–2018). *McLuhan in an Age of Social Media*. Connected Editions. Kindle Edition.

Levinson, Paul. (2013, 2nd edition). *New New Media*. Pearson

Lippmann, Walter. (1929 [1922]). *Public Opinion.* New York: The Macmillan Company. https://en.wikisource.org/wiki/Public_Opinion

Logan, Robert. (2011). "Figure/ground: Cracking the McLuhan code." Revista da Associação Nacional dos Programas de Pós-Graduação em Comunicação E-compós, 14:3.

Lotman, Yuri M. (2010). *Unpredictable mechanisms of culture.* Tallinn University. / Лотман Юрий Михайлович. (2010). Непредсказуемые механизмы культуры. Издательство Таллиннского Университета.

Mailer, Norman. (1973). *Marilyn, a biography.* New York: Grosset & Dunlap.

Mailer, Norman. (1988). *Conversations with Norman Mailer.* Edited by J. Michael Lennon. University Press of Mississippi.

McChesney, Robert W. (2015 [1999]). *Rich Media, Poor Democracy: Communication Politics in Dubious Times.* New York: The New Press.

McIntyre, Lee. (2018). *Post-Truth.* Cambridge, Massachusetts: The MIT Press.

McLuhan, Marshall (1969). "Playboy interview." *Playboy Magazine.* March.

McLuhan, Marshall, and Carson, David. (2011). *The Book of Probes.* Ed. Eric McLuhan and William Kuhns. Corte Madera, CA: Gingko Press.

McLuhan, Marshall, and Fiore, Quentin. (1967). *The Medium is the Massage: An Inventory of Effects.* Co-ordinated by J. Agel. New York, London, Toronto: Bantam Books.

McLuhan, Marshall, and McLuhan, Eric. (1988). *Laws of media: The new science.* Toronto: University of Toronto Press

McLuhan, Marshall. (1962). *The Gutenberg Galaxy: The making of typographic man.* Toronto: University of Toronto Press.

McLuhan, Marshall. (1994 [1964]). *Understanding Media. The Extension of Man.* The MIT Press.

McLuhan, Marshall. (2005 [1951]). The mechanical bride: folklore of industrial man. In: *Essential McLuhan.* Edited by Eric McLuhan and Frank Zingrone. London: Routledge.

McQuail, Denis, and Windahl, Sven. (1993 [1982]). *Communication Models for the Study of Mass Communication.* London and New York: Routledge.

Meggs, Philip B. (1998). *A History of Graphic Design* (Third ed.). John Wiley & Sons, Inc.

Miroshnichenko, Andrey. (2014). *Human as media. The Emancipation of authorship.*

Miroshnichenko, Andrey. (2016). "Extrapolating on McLuhan: How Media Environments of the Given, the Represented, and the Induced Shape and Reshape Our Sensorium." *Philosophies*, 1, no. 3: 170–189.

Miroshnichenko, Andrey. (2020). "The hardware and software of Trumpism: A figure/ground analysis." *Explorations in Media Ecology*, Volume 19, Number 1, March, pp. 55–84. https://www.ingentaconnect.com/content/intellect/eme/2020/00000019/00000001/art00005

Morison, Stanley. (1954). "The Origins of the Newspaper." In: Morison, Stanley. (1980). *Selected Essays on the History of Letter-Forms in Manuscript and Print.* Vol. 2. Cambridge: Cambridge University Press.

Mullen, Andrew, and Klaehn, Jeffery. (2010). "The Herman–Chomsky Propaganda Model: A Critical Approach to Analysing Mass Media Behaviour." *Sociology Compass*, 4/4 (2010), pp. 215–229.

Mullen, Andrew. (2009). "The Propaganda Model after 20 Years: Interview with Edward S. Herman and Noam Chomsky." *Westminster Papers in Communication and Culture.* Vol. 6(2): 12–22. ISSN 1744–6708 (Print); 1744–6716 (Online). London: University of Westminster.

Murdock, Graham. (1983). "Large Corporations and the Control of the Communications Industries." In: Bennett, Tony, Curran, James, Gurevitch, Michael, and Wollacott, Janet (Eds.), *Culture, Society and the Media.* London: Methuen. Pp. 118–122.

Nabokov, Vladimir. (1958). "Writers, censorship and readers in Russia." In *The lectures on Russian literature.* / Набоков, Владимир. (1958). «Писатели, цензура и читатели в России». *Лекции по русской литературе.* http://nabokov-lit.ru/nabokov/kritika-nabokova/lekcii-po-russkoj-literature/pisateli-cenzura-i-chitateli.htm

Napoli, Philip, and Dwyer, Deborah L. (2018). "U.S. media policy in a time of political polarization and technological evolution." *Publizistik.* DOI 10.1007/s11616-018-0440-2

Nerone, J. C. (1987). "The Mythology of the Penny Press." *Critical Studies in Mass Communication*, 87(4), pp. 376–404.

Ortega y Gasset, José. (1985 [1930]). *The Revolt of the Masses.* Indiana, US: University of Notre Dame Press.

Owen, Diana. (2019). "The past decade and future of political media: The ascendance of social media." in *Towards a New Enlightenment? A Transcendent Decade.* Madrid: BBVA and OpenMind project, pp. 347–65.

https://www.bbvaopenmind.com/en/articles/the-past-decade-and-future-of-political-media-the-ascendance-of-social-media/.

Palazzo, Chiara. (2016). "The Venetian News Network in the Early Sixteenth Century: The Battle of Chaldiran." In: Palazzo, Chiara. *News Networks in Early Modern Europe*. Pp. 849–869.

Pariser, Eli. (2011). *The Filter Bubble. What the Internet Is Hiding from You*. NY: The Penguin Press.

Pedro-Carañana, Joan, Broudy, Daniel, and Klaehn, Jeffery (2018). Introduction. In: Pedro-Carañana, J., Broudy, D. and Klaehn, J. (eds.). *The Propaganda Model Today: Filtering Perception and Awareness*. London: University of Westminster Press. Pp. 1–18.

Postman, Neil. (1985). *Amusing Ourselves to Death: Public Discourse in the Age of Show Business*. New York: Viking.

Pruska-Oldenhof, Izabella, and Logan, Robert K. (2017). "The spiral structure of Marshall McLuhan's thinking." *Philosophies*, 2, 2:9, https://www.mdpi.com/2409-9287/2/2/9.

Rushkoff, Douglas. (1994). *Media Virus! Hidden Agendas in Popular Culture*. Random House Publishing Group.

Salomon, Ludwig. (1907). *Allgemeine Geschichte des Zeitungswesens*. (General History of the Press. In the Russian edition: Л. Саламон. *Всеобщая история прессы*. Я. Н. Засурский, Е. Л. Вартанова. *История печати. Антология*. Т. 1. М., 2001.)

Sclater, Karla Kelling. (2009). "The Labor and Radical Press. 1820 – the Present." *The Labor Press Project*. University of Washington. https://depts.washington.edu/labhist/laborpress/Kelling.shtml

Scott, Martin, Bunce, Mel, & Wright, Kate. (2019). "Foundation Funding and the Boundaries of Journalism." *Journalism Studies*, Volume 20, Issue 14, 2034–2052. https://www.tandfonline.com/doi/full/10.1080/321

Shirky, Clay. (2010). *Cognitive Surplus: Creativity and Generosity in a Connected Age*. Penguin Books.

Smythe, Dallas W. (1977). "Communications: Blindspot of Western Marxism". *Canadian Journal of Political and Society Theory*. 1 (3), pp. 1–28.

Smythe, Dallas W. (2012 [1981]). On the audience commodity and its work. In: M. Durham and D. M. Kellner (Eds.), *Media and cultural studies: Keyworks*. Oxford: Wiley-Blackwell. Pp. 185-204.

Sokal, Alan D. (1996), "Transgressing the Boundaries: Toward a Transformative Hermeneutics of Quantum Gravity." *Social Text*, 46–47:

217–252. https://physics.nyu.edu/faculty/sokal/transgress_v2/transgress_v2_singlefile.html

Strate, Lance. (2008). "Studying media as media: McLuhan and the media ecology approach." *MediaTropes*, 1:1, pp. 127–42. https://mediatropes.com/index.php/Mediatropes/article/view/3344.

Thrift, Nigel J. (2005). *Knowing Capitalism*. London: SAGE Publications.

Usher, Nikki, Holcomb, Jesse, and Littman, Justin. (2018). "Twitter makes it worse: Political journalists, gendered echo chambers, and the amplification of gender bias." *International Journal of Press/Politics*, 23:3, pp. 1–21, http://journals.sagepub.com/doi/10.1177/1940161218781254.

Vasilyeva, Tatyana. (1977). "Preface" to *Karl Marx and Frederick Engels, Collected Works*. Volume 7: Marx and Engels, 1848. New York: International Publishers.

Vygotsky, Lev S. (1986). *Thought and Language*. Cambridge, MA: The MIT Press.

Wanless, Alicia, and Berk, Michael. (2017). "Participatory Propaganda: The Engagement of Audiences in the Spread of Persuasive Communications." Conference paper: *Social Media & Social Order, Culture Conflict 2.0*. Oslo, November 2017. https://www.researchgate.net/publication/329281610_Participatory_Propaganda_The_Engagement_of_Audiences_in_the_Spread_of_Persuasive_Communications

Würgler, Andreas. (2012). "National and Transnational News Distribution 1400–1800." *EGO – European History Online*. http://ieg-ego.eu/en/threads/european-media/national-and-transnational-news-distribution/national-and-transnational-news-distribution

Yechiam, Eldad, and Hochman, Guy. (2013). "Losses as modulators of attention: Review and analysis of the unique effects of losses over gains." *Psychological Bulletin*, 139(2), pp. 497–518. https://psycnet.apa.org/doiLanding?doi=10.1037%2Fa0029383

Zollmann, Florian. 2018. "Corporate-Market Power and Ideological Domination: The Propaganda Model after 30 Years – Relevance and Further Application." In: Pedro-Carañana, J., Broudy, D. and Klaehn, J. (eds.). *The Propaganda Model Today: Filtering Perception and Awareness*. London: University of Westminster Press. Pp. 223–236.

Printed in Great Britain
by Amazon